W0008563

Study Guide and Student Workbook

to accompany

MUSIC: AN APPRECIATION

Fifth Brief Edition

Roger Kamien
Zubin Mehta Chair in Musicology, Emeritus
The Hebrew University of Jerusalem

=============================

Prepared by:
Raoul F. Camus
Emeritus Professor
Queensborough Community College
of the City University of New York

Revised by:
Susan Lindahl
Central Michigan University

Boston   Burr Ridge, IL   Dubuque, IA   Madison, WI   New York   San Francisco   St. Louis
Bangkok   Bogotá   Caracas   Kuala Lumpur   Lisbon   London   Madrid   Mexico City
Milan   Montreal   New Delhi   Santiago   Seoul   Singapore   Sydney   Taipei   Toronto

The McGraw·Hill Companies

Higher Education

Study Guide and Student Workbook to accompany
MUSIC: AN APPRECIATION, FIFTH BRIEF EDITION
Roger Kamien

Published by McGraw-Hill, an imprint of the McGraw-Hill Companies, Inc., 1221 Avenue of the Americas, New York, NY 10020. Copyright © 2006, 2002, 1998, 1994, 1990 by the McGraw-Hill Companies, Inc. All rights reserved.
No part of this publication may be reproduced or distributed in any form or by any means, or stored in a database or retrieval system, without the prior written consent of The McGraw-Hill Companies, Inc., including, but not limited to, in any network or other electronic storage or transmission, or broadcast for distance learning.

1 2 3 4 5 6 7 8 9 0 QDP/QDP 0 9 8 7 6 5

ISBN 0-07-321273-3

www.mhhe.com

CONTENTS

To the Student   v
Introduction to Technology   vi
Table of URLS   viii
Pre-Course Questionnaire   ix

I. ELEMENTS
I-1.   Sound: Pitch, Dynamics, and Tone Color   1
        Multimedia Companion: The Elements
        of Music: Sound   2
        Pitch discrimination   3
        Timbres: Tone colors and combinations   3
        Timbres: Performing media   4
        Multimedia Companion: The Elements
        of Music: Timbre   4
        Multimedia Companion: The Elements
        of Music: Timbre comparison   5
        Pre-Course Listening Analysis   6
I-2.   Performing Media: Voices and
        Instruments   7
        Voices and instruments   10
        Seating plans   13
I-3.   Rhythm   15
I-4.   Music Notation   16
I-5.   Melody   18
        Multimedia Companion: The Elements
        of Music: Melody   19
I-6.   Harmony   20
        Kamien/Chopin's *Prelude in E Minor*   21
I-7.   Key   22
I-8.   Musical Texture   23
        Multimedia Companion: The Elements
        of Music: Texture   24
I-9.   Musical Form   25
        Listening for form   25
I-10.   Musical Style   26
        Multimedia Companion: The Elements
        of Music: Form   26
        Stylistic periods   27
        Unit Quiz I   29

II. THE MIDDLE AGES AND RENAISSANCE
II-1.   Music in the Middle Ages (450–1450)   31
        The medieval period   33
        The church modes   35
        The Mass   36
        Parrott/*Agnus Dei* from Machaut's
        Notre Dame Mass   37
II-2.   Music in the Renaissance (1450–1600)   38
        People and events in the Renaissance   40
        Differences between the Middle Ages
        and the Renaissance   40
        A comparison of the Medieval and
        Renaissance styles   41
        Renaissance instruments   42
        Period and modern instruments   43
        Dances of the Renaissance   44
        Unit Quiz II   45

III. THE BAROQUE PERIOD
III-1.   Baroque Music (1600–1750)   47
         A comparison of the Renaissance and
         early baroque styles   48
III-2.   Music in Baroque Society   49
III-3.   The Concerto Grosso and Ritornello
         Form   49
         A *Brandenburg* Concerto   50
III-4.   The Fugue   51
         Bach's Organ Fugue in G Minor   52
         Transcriptions of Bach's Organ Fugue
         in G Minor   52
III-5.   The Elements of Opera   53
         Preparing for a visit to the opera   54
III-6.   Opera in the Baroque Era   55
III-7.   Claudio Monteverdi   56
III-8.   Henry Purcell   56
III-9.   The Baroque Sonata   57
III-10. Antonio Vivaldi   57
         Lamon/Vivaldi's *Spring* Concerto   58
III-11. Johann Sebastian Bach   59
III-12. The Baroque Suite   60
         Comparing two baroque suites   60
III-13. The Chorale and Church Cantata   61
III-14. The Oratorio   61
III-15. George Frideric Handel   62
         Handel oratorios   63
         Handel operas   63
         Biographical Sketch—A baroque
         composer   64
         Unit Quiz III   65

IV. THE CLASSICAL PERIOD
IV-1.   The Classical Style (1750–1820)   67
         A comparison of the late baroque and
         classical styles   68
IV-2.   Composer, Patron, and Public in the
         Classical Period   69
IV-3.   Sonata Form   70
IV-4.   Theme and Variations   71
IV-5.   Minuet and Trio   71
IV-6.   Rondo   72
         Multimedia Companion: Rondo   72
IV-7.   The Classical Symphony   73
         A classical symphony   74
IV-8.   The Classical Concerto   75
IV-9.   Classical Chamber Music   76
IV-10.   Joseph Haydn   77
         Nicknames in Haydn's music   77
         Biographical Sketch—Joseph Haydn
         or Wolfgang Amadeus Mozart   78
IV-11.   Wolfgang Amadeus Mozart   79
         Perahia/Mozart's Piano Concert in
         A Major, K. 488   80
IV-12.   Ludwig van Beethoven   81
         Biographical Sketch—Ludwig
         van Beethoven   82
         Unit Quiz IV   83

V. THE ROMANTIC PERIOD

V-1.	Romanticism in Music (1820–1900)	85
	A comparison of the classical and romantic styles	86
V-2.	Romantic Composers and Their Public	87
V-3.	The Art Song	88
V-4.	Franz Schubert	88
V-5.	Robert Schumann	89
	Lieder	89
V-6.	Clara Wieck Schumann	90
V-7.	Frédéric Chopin	91
V-8.	Franz Liszt	92
V-9.	Felix Mendelssohn	93
V-10.	Program Music	94
	The program symphony	95
	The concert overture	96
	The symphonic poem	97
	Incidental music	98
V-11.	Hector Berlioz	99
	The changing orchestra	100
V-12.	Nationalism in Nineteenth-Century Music	102
	Nationalism in music	103
	Nationalistic composers	103
V-13.	Antonin Dvořák	104
V-14.	Peter Ilyich Tchaikovsky	105
	Tchaikovsky's ballets	105
V-15.	Johannes Brahms	106
	Brahms's music	107
V-16	Giuseppe Verdi	108
	My favorite Verdi or Puccini opera	109
V-17.	Giacomo Puccini	110
	Verismo opera	111
	Pavarotti/*Che gelida manina* from Puccini's *La Bohème*	112
	Multimedia Companion: Opera	113
V-18.	Richard Wagner	114
	The Ring of the Nibelung	115
	Biographical Sketch—A romantic composer	116
	Unit Quiz V	117

VI. THE TWENTIETH CENTURY AND BEYOND

VI-1.	Musical Styles: 1900–1945	119
	The twentieth-century context	120
	A comparison of twentieth-century styles	121
VI-2.	Music and Musicians in Society	122
VI-3.	Impressionism and Symbolism	123
VI-4.	Claude Debussy	124
VI-5.	Neoclassicism	125
	The music of Igor Stravinsky	125
VI-6.	Igor Stravinsky	126
VI-7.	Expressionism	127
VI-8.	Arnold Schoenberg	128
	The music of Arnold Schoenberg	128
VI-9.	Alban Berg	129
VI-10.	Anton Webern	129
VI-11.	Béla Bartók	130
VI-12.	Charles Ives	131
VI-13.	George Gershwin	132
VI-14.	William Grant Still	133
VI-15.	Aaron Copland	134
	Biographical Sketch—An American composer	135
VI-16.	Musical Styles since 1945	136
	An overview of musical developments since 1945	137
VI-17.	Music since 1945: Four Representative Pieces	139
	Biographical Sketch—A twentieth-century composer	140
	Sic transit gloria mundi	141
	Is art music alive and well in the twenty-first century? A survey	141
VI-18.	Jazz	142
	Roots of jazz	144
	Blues lyrics	144
	Smith/*Lost Your Head Blues*	145
	Jazz styles	146
VI-19.	The American Musical and Music in Film	148
	Musical theater	150
	Film music exploration	151
	Leitmotifs in film music	152
	Film music composers	152
VI-20.	Rock	153
	The diversity of rock styles—an analysis	154
	Biographical Sketch—A performer or composer of jazz or rock	155
	Some popular rock groups today—a comparison	156
	Unit Quiz VI, part 1: The Twentieth Century	157
	Unit Quiz VI, part 2: Jazz and Rock	159

VII. NONWESTERN MUSIC

VII-1.	Music in Nonwestern Cultures	161
	Other nonwestern musics	162
	Nonwestern instruments	163
VII-2.	Music in Sub-Saharan Africa	164
VII-3.	Classical Music of India	165
	Shankar/*Maru-Bihag*	166
	Unit Quiz VII	167

APPENDIX

Going to a Concert	169
Concert Reports	171
Concert Report 1	173
Concert Report 2	175
Concert Report 3	177
Post-Course Listening Analysis	179
Post-Course Evaluation	180
Answer Key for Self-Test Questions	181

TO THE STUDENT

This *Study Guide and Student Workbook* is designed to accompany Roger Kamien's *Music: An Appreciation*, fifth brief edition, on which it is based. As the title indicates, this manual has two basic purposes:

1. The *Study Guide* is designed to help you in your preparation for class by reviewing the materials in the text through lists of "Basic Terms" and through "Self-Tests" consisting of multiple-choice, matching, or fill-in questions.

2. The *Student Workbook* contains exercises, research projects, and worksheets. Some are explorative, some argumentative, but all are designed to encourage thought and interaction in and outside of class. These pages may be used for

- classroom discussion
- listening or written assignments
- broadening the scope of understanding music in its relationship to the cultural periods and the other humanities
- reviewing the biographical details of some of the major composers and performers
- supplementing topics discussed in the text

SUGGESTIONS FOR USING THE STUDY GUIDE

The text on which this work is based is divided into seven major parts, with eighty sections. Most likely, the course you are taking will not cover all these sections because of time limitations, so you can use the Contents as a course outline by checking off those topics that will be covered. After reading an assignment, answer the questions in the Study Guide. Then, check your answers against those given in the back of this book. Reread the text, if necessary, for any questions that might still be unresolved.

At the end of each of the major units (corresponding to parts I through VII in the text), there is a unit quiz. Since the answers to the quiz questions are not given in this manual, the quizzes may be used by the instructor for review in class, for outside assignment, or for collection. If your instructor does not plan to use the unit quizzes in this way, please ask him or her to provide you with a photocopy of the answer page from the instructor side of the Online Learning Center, so that you may do the work and check it on your own.

The text and accompanying materials have been designed to help you develop an understanding and appreciation of music, including different artistic styles and historical periods, something that can provide you with a lifelong source of pleasure, inspiration, and cultural enrichment. We sincerely hope you will give them a chance to do so, and we hope you will enjoy the time you spend in discovering that, like "reading, 'riting, and 'rithmetic," *music is basic!*

INTRODUCTION TO TECHNOLOGY
by Rebecca Kaufman

The world of technology has but one constant—it's always changing! New developments and technologies come out at a dizzying pace, making us wonder if we can keep up or should even try. Computer software can present information, provide out-of-class drills, establish a creative environment, or encourage the development of problem-solving skills. It can enhance our learning efforts in creative and effective ways, if we understand how it can work for us.

Technology also includes the mysterious realm of cyberspace, that is, the Internet and the World Wide Web. What is to be gained by entering the "information superhighway"? For one thing, we can access information that used to be inaccessible or very difficult to pursue, such as rare music manuscripts or research materials. We can also connect with new sources of current information and establish contact with others in our areas of interest. We can listen to or download music files for instant sound through the computer without an instrument or CD player. Last, but not least, we can explore or "surf" the World Wide Web for fun. It's a big information world out there. We can take in as little or as much as we want. But to do so, we must be explorers, ready to jump on board and go along for the ride, learning as we go. To be willing to learn new things is a valuable skill in the information age.

Once a common network language for computers was developed in 1969, computers could be linked together and the Internet was born. In 1991, a graphical user interface with icons and images gave rise to the World Wide Web (WWW), or Web for short. Information from the Web can be in the form of text, images, sounds, or movies.

To gain access to the Web, there are some basic requirements: (1) a computer with at least 8 MB of RAM (preferably more); (2) a modem (the faster the better) and an account with an Internet service provider or a direct Internet connection via your school; and (3) software to access the Internet.

The Web can be accessed with a *browser,* which is software that acts as a gateway to the Web. The browser on your computer contacts another computer and sets up the link. It then displays the information it receives on your computer screen. The technical terms for this arrangement are *client* and *server*. The client is your computer, which requests information, and the server is the computer that provides that information. Your browser contacts a server via its address, much like regular mail. This address is called a URL, or universal resource locator. This is a sample URL: **http://www.mhhe.com**. To make it easier to read and avoid confusion, from here on all URLs, or parts of URLs, will be enclosed in angle brackets, but the angle brackets are not part of the URL:

<http://www.mhhe.com>

This URL contains several parts. The first few characters, <http://>, are the protocol and you will see them at the beginning of all Web URLs. Other older but still active protocols include <ftp://> and <gopher://>. The actual server is listed next, in this case, <www.mhhe>. Many Web addresses begin with <www.>. At the end of the URL is <.com>. This is the domain, which gives you a clue as to the type of server. Some common domains are *.com* for commercial, *.edu* for an educational institution, *.gov* for government, *.mil* for military, and *.org* for organization. Foreign sites have an additional letter code at the end of the domain, such as *.au* for Australia, *.nl* for Netherlands, and *.uk* for the United Kingdom. Each character must be correct in a URL or the link won't be established. If you have access to the Web, test the waters by visiting the McGraw-Hill site at <http://www.mhhe.com>. Once you are there, see if you can find your way to a citation of this book or a reference to Roger Kamien. What did you have to do to find the information? Although Web sites can be organized differently, there are many similarities among them.

How do we get URLs? Perhaps someone has given you a URL to check out or you have noticed a URL as part of a company's advertisement. You can visit that site by typing in the correct URL in your browser's entry line, called the GoTo line. To find sites without knowing the URL, you can use a directory or a search engine. A directory lists categories of information, categories that become more detailed as selections are made. If you feel like browsing, use a directory. If you want something specific, use a search engine. With a search engine, you may enter one or several keywords and let the search engine find possible matches. Because of the dynamic nature of the Web, to stay current it makes sense to do fresh searches each time you want specific information.

To do effective searches on the Web, it helps to know what makes for a good search. Each search engine does a search a bit differently, so take the time to read their tips for successful searches. A general search for "music" might return 800,000 sites (called "hits" in Web terminology). It doesn't make sense to wade through 800,000 hits to find the perfect crumhorn site. Again, if you want to browse, use a directory. For a specific search, use restrictors, such as AND, NOT, and OR. The presence of the restrictor AND, or a plus sign (+) in some search engines, as in "Mozart AND clarinet," searches for sites that contain both terms. The restrictor NOT, or a minus sign (-), eliminates certain sites and tightens up the search. The restrictor OR increases the number of hits by including all sites that mention either of the terms used in the search. AND and NOT will benefit you the most in the long run. For practice, check out the Infoseek Ultra search engine at <**http://ultra.infoseek.com**> and do a search with these keywords: +Clara Schumann, +Johannes Brahms (this is the correct format for an Infoseek Ultra search). The search engine will find all sites with both names mentioned. See if you can find a site that follows the correspondence between the two composers. How would you refine the search even more if all you wanted was the correspondence? Each search engine takes practice to learn, so be patient and experiment with how you use keywords. Keep refining your search parameters until you have a short list of sites. To avoid searching with several search engines, you might want to try a metasearch, which is one service searching with several search engines and posting all of the results. The table of URLs on the next page lists a number of search engines and some popular metasearch sites.

At the heart of the Web is the Web *page,* which is the primary medium for information. A Web page is what you see when you connect with a site. A Web page displays information, but its most important feature is *hypermedia,* or links to other web pages on other computers. *Hypertext* is text in a different color or underlined, which means you can click on the text to go to another Web page. Pictures can also be links, such as a map that lets you zoom in on a particular area through a series of clicks and end up at a site with relevant tourist information. English is the most common language on the Web, but there are other languages, too.

Because the Web depends on connections between computers and Web traffic is increasing rapidly, interruptions happen frequently. If your request to connect with a site is rejected or doesn't go through, try again later. If a page starts to load but doesn't finish or you see the message "transfer interrupted," reload the page from your browser's options. Be persistent and patient.

Once you start exploring, it's easy to get lost and forget where you started or where you were headed. Luckily, the browser keeps track of the sites visited and you can retrace your steps through either the Go menu, which lists the most recent sites visited, or the Back and Forward buttons, which let you step back and forward through your most recent sites. You can set up bookmarks at your favorite sites so that it is easy to return to them, but keep in mind that bookmarks need to be updated, too. Return visits to favorite sites can yield valuable new information and new links to other sites. A well-maintained Web site with updated links to specific sites is your best bet to stay current. Chances are the technology you discover will spur you on to further explorations. The table on the next page lists some good sites from which to start your exploring. In the parlance of the Web, happy surfing!

TABLE OF URLS

Site Name	Description	URL
Internet Tutorials		
Learn the Net	tutorial and information in four languages	http://www.learnthenet.com
Help Web	guide to getting started on the Internet	http://www.imagescape.com/helpweb
Internet Web Text	hypertext guide to Internet resources	http://www.december.com/web/text
Search Engines		
AltaVista	for simple and advanced searches	http://www.altavista.digital.com
Lycos	thorough search of Internet by keyword	http://www.lycos.com
Magellan Internet Guide	search engine plus four-star rating system	http://magellan.excite.com
MetaCrawler	parallel search with nine services	http://www.metacrawler.com
ProFusion	design-your-own metasearch	http://www.profusion.com
SavvySearch	detailed search with 28+ search engines	http://www.search.com
WebCrawler	detailed search by keyword	http://www.webcrawler.com
Yahoo	subject-oriented directory	http://www.yahoo.com
Music Resources		
Worldwide Internet Music Resources	directory of music resources links	http://www.music.indiana.edu/music_resources
Internet Resources for Music Scholars	research directory	http://www.rism.harvard.edu/MusicLibrary/InternetResources.html
Music Resources from the Sibelius Academy	extensive lists of music sites	http://www.siba.fi:80/Kulttuuripalvelut/music.html
WWW Virtual Library	music directory and alphabetical index	http://www.gprep.org/classical
Classical Net Home Page	index and links to classical music sites	http://www.classical.efront.com
MUSIClassical.com	links to various music sites	http://www.angelfire.com/biz/musiclassical/index.html
Bringing American Music Home	guide for teachers of music history	http://falcon.cc.ukans.edu/~bclark/groubody.html
Historic American Sheet Music	index and illustrations of sheet music	http://scriptorium.lib.duke.edu/sheetmusic
Dance Resources		
American Ballet Theatre	repertory archives, photos, dictionary	http://abt.org
American Ballroom Companion	dance instruction manuals, c1490–1920	http:memory.loc.gov/ammem/dihtml/dihome.html
Dance Heritage Coalition	tutorial for in-depth dance research	http://www.danceheritage.org
Music Organizations		
College Music Society	info and links to resources	http://www.music.org
American Musicological Society	info and links to musicological sites	http://www.ams-net.org
Recording Companies		
BMG Classics World	catalog of releases, classical music guides	http://www.getmusic.com/classical/bmg
Sony Online	catalog of Sony products and ventures	http://www.sony.com
Other Sites of Interest		
WebMuseum	catalog of art works for display	http://SunSITE.sut.ac.jp/wm/
Classical MIDI Archives	many classical MIDI files	http://www.prs.net/midi.html
MIDI Farm	directory of MIDI files	http://www.midifarm.com/directory.htm
Classical Composers Archive	small pictures and brief biographies	http://spight.physics.unlv.edu/picgalr2.htm
Library of Congress	LoC online resources	http://lcweb.loc.gov

Name_____ Class/section_____ Date_____

PRE-COURSE   Class: ___Freshman ___Sophomore ___Junior ___Senior ___Graduate
QUESTIONNAIRE   Major:_____ Minor:_____

Technology: I ___do ____do not have a computer. I ____do ____do not have access to the Internet.

Background in music:
  Junior high school: ___none ___general music course
      ___performing group:_____
  High school: ___none ___general music course ___theory ___other
    ___chorus (voice:_____) ___stage band/combo
    ___band ___orchestra (instrument:_____)
  College courses: ___none ___survey/appreciation ___theory
    ___performing group:_____(instrument:_____)
  Private lessons: ___none ___years of piano ___years of _____

Reason for taking the present course (check as many as apply):
  ____college requirement for degree program
  ____personal enrichment
  ____recommended by advisor
  ____only class I could fit into my program
  ____other:_____

Musical habits:
  I attend about _____ concerts per _____, most of which are _____(style).
  I listen to about _____ hours per _____ of music on the radio, most of which
    is _____ (style), on station(s) _____.
  I buy about _____ cassettes/CDs per _____, most of which are _____(style).

I have had the following musical experiences:

	PERFORMER OR WORK	WHEN	REACTION
ballet	_____	_____	_____
chamber music	_____	_____	_____
chorus or choir	_____	_____	_____
jazz group	_____	_____	_____
opera or musical	_____	_____	_____
recital	_____	_____	_____
rock group	_____	_____	_____
stage band	_____	_____	_____
symphonic band	_____	_____	_____
symphonic orchestra	_____	_____	_____
other: _____	_____	_____	_____

Preferences in music:

My favorite musical compositions are:

TITLE	COMPOSER
1. _____	_____
2. _____	_____
3. _____	_____

My favorite composers are:

1. _____
2. _____
3. _____

My favorite performers are:

INDIVIDUALS	GROUPS
1. _____	_____
2. _____	_____
3. _____	_____

Identify and describe in your own words the following musical styles.

baroque: _____

blues: _____

classical: _____

jazz: _____

rap: _____

rock: _____

romantic: _____

Define the following musical terms.

pitch: _____

dynamics: _____

harmony: _____

melody: _____

rhythm: _____

tempo: _____

timbre: _____

What do you hope to achieve, other than the necessary credit, from this course?

I. ELEMENTS

I-1. SOUND: PITCH, DYNAMICS, AND TONE COLOR

BASIC TERMS:

sound	interval	dynamics
pitch	octave	accent
tone	pitch range (range)	tone color (timbre)

SELF-TEST Multiple-choice: Circle the answer that best completes each item.

1. *Timbre* is synonymous with
   - a. sound
   - b. vibrations
   - c. tone color
   - d. dynamic accent

2. Degrees of loudness and softness in music are called
   - a. dynamics
   - b. pitches
   - c. notes
   - d. tone colors

3. The relative highness or lowness of a sound is called
   - a. timbre
   - b. pitch
   - c. dynamics
   - d. octave

4. The distance between the lowest and highest tones that a voice or instrument can produce is called
   - a. pitch range
   - b. an octave
   - c. timbre
   - d. dynamic accent

5. The Italian dynamic markings traditionally used to indicate very soft, loud, and very loud are (respectively)
   - a. piano, mezzo forte, forte
   - b. mezzo piano, forte, fortissimo
   - c. pianissimo, piano, forte
   - d. pianissimo, forte, fortissimo

6. The pitch of a sound is decided by the _____ of its vibrations.
   - a. amplitude
   - b. timbre
   - c. frequency
   - d. dynamics

7. The distance in pitch between any two tones is called
   - a. duration
   - b. dynamic accent
   - c. timbre
   - d. an interval

8. When two different tones blend so well when sounded together that they almost seem to merge into one tone, the interval is called a(n)
   - a. dynamic accent
   - b. octave
   - c. interval
   - d. pitch range

9. The frequency of vibrations is measured in
   - a. cycles per minute
   - b. cycles per second
   - c. dynamic levels
   - d. Italian words

10. A dynamic accent occurs in music when a performer
    a. emphasizes a tone by playing it more loudly than the tones around it
    b. plays all the notes loudly
    c. stamps his or her foot on the floor
    d. begins speeding up the music

11. A gradual increase in loudness is known as a
    a. decrescendo
    b. crescendo
    c. fortissimo
    d. diminuendo

12. In music, a sound that has a definite pitch is called a
    a. noise
    b. dynamic accent
    c. sound
    d. tone

13. The symbol ⟩ indicates to the performer that the music should
    a. gradually increase in loudness
    b. gradually decrease in pitch
    c. gradually decrease in loudness
    d. be played faster

14. Music can be defined as
    a. sounds produced by musical instruments
    b. sounds that are pleasing, as opposed to noise
    c. an art based on the organization of sounds in time
    d. a system of symbols that performers learn to read

15. In general, the smaller the vibrating element, the _____ its pitch.
    a. higher
    b. softer
    c. lower
    d. louder

MULTIMEDIA COMPANION The Elements of Music: Sound
Sound Journal

Observe carefully and record in a journal all of the different sounds you experience in one day. In your journal write a brief description of each of the sounds, the cause of the sound, and what effect the sound had on you. Make specific reference to the dynamic of the sound and the *color* of the sound. How did the dynamic and *color* of the sound impact your response?

LISTENING EXERCISE   Pitch discrimination:

Some people believe they are monotones, unable to sing on pitch or tell one piece of music from another. It is very rare that this is true, but there are individual differences in the ability to discriminate pitches. Just as we learn through practice to differentiate colors with our eyes, we can develop pitch differentiation.

To see how well you can hear pitch differences, try the following exercise. The instructor will play two pitches in succession (or you can ask a friend to do this outside of class). Is the second pitch higher, lower, or the same as the first? Check your responses.

1. ____higher   ____lower   ____unison   ____octave
2. ____higher   ____lower   ____unison   ____octave
3. ____higher   ____lower   ____unison   ____octave
4. ____higher   ____lower   ____unison   ____octave
5. ____higher   ____lower   ____unison   ____octave
6. ____higher   ____lower   ____unison   ____octave
7. ____higher   ____lower   ____unison   ____octave
8. ____higher   ____lower   ____unison   ____octave
9. ____higher   ____lower   ____unison   ____octave
10. ____higher   ____lower   ____unison   ____octave

LISTENING EXERCISE   Timbres—Tone colors and combinations:

Just as we can develop pitch discrimination through practice, so too can we develop the ability to recognize the sounds of the various instruments and their combinations. To see how well you can recognize individual voice ranges or instruments, identify them in each of ten excerpts played in class.

1.

2.

3.

4.

5.

6.

7.

8.

9.

10.

LISTENING EXERCISE Timbres—Performing media:
   To see how well you can recognize combinations of sounds in their normal groupings, identify the medium—such as orchestra, band, rock group, jazz combo, or chorus—of each of ten excerpts played in class.

1.

2.

3.

4.

5.

6.

7.

8.

9.

10.

MULTIMEDIA COMPANION The Elements of Music: Timbre
Listening for timbre contrasts while surfing the FM dial

   This exercise will help you explore the many varieties of musical timbre. Begin with the FM dial of your radio set all the way to the left and then slowly work your way through the stations. Stop each time you hear a musical selection and listen for several minutes. Record each station you stop at, as well as your observations of the various musical timbres you hear. List the instruments you hear and then describe the *color* of the sound.

MULTIMEDIA COMPANION The Elements of Music: Timbre
Timbre comparison

Go to the Additional Recordings section of the Multimedia Companion. Listen to the *Air* in D Major from Suite No. 3 by J. S. Bach in the Baroque music section. Discuss your impressions of the movement in regard to the *color*. Compare this recording with another of the same piece that has been arranged for different instrumentation (e.g., the arrangement for brass choir performed by Summit Brass on their *Toccata and Fugue* CD, 1989). How does the change in timbre affect your impressions of the movement? How important do you feel timbre is to the overall impact of a piece upon the listener? Cite music from other styles of music that you are aware of.

PRE-COURSE LISTENING ANALYSIS

Listen to **Scene 2 of Igor Stravinsky's** *The Firebird.* Write your personal and emotional reactions to the work, and try to analyze the music and its technical aspects as completely and specifically as you can.

Now listen to *C-Jam Blues* as performed by Duke Ellington and his orchestra. Once again, write your personal and emotional reactions to the work, and try to analyze the music and its technical aspects as completely and specifically as you can, comparing it with Stravinsky's scene from *The Firebird*.

I-2. PERFORMING MEDIA: VOICES AND INSTRUMENTS

BASIC TERMS:

Voices
  soprano
  mezzo-soprano
  alto (or contralto)
  tenor
  baritone
  bass

Musical Instruments
  register

String Instruments
  violin
  viola
  cello (violoncello)
  double bass
  bow
  pizzicato
  stop (double, triple, quadruple)
  vibrato
  mute
  tremolo
  harmonics
  plectrum (plectra)
  harp
  guitar

Woodwind Instruments
  piccolo
  flute
  recorder
  single-reed woodwinds
    clarinet
    bass clarinet
    saxophone
  double-reed woodwinds
    oboe
    english horn
    bassoon
    contrabassoon

Brass Instruments
  trumpet
  cornet
  french horn (horn)
  trombone
  baritone horn
  euphonium
  tuba
  mute

Percussion Instruments: definite pitch
  timpani (kettledrums)
  glockenspiel
  xylophone
  celesta
  chimes

Percussion Instruments: indefinite pitch
  snare drum (side drum)
  bass drum
  tambourine
  triangle
  cymbals
  gong (tam-tam)

Keyboard Instruments
  piano
  harpsichord
  pipe organ
  accordion

Electronic Instruments
  tape studio
  synthesizer
  analog synthesis
  digital frequency modulation (FM)
    synthesis
  effects devices
  sampling
  musical instrument digital interface (MIDI)
  computer

SELF-TEST Multiple-choice: Circle the answer that best completes each item.

1. A thin piece of cane, used singly or in pairs by woodwind players, is called a
   a. reed
   b. mute
   c. double stop
   d. mouthpiece

2. The strings of a violin are tuned
   a. by moving the bridge
   b. by putting on new strings
   c. by tightening or loosening the pegs
   d. at the factory

3. The lowest instrument in the orchestra is the
   a. piccolo
   b. tuba
   c. double bass
   d. contrabassoon

4. Systems of electronic components that generate, modify, and control sound are called
   a. amplifiers
   b. computers
   c. synthesizers
   d. stereo sets

5. A part of an instrument's total range is called a
   a. mute
   b. register
   c. pizzicato
   d. range

6. It is difficult to sing well because _____ than in speaking.
   a. singing demands a greater supply and control of breath
   b. wider ranges of pitch and volume are used
   c. vowel sounds are held longer
   d. all of the above

7. The bow that string players usually use to produce sound on their instruments is a slightly curved stick strung tightly with
   a. catgut
   b. horsehair
   c. string
   d. flax

8. The highest woodwind instrument in the orchestra is the
   a. piccolo
   b. flute
   c. oboe
   d. clarinet

9. If a string player uses vibrato—rocking of the left hand to produce small pitch fluctuations—it is because
   a. using vibrato is easier than not using it, and no one can hear the fluctuations anyway
   b. the performer is nervous
   c. the performer is unsure of the correct pitch
   d. using vibrato makes the tone warmer and more expressive

10. Plucking the string with the finger instead of using a bow is called
    a. tremolo
    b. pizzicato
    c. vibrato
    d. pluckato

11. Symphonic bands differ from symphonic orchestras in that they
   a. are smaller
   b. have a drum major instead of a conductor
   c. play only marches
   d. do not contain a string section

12. A hollow, funnel-shaped piece of wood or plastic that brass players use to alter the tone of their instruments is called a
   a. tailpiece
   b. crook
   c. mute
   d. reed

13. Woodwind instruments are so named because they
   a. are made of wood
   b. use a wooden reed
   c. have wooden key mechanisms
   d. were originally made of wood

14. The range of a singer's voice depends on
   a. training
   b. physical makeup
   c. training and physical makeup
   d. which microphone the singer uses

15. The very high-pitched tones that are produced when a string player lightly touches certain points on a string are called
   a. harmonics
   b. vibrato
   c. pizzicato
   d. tremolo

16. The main tool of composers of electronic music during the 1950s was the
   a. synthesizer
   b. tape studio
   c. piano
   d. sampler

SELF-TEST Matching: Match each term with its definition.

17. analog synthesis

18. digital synthesis

19. MIDI

20. sampling

a. technology based on placing brief digital recordings of live sounds under the control of a synthesizer keyboard

b. technology based on representing data in terms of measurable physical quantities

c. a standard adopted by manufacturers for interfacing synthesizer equipment

d. technology based on representing physical quantities as numbers

EXERCISE   Voices and instruments: Complete the following charts by placing each voice or instrument listed in "Basic Terms" (page 7) in its proper place.

1. Voices and strings

FAMILY	VOICE	STRING (CHORDOPHONES)	
VIBRATING ELEMENT:	Vocal chords	Stretched strings	
		BOWED	PLUCKED
PITCH RANGE: Sopranino			
Soprano			
Alto			
Tenor			
Baritone			
Bass			
Contrabass			
Exceptions			

2. Woodwinds and brasses

WOODWIND (AEROPHONES)			BRASS (AEROPHONES)
VIBRATING ELEMENT: a vibrating column of air			Lips
WITHOUT A REED	SINGLE-REED	DOUBLE-REED	

3. Percussion instruments

STRETCHED MEMBRANE (MEMBRANOPHONES)	
DEFINITE PITCH	INDEFINITE PITCH
SELF-SOUNDING (IDIOPHONES)	
DEFINITE PITCH	INDEFINITE PITCH

4. Keyboard instruments

INSTRUMENT	VIBRATING ELEMENT	MANNER OF TONE PRODUCTION
piano		
harpsichord		
organ		
accordion		
synthesizer		

RESEARCH PROJECT Seating plans: Fill in the blank spaces as appropriate.

1. Your local professional orchestra.

   Name of orchestra: _____

2. Your local college or community orchestra.

   Name of orchestra: _____

3. Your local college or community choir or choral society.

Name of group: _____

4. Your local professional, college, or community symphonic band.

Name of group: _____

I-3. RHYTHM

BASIC TERMS:

beat	meter (duple, triple,	upbeat	tempo indication
rhythm	quadruple, quintuple,	accent	metronome
measure	sextuple, septuple)	syncopation	accelerando
	downbeat	tempo	ritardando

SELF-TEST Matching: Match each term with its description.

1. accent

2. beat

3. downbeat

4. measure

5. meter

6. metronome

7. rhythm

8. syncopation

9. tempo

10. upbeat

a. unit or group containing a fixed number of beats

b. organization of beats into regular groupings

c. stress or emphasis on a note

d. particular arrangement of note lengths in a piece of music; the ordered flow of music through time

e. putting an accent in music where it would not normally be expected

f. rate of speed of the beat of music

g. unaccented pulse preceding the downbeat

h. first, or stressed, beat of the measure

i. regular, recurrent pulsation that divides music into equal units of time

j. device that produces ticking sounds or flashes of light at any desired musical speed

MATCHING: Match each Italian tempo marking with its English translation.

11. accelerando
12. adagio
13. allegro
14. andante
15. largo
16. molto
17. non troppo
18. prestissimo
19. ritardando
20. vivace

k. as fast (quickly) as possible
l. very slow; broad
m. gradual speeding up of tempo
n. lively
o. slow
p. much
q. gradual slowing down of tempo
r. not too much
s. fast
t. moderately slow, a walking pace

I-4. MUSIC NOTATION

BASIC TERMS:

notation	natural sign (♮)	stem	tie
note	treble clef	flag	triplet
staff (staves)	bass clef	beam	rest
ledger lines	grand staff	dotted note	time (meter) signature
sharp sign (♯)	middle C	dotted rhythm	score
flat sign (♭)			

SELF-TEST Completion: Write the letter name of each of the notes in these measures:

EXERCISES Practice in notation:

1. Draw five treble and five bass clefs, copying the pattern.

2. Draw each of the accidental signs, following the examples.

3. Practice drawing whole notes by copying the C major scale.

4. Practice drawing notes by copying *The Farmer in the Dell* (see text).

5. Write three of each rest, following the examples in your text.

Whole rests   Half rests   Quarter rests   Eighth rests   Sixteenth rests

6. Some blank staves for practice, assignments, or original compositions:

I-5. MELODY

BASIC TERMS:

melody	legato	cadence
step	staccato	incomplete cadence
leap	phrase	complete cadence
climax	sequence	theme

SELF-TEST Multiple-choice: Circle the answer that best completes each item.

1. A melodic phrase ending that sets up expectations for continuation is known as a(n)
   a. incomplete cadence
   b. complete cadence
   c. sentence
   d. theme

2. A series of single tones that add up to a recognizable whole is called a
   a. cadence
   b. rhythm
   c. melody
   d. sequence

3. The emotional focal point of a melody is called the
   a. sequence
   b. theme
   c. cadence
   d. climax

4. The repetition of a melodic pattern at a higher or lower pitch is called a
   a. climax
   b. sequence
   c. cadence
   d. phrase

5. A resting place at the end of a phrase is called a
   a. climax
   b. melody
   c. stop
   d. cadence

6. A part of a melody is called a
   a. cadence
   b. sequence
   c. phrase
   d. step

7. *Legato* refers to playing or singing a melody
   a. in a short, detached manner
   b. in a smooth, connected style
   c. at a higher or lower pitch
   d. by small steps

8. A melody that serves as the starting point for a more extended piece of music is called a
   a. theme
   b. tune
   c. climax
   d. cadence

9. A melody is said to move by steps if it moves by
   a. repeating the same notes
   b. having rests between the notes
   c. large intervals
   d. adjacent scale tones

10. A short, detached style of playing a melody is known as
    a. legato
    b. staccato
    c. glissando
    d. vibrato

MULTIMEDIA COMPANION The Elements of Music: Melody
Mapping the phrase structure of simple melodies

Continue your exploration of melodic form by "mapping" the phrase structure for each of the following melodies.

With each melody consider the following:
1. How many phrases does each melody have?
2. Are the phrases the same or different?
3. Do each of the phrases have the same length?

Melody No. 1: *Twinkle, Twinkle Little Star*

Melody No. 2: *Happy Birthday*

Melody No. 3: *Rock-a-bye Baby*

Provide some additional melodic examples:

I-6. HARMONY

BASIC TERMS:

harmony	dissonance	dominant chord
chord	resolution	cadence
progression	triad	broken chord (arpeggio)
consonance	tonic chord	

SELF-TEST Multiple-choice: Circle the answer that best completes each item.

1. A combination of three or more tones sounded at the same time is called
   a. harmony   b. consonance   c. a chord   d. dissonance

2. *Harmony* refers to
   a. the way chords are constructed and how they follow each other
   b. living in peace with other people
   c. a pattern of beats per measure
   d. a chord built on the first step of the scale

3. The triad built on the fifth step of the scale is called the
   a. tonic chord   c. progression
   b. dominant chord   d. resolution

4. *Resolution* refers to a(n)
   a. dissonant chord moving to a consonant chord   c. composer resolving to write a composition
   b. consonant chord moving to a dissonant chord   d. arpeggio

5. _____ in music adds support, depth, and richness to a melody.
   a. Rhythm   c. Meter
   b. Tempo   d. Harmony

6. When the individual tones of a chord are sounded one after another instead of simultaneously, it is called a *broken chord,* or
   a. cadence   c. allegro
   b. arpeggio   d. progression

7. A combination of tones that is considered unstable and tense is called a
   a. consonance   c. dissonance
   b. progression   d. chord

8. Traditionally, a composition would almost always end on a
   a. progression   c. dominant chord
   b. dissonant chord   d. tonic chord

9. A series of chords is called a(n)
   a. triad   c. arpeggio
   b. progression   d. consonance

10. A combination of tones that is considered stable and restful is called a
    a. consonance   b. dissonance   c. progression   d. chord

PERFORMANCE PERSPECTIVE
Roger Kamien, pianist, playing Chopin's *Prelude in E Minor*

Roger Kamien discussed some of the decisions he made regarding his performance of the Chopin *Prelude in E Minor*. Take his suggestion and compare his performance of the *Prelude* to that of two other pianists. How do the performances differ in expression, tempo, dynamic range, and relationship between melody and accompaniment?

Example No. 1
Performer: Roger Kamien

Expression:

Tempo:

Dynamic Range:

Melody/Accompaniment:

Example No. 2
Performer:

Expression:

Tempo:

Dynamic Range:

Melody/Accompaniment:

Example No. 3
Performer:

Expression:

Tempo:

Dynamic Range:

Melody/Accompaniment:

Which performer's interpretation do you prefer, and why?

I-7. KEY

BASIC TERMS:

keynote (tonic)   key signature   chromatic scale
key (tonality)   half step   modulation
scale   whole step   tonic key (home key)
major scale   minor scale

SELF-TEST Multiple-choice: Circle the answer that best completes each item.

1. *Key* refers to
    a. the major scale   c. any twelve random pitches
    b. a central tone, chord, and scale   d. a musical symbol placed at
                                               the beginning of the staff

2. Another term for *key* is
    a. tonality   c. chromaticism
    b. scale   d. dominant

3. In traditional western music, the _____ is the smallest interval between successive tones
   of a scale.
    a. quarter step   c. half step
    b. whole step   d. octave

4. A shift from one key to another within the same composition is called
    a. key   c. scale
    b. resolution   d. modulation

5. The central tone around which a musical composition is organized is called the
    a. scale   c. tonic
    b. dominant   d. modulation

EXERCISE Scales: Write the following scales (don't forget the clef):

G major   D major

E♭ major   F major

D minor (harmonic form)   D minor (melodic form)

I-8. MUSICAL TEXTURE

BASIC TERMS:

musical texture	unison	counterpoint	homophonic texture
monophonic texture	polyphonic texture	imitation	

SELF-TEST Multiple-choice: Circle the answer that best completes each item.

1. *Musical texture* refers to
   a. how many different layers of sound are heard at the same time
   b. what kind of layers of sound are heard (melody or harmony)
   c. how layers of sound are related to each other
   d. all of the above

2. When a melodic idea is presented by one voice or instrument and then restated immediately by another voice or instrument, the technique is called
   a. counterpoint   c. copying
   b. imitation   d. all of the above

3. A *round* is an example of
   a. homophonic texture   c. strict imitation
   b. monophonic texture   d. sloppy singing

4. When there is one main melody accompanied by chords, the texture is
   a. polyphonic   b. homophonic   c. monophonic   d. imitative

5. The texture of a single melodic line without accompaniment is
   a. contrapuntal   b. homophonic   c. monophonic   d. polyphonic

6. Performance of a single melodic line by more than one instrument or voice is described as playing or singing in
   a. unison   b. counterpoint   c. harmony   d. imitation

7. The technique of combining several melodic lines into a meaningful whole is called
   a. texture   b. imitation   c. unison   d. counterpoint

8. An example of homophonic texture could be a
   a. hymn   c. folksinger accompanied by a guitar
   b. barbershop quartet   d. any of the above

9. When two or more melodic lines of equal interest are performed simultaneously, the texture is
   a. monophonic   c. polyphonic
   b. homophonic   d. heterophonic

10. *Contrapuntal texture* is sometimes used in place of the term
    a. monophonic texture   c. polyphonic texture
    b. homophonic texture   d. unisonal performance

MULTIMEDIA COMPANION The Elements of Music: Texture
Listening for musical texture contrasts while surfing the FM dial

This exercise will help you explore the many varieties of musical texture. Begin with the FM dial of your radio set all the way to the left and then slowly work your way through the stations. Stop each time you hear a musical selection and listen for several minutes. Record each radio station you stop at, as well as your observations of the various musical textures you hear. In your observations, include any instruments you hear as well as any dynamic contrasts you notice.

I-9. MUSICAL FORM

BASIC TERMS:

form	contrast	three-part form (A B A)
repetition	variation	two-part form (A B)

SELF-TEST Multiple-choice: Circle the answer that best completes each item.

1. Retaining some features of a musical idea while changing others is called
   - a. form
   - b. contrast
   - c. repetition
   - d. variation

2. Three-part form can be represented as
   - a. A B A
   - b. A B A'
   - c. statement, contrast, return
   - d. all of the above

3. The organization of musical ideas in time is called
   - a. form
   - b. repetition
   - c. ternary
   - d. variation

4. Repetition is a technique widely used in music because it
   - a. creates a sense of unity
   - b. helps engrave a melody in the memory
   - c. provides a feeling of balance and symmetry
   - d. any of the above

5. The form consisting of a musical statement followed by a counterstatement would be called
   - a. ternary
   - b. binary
   - c. free
   - d. any of the above

LISTENING EXERCISE Listening for form:

As you listen to music, try to become aware of the form. Hum some old, familiar melodies, listen to the radio or television, or attend a concert, and list as many forms as you can recognize. Two examples are provided.

BINARY FORMS		TERNARY FORMS	
America	ab	*Home on the Range*	aa'ba'

_____   _____

_____   _____

_____   _____

_____   _____

I-10. MUSICAL STYLE

BASIC TERM:
  style

SELF-TEST Multiple-choice: Circle the answer that best completes each item.
  1. Which of the following would be a good example of a change in musical style?
      a. The men in the New York Philharmonic wear white tie and tails during the winter season, but for the summer concerts they wear black tie and white dinner jackets.
      b. The major and minor scales were the basic scales of western music from the 1600s to the 1900s, but in the twentieth century many composers abandoned tonality.
      c. The treble clef is used for relatively high pitch ranges, but the bass clef is used for lower ranges.
      d. all of the above.

  2. Changes in musical style from one historical period to the next are usually
      a. continuous
      b. recognizable only by scholars and professional musicians
      c. very abrupt
      d. for the worse

  3. We know little about the music of very ancient civilizations because
      a. there probably was almost none
      b. it was too primitive to interest later generations
      c. it is too difficult to be played today
      d. hardly any notated music has survived from these cultures

MULTIMEDIA COMPANION The Elements of Music: Form
Creating a Listening Guide

  Pick one of your favorite pieces or songs, any style, and create a listening guide that reflects the formal organization of the piece. Include any similarities or differences in the musical characteristics of the piece (i.e., melody/harmony, rhythm, timbre, and dynamic) that would support your outline of the piece.

EXERCISE Stylistic periods:

Although there is no substitute for memorizing the styles and their approximate dates given in the textbook, the task will be easier if you associate each period with famous personalities; costume styles; dances; works of literature, art, and architecture; and historical and cultural events. Using the chart on the next page, make as many meaningful associations with each period as you can, and at the same time see how many musicians you can name. Some major events and personalities may be found in the textbook (see the Time-line for each stylistic period).

STYLISTIC PERIOD	Historical and Cultural Events	Famous Personalities	Musicians
Middle Ages (450–1450)			
Renaissance (1450–1600)			
Baroque (1600–1750)			
Classical (1750–1820)			
Romantic (1820–1900)			
Twentieth century to 1945			
1945 to the present			

UNIT QUIZ I
ELEMENTS

Name_____

Class/section_____ Date_____

Matching: Match each term with its definition.

1._____ shifting from one key to another within a musical composition

2._____ tone color; quality of sound

3._____ stable combination of tones; points of rest

4._____ degrees of loudness and softness in music; intensity of sound

5._____ series of single tones that add up to a recognizable whole; musical sentence

6._____ distance in pitch between any two tones

7._____ chord built on the first step of the scale; central key around which a musical composition is organized

8._____ progression of chords leading to a feeling of repose at the end of a phrase; musical punctuation mark

9._____ repetition of a melodic pattern at a higher or lower pitch

10._____ relative highness or lowness of sound; frequency of vibrations

11._____ part of a melody

12._____ particular arrangement of note lengths in a piece of music; ordered flow of music through time

13._____ how chords are constructed and follow each other

14._____ combination of three or more tones sounded at the same time

15._____ placing an accent in music where it would not normally be expected

16._____ organization of beats into regular groupings; time signature

17._____ speed of a beat

18._____ triad built on the fifth step of the scale

19._____ melody that serves as the starting point for a more extended piece of music

20._____ unstable combination of tones; tension demanding onward motion

a. cadence

b. chord

c. consonance

d. dissonance

e. dominant

f. dynamics

g. harmony

h. interval

i. melody

j. meter

k. modulation

l. phrase

m. pitch

n. rhythm

o. sequence

p. syncopation

q. tempo

r. theme

s. timbre

t. tonic

Unit Quiz I (cont.)

Matching: Match each instrument with its family grouping.

21._____ trumpet

22._____ saxophone   a. strings

23._____ cello

24._____ english horn   b. woodwinds

25._____ vibraphone

26._____ trombone   c. brass

27._____ violin

28._____ oboe   d. percussion

29._____ timpani

30._____ bassoon

Matching: Match each term with its definition.

31._____ short, detached style of playing or singing a melody   a. allegro

32._____ tempo marking for *fast*   b. andante

33._____ plucking the strings of a string instrument instead of using a bow   c. arpeggio

d. crescendo

34._____ gradual increase in loudness

e. homophonic

35._____ sounding the individual tones of a chord one after another, instead of together; broken chord   f. legato

g. monophonic

36._____ smooth, connected style of playing or singing a melody

h. pizzicato

37._____ texture in which two or more melodies of equal interest are performed at the same time   i. polyphonic

j. staccato

38._____ texture in which one main melody predominates over a subordinate chordal accompaniment

39._____ texture of a single melodic line without accompaniment

40._____ tempo marking for moderately slow; a walking pace

II. THE MIDDLE AGES AND RENAISSANCE

II-1. MUSIC IN THE MIDDLE AGES (450–1450)

BASIC TERMS:

Gregorian chant   drone   mass ordinary
church modes   organum

SELF-TEST Multiple-choice: Circle the answer that best completes each item.

1. Gregorian chant
   a. is monophonic in texture
   b. is polyphonic in texture
   c. is homophonic in texture
   d. has no texture

2. The wandering minstrels, or *jongleurs,* of the Middle Ages
   a. performed music and acrobatics in castles, taverns, and town squares
   b. lived on the lowest level of society
   c. played instrumental dances on harps, fiddles, and lutes
   d. all of the above

3. The notation of the secular songs of the Middle Ages does not indicate
   a. rhythm   b. pitch   c. duration   d. any of the above

4. The church modes are
   a. different from the major and minor scales in that they consist of only six different tones
   b. different from the major and minor scales in that they consist of only five different tones
   c. like the major and minor scales in that they consist of seven tones and an eighth tone
      that duplicates the first an octave higher
   d. completely different from any other form of scale

5. The first large body of secular songs that survives in decipherable notation was composed during
   a. the ninth century by monks for church services
   b. the twelfth and thirteenth centuries by French nobles called *troubadours* and *trouvères*
   c. the fourteenth century by Guillaume de Machaut and his contemporaries
   d. the fifteenth century by wandering minstrels called *jongleurs*

6. The *ars nova,* or *new art,* of the fourteenth century differed from older music in that
   a. a new system of notation permitted composers to specify almost any rhythmic pattern
   b. the subjects were all secular
   c. there was no syncopation
   d. the music emphasized homophonic texture

7. The first steps toward the development of polyphony were taken sometime
   between 700 and 900, when
   a. musicians composed new music to accompany dancing
   b. the French nobles began to sing hunting songs together
   c. monks in monastery choirs began to add a second melodic line to Gregorian chant
   d. all of the above

8. The *Notre Dame* Mass by Guillaume de Machaut was
    a. written for three voices without instrumental accompaniment
    b. written for the Cathedral of Notre Dame in Paris
    c. the first polyphonic treatment of the mass ordinary by a known composer
    d. all of the above

9. Leonin and Perotin are notable because they
    a. are the first important composers known by name
    b. indicated definite time values and a clearly defined meter in their music
    c. were the leaders of the school of Notre Dame
    d. all of the above

10. Secular music in the fourteenth century
    a. became more important than sacred music
    b. was not based on Gregorian chant
    c. included drinking songs and pieces in which bird calls, barks of dogs,
        and hunting shouts are imitated
    d. all of the above

11. Gregorian chant is named after Pope Gregory I, who
    a. composed all the chants presently in use
    b. was credited by medieval legend with having created it, even though it evolved
        over many centuries
    c. had his name put on the first printed edition
    d. wrote the texts for the chants

12. The center of polyphonic music in Europe after 1150 was
    a. Paris   b. Rome   c. Reims   d. London

13. Gregorian chant
    a. was the official music of the Roman Catholic church for more than 1,000 years
    b. retained some elements of the Jewish synagogue of the first centuries after Christ
    c. is set to sacred Latin texts
    d. all of the above

14. The French secular songs of the Middle Ages usually dealt with
    a. the Crusades   c. love
    b. spinning   d. all of the above

15. In the recording of the medieval *estampie*, the melody line is played on a rebec, a
    a. medieval drum   c. tubular wind instrument
    b. bowed string instrument   d. plucked string instrument

16. Medieval music that consists of Gregorian chant and one or more additional melodic lines is called
    a. *ars nova*   c. alleluia
    b. organum   d. cantus firmus

17. The foremost composer of fourteenth-century France was
    a. Guillaume de Machaut   c. Charles V
    b. Hildegard of Bingen   d. Perotin

18. Gillaume de Machaut's love song *Puis qu'en oubli sui de vous* is an example of
    a. rondeau   c. chant
    b. estampie   d. organum

EXERCISE The medieval period:

The term *Middle Ages* implies little more than the period between the "good old days" of Rome, and the "wonderful new days" of the Renaissance. But during this time — a thousand years of human history — something must have happened that would deserve greater distinction. Try to get an overall feeling for the period (actually three distinct periods) by filling in the following chart.

MIDDLE AGES: (450–1450)	DARK AGES (–)	ROMANESQUE (–)	GOTHIC (–)
Personalities			
Events			
Political and economic conditions			
Social life			
Education			
Literature			

The medieval period (cont.)

MIDDLE AGES: (450–1450)	DARK AGES (–)	ROMANESQUE (–)	GOTHIC (–)
Architecture			
Art			
Costume			
Dance			
Vocal music			
Instrumental music			

EXERCISE The church modes:

The church modes were the basic scales of western music during the Middle Ages and the Renaissance and were used in secular as well as sacred music. Originally there were four authentic and four plagal modes, but by the sixteenth century two more of each were added, making a total of twelve modes.

Because these modes are so important to the music of that period, and also to some extent to the music of the twentieth century, you might want to take a closer look at them. For the moment, let us consider only the authentic modes, those whose first step of the scale is also the tonic or *finalis*. Using only the natural notes of the scale (the white keys of the piano), write, and then sing or play, each of the following modes.

THE FOUR AUTHENTIC CHURCH MODES

Dorian
(D-D)

Phrygian
(E-E)

Lydian
(F-F)

Mixolydian
(G-G)

SIXTEENTH-CENTURY ADDITIONS

Aeolian
(A-A)

Ionian
(C-C)

RESEARCH PROJECT   The Mass:
   The most solemn service of the Roman Catholic church, the Mass is the ritual celebration of the Eucharist. The liturgy, or public form of worship, is divided into texts that remain the same each day (the *ordinary*) and texts that vary from day to day (the *proper*). Using the framework below, check those sections that were usually set to music. Note particularly their place within the complete ceremony. (If you have the opportunity of hearing a High Mass, see if you can follow the various sections.)

MASS PROPER	MASS ORDINARY
(changing)	(constant)
_____1. Introit	
	_____2. *Kyrie eleison* (Lord have mercy on us)
	_____3. *Gloria in excelsis Deo* (Glory to God in the highest)
_____4. Collect (Prayer)	
_____5. Epistle [New Testament]	
_____6. Gradual [Psalms]	
_____7. Alleluia (or Tract)	
_____8. Gospel [New Testament]	
	_____9. *Credo in unum Deum* (I believe in one God)
_____10. Offertory	
_____11. Secret	
_____12. Preface	
	_____13. *Sanctus* (Holy, Holy, Holy); *Benedictus qui venit in nomine Domini* (Blessed is he that comes in the name of the Lord)
	_____14. Canon [prayers before and after the Consecration]
	_____15. *Agnus Dei, qui tollis peccata mundi* (Lamb of God, who takest away the sins of the world)
_____16. Communion	
_____17. Post-Communion	
	_____18. *Ite, missa est* (Go, you are sent forth) [congregation dismissed]

PERFORMANCE PERSPECTIVE
Andrew Parrott conducting the *Agnus Dei* from Machaut's *Notre Dame* Mass

Andrew Parrott discusses some of the philosophies surrounding the use of modern versus period instruments and the performance techniques used when performing works prior to the early nineteenth century. Listen to a recording from the fourteenth or early fifteenth century that has been recorded using period instruments. Discuss your impressions of the impact these instruments have on the *color* of the performance.

Composition:

Composer:

Observations
Timbre:

Balance:

Interpretation:

Technical execution:

Opinion and discussion:

II-2. MUSIC IN THE RENAISSANCE (1450–1600)

BASIC TERMS:

word painting	motet	madrigal
a cappella	mass	lute

SELF-TEST Multiple-choice: Circle the answer that best completes each item.

1. The texture of Renaissance music is chiefly
   a. monophonic   b. homophonic   c. polyphonic   d. heterophonic

2. The Renaissance madrigal began around 1520 in
   a. England   b. France   c. Italy   d. Flanders

3. Much of the instrumental music composed during the Renaissance was intended for
   a. the concert hall   c. dancing
   b. religious worship   d. the piano

4. The dominant intellectual movement of the Renaissance was called
   a. feudalism   b. humanism   c. classicism   d. paganism

5. *A cappella* refers to
   a. unaccompanied choral music
   b. men taking their hats off in church
   c. singing in a hushed manner because one is in church
   d. any form of music appropriate for church use

6. The _____ is a stately dance in duple meter similar to the pavane.
   a. galliard   b. passamezzo   c. saltarello   d. minuet

7. Palestrina's career centered in
   a. the Netherlands   b. Florence   c. Naples   d. Rome

8. Renaissance melodies are usually easy to sing because
   a. the level of musicianship in the Renaissance was not very high, and so easy music
      was composed
   b. the music was mostly homophonic, so that one could sing it with a group
   c. there was a sharply defined beat, which kept the performers together
   d. the melody usually moves along a scale with few large leaps

9. Palestrina's *Pope Marcellus* Mass sounds fuller than Josquin's *Ave Maria* because
   a. Palestrina was a better composer
   b. it is set for six voices instead of four
   c. the recording engineer adjusted the levels differently
   d. all of the above

10. The *Kyrie* from Palestrina's *Pope Marcellus* Mass
    a. has rich polyphonic texture based on imitation
    b. is written in three different sections
    c. contains upward leaps in the melody that are balanced by downward steps
    d. all of the above

11. Josquin Desprez was a contemporary of
    a. Christopher Columbus
    b. Perotin
    c. Palestrina
    d. Queen Elizabeth of England

12. The madrigal anthology *The Triumphes of Oriana* was written in honor of
    a. Queen Anne
    b. King Henry VIII
    c. the goddess Diana
    d. Queen Elizabeth I

13. A madrigal, like a motet, is a vocal composition that combines homophonic and polyphonic textures; but it differs from the motet in that it
    a. uses a vernacular rather than Latin text
    b. more often uses word painting and unusual harmonies
    c. both a and b
    d. neither a nor b

14. Thomas Weelkes's *As Vesta Was Descending* is notable for its
    a. word painting
    b. completely homophonic texture
    c. instrumental accompaniment
    d. monophonic texture

15. The development of the English madrigal can be traced to 1588 and considered a result of
    a. the Spanish armada
    b. a decree by Queen Elizabeth
    c. the writings of Shakespeare
    d. the publication in London of a volume of translated Italian madrigals

Completion: Supply the missing information.

16. The two main forms of sacred Renaissance music are

    the _____ and the _____.

17. The sections of the Renaissance mass are _____, _____,

    _____, _____, and _____.

18. Performing choral music without instrumental accompaniment is

    called _____.

Listen to Josquin's *Ave Maria,* and then complete the following:

19. The work is written for _____ voices.

20. A feeling of continuous flow is created by _____.

21. The opening section, like many later sections, uses polyphonic

    _____, a technique typical of the period.

EXERCISE   People and events in the Renaissance:

Although some historians place the beginning of the Renaissance as early as 1400, or even earlier, the textbook prefers 1450. Using either 1400 or 1450, list some of the more important personalities and significant events of that period.

PERSONALITIES   EVENTS (include dates)

EXERCISE   Differences between the Middle Ages and the Renaissance:

Referring to the chart you made for the Middle Ages (pages 33–34), explain the differences, if any, between the Middle Ages and the Renaissance in each of the following areas.

Economic conditions:

Social life:

Education:

Literature:

Architecture:

Art:

Costume:

Dance:

Vocal music:

Instrumental music:

LISTENING EXERCISE A comparison of the Medieval and Renaissance styles:
    As you listen to three examples provided by your instructor, check those characteristics that are predominant in each composition. When this analysis is completed, decide which style each example represents.

	1.	2.	3.
Melody: angular, rhythmic, narrow range	___	___	___
basically conjunct, greater range, arches	___	___	___
Texture: use of cantus firmus	___	___	___
free polyphony	___	___	___
Rhythm: greater use of syncopation	___	___	___
gently flowing	___	___	___
Harmony: occasional dissonant clashes between parts	___	___	___
basically consonant, triadic	___	___	___
Sonority: two or three voices in upper ranges	___	___	___
full four- to six-voice choirs, with bass range	___	___	___
Language: predominantly Latin	___	___	___
greater use of vernacular	___	___	___

Example 1:

    style:

    composer: title:

Example 2:

    style:

    composer: title:

Example 3:

    style:

    composer: title:

RESEARCH PROJECT Renaissance instruments:
  It has been said that the Renaissance had a greater variety of instrumental timbres than we have at present. Classify each of the following Renaissance instruments according to the correct family grouping, and identify the specific characteristics that distinguish it from the other members of the same family.

	FAMILY	CHARACTERISTICS
Bagpipe		
Cornett		
Crumhorn		
Curtal		
Fiddle		
Lute		
Mandora		
Pipe and tabor		
Regal		
Sackbut		
Serpent		
Shawm		
Theorbo		
Viol		

LISTENING EXERCISE Period and modern instruments:
Listen to a Renaissance composition played on modern instruments; then listen to the same composition played on period instruments. Compare the performances with regard to balance, appropriateness of combination, interpretation, and technical execution, indicating similarities and differences. Evaluate the results of each.

Title: Composer:

Modern instruments (performers):

    Comments:

Period instruments (performers):

    Comments:

RESEARCH PROJECT Dances of the Renaissance:
    Dancing was very popular among all social classes in the Renaissance, and skill in dancing was a very important mark of a gentleman or gentlewoman. Listen to some of the dances popular at that time, and identify the character, purpose (if any), tempo, meter, and basic rhythmic pattern of each.

Allemande:

Basse danse:

Branle:

Canario:

Courante:

Galliard:

Passamezzo:

Pavane:

Saltarello:

Sarabande:

Tourdion:

Volta:

THE MIDDLE AGES AND RENAISSANCE

Matching: Match each term with its definition.

1._____ medieval music consisting of Gregorian chant and one or more additional lines

2._____ wandering minstrels of the Middle Ages

3._____ poet-musicians of the French nobility

4._____ musical representation of specific poetic images

5._____ plucked string instrument with a body shaped like half a pear

6._____ family of bowed string instruments

7._____ unaccompanied choral singing

8._____ scales consisting of seven different tones, whose patterns are different from the major and minor scales

9._____ melody sung without accompaniment

10._____ text portions of the Roman Catholic Mass that remain the same each day

11._____ text portions of the Roman Catholic Mass that change from day to day

12._____ polyphonic choral work set to a sacred Latin text

13._____ stately dance in duple meter

a. a cappella

b. chant

c. church modes

d. jongleurs

e. lute

f. mass ordinary

g. mass proper

h. motet

i. organum

j. passamezzo

k. trouvères

l. viol

m. word painting

Matching: Match each composition with its composer.

14._____ *Notre Dame* Mass

15._____ *Pope Marcellus* Mass

16._____ *As Vesta Was Descending*

17._____ *Ave Maria . . . virgo serena*

18._____ *Terpsichore*

a. Josquin Desprez

b. Guillaume de Machaut

c. G. P. da Palestrina

d. Michael Praetorius

e. Thomas Weelkes

Unit Quiz II (cont.)

Multiple-choice: Choose the answer that best completes each item.

19. The intellectual movement called *humanism*
    a. condemned any remnant of pagan antiquity
    b. focused on human life and its accomplishments
    c. treated the madonna as a childlike earthly creature
    d. focused on the afterlife in heaven and hell

20. Which of the following is not a part of the Renaissance mass?
    a. Ave Maria   b. Gloria   c. Kyrie   d. Credo

21. An outstanding composer of the *ars nova* was
    a. Perotin
    b. Guillaume de Machaut   c. Leonin
                                            d. Pope Gregory I

22. The first large body of secular songs that survives in decipherable notation was composed
    a. during the twelfth and thirteenth centuries   c. from 590 to 604
    b. during the ninth century   d. during the fifteenth century

23. Which of the following is *not* true of Gregorian chant?
    a. It conveys a calm, otherworldly quality.
    b. Its rhythm is flexible, without meter.
    c. The melodies tend to move stepwise within a narrow range of pitches.
    d. It is usually polyphonic in texture.

24. One of the major characteristics of *ars nova* music is its use of
    a. syncopation   c. Gregorian chant
    b. organum   d. monophonic texture

25. An outstanding composer of the Notre Dame school was
    a. Perotin
    b. Guillaume de Machaut   c. Hildegard of Bingen
                                            d. Pope Gregory I

Listening or essay question: To be provided by your instructor.

_____

_____

_____

_____

III. THE BAROQUE PERIOD

III-1. BAROQUE MUSIC (1600–1750)

BASIC TERMS:

terraced dynamics   basso continuo (figured bass)
clavichord   movement

SELF-TEST Completion: Supply the missing information.

1. The medieval church modes gradually gave way to the _____

   and _____ scales in the middle baroque.

2. The two musical giants of the baroque were _____ and _____.

3. A bass part together with numbers (figures) specifying the chords to be played above it,

   characteristic of the baroque, is called _____.

4. The alternation between soft and loud dynamics in baroque music

   is known as _____.

5. A section that sounds fairly complete and independent but is part of a larger composition

   is called a_____.

SELF-TEST Multiple-choice: Circle the answer that best completes each item.

6. One of the most revolutionary periods in music history was the
   a. Renaissance   c. middle baroque
   b. early baroque   d. late baroque

7. The early baroque was characterized by
   a. elaborate counterpoint
   b. homophonic texture
   c. development of the standardized orchestra
   d. diffusion of the style into every corner of Europe

8. The middle baroque was characterized by
   a. elaborate counterpoint
   b. homophonic texture
   c. development of the standardized orchestra
   d. diffusion of the style into every corner of Europe

9. A popular keyboard instrument in which sound was produced
   by means of brass blades striking the strings was the
   a. clavichord   c. organ
   b. harpsichord   d. basso continuo

10. *Affections* in baroque usage refers to
    a. the nobility's manner of deportment   c. terraced dynamics
    b. the doctrine of universal brotherhood   d. emotional states or moods of music

LISTENING EXERCISE A comparison of the Renaissance and early baroque styles:
   As you listen to three examples provided by your instructor, check those characteristics that are predominant in each composition. When this analysis is completed, decide which style each example represents.

	1.	2.	3.
Medium: large choral group, a cappella	___	___	___
small vocal ensemble, with basso continuo	___	___	___
Melody: basically conjunct, easy to sing	___	___	___
elaborate, ornamented; difficult to sing	___	___	___
Texture: basically polyphonic	___	___	___
basically homophonic	___	___	___
Rhythm: gently flowing	___	___	___
emphatically rhythmic	___	___	___
Harmony: consonant, triadic, church modes	___	___	___
greater use of dissonances, major and minor tonalities	___	___	___
Dynamics: basically constant	___	___	___
terraced	___	___	___
Timbres: specialized instruments	___	___	___
violin family, familiar instruments, basso continuo	___	___	___

Example 1:

   style:

   composer: title:

Example 2:

   style:

   composer: title:

Example 3:

   style:

   composer: title:

III-2. MUSIC IN BAROQUE SOCIETY

SELF-TEST Multiple-choice: Circle the answer that best completes each item.

1. In the baroque period, the ordinary citizen's opportunities for hearing music usually came from the
   a. court   b. church   c. concert hall   d. corner tavern

2. Frederick the Great, king of Prussia, was a
   a. flutist   c. composer
   b. general   d. all of the above

3. In Italy, music schools were often connected with
   a. orphanages   c. public schools
   b. courts of the nobility   d. universities

4. The music director of a court in the baroque period
   a. supervised and directed the musical performances
   b. composed much of the music required
   c. was responsible for the discipline of the other musicians
   d. all of the above

5. A large court during the baroque period might employ about _____ performers.
   a. 18   b. 24   c. 80   d. 120

III-3. THE CONCERTO GROSSO AND RITORNELLO FORM

BASIC TERMS:

concerto grosso   ritornello form
tutti   ritornello

SELF-TEST Completion: Supply the missing information.

1. A concerto grosso usually has _____ movements.

2. The tempo markings of the movements of a concerto grosso are

   usually _____, _____, and _____.

3. The large group of players in a concerto grosso is known as the _____.

4. The first and last movements of the concerto grosso are often in _____ form.

5. The solo instruments in Bach's *Brandenburg* Concerto No. 5 are the

   _____, _____, and _____.

LISTENING EXERCISE A *Brandenburg* Concerto:
    Having studied Bach's *Brandenburg* Concerto No. 5, listen to one of the other five concertos and find similarities and differences. While listening, complete the following.

Johann Sebastian Bach: *Brandenburg* Concerto No.____

Performers:
    _____live performance   _____recorded performance

Instrumentation:
    concertino (solo group):
    ripieno (tutti):

Order of movements:
    For each movement, in addition to the tempo, form, and mood requested, give any other characteristics you recognize, such as terraced dynamics, changes in texture, strong rhythmic drive, basso ostinato, improvisation, the realization of a basso continuo, or elaborate ornamentation.

First movement:
    tempo: form: mood:

    comments:

Second movement:
    tempo: form: mood:

    comments:

Third movement:
    tempo: form: mood:

    comments:

Fourth movement:
    tempo: form: mood:

    comments:

Comparison with the *Brandenburg* Concerto No. 5:
    similarities:

    differences:

III-4. THE FUGUE

BASIC TERMS:

fugue	pedal point (organ point)
subject	inversion
answer	retrograde
countersubject	augmentation
episode	diminution
stretto	prelude

SELF-TEST Matching: Match each term with its description.

1. answer

2. augmentation

3. countersubject

4. diminution

5. episodes

6. inversion

7. pedal point

8. retrograde

9. stretto

10. subject

a. presentation of a subject from right to left, or beginning with the last note and proceeding backward to the first

b. main theme of a fugue

c. imitation of a subject before it is completed

d. subject of a fugue presented in the dominant

e. presentation of a subject in lengthened time values

f. presentation of a subject in shortened time values

g. melodic idea that constantly accompanies the subject of a fugue

h. turning the subject of a fugue upside down, or reversing the direction of each interval

i. single tone, usually in the bass, that is held while the other voices produce a series of changing harmonies against it

j. transitional sections of a fugue that offer either new material or fragments of the subject or countersubject

LISTENING EXERCISE Bach's Organ Fugue in G Minor:

After listening several times to the subject of Bach's Organ Fugue in G Minor (*Little* Fugue), you should be able to recognize it regardless of accompanying material. Complete the following diagram by sketching in the relative pitch levels of the entrances of the subject (the first two are already indicated). Draw vertical lines to indicate episodes where the subject is not presented in its entirety.

1————————
    2————————

RESEARCH PROJECT Transcriptions of Bach's Organ Fugue in G Minor:

Compare the original organ version of Bach's *Little* Fugue with two transcriptions. Which do you prefer from an aesthetic point of view? Why? Which do you prefer for personal listening? Why?

Medium: organ   _____   _____

Performer:

Comments:

Preferences:
(include reasons)

III-5. THE ELEMENTS OF OPERA

BASIC TERMS:

opera	aria
libretto	recitative
librettist	ensemble
voice categories of opera	prompter
overture (prelude)	

SELF-TEST Matching: Match each term with its description.

1. aria

2. basso buffo

3. basso profundo

4. conductor

5. duet

6. ensemble

7. libretto

8. opera

9. overture

10. prompter

11. recitative

12. supernumeraries

a. play, set to music and sung to orchestral accompaniment, with scenery, costumes, and action

b. singer with a low range who usually takes comic roles

c. musical number for two solo voices with orchestral accompaniment

d. song for solo voice with orchestral accompaniment

e. singer with a very low range and powerful voice, who usually takes roles calling for great dignity

f. vocal line that imitates the rhythms and pitch fluctuations of speech

g. person who beats time, indicates expression, cues in musicians, and controls the balance among instruments and voices

h. people on the opera stage who do not sing, but carry spears, fill out crowds, drink wine, or do other things that add to the opera's effect

i. text, or book, of a musical dramatic work

j. operatic number in which three or more lead singers are involved

k. orchestral composition performed before the curtain rises on a dramatic work

l. person who gives cues and reminds singers of words or pitches if they momentarily lose their place

RESEARCH PROJECT Preparing for a visit to the opera:
    Either on your own or as part of a class project, begin preparing for a visit to the opera. Whether for a live performance, a television broadcast, or a Saturday radio broadcast by the Metropolitan Opera, a little advance preparation can greatly enhance your appreciation and enjoyment of the performance.

Name of the opera:

Composer: Language:

Historical time: Place:

Comic or tragic:

Main characters:

Summary of plot or argument:

High points to look and listen for:

"Hit tunes":

III-6. OPERA IN THE BAROQUE ERA

BASIC TERMS:

Camerata	da capo aria	secco recitative
castrato (castrati)	da capo	accompanied recitative

SELF-TEST Multiple-choice: Circle the answer that best completes each item.

1. Most early baroque operas were based on Greek mythology and
   a. contemporary political events
   b. contemporary lyric poetry
   c. contemporary exploration of the new world
   d. ancient history

2. Members of the Camerata wanted to create a new vocal style based on the
   a. music of the ancient Greek tragedies
   b. glories of their aristocratic patrons
   c. organum of the Middle Ages
   d. polyphonic madrigal

3. A typical baroque operatic form was the da capo aria in ABA form in which the singer
   a. would make a literal repetition of the opening A section after the B section
   b. was expected to embellish the returning melody with ornamental tones
   c. would insert recitatives between the sections for added variety
   d. improvise new words for the returning A section

4. The first opera house in Europe to offer entry to anyone with the price of admission opened in 1637 in
   a. Hamburg   b. London   c. Rome   d. Venice

5. The members of the Camerata wanted the vocal line of their music to follow
   a. standard rules of musical theory
   b. the rhythms and pitch fluctuations of speech
   c. the lines of contrapuntal writing
   d. set metrical and melodic patterns

6. Speechlike melody accompanied only by a basso continuo is called
   a. secco recitative
   b. accompanied recitative
   c. castrato
   d. basso ostinato

7. Embellishments are
   a. ornamental tones not printed in the music that seventeenth- and eighteenth-century performers were expected to add to the melody
   b. music created at the same time it is performed
   c. notes printed in the music that embellish the melody
   d. obsolete in contemporary performances

III-7. CLAUDIO MONTEVERDI

SELF-TEST Multiple-choice: Circle the answer that best completes each item.

1. Monteverdi spent the greater part of his career in the most important church post in Italy, that of
   - a. Notre Dame, Paris
   - b. The Duomo, Florence
   - c. St. Mark's, Venice
   - d. the Vatican, Rome

2. To achieve intensity of expression, Monteverdi used _____ with unprecedented freedom and daring.
   - a. consonance
   - b. dissonance
   - c. basso continuo
   - d. texts

3. Orpheus goes to Hades in the hope of bringing _____ back to life.
   - a. Eurydice
   - b. Phyllis
   - c. Persephone
   - d. Oriana

4. Which of the following statements is *not* true?
   - a. Monteverdi's *Orfeo,* written in 1607, is considered to be the earliest operatic masterpiece.
   - b. All twelve of Monteverdi's operas are regularly performed in Europe and America.
   - c. Monteverdi creates variety in *Orfeo* by using many kinds of music, combining recitatives, arias, duets, choruses, and instrumental interludes into one dramatic whole.
   - d. Monteverdi's works form a musical bridge between the sixteenth and seventeenth centuries and greatly influenced composers of the time.

5. To evoke angry or warlike feelings in some of his texts, Monteverdi introduced new orchestral effects, including pizzicato and
   - a. tremolo
   - b. double stops
   - c. sul ponticello
   - d. col legno

6. Monteverdi's vocal music was ordinarily supported by a _____ and other instruments.
   - a. bassoon
   - b. trumpet
   - c. basso continuo
   - d. string bass

III-8. HENRY PURCELL

BASIC TERM:
   ground bass (basso ostinato)

SELF-TEST Completion: Supply the missing information.

1. A common variation form in the baroque is the ground bass, or _____.

2. *Dido and Aeneas,* which many people consider the finest opera ever written to an English text, was inspired by Virgil's epic poem, the _____; it was written for students at a _____; it has a great number of dances (more so than is usual in opera) because _____; and it is scored for _____.

3. Some indication of the acclaim and respect given Purcell by his contemporaries in England can be seen from the fact that he is buried in _____.

THE BAROQUE PERIOD   57

III-9. THE BAROQUE SONATA

BASIC TERMS:
    sonata   trio sonata   opus

SELF-TEST Multiple-choice: Circle the answer that best completes each item.
1. Baroque trio sonatas usually involve _____ performers.
    a. two   b. three   c. four   d. five

2. The sonata in the baroque period was a composition in several movements for
    a. a solo instrument   c. two to four instruments
    b. three solo instruments   d. one to eight instruments

3. Corelli's Trio Sonata in A Minor, Op. 3, No. 10, is scored for
    a. two violins   c. two violins and basso continuo
    b. solo violin and orchestra   d. piano, violin, and cello

4. Characteristic of baroque trio sonatas, the second movement of Corelli's Trio Sonata in A Minor, Op. 3, No. 10, is
    a. slow and dignified   b. songlike   c. fuguelike   d. a dance

5. The abbreviation *op.* stands for *opus,* Latin for
    a. a cartoon character   b. Spring   c. work   d. opulent

III-10. ANTONIO VIVALDI

BASIC TERMS:
    solo concerto   trill

SELF-TEST Multiple-choice: Circle the answer that best completes each item.
1. Vivaldi is closely identified with the musical life of
    a. Rome   b. Venice   c. Florence   d. Cremona

2. Vivaldi wrote approximately _____ concertos.
    a. 10   b. 30   c. 95   d. 450

3. Vivaldi wrote concertos
    a. only for string instruments   c. for a great variety of instruments
    b. only for violins with continuo   d. only for keyboard instruments

4. Vivaldi was famous and influential as a virtuoso
    a. harpsichordist   b. opera singer   c. lutenist   d. violinist

5. A Vivaldi concerto usually has _____ movements.
    a. a variable number of   b. two   c. three   d. four

6. A musical ornament consisting of rapid alternation of two tones that are a whole step or half step apart is a _____.
    a. trill   b. shake   c. blurb   d. wobble

PERFORMANCE PERSPECTIVE
Jeanne Lamon, violinist, plays and conducts Vivaldi's *Spring* Concerto

Lamon both conducts and directs Tafelmusik, a Canadian period-instrumental group. Listen to another one of the concertos from their recording of Vivaldi's *The Four Seasons* and read the poetry associated with the concerto. How does the concerto "come to life" through the programmatic elements Vivaldi writes into the music? How does Lamon's interpretation enhance these programmatic elements?

III-11. JOHANN SEBASTIAN BACH

BASIC TERM:
improvisation

SELF-TEST Completion: Supply the missing information.

1. The longest period of Bach's professional life was spent as director of music at St. Thomas Church

   in _____.

2. Bach's church music uses operatic forms such as the _____

   and _____.

3. A collection of compositions that displays all the resources of fugue writing is Bach's

   _____.

4. Bach's works are unique in their combination of rich _____

   and _____ texture.

5. A collection of twice twenty-four preludes and fugues, one in each major and minor key, basic to

   the repertory of keyboard players today, is Bach's _____.

SELF-TEST Multiple-choice: Circle the answer that best completes each item.

6. Bach achieves unity of mood in his compositions by using
   a. homophonic texture
   b. musical symbolism
   c. an insistent rhythmic drive
   d. simple melodic ideas

7. Of Bach's twenty children, _____ went on to become well-known composers.
   a. two
   b. three
   c. four
   d. five

8. Bach created masterpieces in every baroque form except the
   a. opera
   b. concerto
   c. fugue
   d. sonata

9. Bach's personal music style was drawn from
   a. Italian concertos
   b. French dance pieces
   c. German church music
   d. all of the above

10. Bach was recognized as the most eminent _____ of his day.
    a. organist
    b. composer
    c. violinist
    d. cellist

III-12. THE BAROQUE SUITE

BASIC TERMS:
suite   French overture

SELF-TEST Multiple-choice: Circle the answer that best completes each item.
1. Baroque suites frequently begin with a
   a. French overture   b. gavotte   c. gigue   d. sarabande

2. Although all the movements of a baroque suite are written in the same key, they differ in
   a. meter   b. national origin   c. tempo   d. all of the above

3. Which of the following is *not* a part of the baroque suite?
   a. allemande   b. waltz   c. sarabande   d. gigue

4. The various dances of the baroque suite are usually
   a. polyphonic in texture   c. in AABB form
   b. in theme and variation form   d. in ABA form

5. The French overture has
   a. two sections: slow-fast   c. three sections: fast-slow-fast
   b. two sections: fast-slow   d. one continuous section

LISTENING EXERCISE Comparing two baroque suites:
   Listen to any two baroque suites. See if all the movements are in the same key, indicate any differences from the traditional order of movements, and note the tempo, meter, and character of the individual movements. Distinguish between those movements that are dance-inspired and those that are not.

Traditional order of movements:	FIRST EXAMPLE composer: title:	SECOND EXAMPLE composer: title:

Prelude or introduction

Allemande
(moderate dance from Germany)

Courante
(fast dance from France)

Sarabande
(slow and solemn dance from Spain)

Optional
(gavotte, passepied, loure, air, *etc.*)

Gigue
(fast dance from England and Ireland)

III-13. THE CHORALE AND CHURCH CANTATA

BASIC TERMS:
    chorale   chorale prelude   cantata

SELF-TEST Multiple-choice: Circle the answer that best completes each item.

1. The _____ is an instrumental composition based on a chorale.
    a. cantata   c. chorale prelude
    b. solo concerto   d. French overture

2. In Bach's day, the Lutheran church service lasted about _____ hour(s).
    a. one   b. two   c. three   d. four

3. The _____ is a Lutheran congregational hymn tune.
    a. cantata   b. chorale   c. chorale prelude   d. recitative

4. In their use of aria, duet, and recitative, Bach's cantatas closely resembled the _____ of the time.
    a. suites   b. operas   c. concertos   d. sonatas

5. A sung piece, or choral work with or without vocal soloists, usually
   with orchestral accompaniment, is the
    a. cantata   c. concerto grosso
    b. chorale prelude   d. sonata

III-14. THE ORATORIO

BASIC TERM:
    oratorio

SELF-TEST Multiple-choice: Circle the answer that best completes each item.

1. Oratorios first appeared in
    a. Germany   b. England   c. Italy   d. France

2. The first oratorios were based on
    a. Greek mythology   c. Greek and Roman literature
    b. contemporary literature   d. stories from the Bible

3. Oratorio differs from opera in that it has no
    a. orchestral accompaniment   c. choral parts
    b. acting, scenery, or costumes   d. vocal soloists

4. In oratorio, the story is carried forward by the
    a. arias   b. chorus   c. narrator's recitatives   d. duets

5. An element of the oratorio that is especially important and serves to comment on or participate
   in the drama is the
    a. narrator   b. chorus   c. orchestra   d. vocal soloist

III-15. GEORGE FRIDERIC HANDEL

SELF-TEST Multiple-choice: Circle the answer that best completes each item.
1. George Frideric Handel was born in 1685, the same year as
   a. Johann Sebastian Bach
   b. Arcangelo Corelli
   c. Claudio Monteverdi
   d. Antonio Vivaldi

2. Although Handel wrote a great deal of instrumental music, the core of his huge output consists of English oratorios and Italian
   a. operas   b. songs   c. chorales   d. madrigals

3. Handel's oratorios are usually based on
   a. the Old Testament
   b. Greek mythology
   c. the New Testament
   d. Roman history

4. In addition to being a composer and opera impresario, Handel was a virtuoso
   a. violinist   b. organist   c. cellist   d. trumpeter

5. Handel's *Messiah* is an example of
   a. an oratorio   b. an opera   c. musical theater   d. a song

6. Handel spent the major portion of his life in
   a. Germany   b. England   c. Italy   d. Ireland

7. Which of the following oratorios is *not* by Handel?
   a. *Messiah*   b. *Elijah*   c. *Israel in Egypt*   d. *Joshua*

8. The focus of a Handel oratorio is usually the
   a. soprano soloist   b. chorus   c. orchestra   d. conductor

RESEARCH PROJECTS

Handel oratorios:

List some of the other oratorios by Handel with which you may be familiar.

Handel operas:

List some of the operas of Handel that have been revived, with a brief synopsis of their plots, or list some famous arias from his operas that are still performed.

BIOGRAPHICAL SKETCH A baroque composer: _____

Born (year, place):
Died (year, place):

Personal life:

    family:

    health and physiognomy:

    personality:

Career:

    significant places:

    significant people:

    employers or patrons:

    means of earning a living:

    financial situation:

Music:

    style of composition:

    general characteristics:

Output (List some of the major forms in which the composer worked, including the approximate number of compositions if significant. List some of the major compositions in each category, check those which you have heard, and circle those which you have studied):

Category: _____   _____   _____

Works:

Category: _____   _____   _____

Works:

UNIT QUIZ III
THE BAROQUE PERIOD

Name_____

Class/section_____ Date_____

Matching: Match each term with its definition.

1._____ play, set to music and sung to orchestral accompaniment, with scenery, costumes, and action

2._____ set of dance-inspired movements

3._____ large-scale composition for chorus, vocal soloists, and orchestra, usually set to a narrative biblical text

4._____ text, or book, of a musical dramatic work

5._____ orchestral composition performed before the curtain rises on a dramatic work

6._____ song for solo voice with orchestral accompaniment

7._____ sung piece; choral work with or without vocal soloists; usually with orchestral accompaniment

8._____ hymn tune for congregational use

9._____ instrumental composition in which a small group of soloists is pitted against a larger group

10._____ imitation of a fugue subject before it is completed

11._____ instrumental composition based on a chorale

12._____ single tone, usually in the bass, that is held while the other voices produce a series of changing harmonies against it

13._____ bass part together with numbers (figures) specifying the chords to be played above it

14._____ polyphonic composition based on one main theme

15._____ section of a musical work that sounds fairly complete and independent, but is part of a larger composition

16._____ vocal line that imitates the rhythms and pitch fluctuations of speech

17._____ instrumental composition in several movements

18._____ ornament consisting of the rapid alternation of two tones that are a whole or half step apart

a. aria

b. basso continuo

c. cantata

d. chorale

e. chorale prelude

f. concerto grosso

g. fugue

h. libretto

i. movement

j. opera

k. oratorio

l. overture

m. pedal point

n. recitative

o. sonata

p. stretto

q. suite

r. trill

Unit Quiz III (cont.)

Matching: Match each work with its composer.

19._____ Fugue in G Minor (*Little* Fugue)   a. Johann Sebastian Bach

20._____ *Orfeo*   b. Arcangelo Corelli

21._____ *Brandenburg* Concerto No. 5   c. George Frideric Handel

22._____ *Wachet auf, ruft uns die Stimme*   d. Claudio Monteverdi

23._____ *Messiah*   e. Henry Purcell

24._____ *Dido and Aeneas*   f. Antonio Vivaldi

25._____ *Spring* Concerto, Op. 8, No. 1, from *The Four Seasons*

Listening or essay question: To be provided by your instructor.

_____

_____

_____

_____

_____

_____

_____

_____

_____

_____

_____

IV. THE CLASSICAL PERIOD

IV-1. THE CLASSICAL STYLE (1750–1820)

SELF-TEST Completion: Complete the following comparison of the baroque and classical periods by checking the column of the period with which each description is most closely associated.

	BAROQUE	CLASSICAL
1. Interest in forming a total illusion; theatrical	____	____
2. Fills the space with action and movement	____	____
3. Emphasis on balance and clarity of structures	____	____
4. "Age of enlightenment"	____	____
5. Louis XIV as the epitome of his age	____	____
6. Impartial in approach; reality rather than illusion	____	____
7. Complex mixture of rationalism, sensuality, materialism, and spirituality	____	____
8. New approach to science based on the union of mathematics and experiment	____	____
9. Attempt to recapture the "noble simplicity and calm grandeur" of ancient Greece and Rome	____	____
10. Evolution of the standard orchestra of four sections	____	____
11. Free interchange of instrumental parts	____	____
12. Emergence of major and minor as basis of tonality	____	____
13. End of the basso continuo	____	____
14. Faith in the power of reason as the best guide to human conduct	____	____
15. "Age of grandeur"	____	____
16. Period of Voltaire, Diderot, David, Goya, and Hogarth	____	____
17. Exploitation of individual tone colors in orchestration	____	____
18. Emotional restraint and "good taste"	____	____
19. Basso continuo as the nucleus of the instrumental ensemble	____	____
20. Period of Galileo, Newton, Bernini, Rubens, and Rembrandt	____	____

LISTENING EXERCISE A comparison of the late baroque and classical styles:

As you listen to three examples provided by your instructor, check those characteristics that are predominant in each composition. When this analysis is completed, decide which style each example represents.

	1.	2.	3.
Mood: unified	___	___	___
variety and contrast	___	___	___
Rhythm: single continuous figure	___	___	___
varied, changing, flexible	___	___	___
Texture: predominantly polyphonic	___	___	___
basically homophonic	___	___	___
Melody: elaborate, ornamented, continuously expanding	___	___	___
balanced, symmetrical	___	___	___
Themes: one main theme	___	___	___
contrasting themes	___	___	___
Improvisation: essential	___	___	___
limited to cadenzas	___	___	___
Dynamics: terraced	___	___	___
gradual changes	___	___	___
Timbres: subordinate to other elements	___	___	___
exploitation of instrumental timbres	___	___	___
Orchestra: based on the violin family with basso continuo	___	___	___
standard orchestra of four families	___	___	___

Other characteristics:

Example 1:
  style:

  composer: title:

Example 2:
  style:

  composer: title:

Example 3:
  style:

  composer: title:

IV-2. COMPOSER, PATRON, AND PUBLIC IN THE CLASSICAL PERIOD

SELF-TEST Multiple-choice: Circle the answer that best completes each item.

1. Joseph Haydn was content to spend most of his life
    a. serving a wealthy aristocratic family
    b. as a church musician and organist
    c. as an independently wealthy composer
    d. as a professional freelance musician

2. In the classical period, comic operas sometimes
    a. were based on the Old Testament
    b. ridiculed the aristocracy
    c. were in Latin
    d. all of the above

3. Haydn's contract of employment shows that he was considered
    a. a skilled servant
    b. a freelance musician
    c. a visiting guest composer
    d. an equal by his employer

4. Social mobility during the classical period was
    a. a limited sociological factor
    b. ruthlessly stamped out by the aristocracy
    c. promoted and encouraged by the church
    d. an important factor in the rise of the middle class

5. Vienna in 1800
    a. was the fourth-largest city in Europe
    b. had a population of almost 250,000
    c. was the seat of the Holy Roman Empire
    d. all of the above

6. In Vienna, Haydn and Mozart
    a. avoided each other
    b. became close friends
    c. were jealous of each other
    d. never met

7. In the classical period, serious composition was flavored by
    a. folk and popular music
    b. heroic and mythological plots
    c. elaborately ornamented melodies
    d. all of the above

8. The prospering middle class in the classical period sought aristocratic luxuries such as
    a. theater   b. literature   c. music   d. all of the above

9. The *Concert des Amateurs,* an organization in Paris devoted to presenting public concerts, was conducted in the 1770s by
    a. Johann Christian Bach
    b. the Chevalier de Saint-Georges
    c. Ludwig van Beethoven
    d. Joseph Haydn

10. Haydn and Mozart wrote many outdoor entertainment pieces, which they called
    a. sonatas   b. divertimentos   c. concertos   d. symphonies

IV-3. SONATA FORM

BASIC TERMS:

sonata form   bridge (transition)   motive   coda
exposition   development   recapitulation

SELF-TEST Completion: Supply the missing information.

1. Sonata form consists of three main sections: _____,

_____, and _____.

2. A movement in sonata form may be preceded by a slow _____

that creates a strong feeling of expectancy.

3. A transitional passage that leads to a contrasting section is called a _____.

4. The three main sections of a sonata-form movement are often followed by a concluding section

known as the _____.

5. Short musical ideas developed within a composition are called fragments or _____.

6. The "K" number that appears after Mozart's works refers to

_____.

Multiple-choice: Circle the answer that best completes each item.

7. Sonata form should be viewed as
   a. a rigid mold into which musical ideas are poured
   b. another term for the symphony
   c. a set of principles that serve to shape and unify contrasts of theme and key
   d. a set of variations on a theme

8. In the exposition of a sonata-form movement,
   a. the closing theme is in the tonic key   c. the second theme is in a new key
   b. a new theme is always presented in the bridge d. a new meter enters with the second theme

9. Sonata form is used frequently as the form for the _____ movement of a multimovement work.
   a. first
   b. slow   c. final fast
                                                      d. all of the above

10. In the recapitulation of a sonata-form movement,
    a. all the principal material is in the tonic key   c. the second theme is in a new key
    b. a new theme is presented in the bridge   d. there is no second theme

11. At the end of a classical exposition there usually is a
    a. new tempo indication   c. repeat sign
    b. new time signature   d. coda sign

IV-4. THEME AND VARIATIONS

BASIC TERMS:
countermelody   theme and variations

SELF-TEST Multiple-choice: Circle the answer that best completes each item.
1. Theme-and-variations form may be schematically outlined as
   a. AABB   b. AA'A''A'''A''''   c. ABA   d. ABACADA

2. Each successive variation in a theme with variations
   a. retains some elements of the theme   c. is usually in the same key
   b. is usually in a new key   d. presents a new melodic idea

3. The _____ movement of Haydn's *Surprise* Symphony is in theme-and-variations form.
   a. first   b. second   c. third   d. fourth

IV-5. MINUET AND TRIO

BASIC TERMS:
minuet and trio (minuet)   da capo   scherzo   serenade

SELF-TEST Multiple-choice: Circle the answer that best completes each item.
1. The minuet is generally the _____ movement of a classical symphony.
   a. first   b. second   c. third   d. fourth

2. The minuet as a whole may be outlined as
   a. ABA   b. AABB   c. ABC   d. AABBCC

3. In many of Beethoven's works, there is a _____ movement instead of the minuet.
   a. presto   b. scherzo   c. fugato   d. ritornello

4. The minuet first appeared around 1650 as a(n)
   a. instrumental composition for concert performance
   b. prayer in Germany at the end of the Thirty Years' War
   c. dance at the court of Louis XIV of France
   d. country dance in England

5. The character of the minuet is best described as
   a. brisk and lively   c. heavy and ponderous
   b. quiet and relaxed   d. stately and dignified

6. The scherzo differs from the minuet in that it
   a. moves more quickly   c. has a different meter
   b. has a different form   d. all of the above

7. As is typical in classical music, the double bass part in Mozart's *Eine kleine Nachtmusik*
   a. sounds the same as the cello part   c. is a separate and distinct bass part
   b. is frequently left out in performance   d. sounds an octave lower than the cello part

IV-6. RONDO

BASIC TERMS:
rondo   sonata-rondo

SELF-TEST Multiple-choice: Circle the answer that best completes each item.
1. Because of its character, the rondo most often serves as a
   a. slow movement   b. first movement   c. set of variations   d. finale

2. A common rondo pattern is
   a. ABACA   b. ABACBA   c. ABBABC   d. ABCBA

3. The main theme of the rondo
   a. returns only once in the movement   c. seldom ends the movement
   b. is usually slow and dignified   d. is usually in the tonic key

4. Another common rondo pattern is
   a. ABCBCD   b. ABACABA   c. ABCBAC   d. ABACDC

5. The rondo was used
   a. exclusively in the classical period   c. as late as the twentieth century
   b. only as an independent composition   d. only in the classical symphony and quartet

MULTIMEDIA COMPANION Activities: Rondo
Mapping an additional rondo form movement

Once you have worked your way through the fourth movement of Beethoven's String Quartet in C Minor, Op. 18, No. 4 in rondo form (included in the "activities section" of the Multimedia Companion CD-Rom), you should be ready to try your hand at "mapping" out a musical form on your own. Listen to the second movement of Beethoven's Piano Sonata in C Minor, Op. 13 (*Pathétique*). You can find a recording of this movement in the Classical music section under "additional recordings" on the Multimedia Companion. This movement is in rondo form. Create a brief listening guide for this movement that reflects the formal organization of the movement. Make reference to specific musical characteristics that support the form.

IV-7. THE CLASSICAL SYMPHONY

BASIC TERM:

symphony

SELF-TEST Multiple-choice: Circle the answer that best completes each item.
1. *Symphony* may be defined as a(n)
    a. musical composition for orchestra, usually in four movements
    b. sonata for orchestra
    c. extended, ambitious composition exploiting the expanded range of tone color and dynamics
        of the classical orchestra
    d. all of the above

2. The usual order of movements in a classical symphony is
    a. fast, dance-related, slow, fast
    b. fast, slow, dance-related, fast
    c. fast, slow, fast, slow
    d. slow, fast, slow, fast

3. The first movement of a classical symphony is almost always fast and in _____ form.
    a. sonata   b. rondo   c. minuet   d. ABA

4. ABA form is typical of the minuet or scherzo movement and is also common in the
    a. finale   b. first movement   c. slow movement   d. all of the above

5. A symphony is unified partly by the use of the same
    a. key in three of its movements
    b. theme for each of its movements
    c. tempo throughout
    d. all of the above

LISTENING EXERCISE A classical symphony:

Either on your own or as part of a class project, prepare for a live or televised performance of a classical symphony. As with opera—indeed with any form of music—a little advance preparation can greatly enhance your appreciation and enjoyment of the performance.

Title:_____

Composer:_____ Date of composition:_____

Instrumentation:_____

First movement: tempo_____ meter_____ key_____

           form_____ mood_____

   themes:

   comments:

Second movement: tempo_____ meter_____ key_____

           form_____ mood_____

   themes:

   comments:

Third movement: tempo_____ meter_____ key_____

           form_____ mood_____

   themes:

   comments:

Fourth movement: tempo_____ meter_____ key_____

           form_____ mood_____

   themes:

   comments:

IV-8. THE CLASSICAL CONCERTO

BASIC TERMS:
concerto   cadenza   fermata

SELF-TEST Multiple-choice: Circle the answer that best completes each item.
1. A classical concerto is a three-movement work for
   a. instrumental soloist and orchestra   c. instrumental soloist and piano
   b. symphonic orchestra   d. vocal soloist and orchestra

2. An unaccompanied showpiece for the concerto's soloist is known as a
   a. fermata   c. concerto's solo
   b. cadenza   d. pause

3. The symphonic movement usually lacking in the concerto is the
   a. sonata-form movement   c. minuet or scherzo
   b. slow movement   d. rondo finale

4. The favored solo instrument in the classical concerto was the
   a. violin   b. cello   c. piano   d. clarinet

5. A pause in the score of a concerto is indicated by a
   a. signal from the soloist   c. signal from the conductor
   b. signal from the concertmaster   d. fermata

6. The first movement of a classical concerto
   a. is in the same form as a classical symphony   c. is usually a long cadenza
   b. has two expositions   d. does not have a development section

IV-9. CLASSICAL CHAMBER MUSIC

BASIC TERMS:
chamber music   string quartet

SELF-TEST Multiple-choice: Circle the answer that best completes each item.
1. Classical chamber music is designed
   a. to display the virtuosity of the players
   b. for the intimate setting of a small room
   c. exclusively for performance by paid professional musicians
   d. to be conducted by experienced orchestral directors

2. The classical string quartet is a musical composition for
   a. violin, viola, cello, and bass   c. violin, guitar, viola, and cello
   b. two violins, viola, and cello   d. all of the above

3. The most important form of classical chamber music is the
   a. piano trio   c. string quartet
   b. string quintet   d. violin and piano sonata

4. The piano trio is a musical composition for
   a. three pianos   c. violin, cello, and piano
   b. violin and piano   d. all of the above

5. The usual order of movements in a classical string quartet is
   a. fast, slow, minuet or scherzo, fast   c. slow, fast, slow, fast
   b. fast, slow, fast, slow   d. fast, slow, fast

6. A major factor that distinguishes chamber music from the symphony or concerto is that
   chamber music
   a. does not use sonata form   c. does not have difficult parts
   b. is performed in concert in concert halls d. is performed by one player per part

IV-10. JOSEPH HAYDN

SELF-TEST Completion: Supply the missing information.

1. Haydn was fortunate in having a long and fruitful, as well as financially stable, relationship with the noble Hungarian family of _____.

2. The twelve symphonies Haydn wrote for the concert manager J. P. Salomon for performance at his public concerts are also known as the _____ symphonies, for the city in which they were first performed.

3. Haydn was a prolific composer, as demonstrated in part by his 68 _____ and 104 _____.

4. Haydn's two popular oratorios are entitled _____ and _____.

SELF-TEST Multiple-choice: Circle the answer that best completes each item.

5. Along with his symphonies, Haydn's _____ are considered his most important works.
   a. operas   b. string quartets   c. baryton trios   d. serenades

6. Haydn's duties while in the service of the Esterházys included
   a. composing all the music requested by his patron
   b. conducting the orchestra of about twenty-five players
   c. coaching the singers for operatic performances
   d. all of the above

7. Which of the following is *not* a characteristic of Haydn's music?
   a. The music is robust and direct, radiating a healthy optimism.
   b. The minuets often romp and stomp rather than bow and curtsy.
   c. There are few changes in texture and orchestration.
   d. Many works have a folk flavor, due to the use of actual peasant tunes and original melodies in folklike style.

LISTENING EXERCISE Nicknames in Haydn's music:

Many of Haydn's symphonies and string quartets have nicknames. From your listening experiences, identify some of these compositions, and give the nickname and the factors that caused the association.

Work: Nickname:

   Reason:

Work: Nickname:

   Reason:

Work: Nickname:

   Reason:

BIOGRAPHICAL SKETCH A classical composer: Joseph Haydn *or* Wolfgang Amadeus Mozart

Born (year, place):
Died (year, place):

Personal life:

    family:

    health and physiognomy:

    personality:

Career:

    significant places:

    significant people:

    employers or patrons:

    means of earning a living:

    financial situation:

Music:

    style of composition:

    general characteristics:

Output (List some of the major forms in which the composer worked, including the approximate number of compositions if significant. List some of the major compositions in each category, check those which you have heard, and circle those which you have studied):

Category: _____ _____ _____

Works:

Category: _____ _____ _____

Works:

IV-11. WOLFGANG AMADEUS MOZART

SELF-TEST Multiple-choice: Circle the answer that best completes each item.

1. By the age of six, Mozart could
   a. play the harpsichord and violin
   b. improvise fugues and write minuets
   c. read music perfectly at sight
   d. all of the above

2. Don Giovanni, in Mozart's opera of that name, is
   a. a despotic Italian nobleman
   b. the legendary Spanish lover
   c. Sir John Falstaff
   d. the servant to Leporello

3. Mozart's Requiem was
   a. composed by a nobleman using Mozart's name
   b. a high point in his career
   c. an early work
   d. finished by one of his pupils

4. Mozart's trips to Italy
   a. enabled him to study and master the Italian operatic style
   b. were quite rare
   c. were the scenes of his greatest triumphs
   d. enabled him to secure several permanent posts

5. Between the ages of six and fifteen, Mozart
   a. received an excellent formal education in Salzburg
   b. went to Vienna to study with Haydn
   c. was continually on tour in England and Europe
   d. played in the archbishop's orchestra in Salzburg

6. Mozart's Symphony No. 40
   a. is in G major
   b. has only three movements
   c. is one of his last three symphonies
   d. all of the above

7. Mozart's finest German opera was
   a. *The Magic Flute*
   b. *The Marriage of Figaro*
   c. *Don Giovanni*
   d. *Fidelio*

8. Mozart was born in
   a. Salzburg, Austria   b. Eisenach, Germany   c. Bonn, Germany   d. Rohrau, Austria

9. Which of the following is *not* one of Mozart's three masterpieces of Italian opera?
   a. *The Marriage of Figaro*
   b. *Cosi fan tutte*
   c. *Orfeo*
   d. *Don Giovanni*

10. The cadenza in the first movement of Mozart's Piano Concerto No. 23 in A Major is unusual in that
    a. it serves as a transition to the recapitulation
    b. the performer is expected to improvise at the performance
    c. it was composed by Mozart himself
    d. it was composed by Beethoven

PERFORMANCE PERSPECTIVE
Murray Perahia, pianist, playing and conducting the first movement of Mozart's Piano Concerto in A Major, K. 488.

Perahia describes Mozart's Piano Concerto in A Major, K. 488 as being more lyric and passionate when compared to his other piano concertos, which he describes as being symphonic in dimension. Pick another one of Mozart's piano concertos and listen to the first movement. Compare and contrast the movement you pick with the first movement of the A Major concerto in regard to tone color, dynamic range, the piano style (virtuosic vs. lyric), and the expressive qualities of the melody.

Composition No. 1: Mozart's Piano Concerto in A Major, K. 488, first movement

Musical Elements
Tone color:

Dynamic range:

Piano style:

Expressive qualities:

Composition No. 2:

Musical Elements
Tone color:

Dynamic range:

Piano style:

Expressive qualities:

Compare/Contrast:

IV-12. LUDWIG VAN BEETHOVEN

SELF-TEST Completion: Supply the missing information.

1. Beethoven's Ninth Symphony is unusual in that it is scored for _____ and _____ as well as orchestra.

2. We have a record of Beethoven's struggle with his musical material because of his habit of carrying _____.

3. Beethoven's only opera is entitled _____.

4. Beethoven's Third Symphony was originally composed to commemorate the deeds of _____ as the embodiment of heroism and democratic ideals. It is said that when Beethoven heard what this person had done, he tore up the title page, and the symphony is now known as the _____.

5. Beethoven, as the musical heir of Haydn and Mozart, bridged the _____ and _____ periods.

SELF-TEST Multiple-choice: Circle the answer that best completes each item.

6. Beethoven's greatest liturgical music is to be found in his
   a. Mass in B Minor
   b. *Missa Solemnis*
   c. *Fidelio*
   d. Eighth Symphony

7. Beethoven's late works, composed after he was totally deaf, include
   a. piano sonatas
   b. string quartets
   c. the Ninth Symphony
   d. all of the above

8. Beethoven greatly expanded the _____ section of the sonata-form movement and made it more dramatic.
   a. introduction
   b. exposition
   c. development
   d. recapitulation

9. The choral finale of Beethoven's Ninth Symphony is based on
   a. Dante's *Inferno*
   b. Shakespeare's *Midsummer Night's Dream*
   c. Schiller's *Ode to Joy*
   d. Shelley's *Ode to the West Wind*

10. Beethoven's sixteen _____ are generally considered among the greatest music ever composed.
   a. piano concertos
   b. string quartets
   c. piano sonatas
   d. symphonies

BIOGRAPHICAL SKETCH Ludwig van Beethoven

Born (year, place):
Died (year, place):

Personal life:

   family:

   health and physiognomy:

   personality:

Career:

   significant places:

   significant people:

   employers or patrons:

   means of earning a living:

   financial situation:

Music:

   style of composition:

   general characteristics:

Output (List some of the major forms in which the composer worked, including the approximate number of compositions if significant. List some of the major compositions in each category, check those which you have heard, and circle those which you have studied):

Category: _____   _____   _____

Works:

Category: _____   _____   _____

Works:

UNIT QUIZ IV
THE CLASSICAL PERIOD

Name_____

Class/section_____ Date_____

Multiple-choice: Choose the answer that best completes each sentence.

1. The character of the minuet is best described as
   a. heavy and ponderous
   b. brisk and lively
   c. stately and dignified
   d. quiet and relaxed

2. A common rondo pattern is
   a. AABB
   b. ABA
   c. ABCBA
   d. ABACABA

3. brilliant solo section in a concerto designed to display the performer's virtuosity   is called
   a. a cadenza
   b. a fermata
   c. a pause
   d. da capo

4. The usual order of movements in a classical symphony is
   a. fast, slow, fast
   b. slow, fast, slow, fast
   c. fast, slow, dance-related, fast
   d. slow, fast, fast

5. The typical orchestra of the classical period consisted of
   a. a loose ensemble of available instruments
   b. strings, pairs of woodwinds, horns, trumpets, and timpani
   c. strings with harpsichord continuo
   d. woodwinds, trombones, drums, and strings

6. In many of Beethoven's works there is a _____ movement instead of the minuet.
   a. presto
   b. scherzo
   c. fugato
   d. theme-and-variations

7. A symphony is a
   a. sonata for orchestra
   b. work for solo instrument
   c. work for chorus and orchestra
   d. work for piano solo

8. The standard catalog of the compositions of Mozart was made by
   a. Ludwig von Köchel
   b. Franz X. Süssmayr
   c. Lorenzo da Ponte
   d. Friedrich Kuhlau

9. Chamber music is characterized by
   a. having one performer per part
   b. having each player play very difficult solo passages
   c. a lack of repertoire
   d. being worth playing only in intimate chambers

10. A string quartet is a musical composition for
    a. flute, violin, viola, and cello
    b. violin, guitar, viola, and cello
    c. violin, viola, cello, and bass
    d. two violins, viola, and cello

Unit Quiz IV (cont.)

11. Classicism, as a stylistic period in music, figured prominently during the years
    a. 1450–1600   c. 1750–1820
    b. 1600–1750   d. 1820–1900

12. Theme-and-variations form may be schematically outlined as
    a. AABB   b. ABA   c. AA'A''A'''A''''   d. ABACA

13. The minuet is generally the _____ movement of a classical symphony.
    a. first   c. third
    b. second   d. fourth

14. The classical concerto is a large-scale work in three movements for
    a. solo instrument and piano   c. solo instrument
    b. solo instrument and orchestra   d. orchestra

15. A piano sonata is a musical composition in two or more movements for
    a. piano   c. piano and orchestra
    b. piano, violin, and cello   d. flute and piano

Completion: Name the basic parts of sonata-allegro form.

16._____

17._____

18._____

19. Optional part before 16:_____

20. Optional part after 18:_____

Matching: Match each composition with its composer.

21._____ *Eine kleine Nachtmusik*   a. Ludwig van Beethoven

22._____ Symphony No. 94 in G (*Surprise*)   b. Joseph Haydn

23._____ Symphony No. 40 in G Minor   c. Wolfgang Amadeus Mozart

24._____ Sonata in C Minor (*Pathétique*)

25._____ *Don Giovanni*

26._____ *The Magic Flute*

27._____ *The Creation*

28._____ Symphony No. 3 in E♭ (*Eroica*)

29._____ *Fidelio*

30._____ *The Marriage of Figaro*

V. THE ROMANTIC PERIOD

V-1. ROMANTICISM IN MUSIC (1820–1900)

BASIC TERMS:

nationalism	program music	rubato
exoticism	chromatic harmony	thematic transformation

SELF-TEST Completion: Complete the following comparison of the classical and romantic periods by checking the column of the period with which each description is most closely associated.

	CLASSICISM	ROMANTICISM
1. Impartial in approach; reality rather than illusion	_____	_____
2. Aristocratic patronage of the arts	_____	_____
3. Emphasis on balance and clarity of structures	_____	_____
4. Emotional subjectivity; fantasy	_____	_____
5. Interest in the strange and the unknown	_____	_____
6. Wide range of emotional expression	_____	_____
7. Nationalism	_____	_____
8. Traditionalism; adherence to established methods	_____	_____
9. Enthusiasm for the culture of the Middle Ages	_____	_____
10. Exoticism	_____	_____
11. Belief in the supernatural; personification	_____	_____
12. Art and culture of ancient Greece as a basic influence	_____	_____
13. Brilliant colors and dynamic motion	_____	_____
14. Emotional restraint and "good taste"	_____	_____
15. Nature as the mirror of the human heart	_____	_____
16. Frequently autobiographical	_____	_____
17. Period of the industrial revolution	_____	_____
18. Individualism	_____	_____
19. Faith in the power of reason	_____	_____
20. Period of the American and French revolutions	_____	_____

LISTENING EXERCISE A comparison of the classical and romantic styles:
    As you listen to three examples provided by your instructor, check those characteristics that are predominant in each composition. Then, decide which style each example represents.

	1.	2.	3.
Style: traditional	___	___	___
individualistic	___	___	___
Mood: restrained, ordered	___	___	___
flamboyant, unpredictable, melancholy	___	___	___
Content: absolute	___	___	___
programmatic, exotic, nationalistic	___	___	___
Melody: balanced, symmetrical	___	___	___
lyrical, individualized	___	___	___
Timbre: moderate variety	___	___	___
rich and sensuous	___	___	___
Orchestra: mainly strings with paired winds and timpani	___	___	___
large size, full instrumentation	___	___	___
Harmony: predominantly diatonic; relatively mild dissonances	___	___	___
prominent chromaticism; more dissonant	___	___	___
Dynamics: moderate range	___	___	___
wide range, sharp contrasts	___	___	___
Pitch: moderate range	___	___	___
wide range; exploitation of extremes	___	___	___
Tempo: relatively constant	___	___	___
fluctuations; use of rubato	___	___	___
Form: moderate in size	___	___	___
miniatures or monumental	___	___	___

Example 1:

    style:

    composer: title:

Example 2:

    style:

    composer: title:

Example 3:

    style:

    composer: title:

V-2. ROMANTIC COMPOSERS AND THEIR PUBLIC

SELF-TEST Multiple-choice: Circle the answer that best completes each item.
1. The composer whose career was a model for many romantic composers was
   a. Wolfgang Amadeus Mozart
   b. Johann Sebastian Bach
   c. Joseph Haydn
   d. Ludwig van Beethoven

2. A composer who earned his/her living as a violin virtuoso was
   a. Clara Schumann
   b. Niccolò Paganini
   c. Robert Schumann
   d. Frédéric Chopin

3. One of the few composers fortunate enough to be supported by private patrons was
   a. Franz Liszt
   b. Franz Schubert
   c. Hector Berlioz
   d. Peter Ilyich Tchaikovsky

4. Music criticism was a source of income for both Berlioz and
   a. Robert Schumann
   b. Franz Liszt
   c. Niccolò Paganini
   d. Giuseppe Verdi

5. When music conservatories were founded, women
   a. were admitted only as vocalists or pianists
   b. were at first accepted only as students of performance, but by the late 1800s
      could study musical composition
   c. could study only musical composition, since performance was considered undignified
   d. were not admitted

SELF-TEST Completion: Supply the missing information.

6. Because of the _____ and _____, many aristocrats
   could no longer afford to maintain private opera houses, orchestras, and "composers
   in residence."

7. A very important musical part of every middle-class home during the romantic period
   was the _____.

8. Public concerts had developed during the eighteenth century, but only in the nineteenth
   century did regular _____ concerts become common.

9. It is interesting to note that an American orchestra, the _____, is one
   of two orchestras that are the third-oldest in the world.

10. Music conservatories were founded in Europe in the first half of the nineteenth century.
    In the United States, during the 1860s, conservatories were founded in
    _____, _____, _____, _____, and
    _____.

V-3. THE ART SONG

BASIC TERMS:

art song   through-composed form
postlude   modified strophic form
strophic form   song cycle

SELF-TEST Completion: Supply the missing information.

1. The word _____ is commonly used for a romantic art song with a German text.

2. When music is repeated for all the stanzas of a song, the form is known as _____.

3. When new music is written for each stanza of a song, the form is known as _____.

4. The German composers of art songs favored, among others, the lyric poetry of

_____ and _____.

5. The mood of a song is often set by a brief _____, and then summed

up at the end by a(n) _____, both performed on the accompanying

instrument, the _____.

V-4. FRANZ SCHUBERT

SELF-TEST Multiple-choice: Circle the answer that best completes each item.
1. Schubert
    a. was widely acknowledged as a composer in his lifetime
    b. was very self-critical, which accounts for his meager output
    c. produced his greatest works after the age of forty
    d. was the first great master of the romantic art song

2. The piano's relentless rhythm in *Erlkönig (The Erlking)* unifies the song's episodes and suggests the
    a. galloping horse   c. calmness of the father
    b. joy of the child   d. approach of death

3. Schubert's songs number more than
    a. 50   b. 100   c. 250   d. 600

4. The Erlking, in Schubert's song of that name, is a romantic personification of
    a. ghosts   b. death   c. nature   d. a galloping horse

5. *The Erlking* is a poem by
    a. Heinrich Heine   c. Johann Wolfgang von Goethe
    b. Schubert himself   d. Robert Schumann

6. The form of *The Erlking* is
    a. strophic   c. through-composed
    b. modified strophic   d. none of the above

V-5. ROBERT SCHUMANN

SELF-TEST Multiple-choice: Circle the answer that best completes each item.

1. Schumann's works are
   a. intensely autobiographical
   b. usually linked with descriptive titles, texts, or programs
   c. essentially lyrical in nature
   d. all of the above

2. Robert Schumann's *Carnaval* is a(n)
   a. étude for piano students   c. composition for orchestra
   b. song cycle   d. cycle of piano pieces

3. Clara Wieck was
   a. the daughter of Schumann's piano teacher
   b. a virtuoso pianist
   c. Schumann's wife
   d. all of the above

4. During the first ten years of his creative life, Schumann published only
   a. songs   b. piano pieces   c. symphonies   d. musical criticism

5. As a writer and critic, Schumann
   a. founded and edited the *New Journal of Music*
   b. discovered and made famous some of the leading composers of his day
   c. wrote appreciative reviews of young "radical" composers like Chopin and Berlioz
   d. all of the above

LISTENING EXERCISE Lieder: Explore the fascinating world of lieder by listening to some songs of your own choice by Schubert, Schumann, or both.

1. Composer: Title: Form:

   Plot summary:

   Comments:

2. Composer: Title: Form:

   Plot summary:

   Comments:

3. Composer: Title: Form:

   Plot summary:

   Comments:

V-6. CLARA WIECK SCHUMANN

BASIC TERM:
modified strophic form

SELF-TEST Multiple-choice: Circle the answer that best completes each item.
1. Clara Wieck Schumann was
    a. a composer
    b. a concert pianist
    c. the mother of a large family
    d. all of the above

2. Clara Schumann's song *Leibst du um Schönheit* is written in
    a. strophic form
    b. modified strophic form
    c. through-composed form
    d. none of the above

3. Clara Schumann frequently performed the works of her husband and her close friend
    a. Hector Berlioz
    b. Richard Wagner
    c. Johann Sebastian Bach
    d. Johannes Brahms

4. Clara Schumann
    a. composed many works for orchestra
    b. stopped composing at the age of thirty-six when her husband died
    c. gave up concertizing when she got married
    d. continued to compose music throughout her life

5. As a composer, Clara Schumann
    a. wrote songs, piano pieces, a piano concerto, and a trio for piano, violin, and cello
    b. wrote only operas
    c. wrote only short lyrical piano pieces
    d. never performed her own music

V-7. FRÉDÉRIC CHOPIN

BASIC TERMS:

nocturne   étude   polonaise

SELF-TEST Multiple-choice: Circle the answer that best completes each item.

1. In the 1830s, Paris was
    a. a center of romanticism
    b. the artistic capital of Europe
    c. the home of Victor Hugo, Honoré de Balzac, and Heinrich Heine
    d. all of the above

2. Chopin was
    a. an extroverted virtuoso   c. sloppy and careless in dress
    b. robust and flamboyant   d. shy and reserved

3. Most of Chopin's pieces
    a. are exquisite miniatures   c. have a limited variety of moods
    b. are for a wide range of media   d. have literary programs or titles

4. Chopin's *Revolutionary* Étude in C Minor develops the pianist's left hand because
    a. the left hand must play rapid passages throughout
    b. it is played only by the left hand
    c. it takes nearly an hour to perform
    d. the left hand plays the main melody

SELF-TEST Completion: Supply the missing information.

5. A study piece, designed to help a performer master specific technical difficulties,

   is known as a(n) _____.

6. A slow, lyrical, intimate composition for piano, associated with nighttime,

   is known as a(n) _____.

7. The _____ is a dance in triple meter that originated as a stately processional

   for the Polish nobility.

8. Chopin expressed his love of Poland by composing _____

   and _____.

V-8. FRANZ LISZT

BASIC TERMS:
symphonic poem   tone poem

SELF-TEST Multiple-choice: Circle the answer that best completes each item.
1. Among Liszt's favorite inspirations were the literary works of
   a. Johann Wolfgang von Goethe   c. Heinrich Heine
   b. Carolyne Sayn-Wittgenstein   d. Richard Wagner

2. Liszt typified the romantic movement because he
   a. had a charismatic personality   c. was an innovative composer
   b. was a stupendous performer   d. all of the above

3. Liszt's piano works are characterized by
   a. arpeggios   c. an unprecedented range of dynamics
   b. rapid octaves and daring leaps   d. all of the above

4. In many of his works, Liszt unified contrasting moods by a process known as
   a. motivic repetition   c. sequential restatement
   b. thematic transformation   d. cohesive unification

5. During his teens and twenties, Liszt lived in
   a. Rome   b. Weimar   c. Paris   d. Budapest

6. As a youth, Liszt was influenced by the performances of
   a. Richard Wagner   c. Robert Schumann
   b. Hector Berlioz   d. Niccolò Paganini

7. Liszt created the _____, a one-movement orchestral composition based
   to some extent on a literary or pictorial idea.
   a. concert overture   c. piano concerto
   b. symphonic poem   d. sonata

8. Liszt abandoned his career as a traveling virtuoso to become court conductor at _____,
   where he championed works by contemporary composers.
   a. Rome   b. Weimar   c. Paris   d. Budapest

9. Until the age of thirty-six, Liszt toured Europe as a virtuoso
   a. pianist   c. cellist
   b. conductor   d. all of the above

V-9. FELIX MENDELSSOHN

SELF-TEST Multiple-choice: Circle the answer that best completes each item.

1. The high point of Mendelssohn's career was the triumphant premiere of his oratorio
   _____ in England.
   a. *Elijah*
   b. *Hebrides*
   c. A *Midsummer Night's Dream*
   d. *Fingal's Cave*

2. Mendelssohn's Concerto for Violin in E Minor opens with a(n)
   a. orchestral exposition typical in concertos
   b. soloist, who presents the main theme
   c. slow introduction by the orchestra
   d. single bassoon tone

3. The three movements of Mendelssohn's Concerto for Violin
   a. are unified by the process of thematic transformation
   b. are all in the same key
   c. all have separate cadenzas
   d. are played without pause

4. In the first movement of the Concerto for Violin, the cadenza
   a. is left to the performer to improvise
   b. appears at the end of the recapitulation, as is common in classical concertos
   c. appears at the end of the development section as a transition to the recapitulation
   d. is frequently omitted in performance

5. Mendelssohn is known as the man who rekindled an interest in the music of
   a. Giovanni Pierluigi da Palestrina
   b. Johann Sebastian Bach
   c. George Frideric Handel
   d. Franz Schubert

V-10. PROGRAM MUSIC

BASIC TERMS:

program music	program symphony	tone poem
program	concert overture	incidental music
absolute music	symphonic poem	

SELF-TEST Matching: Match each composition with the category it represents.

1. *The Sorcerer's Apprentice* (Dukas)

2. *A Midsummer Night's Dream* (Mendelssohn)

3. *Symphonie fantastique (Fantastic Symphony)* (Berlioz)

4. *The Moldau* (Smetana)

5. *Romeo and Juliet* (Tchaikovsky)

6. Symphony No. 40 in G Minor (Mozart)

7. *Les Préludes* (*The Preludes*) (Liszt)

8. *Overture 1812* (Tchaikovsky)

9. *Hebrides* Overture (Mendelssohn)

10. Concerto for Violin and Orchestra (Mendelssohn)

a. absolute music

b. concert overture

c. incidental music

d. program symphony

e. symphonic poem

Multiple-choice: Circle the answer that best completes each item.

11. The work referred to by Beethoven as an "expression of feeling rather than painting" was his
   a. Symphony No. 5
   b. *Fidelio* Overture
   c. *Eroica* Symphony
   d. Symphony No. 6

12. A _____ is a one-movement orchestral composition based to some extent on a literary or pictorial idea.
   a. mazurka
   b. program symphony
   c. symphonic poem
   d. nocturne

13. The composer who developed the symphonic poem was
   a. Franz Liszt
   b. Ludwig van Beethoven
   c. Franz Schubert
   d. Richard Strauss

14. Today's movie scores may be regarded as examples of
   a. pure music
   b. incidental music
   c. folk music
   d. absolute music

15. Nonprogram music is also known as _____ music.
   a. pure   b. absolute   c. concert   d. symphonic

RESEARCH PROJECT The program symphony:
    A program symphony, as its name implies, is a symphony with a program. Each movement of the symphony usually has a descriptive title, and the music suggests or evokes literary or pictorial ideas.

1. List some examples of program symphonies:

TITLE	COMPOSER
_____	_____
_____	_____
_____	_____
_____	_____

2. Listen to one example of your own choice, and complete the following.

Title: Composer:

First movement: title:
    plot summary:

    tempo: mood: form:

    pictorial techniques:

Second movement: title:
    plot summary:

    tempo: mood: form:

    pictorial techniques:

Third movement: title:
    plot summary:

    tempo: mood: form:

    pictorial techniques:

Fourth movement: title:
    plot summary:

    tempo: mood: form:

    pictorial techniques:

(Add fifth movement if there is one).

RESEARCH PROJECT The concert overture:
    As we have seen, an overture is defined as a musical composition performed before the curtain rises on a dramatic work. In this section, we find that the concert overture is not intended to precede a stage work. Instead of the medley type so popular with dramatic overtures, concert overtures are usually in sonata form. List some examples of concert overtures, as contrasted with overtures intended for dramatic works, from your own background, classroom discussion, or the text.

1. List some examples of concert overtures.

TITLE	COMPOSER
_____	_____
_____	_____
_____	_____
_____	_____

2. Listen to one example of your own choice, determine its form, give a brief summary of the plot, and identify those musical characteristics that evoke or suggest programmatic associations.

Title:

Composer:

Form:

Plot summary:

Sound effects (if any):

Musical techniques that evoke literary or pictorial ideas:

RESEARCH PROJECT The symphonic poem:
    A symphonic poem—a one-movement instrumental composition associated with a story, poem, idea, or scene—may take many traditional forms (sonata form, rondo, or theme and variations), as well as irregular forms. It is this flexibility of form that separates the symphonic poem, or tone poem, from the concert overture, which is usually in sonata form.

1. List some examples of symphonic poems.

TITLE	COMPOSER	FORM

2. Listen to one example of your own choice, determine its form, give a brief summary of the plot, and identify those musical characteristics that evoke or suggest programmatic ideas.

Title:

Composer:

Form:

Plot summary:

Sound effects (if any):

Musical techniques that evoke literary or pictorial ideas:

RESEARCH PROJECT Incidental music:

If a play is set to music and sung throughout, we call it an *opera*. Some composers wrote music intended to be performed before and during a play. We call such music *incidental* music, for it is intended to set a mood for certain scenes or highlight a particular action on the stage. Movie scores, for example, are categorized as incidental music.

1. List some examples of incidental music.

TITLE	COMPOSER	PLAY AND PLAYWRIGHT
_____	_____	_____
_____	_____	_____
_____	_____	_____
_____	_____	_____

2. Listen to one example of your own choice, and complete the following.

Title: Composer:

Movement or section:

   mood:

   action on stage:

   means of musical reinforcement of action or mood:

Movement or section:

   mood:

   action on stage:

   means of musical reinforcement of action or mood:

Movement or section:

   mood:

   action on stage:

   means of musical reinforcement of action or mood:

Movement or section:

   mood:

   action on stage:

   means of musical reinforcement of action or mood:

V-11. HECTOR BERLIOZ

BASIC TERM:
  idée fixe

SELF-TEST Multiple-choice: Circle the answer that best completes each item.
1. In order to support his family, Berlioz turned to
   a. medicine
   b. musical journalism
   c. teaching
   d. arranging concerts

2. Parisians were startled by Berlioz's *Fantastic Symphony* because of its
   a. sensationally autobiographical program
   b. amazingly novel orchestration
   c. vivid description of the weird and diabolical
   d. all of the above

3. In 1830 the Paris Conservatory awarded Berlioz
   a. a graduate fellowship
   b. a scholarship
   c. a position on the faculty
   d. the Prix de Rome

4. The liturgical melody quoted in the last movement of the *Fantastic Symphony* is the
   a. *Ave Maria*
   b. alleluia
   c. benedictus
   d. *Dies irae*

5. Outside France, Hector Berlioz enjoyed a great career as a(n)
   a. conductor   b. concert pianist   c. singer   d. impresario

6. Berlioz's *Fantastic Symphony* is unified by the recurrence of a theme known as the
   a. germ motive
   b. *thème varié*
   c. *idée fixe*
   d. basic motive

7. The *Fantastic Symphony* reflects Berlioz's
   a. intense nationalism
   b. experiences in Rome
   c. love for the actress Harriet Smithson
   d. interest in composing for small, intimate ensembles

8. The fourth movement of the *Fantastic Symphony* depicts a
   a. march to the scaffold
   b. ball
   c. dream of a witches' sabbath
   d. scene in the country

9. Which of the following was not composed by Berlioz?
   a. *Romeo and Juliet*
   b. *The Damnation of Faust*
   c. *The Sorcerer's Apprentice*
   d. Requiem

10. The second movement of the *Fantastic Symphony* is a _____, the most popular dance of the romantic era.
    a. waltz   b. minuet   c. country dance   d. gavotte

RESEARCH PROJECT The changing orchestra:

The text states "as an orchestrator, Berlioz was extraordinarily imaginative and innovative. At a time when the average orchestra had about sixty players, he often assembled hundreds of musicians to achieve new power, tone colors, and timbres." In order to visualize the growth of the orchestra from the baroque through the romantic periods, compare one representative work from each period. Fill in the instrumentation table (see text references), and then arrange the performers into the proper seating plans.

1. Instrumentation table

INSTRUMENTS	Bach (1721)	Haydn (1791)	Berlioz (1830)
piccolo			
flutes			
oboes			
english horn			
clarinets			
bass clarinet			
bassoons			
horns			
cornets			
trumpets			
trombones			
tubas			
timpani			
snare drum			
bass drum			
cymbals			
gong			
bells			
harps			
1st violins	3–5	3–12	12–16
2d violins	3–5	3–12	12–16
violas	1–3	1–8	10–12
cellos	1–3	1–6	8–10
basses	1–2	1–4	4–6
harpsichord			

2. Baroque orchestra, 10–40 players (see text, III-1)

Johann Sebastian Bach: *Brandenburg* Concerto No. 5 in D Major, 1721 (see text, p. 106)

3. Classical orchestra, 20–60 players (see text, IV-1)
   Joseph Haydn: Symphony No. 94 in G Major (*Surprise*), 1791 (see text, p. 168)

4. Romantic orchestra, approximately 100 players (see text, V-1)
   Hector Berlioz: *Fantastic Symphony*, 1830 (see text, p. 247)

V-12. NATIONALISM IN NINETEENTH-CENTURY MUSIC

BASIC TERM:
nationalism

SELF-TEST Multiple-choice: Circle the answer that best completes each item.
1. The most original, and probably the greatest of the Russian five, was
   a. César Cui
   b. Modest Mussorgsky
   c. Alexander Borodin
   d. Mily Balakirev

2. The founder of Czech national music was
   a. César Cui   b. Antonin Dvořák   c. Bedřich Smetana   d. Boris Godunov

3. Libretti that fanned the public's hatred for its Austrian overlords were deliberately
   chosen by the composer
   a. Gioacchino Rossini
   b. Modest Mussorgsky
   c. Giuseppe Verdi
   d. Richard Wagner

4. Smetana grew up when Bohemia was under _____ domination.
   a. German   b. Austrian   c. Polish   d. Russian

5. Smetana's most popular opera is _____.
   a. *The Bartered Bride*
   b. *My Country*
   c. *Boris Godunov*
   d. *The Moldau*

6. Even though Smetana was deaf at the time, he composed a musical work depicting
   Bohemia's main river as it flows through the countryside. The name of the river, and the
   musical composition, is the
   a. Moldau   b. Seine   c. Danube   d. Thames

7. The first American concert pianist to gain international recognition was
   a. Harry T. Burleigh
   b. Charles Ives
   c. Stephen Foster
   d. Louis Moreau Gottschalk

RESEARCH PROJECT Nationalism in music:

 Describe some of the ways in which a composer can express nationalism in music, giving musical examples for each.

RESEARCH PROJECT Nationalistic composers:

 The text mentions important nationalistic composers of nineteenth-century Poland, Russia, Bohemia, Norway, Finland and America. List some other composers not mentioned in the text whose music has a national flavor.

Culture	Composer	Major Works or Characteristics

V-13. ANTONIN DVOŘÁK

BASIC TERM:
pentatonic scale

SELF-TEST Multiple-choice: Circle the answer that best completes each item.
1. Antonin Dvořák's music was first promoted by
   a. Hector Berlioz   c. Franz Liszt
   b. Richard Wagner   d. Johannes Brahms

2. Dvořák _____ quoted actual folk tunes in his compositions.
   a. never   b. rarely   c. occasionally   d. frequently

3. In the first movement of the *New World* Symphony, Dvořák introduces a gracious
   melody that resembles the spiritual
   a. *Swing Low, Sweet Chariot*   c. *Goin' Home*
   b. *Nobody Knows the Trouble I've Had*   d. *Go Down, Moses*

4. In 1892, Dvořák went to _____, where he spent almost three years as director
   of the National Conservatory of Music.
   a. London   b. New York   c. Prague   d. Leipzig

5. Dvořák "found a secure basis for a new national [American] musical school" in the
   a. music of New York
   b. western art music taught at the National Conservatory of Music
   c. African-American spirituals
   d. traditional folk music of European immigrants

6. The popular character of the Dvořák's *New World* Symphony can be traced to the
   composer's use of _____ often found in folk music.
   a. syncopations   c. modal scales
   b. pentatonic scales   d. all of the above

V-14. PETER ILYICH TCHAIKOVSKY

SELF-TEST Multiple-choice: Circle the answer that best completes each item.
1. Nadezhda von Meck was
    a. one of Tchaikovsky's lovers
    b. a wealthy benefactress who provided Tchaikovsky with an annuity
    c. Tchaikovsky's wife
    d. the inspiration for his *Romeo and Juliet*

2. At its premiere in 1870, Tchaikovsky's *Romeo and Juliet* Overture was
    a. a tremendous success
    b. a dismal failure
    c. performed by a large orchestra, with chorus and cannon
    d. enthusiastically applauded by the tsar

3. Which of the following was *not* composed by Tchaikovsky?
    a. Symphony No. 6 (*Pathétique*)   c. *Marche slave*
    b. *Russian Easter* Overture   d. *Overture 1812*

4. Tchaikovsky's *Romeo and Juliet* is a(n)
    a. opera   c. symphonic poem
    b. program symphony   d. concert overture

5. Tchaikovsky's Sixth Symphony
    a. has five movements   c. is in the usual four-movement form
    b. ends with a slow, despairing finale   d. was left unfinished by the composer

RESEARCH PROJECT Tchaikovsky's ballets:

Tchaikovsky thought of himself as "*Russian* in the fullest sense of the word," yet he is not considered one of the Russian nationalistic composers. This is partly because he fused national and international elements to produce intensely subjective and passionate music. Using his three ballets as examples (as they contain some of his finest music), distinguish the national from the international characteristics of each.

Swan Lake
    plot summary:

    national versus international characteristics:

The Sleeping Beauty
    plot summary:

    national versus international characteristics:

The Nutcracker
    plot summary:

    national versus international characteristics:

V-15. JOHANNES BRAHMS

SELF-TEST Multiple-choice: Circle the answer that best completes each item.

1. Brahms's works, though very personal in style, are rooted in the music of
   a. Joseph Haydn
   b. Wolfgang Amadeus Mozart
   c. Ludwig van Beethoven
   d. all of the above

2. Brahms's musical trademarks included
   a. bombastic flamboyance
   b. the use of two notes against three
   c. the use of da capo arias
   d. all of the above

3. Johannes Brahms's Symphony No. 3 in F Major
   a. is the shortest of his four symphonies
   b. is characterized by thematic connections among its four movements
   c. contains striking contrasts between major and minor
   d. all of the above

4. Which of the following statements about the third movement of Brahms's Symphony No. 3 in F Major is *not* true?
   a. It is intensely lyric in character
   b. It is unique in that the movement is not a scherzo, standard in nineteenth-century symphonies
   c. It utilizes a large orchestra
   d. It reflects Brahms's strong feeling for musical tradition because it possesses qualities that are typical of third movements in classical symphonies

5. The course of Brahms's artistic and personal life was shaped by the influence of the composer
   a. Antonin Dvořák
   b. Richard Wagner
   c. Franz Liszt
   d. Robert Schumann and his wife, Clara

6. In comparison to some earlier composers, Brahms's musical output may be considered small. This is explained in part by the fact that Brahms
   a. was too busy conducting and performing to find time to compose
   b. was insecure and lazy, unable to concentrate on composing
   c. was extremely critical of his own work, and endlessly revised his compositions
   d. died before he had a chance to realize himself fully

LISTENING EXERCISE Brahms's music:
  The text states that Brahms "created masterpieces in all the traditional forms" except opera. List your personal favorites in each of the categories below. (If you don't yet have a favorite in some form, try listening to some of his music in that form, and see if you don't find one very easily.)

symphony:

chamber music:

piano composition:

song with piano:

song with orchestra:

choral music:

V-16. GIUSEPPE VERDI

SELF-TEST Multiple-choice: Circle the answer that best completes each item.

1. Critics were often scandalized by the subject matter of Verdi's operas because they
   a. symbolized a free and unified Italy
   b. commemorated the Suez canal, which was not even in Europe
   c. were based on Shakespearean plays
   d. seemed to condone rape, suicide, and free love

2. Which of the following operas is *not* by Verdi?
   a. *La Traviata*   c. *Il Trovatore*
   b. *Cavalleria rusticana*   d. *Otello*

3. Verdi's great comic masterpiece, written when he was seventy-nine, is
   a. *Il Trovatore*   b. *Otello*   c. *Falstaff*   d. *Aïda*

4. Verdi studied music in _____, the city where Italy's most important opera house, La Scala, is located.
   a. Rome   b. Florence   c. Venice   d. Milan

5. Rigoletto, the title character in Giuseppe Verdi's opera, is
   a. a hunchback   c. a court jester to the duke of Mantua
   b. the father of Gilda   d. all of the above

6. Verdi's first great success, an opera with strong political overtones, was
   a. *Oberto*   c. *Nabucco*
   b. *Aïda*   d. *La Traviata*

7. Verdi mainly composed his operas
   a. for the Italian musical elite   c. to promote Italian unification
   b. to glorify the singers   d. to entertain a mass public

8. The famous aria *La donna è mobile* is taken from Verdi's opera
   a. *Rigoletto*   c. *Falstaff*
   b. *Aïda*   d. *Il Trovatore*

9. The soul of a Verdi opera is
   a. extensive thematic development   c. the situation comedy
   b. expressive vocal melody   d. atmospheric orchestral parts

10. Verdi's later operas differ from his earlier ones in that they have
    a. less difference between aria and recitative   c. more imaginative orchestrations
    b. greater musical continuity   d. all of the above

RESEARCH PROJECT My favorite Verdi or Puccini opera:
    The text mentions some of the operas by Verdi and Puccini that are constantly performed in opera houses throughout the world. Choose your favorite Verdi or Puccini opera, and complete the following (indicate whether you are familiar with the work through recordings or a live performance).

Title:

First performance:

Performance heard or seen (where, when, who):

Characters of the opera, their roles, and voice ranges:

Summary of the plot:

Famous arias:

Romantic characteristics noted:

Why it is my favorite Verdi or Puccini opera:

V-17. GIACOMO PUCCINI

SELF-TEST Multiple-choice: Circle the answer that best completes each item.
1. Puccini's operas have lasting appeal because
    a. he had a marvelous sense of theater
    b. his melodies have short, memorable phrases and are intensely emotional
    c. he minimized the difference between aria and recitative, thus creating a continuous flow of music
    d. all of the above

2. In *La Bohème*, who sings the aria *Che gelida manina (How cold your little hand is!)*?
    a. Mimi   b. Schaunard   c. Rodolfo   d. Marcello

3. Puccini used melodic and rhythmic elements derived from Asian music in his operas
    a. *Turandot* and *Manon Lescaut*   c. *La Bohème* and *Madame Butterfly*
    b. *Madame Butterfly* and *Turandot*   d. *Tosca* and *Turandot*

4. An artistic trend of the 1890s, in which operas dealt with ordinary people and true-to-life situations, was known as
    a. *opera seria*   c. exoticism
    b. *Cavalleria rusticana*   d. *verismo*

5. Which of the following operas was *not* written by Puccini?
    a. *Tosca*   c. *Turandot*
    b. *Madame Butterfly* d. *I Pagliacci*

6. Puccini's first successful opera was
    a. *Madame Butterfly*   c. *Manon Lescaut*
    b. *La Bohème*   d. *Turandot*

7. *La Bohème* takes place in
    a. Seville   b. Milan   c. Rome   d. Paris

8. Mimi and Rodolfo meet for the first time in *La Bohème* because she has come to his door to ask for a
    a. light for her candle   c. dinner date
    b. drink of wine   d. cup of sugar

9. In *La Bohème*, Rodolfo is a young
    a. painter   c. philosopher
    b. poet   d. musician

10. Which of the following operas is considered an example of *verismo*?
    a. *Turandot*   b. *Tosca*   c. *Nabucco*   d. *Die Walküre*

LISTENING EXERCISE Verismo opera:
  Tired of operas dealing with kings, gods, and great heroes, some Italian composers in the 1890s preferred ordinary people and scenes from real life for their subjects. One of the first composers in this movement, known as *verismo,* was Ruggiero Leoncavallo. Since the prologue to his opera *I Pagliacci* can be considered the testament of the *veristi,* it is presented here as an introduction to the discussion of Giacomo Puccini in the textbook.

Ruggiero Leoncavallo: Prologue to I Pagliacci

[Tonio, dressed as Taddeo of the Commedia dell'Arte,
puts his head through the curtain, and then advances]

Si può? [salutando] *Signore! Signori! Scusatemi, se da sol mi presento. Io sono il Prologo!*

Permit me? [bowing] Ladies! Gentlemen! Pardon me, if I appear alone: I am the Prologue!

Poichè in iscena ancor le antiche maschere mette l'autore; in parte ei vuol riprendere le vecchie usanze, e a voi di nuovo inviami.

Once again the author brings the old masks before you; partly to remind you of the old custom, he asks me to address you again.

Ma non per dirvi come pria: "Le lacrime che noi versiam son false! Degli spasimi e de'nostri martir non allarmatevi!"

But not to tell you, as before, "The tears we shed are false ones! And don't be alarmed by the sighs we heave, or our sufferings!"

No! L'autore ha cercato invece pingervi uno squarcio di vita. Egli ha per massima sol che l'artista è un uom e che per gli uomini scrivere ei deve. Ed al vero ispiravasi.

No! Your author intends instead to paint you a fragment of life. It is his conviction that the artist is first of all a man, and that he should write for mankind. And the truth has inspired him.

Un nido di memorie in fondo a l'anima cantava un giorno, ed ei con vere lacrime scrisse, e i singhiozzi il tempo gli battevano!

A nest of memories welled up within his innermost soul one day, and the tears accompanied his writing, while his sobs beat the tempo for him!

Dunque, vedrete amar sì come s'amano gli esseri umani; vedrete de l'odio i tristi frutti. Del dolor gli spasimi, urli di rabbia, udrete, e risa ciniche!

So, then, you'll see love as human beings love; you'll see the sad fruits of hatred. The pain of sorrow, howlings of rage, and scornful laughter!

E voi, piuttosto che le nostre povere gabbane d'istrioni, le nostr'anime considerate, poichè siam uomini di carne e d'ossa, e che di quest'orfano mondo al pari di voi spiriamo l'aere!

And you, rather than think of our poor clown costumes, think of our souls, for we are men of flesh and bone, and we breathe the same air in this orphaned world as you!

Il concetto vi dissi . . . Or ascoltate com'egli è svolto. [gridando verso la scena] *Andiam. Incominciate!*

I've given you the idea. . . . Now watch the plot unfold before you. [calling toward the stage] Come on! Let's begin!

[He returns behind the curtain, and it rises]

PERFORMANCE PERSPECTIVE
Luciano Pavarotti, tenor, singing the part of Rodolfo in Puccini's *La Bohème*

Luciano Pavarotti, Placido Domingo, and Jose Carreras have become more well-known to the general public through their performances as *The Three Tenors*. Compare Pavarotti's performance of the aria *Che gelida manina* from *La Bohème* (included in your textbook) with performances of the same aria by Domingo and Carreras. Whose performance do you prefer, and why? Make specific reference to vocal color, tempo, and dynamic range.

MULTIMEDIA COMPANION Opera
Comparison of Puccini's opera *La Bohème* and Larsen's hit musical *Rent*

Jonathan Larsen's hit show *Rent* is inspired by Puccini's opera *La Bohème*. Compare the scene from *La Bohème* included in the Multimedia Companion with the similar scene from *Rent* (or you can listen to the song from the scene entitled "*Light My Candle*"). Discuss the similarities, and obvious differences, between the music and staging of these two productions.

V-18. RICHARD WAGNER

BASIC TERM:
leitmotif

SELF-TEST Multiple-choice: Circle the answer that best completes each item.

1. The composer who had an overwhelming influence on the young Wagner was
   a. Johann Sebastian Bach
   b. Ludwig van Beethoven
   c. Johannes Brahms
   d. Hector Berlioz

2. Wagner called his works *music dramas* rather than operas because
   a. there is a continuous musical flow within each act
   b. there are no breaks where applause can interrupt
   c. the vocal line is inspired by the rhythms and pitches of the German text
   d. all of the above

3. Wagner's last opera was
   a. *Götterdämmerung (The Twilight of the Gods)*
   b. *Tannhäuser*
   c. *Rienzi*
   d. *Parsifal*

4. The librettos to *The Ring of the Nibelung* were written by
   a. Arrigo Boito
   b. Wagner himself
   c. King Ludwig of Bavaria
   d. Hans von Bülow

5. A short musical idea associated with a person, object, or thought, used by Wagner in his operas, is called
   a. leitmotif
   b. lied
   c. unending melody
   d. speech-song

6. Valhalla, in Wagner's *Ring* cycle, is
   a. a city in New York State
   b. the castle of the gods
   c. the home of Siegfried
   d. the magic ring

7. Wagner had an opera house built to his own specifications in
   a. Munich
   b. Weimar
   c. Dresden
   d. Bayreuth

8. Wagner's first successful opera was
   a. *Tannhäuser*
   b. *Rienzi*
   c. *The Twilight of the Gods*
   d. *Die Walküre*

9. Siegmund, in Wagner's opera *Die Walküre,* is
   a. Sieglinde's brother, then wife
   b. Wotan's son by a mortal woman
   c. Siegfried's father
   d. all of the above

10. Which of the following operas was *not* composed by Wagner?
   a. *Tannhäuser*
   b. *Tristan and Isolde*
   c. *Fidelio*
   d. *Parsifal*

RESEARCH PROJECT Richard Wagner, *The Ring of the Nibelung***:**
Wagner's complete *Ring* cycle was first performed at Bayreuth in 1876. Supply the following for its four operas.

Main characters:

1. *Das Rheingold (The Rhine Gold)*
    plot summary:

    excerpts:

2. *Die Walküre (The Valkyrie)*
    plot summary:

    excerpts:

3. *Siegfried*
    plot summary:

    excerpts:

4. *Götterdämmerung (The Twilight of the Gods)*
    plot summary:

    excerpts:

BIOGRAPHICAL SKETCH A romantic composer: _____

Born (year, place):
Died (year, place):

Personal life:

    family:

    health and physiognomy:

    personality:

Career:

    significant places:

    significant people:

    employers or patrons:

    means of making a living:

    financial situation:

Music:

    style of composition:

    general characteristics:

Output (List some of the major forms in which the composer worked, including the approximate number of compositions if significant. List some of the major compositions in each category, check those which you have heard, and circle those which you have studied):

Category: _____ _____ _____

Works:

Category: _____ _____ _____

Works:

UNIT QUIZ V
THE ROMANTIC PERIOD

Name_____

Class/section_____ Date_____

Matching: Match each composition with its composer.

1._____ *Fantastic Symphony*
2._____ *Rigoletto*
3._____ *Madame Butterfly*
4._____ *Swan Lake*
5._____ *La Bohème*
6._____ *The Ring of the Nibelung*
7._____ *The Erlking*
8._____ *Romeo and Juliet* Overture
9._____ *Romeo and Juliet* Symphony
10._____ *Carnaval (Carnival)*
11._____ *The Moldau*
12._____ Symphony No. 3 in F Major
13._____ *The Sleeping Beauty*
14._____ *Leibst du um Schönheit*
15._____ Symphony No. 9 (*From the New World*)
16._____ *Transcendental Étude* No. 10
17._____ *Die Walküre*
18._____ Étude in C Minor (*Revolutionary*)
19._____ *A Midsummer Night's Dream*
20._____ *The Nutcracker*

a. Hector Berlioz
b. Johannes Brahms
c. Frédéric Chopin
d. Antonin Dvořák
e. Franz Liszt
f. Felix Mendelssohn
g. Giacomo Puccini
h. Franz Schubert
i. Clara Schumann
j. Robert Schumann
k. Bedřich Smetana
l. Peter Ilyich Tchaikovsky
m. Giuseppe Verdi
n. Richard Wagner

Multiple-choice: Choose the answer that best completes each item.

21. Instrumental music endowed with literary or pictorial associations, popular during the romantic period, is called
    a. absolute music
    b. opera
    c. program music
    d. symphony

22. The deliberate intent to draw creative inspiration from the composer's own homeland is known as
    a. exoticism
    b. nationalism
    c. *verismo*
    d. individualism

23. The typical orchestra of the late romantic period numbered about _____ musicians.
    a. 15   b. 24   c. 40   d. 100

24. Music intended to be performed before or during a play, to set the mood for scenes or highlight dramatic action, is known as
    a. play music
    b. incidental music
    c. absolute music
    d. music drama

25. Instrumental music that is written for its own sake, and for which the composer does not provide a program, is called
    a. absolute music
    b. program music
    c. music for its own sake
    d. opera

Unit Quiz V (cont.)

26. Drawing creative inspiration from cultures of lands foreign to the composer is known as
    a. exoticism   b. nationalism   c. program music   d. *verismo*

27. Approximately, the romantic period encompassed the years
    a. 1450–1600   b. 1600–1750   c. 1750–1820   d. 1820–1900

28. All the following composers are associated with the romantic period *except*
    a. Giuseppe Verdi   c. Robert Schumann
    b. Wolfgang Amadeus Mozart   d. Frédéric Chopin

29. Which of the following is *not* a characteristic of romanticism?
    a. nationalism   c. individualism
    b. emotional restraint   d. supernaturalism

30. The movement in opera known as *verismo* is best exemplified by
    a. Claudio Monteverdi   c. Giacomo Puccini
    b. Wolfgang Amadeus Mozart   d. Richard Wagner

Matching: Match each term with its definition.

31._____ song form in which new music is written for each stanza

32._____ study piece, designed to help a performer master specific technical difficulties

33._____ song form in which the music is repeated for each stanza

34._____ short musical idea associated with a person, object, or thought, used by Wagner

35._____ romantic art song with a German text

36._____ slow, intimate composition for piano, associated with nighttime

37._____ instrumental composition in several movements based to some extent on a literary or pictorial idea

38._____ dance in triple meter that originated as a stately procession for the Polish nobility

39._____ one-movement orchestral composition based to some extent on a literary or pictorial idea

40._____ slight holding back or pressing forward of tempo

41._____ form in which two or more stanzas of poetry are set to the same music while other stanzas have new music

a. étude

b. leitmotif

c. lied

d. modified strophic

e. nocturne

f. polonaise

g. program symphony

h. rubato

i. strophic

j. symphonic poem

k. through-composed

VI. THE TWENTIETH CENTURY AND BEYOND

VI-1. MUSICAL STYLES: 1900–1945

BASIC TERMS:

glissando	tone cluster	bitonality	polyrhythm
polychord	polytonality	atonality	ostinato
fourth chord			

SELF-TEST Multiple-choice: Circle the answer that best completes each item.

1. Composers in the twentieth century drew inspiration from
   a. folk and popular music from all cultures
   b. European art music from the Middle Ages through the nineteenth century
   c. the music of Asia and Africa
   d. all of the above

2. The combination of two traditional chords sounding together is known as
   a. polytonality   b. bitonality   c. a tone cluster   d. a polychord

3. Among the unusual playing techniques that are widely used during the twentieth
   century is the _____, a rapid slide up or down a scale.
   a. buzz   b. glissando   c. slip   d. ostinato

4. Which of the following composers was *not* stimulated by the folklore of his native land?
   a. Igor Stravinsky   b. Anton Webern   c. Béla Bartók   d. Charles Ives

5. A chord made of tones only a half step or a whole step apart is known as
   a. polytonality   b. a polychord   c. bitonality   d. a tone cluster

6. The absence of key or tonality in a musical composition is known as
   a. polytonality   b. ostinato   c. a tone cluster   d. atonality

7. To create fresh sounds, twentieth-century composers used
   a. scales borrowed from nonwestern cultures   c. ancient church modes
   b. scales they themselves invented   d. all of the above

8. The use of two or more keys at one time is known as
   a. polytonality   c. atonality
   b. a tone cluster   d. the twelve-tone system

9. A motive or phrase that is repeated persistently at the same pitch throughout a section is called
   a. polytonality   b. glissando   c. ostinato   d. atonality

10. In twentieth-century music,
    a. string players are sometimes called on to use the wood instead of the hair on their bows
    b. percussion instruments have become very prominent and numerous
    c. dissonance has been emancipated
    d. all of the above

EXERCISE The twentieth-century context:

The cry is sometimes raised that contemporary audiences listen to music with nineteenth-century ears. Perhaps there is some justification in that complaint, for the twentieth century has seen radical changes in music and it is difficult for the general public to prevent a musical generation gap from developing. Of course, adjustments seem to have been made in other areas: unless the energy crisis takes an extreme turn, for example, no one seriously advocates a return to the horse and buggy. Yet there are people who still refuse to fly.

To place the changes in music in context with similar changes in the other humanities and the sciences, consider life at the turn of the century, at the midpoint, and today. List some of the major stages of development, trends, "isms," and characteristics of each of the following:

	around 1900	around 1945	today
Scientific technology			
Transportation			
Philosophy			
Literature			
Art			
Architecture			
Drama			
Photography			
Motion pictures			
Costume			
Dance			
Sound recordings			

LISTENING EXERCISE A comparison of twentieth-century styles:
    While listening to three compositions in class, or to three works of your own choosing at home, identify the style of each by checking those characteristics that are dominant in each composition. The upper description is usually associated with music before 1900, while the lower is typical of the twentieth century.

	1.	2.	3.
Melody: easy to sing and remember	__	__	__
difficult to sing; asymmetrical	__	__	__
Timbre: rich and sensuous	__	__	__
less emphasis on blended sound	__	__	__
traditional percussion instruments	__	__	__
greater use of percussion and nonmusical sounds	__	__	__
Meter: unified	__	__	__
changing	__	__	__
conventional	__	__	__
unconventional	__	__	__
Rhythm: unified	__	__	__
polyrhythmic	__	__	__
regular	__	__	__
irregular	__	__	__
no jazz elements	__	__	__
jazz elements	__	__	__
Harmony: tonal	__	__	__
polytonal or atonal	__	__	__
predominantly consonant	__	__	__
predominantly dissonant	__	__	__
Ensembles: traditional	__	__	__
unusual	__	__	__
Performance techniques: traditional	__	__	__
unusual	__	__	__
Piano: mainly as a solo instrument	__	__	__
part of percussion section	__	__	__

	TITLE	COMPOSER	STYLE
Selection 1:			
Selection 2:			
Selection 3:			

VI-2. MUSIC AND MUSICIANS IN SOCIETY

SELF-TEST Completion: Supply the missing information.
1. Radio broadcasts of live and recorded music began to reach large audiences during the
    a. 1900s   b. 1920s   c. 1940s   d. 1960s

2. The first opera created for television was Gian-Carlo Menotti's
    a. *Turandot*   c. *Trouble in Tahiti*
    b. *Amahl and the Night Visitors*   d. *The Telephone*

3. Recordings of much lesser-known music multiplied in 1948 through
    a. the appearance of long-playing disks   c. government grants
    b. audience insistence for new works   d. demand created by radio stations

4. The most influential organization sponsoring new music after World War I was
    a. the New York Philharmonic Orchestra
    b. the National Broadcasting Company and its orchestra
    c. the International Society for Contemporary Music
    d. the United Federation of Musicians

5. The best-known American ensemble created in the 1930s by a radio network to broadcast live music was the
    a. NBC Symphony Orchestra   c. New York Philharmonic Orchestra
    b. Lawrence Welk Orchestra   d. CBS Symphony Orchestra

6. One of the most important teachers of musical composition in the twentieth century was
    a. Amy Beach   b. Nadia Boulanger   c. Sergei Diaghilev   d. Igor Stravinsky

7. Which of the following statements is *not* true?
    a. New technological advances, such as phonograph records, tape recordings, radio, and television, have brought music to a larger audience than ever before, besides vastly increasing the amount and scope of music available.
    b. Audiences in the first half of the twentieth century, as in Mozart's time, demanded and got the latest music, and concert programs consisted mainly of recent works.
    c. Nazi persecution and the onset of World War II led many composers, including Stravinsky, Bartók, Schoenberg, and Hindemith, to emigrate to the United States, where they made enormous contributions to American musical culture.
    d. American colleges and universities have played a vital role in our musical culture, as they have trained and employed many of our leading composers, performers, and scholars, have expanded the horizons and interests of countless students, and have sponsored performing groups specializing in twentieth-century music.

VI-3. IMPRESSIONISM AND SYMBOLISM

SELF-TEST Completion: Supply the missing information.

1. Impressionist painters were primarily concerned with the

   effects of _____, _____, and

   _____.

2. The most important impressionist composer was

   _____.

3. The term *impressionist* derived from a critic's derogatory reaction to Monet's painting

   _____, exhibited in 1874.

4. Symbolist writers emphasized the purely _____

   or _____ effects of words.

5. Many songs by Debussy use texts by the symbolist poet _____.

SELF-TEST Multiple-choice: Circle the answer that best completes each item.

6. Impressionism as a movement originated in
   a. France
   b. Italy
   c. Germany
   d. England

7. Which of the following is *not* considered a symbolist poet?
   a. Stéphane Mallarmé
   b. Paul Verlaine
   c. Victor Hugo
   d. Arthur Rimbaud

8. When viewed closely, impressionist paintings are made up of
   a. fine lines
   b. large bands of color
   c. tiny black dots
   d. tiny colored patches

9. The impressionist painters were particularly obsessed with portraying
   a. water
   b. religious scenes
   c. scenes of ancient glories
   d. battle scenes

10. Debussy's most famous orchestral work was inspired by a poem by
    a. Stéphane Mallarmé
    b. Paul Verlaine
    c. Jean-Paul Sartre
    d. Arthur Rimbaud

VI-4. CLAUDE DEBUSSY

BASIC TERMS:
impressionism   pentatonic scale   whole-tone scale

SELF-TEST Multiple-choice: Circle the answer that best completes each item.
1. Debussy's music tends to
   a. sound free and almost improvisational   c. have a strong rhythmic pulse
   b. affirm the key very noticeably   d. use the full orchestra for massive effects

2. The faun evoked in Debussy's famous composition is a
   a. baby deer   c. beautiful young maiden
   b. creature who is half man, half goat   d. sensitive musician

3. As a result of his summer sojourns away from France during his teens, Debussy developed
   a lifelong interest in the music of
   a. Italy   b. Hungary   c. England   d. Russia

4. Debussy's opera *Pelléas et Mélisande* is an almost word-for-word setting of the symbolist play by
   a. Paul Verlaine   c. Maurice Maeterlinck
   b. Arthur Rimbaud   d. Stéphane Mallarmé

5. At the Paris International Exhibition of 1889, Debussy was strongly influenced by the
   a. advantages of modern technology   c. Eiffel Tower
   b. performances of the music of J. S. Bach   d. performances of Asian music

6. In which of the following areas did Debussy *not* create masterpieces?
   a. symphonies   c. chamber music
   b. art songs   d. piano music

7. The poem that inspired the *Prelude to The Afternoon of a Faun* was written by
   a. Paul Verlaine   c. Maurice Maeterlinck
   b. Arthur Rimbaud   d. Stéphane Mallarmé

8. In order to "drown the sense of tonality," Debussy
   a. turned to the medieval church modes
   b. borrowed pentatonic scales from Javanese music
   c. developed the whole-tone scale
   d. all of the above

9. Which of the following is *not* characteristic of impressionist music?
   a. a stress on tone color   c. clearly defined rhythmical patterns
   b. a stress on atmosphere   d. fluidity

VI-5. NEOCLASSICISM

BASIC TERM:
neoclassicism

SELF-TEST Multiple-choice: Circle the answer that best completes each item.

1. Favoring clear polyphonic textures, neoclassical composers wrote
   a. fugues
   b. baroque dance suites
   c. concerti grossi
   d. all of the above

2. Neoclassical compositions are characterized by
   a. forms and stylistic features of earlier periods
   b. whole-tone scales
   c. harsh dissonances
   d. use of the twelve-tone system

3. Neoclassicism was a reaction against
   a. romanticism and impressionism
   b. humanism
   c. classicism
   d. traditional forms

4. Which of the following is *not* characteristic of neoclassicism?
   a. emotional restraint   b. clarity   c. misty atmosphere   d. balance

5. Neoclassical composers favored
   a. tonality   b. atonality   c. program music   d. large orchestras

6. A painter who went through a neoclassical phase, and who designed sets for Stravinsky's first neoclassical work, was
   a. Claude Monet   b. Pablo Picasso   c. Auguste Renoir   d. Wassily Kandinsky

RESEARCH PROJECT The music of Igor Stravinsky:

The music of Stravinsky's long and productive life has been divided into three general periods. The text mentions a number of his major works, but by no means all. In a spirit of discovery, listen to at least one work from each period (other than those discussed in the text, if possible), and then compare them to the musical elements discussed in the text. Can you hear differences in each period, and yet enough similarities to cause one expert to write they are all a "continuous evolution toward greater purity of style and abstraction of thought"?

	RUSSIAN PERIOD (1909–1918)	NEOCLASSICAL PERIOD (1918–1951)	SERIAL PERIOD (1951–1971)
Title:			
Comparisons:			
Rhythm:			
Melody:			
Form:			
Timbre:			
Harmony:			
Inspiration:			
Comments:			

VI-6. IGOR STRAVINSKY

BASIC TERM:
primitivism

SELF-TEST Multiple-choice: Circle the answer that best completes each item.
1. During the period from about 1920 to 1951, Stravinsky drew inspiration largely from
   a. eighteenth-century music
   b. Webern's serial technique
   c. Russian folklore
   d. African sculpture

2. *Le Sacre du printemps (The Rite of Spring)* is an example of
   a. neoclassicism
   b. primitivism
   c. serialism
   d. romanticism

3. Sergei Diaghilev was the director of the
   a. Moscow Conservatory
   b. Leningrad Philharmonic
   c. Russian Ballet
   d. Orchestre de Paris

4. Stravinsky's *Rite of Spring* is scored for
   a. a small chamber group
   b. vocal soloists and orchestra
   c. an enormous orchestra
   d. a wind ensemble

5. Which of the following ballets is *not* from Stravinsky's Russian period?
   a. *The Rite of Spring*
   b. *The Firebird*
   c. *Pulcinella*
   d. *Petrushka*

6. Stravinsky's composition teacher was
   a. Sergei Diaghilev
   b. Modest Mussorgsky
   c. Nikolai Rimsky-Korsakov
   d. Claude Debussy

7. Stravinsky's second phase is generally known as
   a. neoclassical   b. primitive   c. serial   d. postromantic

8. In the 1950s Stravinsky dramatically changed his style, this time drawing inspiration from
   a. Claude Debussy
   b. Richard Wagner
   c. Anton Webern
   d. Russian folk music

9. The famous riot in 1913 was caused by the first performance of Stravinsky's ballet
   a. *Pulcinella*
   b. *The Fairy's Kiss*
   c. *Agon*
   d. *The Rite of Spring*

10. Stravinsky's enormous influence on twentieth-century music is due to his innovations in
    a. rhythm
    b. harmony
    c. tone color
    d. all of the above

VI-7. EXPRESSIONISM

BASIC TERM:
expressionism

SELF-TEST Multiple-choice: Circle the answer that best completes each item.

1. Expressionism is an art concerned with
   a. depicting the beauties of nature
   b. emotional restraint, clarity, and balance
   c. social protest
   d. all of the above

2. The expressionist movement flourished in the years
   a. 1890–1914   b. 1905–1925   c. 1914–1941   d. 1920–1950

3. The expressionist movement was largely centered in
   a. France
   b. Great Britain
   c. Germany and Austria
   d. Russia

4. Twentieth-century musical expressionism grew out of the emotional turbulence in the works of late romantics such as
   a. Richard Wagner
   b. Richard Strauss
   c. Gustav Mahler
   d. all of the above

5. Expressionist music stresses
   a. harsh dissonance
   b. fragmentation
   c. unusual instrumental effects
   d. all of the above

6. Edvard Munch was an expressionist
   a. poet   b. painter   c. musician   d. playwright

7. The expressionists rejected
   a. conventional prettiness
   b. reality
   c. imagination
   d. morality

8. Expressionism stressed
   a. subtle feeling
   b. intense, subjective emotion
   c. reticence
   d. surface beauty

9. Expressionist painters, writers, and composers used _____ to assault and shock their audience.
   a. pastel colors
   b. deliberate distortions
   c. clearly defined forms
   d. vague nature scenes

10. Expressionist composers
    a. contributed many patriotic songs to the war effort
    b. avoided tonality and traditional chord progressions
    c. tried to capture atmosphere with rich, sensuous harmonies and pleasant subjects
    d. all of the above

VI-8. ARNOLD SCHOENBERG

BASIC TERMS:

atonality   twelve-tone system   *Sprechstimme*   tone row (set, series)

SELF-TEST Multiple-choice: Circle the answer that best completes each item.
1. Schoenberg's teacher was
   a. Johannes Brahms   c. Nikolai Rimsky-Korsakov
   b. Richard Wagner   d. Schoenberg himself

2. Alban Berg and Anton Webern were Schoenberg's
   a. teachers   b. students   c. predecessors   d. jealous rivals

3. In addition to being a composer, Schoenberg showed skill as a
   a. chemist   b. painter   c. music critic   d. economist

4. Schoenberg developed an unusual style of vocal performance, halfway between speaking and singing, called
   a. *Klangfarbenmelodie*   b. *Sprechstimme*   c. atonality   d. serialism

5. Which of the following statements is *not* true of Schoenberg's twelve-tone compositional method?
   a. The tones of a row may be presented at the same time to form chords.
   b. Each tone of a row must be placed in the same register.
   c. The tones of a row may be placed one after another to form a melody.
   d. A tone row may be shifted to any pitch level.

6. When Schoenberg arrived in the United States after the Nazis seized power in Germany, he obtained a teaching position at
   a. Harvard   b. Yale   c. UCLA   d. Columbia

RESEARCH PROJECT The music of Arnold Schoenberg:

Schoenberg's music, like Stravinsky's, has been divided into three general periods. The text mentions a number of his major works and discusses examples from the last two periods. Listen to one composition from each period, and then compare the three works with regard to the musical elements discussed in the text.

	POSTROMANTIC PERIOD (1896–1908)	ATONAL PERIOD (1908–1915)	TWELVE TONE PERIOD (1921–1951)
Title:			
Comparisons:			
Rhythm:			
Melody:			
Form:			
Tone colors:			
Dynamics:			
Harmony:			
Tonality:			
Inspiration:			
Comments:			

VI-9. ALBAN BERG

SELF-TEST Multiple-choice: Circle the answer that best completes each item.
1. Georg Büchner's play *Wozzeck* was written in the
   a. 1830s   b. 1890s   c. 1920s   d. 1940s

2. The vocal lines in *Wozzeck* include
   a. distorted folk songs   c. *Sprechstimme*
   b. speaking   d. all of the above

3. Which musical form provides the basis for the last act of *Wozzeck*?
   a. variations   b. military march   c. passacaglia   d. lullaby

4. Which of the following statements regarding Berg is untrue?
   a. He composed a great quantity of music in all forms.
   b. He synthesized traditional and twentieth-century elements.
   c. As in the music dramas of Wagner, there is a continuous musical flow within each act of his
      opera *Wozzeck*.
   d. He first attracted international attention with his opera *Wozzeck*.

VI-10. ANTON WEBERN

SELF-TEST Multiple-choice: Circle the answer that best completes each item.
1. Webern's melodic lines are
   a. "atomized" into two- or three-note fragments
   b. reinforced by frequent tutti unison passages
   c. folklike, with narrow ranges and frequent repetitions
   d. basically in major and minor keys

2. Webern's twelve-tone works contain many examples of
   a. long singing melodies   c. strict polyphonic imitation
   b. melodic and harmonic repetition d. homophonic texture

3. The least important element in Webern's music is
   a. texture   b. tone color   c. dynamic level   d. tonality

4. Webern's Five Pieces for Orchestra are scored for
   a. a chamber orchestra of eighteen soloists   c. the traditional large romantic orchestra
   b. solo voice, chorus, and orchestra   d. mandolin, harmonium, and strings

5. Webern
   a. had little formal musical training
   b. taught himself piano and cello
   c. earned a doctorate in music history from the University of Vienna
   d. enjoyed frequent performances of his own music

VI-11. BÉLA BARTÓK

SELF-TEST Multiple-choice: Circle the answer that best completes each item.

1. Bartók's principal performing medium was
   a. conducting
   b. piano
   c. violin
   d. flute

2. Bartók evolved a completely individual style that fused folk elements with
   a. changes of meter and a powerful beat
   b. twentieth-century sounds
   c. classical forms
   d. all of the above

3. The melodies Bartók used in most of his works are
   a. authentic folk melodies gathered in his research
   b. original themes that have a folk flavor
   c. reminiscent of nineteenth-century symmetrical themes
   d. exclusively Hungarian and Rumanian folk tunes

4. Bartók's six string quartets are widely thought to be the finest since those of
   a. Dmitri Shostakovich
   b. Ludwig van Beethoven
   c. Joseph Haydn
   d. Igor Stravinsky

5. While remaining within the framework of a tonal center, Bartók often used
   _____ in his music.
   a. harsh dissonances
   b. polychords
   c. tone clusters
   d. all of the above

6. Bartók's Concerto for Orchestra
   a. is his most popular work
   b. received its title because it was written for an orchestra of virtuosi
   c. is romantic in spirit because of its emotional intensity, memorable themes, and vivid
      contrasts of mood
   d. all of the above

VI-12. CHARLES IVES

SELF-TEST Multiple-choice: Circle the answer that best completes each item.

1. *Putnam's Camp, Redding, Connecticut,* is a child's impression of
   a. a summer at camp
   b. a Fourth of July picnic
   c. a fishing trip
   d. army life in the war

2. Charles Ives's father was a(n)
   a. insurance salesman
   b. physician
   c. professional athlete
   d. bandmaster

3. After graduating from Yale, Ives
   a. went into the insurance business
   b. began teaching
   c. began playing the trumpet professionally
   d. went into professional athletics

4. During most of his lifetime, Ives's musical compositions
   a. were enthusiastically received in public performances
   b. were quickly published by a major firm
   c. accumulated in the barn of his Connecticut farm
   d. were sought after by musicians eager to perform them in public

5. Ives's music contains elements of
   a. revival hymns and ragtime
   b. patriotic songs and barn dances
   c. village bands and church choirs
   d. all of the above

6. *Putnam's Camp, Redding, Connecticut,* illustrates Ives's technique of quoting snatches of familiar tunes by presenting fragments of
   a. *Yankee Doodle*
   b. *The British Grenadiers*
   c. both a and b
   d. neither a nor b

7. Ives's large and varied output includes works in many genres, but not
   a. symphonies
   b. operas
   c. songs
   d. chamber music

8. *Putnam's Camp, Redding, Connecticut,* is a movement from Ives's
   a. *Three Places in New England*
   b. *Essays before a Sonata*
   c. *Concord* Sonata
   d. *The Unanswered Question*

VI-13. GEORGE GERSHWIN

SELF-TEST Multiple-choice: Circle the answer that best completes each item.
1. Gershwin left high school at the age of fifteen to
   a. become a pianist demonstrating new songs in a publisher's salesroom
   b. study theory and composition in Paris
   c. work in his father's store
   d. develop his athletic talents

2. The Gershwin song that became a tremendous hit in 1920 was
   a. *La, La, Lucille*   c. *Swanee*
   b. *I Got Rhythm*   d. *Embraceable You*

3. *Porgy and Bess* is a(n)
   a. Broadway musical   c. rhapsody for piano
   b. opera   d. popular song

4. In addition to his musical skills, George Gershwin showed talent as a
   a. lyricist   c. sculptor
   b. clarinetist   d. painter

5. George Gershwin usually collaborated with the lyricist
   a. Jerome Kern   c. Paul Whiteman
   b. Irving Berlin   d. Ira Gershwin

6. Which of the following works is *not* by George Gershwin?
   a. *Of Thee I Sing*   c. *The Desert Song*
   b. *Porgy and Bess*   d. *An American in Paris*

7. *Rhapsody in Blue* opens with
   a. a solo flute
   b. the full orchestra   c. a muted trumpet
                                           d. a solo clarinet

VI-14. WILLIAM GRANT STILL

SELF-TEST Multiple-choice: Circle the answer that best completes each item.
1. "Harlem Renaissance" was the name
    a. sometimes given to a flowering of African American culture during the years 1917–1935
    b. given to a housing project in New York City's Harlem
    c. of a city in Holland
    d. of a symphony by William Grant Still

2. William Grant Still's opera dealing with the Haitian slave rebellion is
    a. *Trouble in Tahiti*   c. *Emperor Jones*
    b. *Troubled Island*   d. *Once on This Island*

3. As a result of his studies in composition with composers from two opposing musical camps, the conservative George Whitefield Chadwick and the modernist Edgard Varèse, Still
    a. composed in a very conservative style
    b. composed in a highly dissonant style.
    c. composed in a mixture of conservative and avant-garde styles
    d. turned away from avant-garde styles and wrote compositions with a uniquely African American flavor.

4. Each movement of William Grant Still's *Afro-American Symphony* is prefaced by lines from a poem by
    a. Paul Laurence Dunbar   c. W. E. B. DuBois
    b. Zora Neale Hurston   d. James Weldon Johnson

5. William Grant Still's works in African American style, such as his *Afro-American Symphony,* were
    a. never performed during his lifetime
    b. severely criticized by audiences and critics
    c. panned by critics, but popular with audiences
    d. performed to critical acclaim in New York

6. After serving in the navy and a brief return to studies at Oberlin College, William Grant Still moved to New York where he
    a. made band arrangements and played in the orchestras of all-black musical shows
    b. practiced medicine
    c. served as a navy recruiter
    d. composed full time to satisfy his many commissions

VI-15. AARON COPLAND

SELF-TEST Multiple-choice: Circle the answer that best completes each item.

1. Copland's name has become synonymous with American music because of his use of
   a. revival hymns, cowboy songs, and other folk tunes
   b. jazz, blues, and ragtime elements
   c. subjects from American folklore
   d. all of the above

2. Copland's turn toward simplicity in the 1930s can be traced in part to
   a. the great depression
   b. dissatisfaction with his own style
   c. the influence of Schoenberg
   d. the influence of religion

3. In 1921 Copland began a three-year period of study in
   a. Germany   b. Austria   c. Italy   d. France

4. Which of the following works was *not* composed by Copland?
   a. *Concord* Sonata
   b. *Rodeo*
   c. *Billy the Kid*
   d. *Music for the Theater*

5. In addition to his compositions, Copland made valuable contributions to music in America by
   a. directing composer's groups
   b. writing books and magazine articles
   c. organizing concerts of American music
   d. all of the above

6. In 1925, and for a few years afterward, Copland's music showed the influence of
   a. impressionism
   b. jazz
   c. neobaroque styles
   d. expressionism

7. An example of Copland's use of serialist technique is
   a. *Music for the Theater*
   b. *Connotations for Orchestra*
   c. *Fanfare for the Common Man*
   d. *Appalachian Spring*

8. *Appalachian Spring* originated as a
   a. program symphony
   b. song cycle
   c. ballet score
   d. chamber opera

9. Copland depicted "Scenes of daily activity for the Bride and her Farmer-husband" in *Appalachian Spring* through
   a. five variations on the Shaker melody *Simple Gifts*
   b. intensely dissonant passages and humorous offbeat accents
   c. strings softly singing a hymnlike melody
   d. a joyful dance tune that is American in flavor

BIOGRAPHICAL SKETCH An American composer: _____

Born (year, place):
Died (year, place):

Personal life:

    family:

    health and physiognomy:

    personality:

Career:

    significant places:

    significant people:

    employers or patrons:

    means of making a living:

    financial situation:

Music

    style of composition:

    general characteristics:

Output (List some of the major forms in which the composer worked, including the approximate number of compositions if significant. List some of the major compositions in each category, check those which you have heard, and circle those which you have studied):

Category: _____ _____ _____

Works:

Category: _____ _____ _____

Works:

VI-16. MUSICAL STYLES SINCE 1945

BASIC TERMS:

serialism   minimalist music   quotation music
chance music (aleatoric music)   microtone

SELF-TEST Multiple-choice: Circle the answer that best completes each item.

1. Minimalist music is characterized by
    a. the development of musical materials through random methods
    b. rapidly changing dynamics and textures
    c. a steady pulse, clear tonality, and insistent repetition of short melodic patterns
    d. the use of twelve-tone techniques to organize the dimensions of music

2. Many composers since the mid-1960s have made extensive use of quotations from earlier
    music as an attempt to
    a. simplify writing original compositions
    b. improve communication between the composer and the listener
    c. capitalize on the popularity of earlier works
    d. continue and develop serialist techniques

3. A major composer associated with the serialist movement is
    a. Philip Glass   b. Milton Babbitt   c. George Crumb   d. Ellen Taaffe Zwilich

4. All of the following are major developments in music since 1950 *except* the
    a. spread of chance music
    b. increased use of the twelve-tone system
    c. continued composition of symphonies in the classical style
    d. composition of music in which tone color, texture, dynamics, and rhythm are as important
       as pitch

5. Intervals smaller than the half step are called
    a. quartertones   b. tone clusters   c. macrotones   d. microtones

6. Twelve-tone compositional techniques used to organize rhythm, dynamics, tone color, and
    other dimensions of music to produce totally controlled and organized music are called
    a. chance music   b. minimalism   c. serialism   d. *Klangfarbenmelodie*

7. In chance or aleatoric music, the composer
    a. writes a rhythmic pattern but leaves it to the performer to determine the actual pitches
    b. takes a chance on which performers will perform the work
    c. chooses pitches, tone colors, and rhythms by random methods
    d. writes the music in a traditional manner, but allows the recording engineer to make changes

EXERCISE An overview of musical developments since 1945:
   The text gives ten major developments in music since 1945. Identify the characteristics that differentiate each from the others, and name some of the major figures with representative compositions in each style.

1. Increased use of the *twelve-tone system*
   Characteristics:

   Special techniques:

   Composers and compositions:

2. *Serialism*—use of twelve-tone system techniques to organize rhythm, dynamics, and tone color
   Characteristics:

   Special techniques:

   Composers and compositions:

3. *Chance music,* in which a composer chooses pitches, tone colors, and rhythms by random methods, or allows a performer to choose much of the musical material
   Characteristics:

   Special techniques:

   Composers and compositions:

4. *Minimalist music,* characterized by a steady pulse, clear tonality, and insistent repetition of short melodic patterns
   Characteristics:

   Special techniques:

   Composers and compositions:

5. Works containing deliberate *quotations* from earlier music
   Characteristics:

   Special techniques:

   Composers and compositions:

MUSICAL STYLES SINCE 1945 (cont.)

6. A *return to tonality*
   Characteristics:

   Special techniques:

   Composers and compositions:

7. *Electronic music*
   Characteristics:

   Special techniques:

   Composers and compositions:

8. *"Liberation of sound"* — greater exploitation of noiselike sounds
   Characteristics:

   Special techniques:

   Composers and compositions:

9. *Mixed media*
   Characteristics:

   Special techniques:

   Composers and compositions:

10. New concepts of *rhythm* and *form*
    Characteristics:

    Special techniques:

    Composers and compositions:

VI-17. MUSIC SINCE 1945: FOUR REPRESENTATIVE PIECES

SELF-TEST Multiple-choice: Circle the answer that best completes each item.

1. *Poème électronique* was designed for the 1958 Brussels World's Fair and was composed in collaboration with the famous architect
   a. I. M. Pei   b. Walter Gropius   c. Le Corbusier   d. Frank Lloyd Wright

2. Ellen Taaffe Zwilich won the 1983 Pulitzer Prize for Music for her composition
   a. String Quartet
   b. Double Quartet for Strings
   c. Symphony No. 1
   d. Concerto for Piano and Orchestra

3. Which of the following is *not* true of John Adams and his musical style?
   a. His music combines the driving pulse, constant repetition, and clear tonality of minimalism with expressive melodies and varied orchestral colors.
   b. He has been described as a postminimalist.
   c. He is a conductor as well as a composer.
   d. His works reflect the influence of American folk music.

4. Around 1940, John Cage invented the prepared piano, a(n)
   a. electronic keyboard capable of producing many percussive sounds
   b. grand piano complete with flowers, candelabra, and elaborate decorations
   c. grand piano whose sound is altered by objects such as bolts, screws, rubber bands, pieces of felt, paper, and plastic inserted between the strings of some of the keys
   d. ensemble of percussion instruments

5. John Adams's *Short Ride in a Fast Machine* is written for a large orchestra that includes
   a. two synthesizers
   b. a sizzle cymbal
   c. crotales
   d. all of the above

6. Ellen Taaffe Zwilish's *Concerto Grosso 1985* is an example of
   a. total serialism
   b. quotation music
   c. minimalism
   d. chance music

7. *Ionisation,* the first important work for percussion ensemble, was composed by
   a. John Cage   b. Edgard Varèse   c. Philip Glass   d. Ellen Taaffe Zwilich

8. John Cage's best-known work for prepared piano, and one of his most widely performed works, is
   a. *Sonatas and Interludes*
   b. *4'33''*
   c. *Imaginary Landscape No. 4*
   d. *Daughters of the Lonesome Isle*

9. Which of the following is *not* a musical characteristic of John Adams's *Short Ride in a Fast Machine*?
   a. rapid tempo
   b. slow-moving ostinato patterns
   c. rhythmic drive
   d. powerful, colorful sonorities

BIOGRAPHICAL SKETCH A twentieth-century composer: _____

Born (year, place):
Died (year, place):

Personal life:

    family:

    health and physiognomy:

    personality:

Career:

    significant places:

    significant people:

    employers or patrons:

    means of making a living:

    financial situation:

Music:

    style of composition:

    general characteristics:

Output (List some of the major forms in which the composer worked, including the approximate number of compositions if significant. List some of the major compositions in each category, check those which you have heard, and circle those which you have studied):

Category: _____ _____ _____

Works:

Category: _____ _____ _____

Works:

RESEARCH PROJECT *Sic transit gloria mundi (Thus passes away the glory of this world):*
In 1896 Sir George Grove brought out the first edition of his *Dictionary of Music and Musicians*. Within its four volumes, he devoted eight pages to Louis Spohr, but only a page and a half to Johannes Brahms. He gave four and a half pages to Johann Dussek, but a mere quarter-page to Smetana. Dvořák received three pages, but not until the final Appendix. Tchaikovsky received less than a page. In *The New Grove Dictionary of Music and Musicians* (sixth edition, 1980), Tchaikovsky is given almost thirty pages. Brahms has thirty-five pages in the later edition, as contrasted with Spohr's six. These figures are not necessarily reliable indications of lasting fame, but they do give some indication of how difficult it is to assess contemporary composers.

Looking back over the composers studied in Part VI (The Twentieth Century and Beyond), which of them do you feel is most significant today? Why? Do you feel that the same composer will be just as significant 100 years from now? If so, why? If not, why not? Is there perhaps an unknown today—another Brahms, for example—who will come and eclipse the glory presently accorded one of our leading composers?

RESEARCH PROJECT **Is art music alive and well in the twenty-first century? A survey:**
The United States seems to be a country of statistics and percentages. Compile some statistics of your own: just how much contemporary art music is actually performed in your area? Make a survey of all the concerts offered in a week—or as much time as you need to make a representative sampling—including professional, community, and university performances. Determine the percentage of contemporary music. Is it a healthy ratio? While you are at it, now that the bicentennial is long over, how much of that percentage is American music?

City (metropolitan area, etc.):
Survey begun:
Survey ended:
Sources consulted (newspapers, advertising flyers, radio broadcasts, magazine listings, etc.):

Number of concerts advertised:

Total number of compositions performed:

Number of twentieth-century works scheduled: Percentage:

Number of American works scheduled: Percentage:

Do you feel these are healthy percentages?

If not, what can you do to change them?

VI-18. JAZZ

BASIC TERMS:

jazz	12-bar blues	New Orleans style	bebop (bop)
call and response	subdominant	front line	cool jazz
ragtime	rhythm section	swing band	free jazz
blues	chorus	riff	jazz rock (fusion)

SELF-TEST Multiple-choice: Circle the answer that best completes each item.

1. Ragtime flourished in the United States
   a. just before the Civil War
   b. from the 1860s to about 1890
   c. from the 1890s to about 1915
   d. between the two world wars

2. A bebop performance generally began and ended with
   a. a statement of the main theme by one or two soloists in unison
   b. a statement of the main theme by the whole combo in unison
   c. improvisational sections by the soloists
   d. free sections by the rhythm instruments to set the beat and tempo

3. The "front line" of a Dixieland group included
   a. cornet, clarinet, and trombone
   b. drums, bass, and banjo
   c. piano
   d. all of the above

4. Cool jazz
   a. was related to bop but was calmer and more relaxed in character
   b. consisted of short pieces freely improvised
   c. used traditional jazz instrumental combinations
   d. all of the above

5. One of the most important solo instruments of the swing era was the
   a. cornet   b. guitar   c. tuba   d. saxophone

6. Which of the following is *not* a characteristic of fusion?
   a. The group typically includes acoustic instruments along with synthesizers, guitar, and bass.
   b. The percussion section is smaller than in earlier jazz.
   c. Rock rhythms and tone colors are combined with the jazz musician's improvisatory approach.
   d. Acoustic instruments are often used with electric attachments that expand the range of tonal effects.

7. The most famous blues singer of the 1920s, known as the "empress of the blues," was
   a. Bessie Smith   b. Nina Simone   c. Diana Ross   d. Mahalia Jackson

8. Bebop was
   a. music with sophisticated harmonies and unpredictable rhythms
   b. usually played by small jazz groups
   c. meant for attentive listening, not dancing
   d. all of the above

9. Two notable blues compositions are *Memphis Blues* and *St. Louis Blues,* by
   a. Bessie Smith
   b. William C. Handy
   c. Louis Armstrong
   d. King Oliver

10. Ragtime is
    a. a style of composed piano music
    b. generally in duple meter
    c. performed at a moderate march tempo
    d. all of the above

11. The most distinctive feature of New Orleans jazz was the
    a. use of a saxophone for playing the melody
    b. collective improvisation by the front line
    c. solo breaks by the rhythm instruments
    d. lack of syncopated melodies

12. The following can be said about free jazz:
    a. It disregarded regular forms and established chord patterns.
    b. It can be compared to chance music.
    c. It began in the early 1960s.
    d. All of the above are true.

13. Blues music is usually written in _____ time.
    a. 4/4   b. 3/4   c. 6/8   d. 2/4

14. Short repeated melodic phrases frequently used during the swing era are called
    a. riffs   b. breaks   c. gigs   d. tags

15. The "king of ragtime" is acknowledged to be
    a. John Philip Sousa
    b. Bessie Smith
    c. Scott Joplin
    d. Louis Armstrong

16. In bebop, the beat of the music was mainly marked by the
    a. piano
    b. bass drum
    c. pizzicato bass
    d. trumpet

17. Duke Ellington was perhaps the most important composer, arranger, and conductor of the
    _____ era(s).
    a. swing   b. ragtime   c. bebop   d. all of the above

18. A major figure in the development of jazz rock or fusion was
    a. Miles Davis
    b. Ornette Coleman
    c. Louis Armstrong
    d. Stan Getz

19. The chord progression usually used in the blues involves only three basic chords: tonic, dominant, and
    a. supertonic   b. mediant   c. subdominant   d. submediant

20. Which of the following is *not* associated with cool jazz?
    a. Ornette Coleman
    b. Lennie Tristano
    c. Stan Getz
    d. Miles Davis

EXERCISE Roots of jazz:
    Early jazz blended elements from many musical cultures, including west African, European, and American. Identify those musical practices and traditions in the following cultures that can be considered influences on early jazz.

West African:

Black African American:

European:

White European American:

Other:

EXERCISE Blues lyrics:
    The text describes blues lyrics as several three-line stanzas, with the second line a repeat of the first. Other writers describe blues lyrics as a rhymed couplet in iambic pentameter (._._._._._), with the first line repeated. Whichever way you think of it, write a few stanzas that could serve as lyrics for vocal blues. As you try your luck, remember that most actual blues songs were improvised on the spot by the great performers.

PERFORMANCE PERSPECTIVE
Bessie Smith singing *Lost Your Head Blues*

Bessie Smith's recordings have not only delighted listeners worldwide but they have also had a powerful impact on several generations of singers. Listen to another recording of one of Bessie Smith's songs (e.g., *St. Louis Blues* or *Empty Bed Blues*) and create your own listening guide. Consider musical elements such as vocal style and timbre as well as dynamic range and tempo.

Song Title:

Form/Text: Musical References:

EXERCISE Jazz styles:
    The text discusses six of the most important styles in the history of jazz. Listen to representative examples of each style, and identify the characteristic features of that style.

1. New Orleans style

    Title:
    Date:

    Performers:

    Instrumentation:

    Similarities:

    Differences:

2. Swing

    Title:
    Date:

    Performers:

    Instrumentation:

    Similarities:

    Differences:

3. Bebop

    Title:
    Date:

    Performers:

    Instrumentation:

    Similarities:

    Differences:

4. Cool jazz

   Title:
   Date:

   Performers:

   Instrumentation:

   Similarities:

   Differences:

5. Free jazz

   Title:
   Date:

   Performers:

   Instrumentation:

   Similarities:

   Differences:

6. Jazz rock (fusion)

   Title:
   Date:

   Performers:

   Instrumentation:

   Similarities:

   Differences:

VI-19. THE AMERICAN MUSICAL and MUSIC IN FILM

BASIC TERMS:
film music   musical (musical comedy)

Matching: Match each term with its definition.

1. the main section of a musical comedy song

2. type of theater that fuses script, acting, and spoken dialogue with music, singing, and dancing, and with scenery, costumes, and spectacle

3. the introductory section of a musical comedy song

4. a variety show without a plot but with a unifying idea

5. musical theater work that combines song, spoken dialogue, and dance with sophisticated musical techniques

6. a variety show with songs, comedy, juggling, acrobats, and animal acts, but no plot

7. music synchronized with images on a movie screen

a. chorus

b. film music

c. musical

d. operetta

e. revue

f. vaudeville

g. verse

SELF-TEST Multiple choice: Circle the answer that best completes each item.

8. Leonard Bernstein was a well-known
   a. conductor
   b. author-lecturer
   c. composer of orchestral and vocal works
   d. all of the above

9. *Slaughter on Tenth Avenue,* the ballet used in the climax of *On Your Toes,* was choreographed by
   a. Stephen Sondheim
   b. Mikhail Baryshnikov
   c. George Balanchine
   d. Agnes de Mille

10. *West Side Story*
    a. is loosely based on Shakespeare's *Romeo and Juliet*
    b. is set in the slums of New York
    c. deals with the conflict between gang rivalry and youthful love
    d. all of the above

11. The lyrics for *West Side Story* were written by
    a. Oscar Hammerstein II
    b. Stephen Sondheim
    c. Jerome Robbins
    d. Leonard Bernstein

12. Which of the following is *not* a source of the American musical?
    a. operetta   b. oratorio   c. vaudeville   d. revue

13. Which of the following American musicals is *not* by Stephen Sondheim?
    a. *Sweeney Todd*
    b. *Of Thee I Sing*
    c. *Sunday in the Park with George*
    d. *Company*

14. During the silent film era, various performing media were used to heighten the emotional effect of the movie. They were
    a. pianists
    b. organists
    c. orchestras
    d. all of the above

15. The sound for the first talking movie, *The Jazz Singer* (1927), was recorded on
    a. piano roll
    b. vinyl disk
    c. celluloid film
    d. none of the above

16. A musical passage used to accompany film scenes is referred to as a(n)
    a. clip   c. cue
    b. score   d. excerpt

17. In movie scores, musical themes that are associated with specific characters, objects, emotions, or ideas in the film are referred to as
    a. programmatic
    b. leitmotifs
    c. character themes
    d. none of the above

RESEARCH PROJECT Musical theater:
   A little advance preparation can greatly enhance your appreciation and enjoyment of any trip to the theater, whether for opera, operetta, ballet, or musical comedy. Either on your own or as part of a class project, begin preparing for such a visit.

Name of the musical:

Composer: Lyricist:

Historical time: Place:

Comic or tragic:

Main characters:

Summary of plot, argument, or concept:

High points to look and listen for:

"Hit tunes":

RESEARCH PROJECT Film music exploration:
    Pick three scenes from your favorite movie(s). Discuss how the music used in the scene enhances or heightens the emotional impact of each of the scenes. Make reference to the character and/or mood of the music, the style of the music, and elements such as timbre, dynamic, rhythm, and melody.

Example No. 1
Movie Title:

Composer:

Summary of Scene:

Discussion:

Example No. 2
Movie Title:

Composer:

Summary of Scene:

Discussion:

Example No. 3
Movie Title:

Composer:

Summary of Scene:

Discussion:

RESEARCH PROJECT *Leitmotifs* **in film music:**

A *leitmotif* is a musical theme associated with specific characters, objects, emotions, or ideas in a film. Search through some of your favorite movies and make a list of any *leitmotifs* you may notice.

RESEARCH PROJECT Film music composers:

One of the most well-known composers of film music is John Williams. Compile a list of film music composed by John Williams. Discuss your favorites.

VI-20. ROCK

BASIC TERM:
 rock

SELF-TEST Matching: Match each term with its definition.

1. country and western

2. heavy metal

3. Motown

4. rhythm and blues

5. rap

6. reggae

7. rock

8. soul

a. dance music of African Americans that fused blues, jazz, and gospel styles

b. folklike, guitar-based style associated with rural white Americans

c. a style of rock music from the West Indies

d. vocal music with a hard, driving beat, often featuring electric guitar accompaniment and heavily amplified sound

e. basic rock with sexually explicit lyrics, bizarre costumes, and tremendous volume

f. emphasis on emotionality, gospel roots, and relationship to the black community

g. blend of rhythm and blues with popular music

h. rhythmic talking accompanied by recordings creating a collage of rhythmic effects

SELF-TEST Multiple-choice: Circle the answer that best completes each item.

9. A typical rock group consists of
    a. sections of brass, reeds, and percussion (rhythm)
    b. vocalist, two acoustic guitars, harmonica, and drums
    c. two electric guitars, electric bass, percussion, and electric keyboard
    d. vocalist, backup singers, and drums

10. The Beatles' influence on American rock music may be seen through later performers' use of
    a. "classical" and nonwestern instruments   c. new electronic and instrumental sounds
    b. unconventional chord progressions   d. all of the above

11. The harmonic progressions of rock are usually
    a. limited to only two chords   c. quite simple
    b. the same as earlier popular music   d. extremely complex

12. Rock is based on a powerful beat in quadruple meter with strong accents on _____ of each bar.
    a. the second and fourth beats   c. the first beat
    b. the first and third beats   d. all four beats

13. A method of singing used by males to reach notes higher than their normal range is called
    a. freaky   b. Yeah! Yeah!   c. disco   d. falsetto

14. The dominant dance music of the 1970s was
    a. the twist   b. the mashed potato   c. the bunny hop   d. disco

15. Which of these recordings can be considered a unified song cycle?
    a. the "white album"   c. *Magical Mystery Tour*
    b. *Sgt. Pepper's Lonely Hearts Club Band*   d. *Abbey Road*

16. Which of the following was *not* a member of the Beatles?
    a. John Lennon   b. Paul McCartney   c. George Harrison   d. Bob Dylan

RESEARCH PROJECT The diversity of rock styles—an analysis:

The text stresses the enormous variety of rock styles. A major factor in this diversity is the tendency of rock to absorb elements and sounds from other styles, including folk music, country music, jazz, Latin music, western art music ranging from the Renaissance to avant-garde movements, and traditional music from Asia. Choose four popular rock pieces that show a definite relationship to other styles of music, identify these influences, and analyze the resulting combination.

1. Title:

   Performers: Style:

   Influenced by:

   Characteristics of the influencing style present in the piece:

   Result:

2. Title:

   Performers: Style:

   Influenced by:

   Characteristics of the influencing style present in the piece:

   Result:

3. Title:

   Performers: Style:

   Influenced by:

   Characteristics of the influencing style present in the piece:

   Result:

4. Title:

   Performers: Style:

   Influenced by:

   Characteristics of the influencing style present in the piece:

   Result:

BIOGRAPHICAL SKETCH A performer or composer of jazz or rock: _____

Born (year, place):
Died (year, place):

Personal life:

    family:

    health and physiognomy:

    personality:

Career:

    significant places:

    significant people:

    employers or patrons:

    means of making a living:

    financial situation:

Music:

    style of composition:

    general characteristics:

Output (List some of the major styles in which this person worked, including groups in which he or she performed. List some of the major compositions in each style, check those which you have heard, and circle those which you have studied):

Style:_____ _____

Works/recordings:

Style:_____ _____

Works/recordings:

RESEARCH PROJECT Some popular rock groups today. A comparison:
Choose four rock groups popular today. List the instrumentation, lead singers, and instrumentalists who also sing in each group. Describe and contrast any theatrical means employed, such as costumes, staging, or special effects. Identify the musical characteristics of each group, and describe how the groups are similar to and different from each other. When you have completed this analysis, what trends, if any, do you find in contemporary rock? Is rock in the process of forming a standardized instrumentation, such as the string quartet or swing's "big" band?

Group 1:
    Lead vocalists:

    Instrumentation (names and instruments; circle those who also sing):

    Theatrical aspects:

    Musical characteristics:

Group 2:
    Lead vocalists:

    Instrumentation:

    Theatrical aspects:

    Musical characteristics:

Group 3:
    Lead vocalists:

    Instrumentation:

    Theatrical aspects:

    Musical characteristics:

Group 4:
    Lead vocalists:

    Instrumentation:

    Theatrical aspects:

    Musical characteristics:

TRENDS:

Name_____

Class/section_____ Date_____

Matching Match each composition with its composer.

1._____ *The Rite of Spring*   a. Béla Bartók

3._____ *Appalachian Spring*   b. Alban Berg

4._____ *A Survivor from Warsaw*   c. Leonard Bernstein

4._____ *Prelude to The Afternoon of a Faun*   d. Aaron Copland

5._____ *West Side Story*   e. Claude Debussy

6._____ *Putnam's Camp, Redding, Connecticut*   f. George Gershwin

7._____ *Concerto Grosso 1985*   g. Charles Ives

8._____ *Afro-American Symphony*   h. Arnold Schoenberg

9._____ *Pierrot Lunaire*   i. William Grant Still

10._____ Wozzeck   j. Igor Stravinsky

11._____ Concerto for Orchestra   k. Anton Webern

12._____ *Rhapsody in Blue*   l. Ellen Taaffe Zwilich

Multiple-choice: Choose the answer that best completes each item.

13. Placing one traditional chord against another at the same time, a technique of twentieth-century music, is known as

   a. a tone cluster   b. a polychord   c. polytonality   d. bitonality

14. The complete rejection of a tonal center, or treating each of the twelve tones as of equal importance, is called

   a. expanded tonality   c. atonality
   b. polytonality   d. modality

15. The main section of a musical comedy song is called the

   a. chorus   c. release
   b. verse   d. all of the above

16. The technique of using two or more tonal centers at the same time is called

   a. expanded tonality   c. atonality
   b. polytonality   d. twelve-tone

17. *Ostinato* refers to a

   a. rapid slide through different pitches
   b. chord made of tones only a half step or whole step apart
   c. combination of two traditional chords sounding together
   d. motive or phrase that is repeated persistently at the same pitch
      throughout a section

18. A variety show without a plot but with a unifying idea is called

   a. vaudeville   b. an operetta   c. a book musical   d. a revue

Unit Quiz VI, part 1, (cont.)

19. There are _____ different tones in the whole-tone scale.
   a. five   c. eight
   b. six   d. ten

20. Which of the following characteristics is *not* usually associated with impressionism?
   a. evocation of mood   c. suggestion
   b. clearly delineated forms   d. symbolism

21. The years from about _____ are generally considered the golden age of the American musical.
   a. 1890 to 1915   c. 1920 to 1960
   b. 1905 to 1925   d. 1960 to 1990

22. Distortion is a technique used primarily in the _____ period.
   a. impressionist   c. expressionist
   b. classical   d. romantic

23. A variety show with songs, comedy, juggling, acrobats, and animal acts, but no plot, is called
   a. vaudeville   c. a revue
   b. an operetta   d. a concept musical

24. An eerily expressive kind of declamation midway between song and speech, introduced
   by the expressionist composers, is
   a. *Pierrot Lunaire*   c. a cappella
   b. stile rappresentativo   d. *Sprechstimme*

Matching: Match each "ism" with its definition.

25._____ music characterized by its steady pulse, clear tonality, and
           insistent repetition of short melodic fragments

26._____ deliberate evocation of unsophisticated power through insistent
           rhythms and percussive sounds

27._____ artistic movement, centered in Germany and Austria from 1905
           to 1925, that stressed intense, subjective emotion

28._____ artistic movement from about 1920 to 1950 that is marked by
           emotional restraint, balance, and clarity

29._____ use of the technique of the twelve-tone system to organize
           rhythm, dynamics, and tone color

30._____ artistic movement, centered in France in the late nineteenth and
           early twentieth centuries, that stressed atmosphere, fluidity, and
           color

a. expressionism

b. impressionism

c. minimalism

d. neoclassicism

e. primitivism

f. serialism

Name_____

Class/section_____ Date_____

Matching: Match each style with its definition.

1._____ piano style generally in duple meter, performed at a moderate march tempo, popular from the 1890s to about 1915

2._____ folklike, guitar-based style associated with rural white Americans

3._____ style that emerged in the early 1950s that was related to bop but calmer and more relaxed in character

4._____ style popular from 1935 to 1945, characterized by arrangements for about fifteen musicians

5._____ dance music of African Americans that fused blues, jazz, and gospel styles

6._____ combination of jazz improvisation with rock rhythms and tone colors

7._____ blend of rhythm and blues with popular music

8._____ style that emerged in the early 1960s that was not based on regular forms or established chord patterns

9._____ style that evolved in the early 1940s, characterized by complex rhythmic patterns, asymmetrical melodic phrases, solo improvisation, and irregular accents

10._____ form of vocal music usually characterized by a 12-bar chord progression over a steady 4/4 beat

11._____ style developed in the early 1900s, characterized by collective improvisation of solo performers over a clearly marked beat

12._____ vocal music with a hard, driving beat, often featuring electric guitar accompaniment and heavily amplified sound

13._____ emphasis on emotionality, gospel roots, and its relationship to the black community

a. bebop

b. blues

c. cool jazz

d. country and western

e. free jazz

f. fusion

g. Motown

h. New Orleans style

i. ragtime

j. rhythm and blues

k. rock

l. soul

m. swing

Multiple-choice: Choose the answer that best completes each sentence.

14. The chord progression usually used in the blues involves only three basic chords: tonic, dominant, and
   a. supertonic
   b. mediant
   c. subdominant
   d. submediant

Unit Quiz VI, part 2

15. Early rock grew mainly out of _____, a dance music of African Americans that fused blues, jazz, and gospel styles.
a. rhythm and blues   c. disco
b. country and western   d. Motown

16. Frequently repeated short melodic phrases commonly used in swing are called
a. riffs   b. breaks   c. gigs   d. tags

Matching: Match each performer with the style with which he or she is most closely associated.

17._____ Charlie "Bird" Parker   a. bebop

18._____ Louis Armstrong   b. blues

19._____ Elvis Presley   c. cool jazz

20._____ Ornette Coleman
                                                            d. disco
21._____ Donna Summer
                                                            e. folk rock
22._____ Duke Ellington
                                                            f. free jazz
23._____ Ice Cube

24._____ Miles Davis   g. Motown

25._____ Aretha Franklin   h. New Orleans style

26._____ Benny Goodman
                                                            i. ragtime
27._____ Diana Ross and the Supremes
                                                            j. rap
28._____ Scott Joplin

29._____ Ella Fitzgerald   k. rhythm and blues

30._____ Stevie Wonder   l. 1950s rock

31._____ Dizzy Gillespie
                                                            m. soul
32._____ Glenn Miller

33._____ Chuck Berry   n. swing

34._____ Bessie Smith

35._____ Ray Charles

36._____ Bob Dylan

37._____ Lester Young

38._____ W. C. Handy

39._____ Joseph "King" Oliver

40._____ Thelonious Monk

VII. NONWESTERN MUSIC

VII-1. MUSIC IN NONWESTERN CULTURES

BASIC TERMS:
membranophones   aerophones   heterophony
chordophones   idiophones

SELF-TEST Multiple-choice: Circle the answer that best completes each item.
1. Nonwestern music is most often transmitted
   a. orally from parent to child or teacher to student
   b. through the imitation of radio broadcasts
   c. through music notation
   d. all of the above

2. Nonwestern musical scales often contain _____ tones.
   a. five   b. six   c. seven   d. all of the above

3. A nasal, intense, and strained tone is cultivated by singers from
   a. Peru   c. the middle east and north Africa
   b. Siberia   d. sub-Saharan Africa

4. Which of the following statements is *not* true?
   a. Music of the nonwestern world is too varied to allow easy generalizations.
   b. Nonwestern traditions have been an important source of inspiration for twentieth-century western music.
   c. Improvisation is nonexistent in nonwestern music.
   d. Some composers in the nonwestern world combine traditional elements with western forms and styles.

SELF-TEST Matching: Match each term with its definition.

5. musical instrument whose sound generator is a stretched string   a. aerophone

6. musical instrument whose sound generator is a column of air   b. chordophone

7. musical instrument whose sound generator is a stretched skin or other membrane   c. idiophone

    d. membranophone

8. musical instrument whose own material is the sound generator

RESEARCH PROJECT Other nonwestern musics:

There is such a wide variety of western and nonwestern music that ethnomusicologists speak of *musics* rather than implying there is one universal form or art of music. The text covers only a few of the main characteristics of this diversity in nonwestern music and concentrates on two traditions: sub-Saharan Africa and the classical music of India. Other traditions, such as the musics of the near and middle east, Japan, China, southeast Asia, and the Native American, are not discussed.

Choosing one of the other nonwestern traditions, see if you can find characteristics in common with those of the traditions discussed (such as similarities in performance practices), unusual instruments, and other significant features. Be sure to include the names and numbers of those recordings you feel are representative of the style and you would recommend for use in a class discussion of the tradition you have chosen.

Culture:

Areas:

Forms:

Characteristics:

Instruments:

Performance characteristics:

Additional comments:

Recordings:

RESEARCH PROJECT Nonwestern instruments:
   The text states that "nonwestern instruments produce a wealth of sounds and come in many sizes, shapes, and materials." In order to experience some of these sounds, explore one culture, or one instrument type from each culture. Determine the correct category (see text) and describe the sound, shape, and use of the instrument.

AFRICA
   drums
   bimpombu, wana
   azibwasi, sakala, towa
   imbila, mbila, ilimba,
      marimba
   mbira, sanza, kalimba
   kora
   kerar
   bwanzi, ihango, dorungu,
      gwanzu

KARNATAK
   mridangam
   vina
   tambura

CHINA
   ch'in
   sheng
   erh hu
   p'i p'a
   san hsien
   chang ku

HINDUSTANI
   sitar
   tabla
   sarod
   tambura

JAPAN
   shakuhachi
   samisen
   koto
   sho
   biwa
   tsuzumi

KOREA
   komunko, hyon kum
   taegum
   haegum
   chang go

NATIVE AMERICAN
   drums
   bull-roarer
   axmal
   panpipes
   whistles

NEAR AND MIDDLE EAST
   ud
   saz
   rabab
   zurna
   naqqara
   dawul

INSTRUMENT   CATEGORY   DESCRIPTION

VII-2. MUSIC IN SUB-SAHARAN AFRICA

BASIC TERMS:
  ompeh   call and response

SELF-TEST Multiple-choice: Circle the answer that best completes each item.
1. Drums in sub-Saharan Africa
    a. come in a wide variety of sizes, shapes, and forms
    b. are essential to many religious and political ceremonies
    c. are usually played in groups of two to four
    d. all of the above

2. Which of the following statements is *not* true with regard to sub-Saharan Africa?
    a. The most common type of instrument is the chordophone.
    b. The human body is often used as a percussion instrument.
    c. The people speak over 700 different languages.
    d. Music is usually performed outdoors.

3. Vocalists in Africa often use the _____ to accompany themselves.
    a. mbira   c. xylophone
    b. nose flute   d. pressure drum

4. A type of music of the Akan-speaking peoples in Ghana is known as
    a. call and response
    b. ompeh
    c. mbira
    d. none of the above

5. A performance style in which the phrases of a soloist are repeatedly answered by those of a chorus
   is known as
    a. yodeling   c. polyphony
    b. call and response   d. campfire singing

6. The *mbira* may be described as a(n)
    a. hourglass-shaped drum
    b. melodic idiophone with tongues of metal or bamboo attached to a sounding board
    c. form of xylophone used in orchestras
    d. African form of string instrument

7. In the song *Ompeh* one of the percussion instruments is an *ogyamba*, a
    a. bamboo slit drum   c. a large barrel-shaped drum
    b. a two-headed cylindrical drum   d. a metal bell

8. The song *Ompeh* features
    a. percussive sounds
    b. a call and response pattern
    c. polyrhythms
    d. all of the above

VII-3. CLASSICAL MUSIC OF INDIA

BASIC TERMS:
tambura   tala   tabla
raga   sitar

SELF-TEST Matching: Match each term with its definition.

1. alap

2. Hindustani music

3. Karnatak music

4. mridangam

5. raga

6. sitar

7. tabla

8. tala

9. tambura

10. vina

a. long-necked lute with four metal strings used to provide a continuous drone

b. pattern of notes used to create a melody

c. fretted long-necked plucked instrument with four melody and three drone strings, popular in south India

d. pair of single-headed drums played by one performer, popular in north India

e. music of south India, which developed more along its own lines

f. music of north India and Pakistan, which absorbed many Persian elements

g. rhapsodic introductory section of a composition

h. long-necked lute with seven strings, nine to thirteen sympathetically vibrating strings, and nineteen to twenty-three movable frets, popular in north India

i. repeated cycle of beats; a rhythmic pattern

j. two-headed barrel drum popular in south India

PERFORMANCE PERSPECTIVE
Ravi Shankar, Sitar player, performing *Maru-Bihag*

Exercise No. 1

   After meeting with Ravi Shankar in 1966, Beatles guitarist George Harrison began to incorporate the sounds of Indian music into some of his songs. One such song was *Love You To* from the album *Revolver*. Listen to the song and discuss your observations and opinions regarding the Indian music influences in the song.

Exercise No. 2

   John McLaughlin was a pioneer in introducing Indian music traditions into Jazz Fusion in the early 1970s. Listen to a song recorded by John McLaughlin and the Mahavishnu Orchestra (e.g., *Birds of Fire*) and discuss the style.

Song Title:

Musical Characteristics
Style:

Timbre:

Rhythm:

Dynamic range:

Melody/Harmony:

Do you like this style? Explain your response.

UNIT QUIZ VII
NONWESTERN MUSIC

Name_____

Class/section_____ Date _____

Matching: Match each term with its definition.

1._____ aerophone

2._____ call and response

3._____ chordophone

4._____ heterophonic texture

5._____ idiophone

6._____ mbira

7._____ membranophone

8._____ pressure drum

9._____ sitar

10._____ tabla

a. membranophone in the shape of an hourglass capable of imitating human speech

b. musical instrument whose sound generator is a stretched string

c. pair of single-headed drums played by one performer, popular in north India

d. melodic idiophone with tongues of metal or bamboo attached to a sounding board

e. musical instrument whose sound generator is a column of air

f. musical instrument whose sound generator is a stretched skin or other membrane

g. musical instrument whose own material is the sound generator

h. texture in which instruments or voices perform the same basic melody but in versions that differ in ornamentation or rhythm

i. performance style in which the phrases of a soloist are repeatedly answered by those of a chorus

j. long-necked lute with seven strings, nine to thirteen sympathetically vibrating strings, and nineteen to twenty-three movable frets, popular in north India

Listening or essay question: To be provided by your instructor.

_____

_____

_____

_____

_____

APPENDIX:
GOING TO A CONCERT

BEFORE YOU GO:

Why go at all? With radio, television, and recordings all around us, why go to the expense and trouble of attending a live concert? For most people the answer is simple: recordings cannot duplicate the presence, quality, and range of live sound. Some performances must be seen as well as heard; some benefit from the interaction between performers and audience; some depend on the physical surroundings for subconscious and emotional involvement not possible through recorded sound. The fact that more concerts are given now than ever before indicates that audiences achieve pleasure and satisfaction from live performances. If you have not already discovered the reason for yourself, why not give it a try? The following comments are intended to help you achieve this goal as comfortably and easily as possible.

Choosing a concert: There are many kinds of concerts, and people quickly develop preferences, although the educated person should be familiar with the full range of possibilities. There are the symphonic orchestra and band concerts involving over 100 performers led by a conductor, and often with famous soloists. On a smaller scale there are chamber music concerts, involving one performer to each part, as in a piano trio, string quartet, woodwind quintet, brass or woodwind choir, or other chamber ensemble. Even smaller is the recital: a solo pianist, or any solo instrumentalist or vocalist, almost always with keyboard accompaniment. Musicals, operettas, operas, and ballets are all dramatic works and really must be seen to have their full impact. Then there are jazz, rock, and pop concerts where audiences frequently become actively involved in the performance.

Newspapers carry advertisements of coming events, especially in weekend sections. Radio stations frequently announce concerts; and college bulletin boards, especially around the offices of the music department, are usually crowded with announcements of professional, community, student, and amateur performances. Tickets should be obtained in advance (especially when seating is reserved), at the box office, by mail, or through ticket services. Frequently there are student tickets or discounts for students, and one should not overlook the many free performances available in churches, colleges, and parks.

Preparation: A concert is an investment of time, effort, and money on your part. A little preparation will usually help you get the most satisfaction from the experience. Find out the program in advance, and read about the various pieces and composers represented (your text will be a good place to start). Try to listen to recordings of the works, especially if a foreign-language text is involved. Many public and college libraries have excellent record collections, some of which circulate. Information about works can frequently be found on record jackets, as well as in the program notes. In the case of a dramatic work such as an opera or a ballet, some knowledge of the plot is essential. While a brief synopsis is published in the program, you may prefer the complete libretto or collections of synopses readily available in the library.

Dress: There was a time when one "dressed" for the opera or theater, which meant formal tuxedos and long evening dresses. Those days, except for special occasions, are long gone; but men often wear a coat and tie for Sunday and evening performances, and women wear the sort of outfit appropriate for going out to dinner. Other performances are normally less formal, and almost anything neat and clean is appropriate.

GOING TO A CONCERT (continued)

Punctuality: Plan to get to the concert hall or theater at least a half hour before the scheduled time of the performance. This will allow time for any last-minute emergencies, finding your seat, reading the program, and enjoying the ambience of the hall. It is not fair to let the people who were on time be distracted by latecomers, and so most concert halls and theaters today permit latecomers to take their seats only during logical breaks, such as the ends of compositions, scenes, or acts. Some halls have closed-circuit television for latecomers to watch while waiting, but imagine your disappointment if you arrive late for a one-act opera only to find that you will not be permitted to take your seat until the end of the act!

AT THE CONCERT:
The program: Most concerts and dramatic presentations will have a printed program that lists the works to be performed, the performers, program notes, and any other information that may be of value. The program is normally given to you by an usher, who will also help you find your seat. In the United States these services are usually provided without charge, but in Europe expect to purchase the program and tip the usher.

Listening: One may go to a concert for the gratification of all the senses, but music is still the art form dealing with sound. Good listening requires a great deal of mental effort, both intellectual and emotional. Naturally, any distractions, such as extraneous sounds, motions, movements, or behavior that interferes with the enjoyment of others, should be avoided. Save comments, foot tapping, humming, unwrapping candy, rustling of programs, and—if possible—even coughing for the intermission.

Applause: Audiences normally show their appreciation to a performer by applause (whistling, screaming, and hooting are quite impolite at most concerts). In order not to break the concentration of the performers and the audience, one generally does not applaud between movements of a symphony, sonata, suite, or any multimovement work. (In spite of this, opera audiences are notorious for breaking into enthusiastic applause after hit songs or arias, but one should at least wait until the music has stopped.) One usually applauds until the soloist or conductor reaches the wings of the stage, so as not to leave him or her walking off to silence. Applause by itself is simply a "thank you." It may range from polite but unenthusiastic through wildly vociferous to the electrifying rhythmic applause increasingly common in Europe. Calls of *bravo* may be heard (*brava* for a female performer; *bravi* for two or more performers), and sometimes even *encore,* which asks the performers to repeat a work or continue with one or more unscheduled compositions. If this is your first experience, just take your cue from the rest of the audience.

AFTER THE CONCERT:
Recordings: Your appreciation of a musical work, regardless of style, will increase through repeated hearings. If you enjoyed a work, listen to it again through recordings and relive the experience.

Concert reports: If the concert was an assignment, no doubt some form of report will be required. Some suggestions for writing a concert report and three simple forms follow, but your instructor will explain his or her specific requirements.

New experiences: We hope that your experience will have been a pleasant one and that you will now be ready to try other possibilities, fully confident of your own *savoir faire.*

CONCERT REPORTS

SOME PRE-CONCERT SUGGESTIONS

1. Plan ahead; get your tickets early for best seating.
2. Reread these instructions just before attending the concert so you can direct your listening.
3. Save your program and ticket to attach to the concert report. You may wish to make a few notes on the program at the concert, but in general this is not necessary.
4. Write your report as soon after the concert as possible while the experience is still fresh in your mind.
5. When writing the report, use your program to remind yourself of what you heard.

WRITING THE CONCERT REPORT
(Please type if possible)

Your instructor will most likely give specific directions, and the outline that follows is only one of many possible. For example, your instructor may wish an essay discussion of all the works on a program (not just those you liked best and least), or some reference to the biographical details of the performers and/or soloists. The suggestions listed below are merely that, and may be adapted to suit your specific requirements. If you use a computer, be sure to run a spell-check program, and remember that even though this may be a music report, it should still reflect your abilities in proper writing techniques.

Paragraph 1. THE CONCERT ENVIRONMENT:
    1. Describe the hall and physical surroundings.
    2. Describe the behavior, dress, and general demeanor of the audience.
    3. Describe the behavior, dress, and general demeanor of the performers.

Paragraph 2. THE MUSIC: the composition I liked *best* (if the concert consisted of one large work, choose the section or movement you liked best):
    1. Title and composer.
    2. Style (classic, romantic, etc.), and why you feel it is of that style.
    3. Why you like this composition best.
    4. Describe the music, considering some of the following points:
        Instrumentation: large or small orchestra, band, chorus, or chamber ensemble?
        Mood: peaceful, exciting, pompous? How did it make you feel? Emotions evoked?
        Programmatic or absolute? Did the music evoke any particular images or pictures in your mind?
        Texture: monodic, homophonic, polyphonic, or a combination?
        Harmony: major, minor, chromatic, modal, or combination? Consonant or Dissonant?
        Form (check concert program): sonata, ABA, rondo, minuet, scherzo?
        Rhythm, meter, and tempo: fast, slow, changing? Syncopated?

Paragraph 3. THE PERFORMANCE: the composition I liked *best*:
    1. How did it sound to you?
    2. Was there sufficient energy (or calm) to bring across the music?
    3. Were the performers playing or singing in tune?
    4. Did the performers seem comfortable with the technical demands of the music?
    5. Was there good ensemble and communication among the performers?
    6. How did the conductor fulfill his/her role (if applicable)?

(Optional paragraph(s) on the composition (or movement) you liked almost as well, using the questions as above)

Paragraph 4. THE MUSIC: the composition I liked *least* (if the concert consisted of one large work, choose the section or movement you liked least):
  1. Title and composer.
  2. Style (classic, romantic, etc.), and why you feel it is of that style.
  3. What did you dislike about this composition?
  4. Describe the music: how did it make you feel? Did the music evoke any particular images or pictures in your mind? What emotions did the music evoke?

Paragraph 5. THE PERFORMANCE: the composition I liked *least*:
  1. How did it sound to you?
  2. Was there sufficient energy (or calm) to bring across the music?
  3. Were the performers playing or singing in tune?
  4. Did the performers seem comfortable with the technical demands of the music?
  5. Was there good ensemble and communication among the performers?
  6. How did the conductor fulfill his/her role (if applicable)?

Paragraph 6. General reactions to the experience of attending this concert:
  1. Was the experience new to you?
  2. How was it different from what you expected?
  3. Was it like or unlike other concerts you may have attended?
  4. Did you enjoy the experience?
  5. Would you recommend concertgoing to others?
  6. Would you go again if it weren't a requirement?

Remember to attach the ticket stub and program to your report.

Name_____

Class/section_____ Date_____

CONCERT REPORT 1

Attach
ticket stub here,
and
program to back

1. Concert attended:

2. Date of concert:

3. Place of concert:

4. Type of concert (performing media):

5. General reaction to the concert environment:

6. Composition I liked best (if any) and why:

    title:

    composer:

    medium (if different from 4, above):

    movements:

    form:

    tempo:

    historical style:

    criticism of the musical work:

    criticism of the performance:

    overall reaction to this one work:

Concert Report 1 (cont.)

7. Composition I liked almost as well, and why:
    title:

    composer:

    medium (if different):

    movements:

    form:

    tempo:

    historical style:

    criticism of the music:

    criticism of the performance:

    overall reaction to this one work:

8. Composition I liked least (if any), and why:
    title:

    composer:

    medium (if different):

    movements:

    form:

    tempo:

    historical style:

    criticism of the music:

    criticism of the performance:

    overall reaction to this work:

9. Criticism and comments on the concert as a whole:

Name_____

Class/section_____ Date_____

CONCERT REPORT 2

Attach
ticket stub here,
and
program to back

1. Concert attended:

2. Date of concert:

3. Place of concert:

4. Type of concert (performing media):

5. General reaction to the concert environment:

6. Composition I liked best (if any) and why:

   title:

   composer:

   medium (if different from 4, above):

   movements:

   form:

   tempo:

   historical style:

   criticism of the musical work:

   criticism of the performance:

   overall reaction to this one work:

Concert Report 2 (cont.)

7. Composition I liked almost as well, and why:
    title:

    composer:

    medium (if different):

    movements:

    form:

    tempo:

    historical style:

    criticism of the music:

    criticism of the performance:

    overall reaction to this one work:

8. Composition I liked least (if any), and why:
    title:

    composer:

    medium (if different):

    movements:

    form:

    tempo:

    historical style:

    criticism of the music:

    criticism of the performance:

    overall reaction to this work:

9. Criticism and comments on the concert as a whole:

Name_____

Class/section_____ Date_____

CONCERT REPORT 3

Attach
ticket stub here,
and
program to back

1. Concert attended:

2. Date of concert:

3. Place of concert:

4. Type of concert (performing media):

5. General reaction to the concert environment:

6. Composition I liked best (if any) and why:

   title:

   composer:

   medium (if different from 4, above):

   movements:

   form:

   tempo:

   historical style:

   criticism of the musical work:

   criticism of the performance:

   overall reaction to this one work:

Concert Report 3 (cont.)

7. Composition I liked almost as well, and why:
   title:

   composer:

   medium (if different):

   movements:

   form:

   tempo:

   historical style:

   criticism of the music:

   criticism of the performance:

   overall reaction to this one work:

8. Composition I liked least (if any), and why:
   title:

   composer:

   medium (if different):

   movements:

   form:

   tempo:

   historical style:

   criticism of the music:

   criticism of the performance:

   overall reaction to this work:

9. Criticism and comments on the concert as a whole:

POST-COURSE LISTENING ANALYSIS

Think back to the very first lesson in the text, when you listened to **Scene 2 of Igor Stravinsky's** *The Firebird* for the first time. Listen to it once more, and again write your personal and emotional reactions to the work, and analyze the music and its technical aspects as completely and specifically as you can.

Now listen again to *C-Jam Blues* as performed by Duke Ellington and his orchestra. Compare it with the Stravinsky's scene from *The Firebird*, using the full range of your knowledge of music.

POST-COURSE EVALUATION What do you think?

Write a brief statement summarizing what, if anything, this course has done for you. Look back at the Pre-Course Questionnaire you completed at the beginning of your studies in music. Did you meet the goals you set at that time? Have your attitudes and tastes changed? Also, please give an evaluation of the course. For example, which topics pleased you; which topics did you like the least (detest?); what would you have liked to see more of and what less of; which pieces did you like best or least? Indicate anything, in other words, that would make the course more interesting and valuable for the students following you.

Thank you.

ANSWER KEY
FOR SELF-TEST QUESTIONS

I. ELEMENTS

I-1.   1-c, 2-a, 3-b, 4-a, 5-d, 6-c, 7-d, 8-b, 9-b, 10-a, 11-b, 12-d, 13-c, 14-c, 15-a

I-2.   1-a, 2-c, 3-d, 4-c, 5-b, 6-d, 7-b, 8-a, 9-d, 10-b, 11-d, 12-c, 13-d, 14-c, 15-a, 16-b, 17-b, 18-d, 19-c, 20-a

I-3.   1-c, 2-i, 3-h, 4-a, 5-b, 6-j, 7-d, 8-e, 9-f, 10-g, 11-m, 12-o, 13-s, 14-t, 15-l, 16-p, 17-r, 18-k, 19-q, 20-n

I-4.   1. BEAD, 2. CABBAGE, 3. DEAF, 4. BADGE, 5. CAGE, 6. FADE

I-5.   1-a, 2-c, 3-d, 4-b, 5-d, 6-c, 7-b, 8-a, 9-d, 10-b

I-6.   1-c, 2-a, 3-b, 4-a, 5-d, 6-b, 7-c, 8-d, 9-b, 10-a

I-7.   1-b, 2-a, 3-c, 4-d, 5-c

I-8.   1-d, 2-b, 3-c, 4-b, 5-c, 6-a, 7-d, 8-d, 9-c, 10-c

I-9.   1-d, 2-d, 3-a, 4-d, 5-b

I-10. 1-b, 2-a, 3-d

II. THE MIDDLE AGES AND RENAISSANCE

II-1. 1-a, 2-d, 3-a, 4-c, 5-b, 6-a, 7-c, 8-c, 9-d, 10-d, 11-b, 12-a, 13-d, 14-d, 15-b, 16-b, 17-a, 18-a

II-2. 1-c, 2-c, 3-c, 4-b, 5-a, 6-b, 7-d, 8-d, 9-b, 10-d, 11-a, 12-d, 13-c, 14-a, 15-d, 16-motet, mass; 17-Kyrie, Gloria, Credo, Sanctus, Agnus Dei; 18-a cappella; 19-four; 20-the overlapping of voices; 21-imitation

III. THE BAROQUE PERIOD

III-1. 1-major, minor; 2-Johann Sebastian Bach, George Frideric Handel; 3-basso continuo; 4-terraced dynamics; 5-movement; 6-b, 7-b, 8-d, 9-a, 10-d

III-2. 1-b, 2-d, 3-a, 4-d, 5-c

III-3. 1-three; 2-fast, slow, fast; 3-tutti; 4-ritornello; 5-flute, violin, harpsichord

III-4. 1-d, 2-e, 3-g, 4-f, 5-j, 6-h, 7-i, 8-a, 9-c, 10-b

III-5. 1-d, 2-b, 3-e, 4-g, 5-c, 6-j, 7-i, 8-a, 9-k, 10-l, 11-f, 12-h

III-6. 1-d, 2-a, 3-b, 4-d, 5-b, 6-a, 7-a

III-7. 1-c, 2-b, 3-a, 4-b, 5-a, 6-c

III-8. 1-basso ostinato; 2-*Aeneid,* girl's boarding school, the director was a dancing master, strings and harpsichord continuo; 3-Westminster Abbey

III-9. 1-c, 2-d, 3-c, 4-c, 5-c

III-10. 1-b, 2-d, 3-c, 4-d, 5-c, 6-a

III-11. 1-Leipzig; 2-aria, recitative; 3-*Art of the Fugue*; 4-harmony, polyphonic; 5-*The Well-Tempered Clavier*; 6-c, 7-c, 8-a, 9-d, 10-a

III-12. 1-a, 2-d, 3-b, 4-c, 5-a

III-13. 1-c, 2-d, 3-b, 4-b, 5-a

III-14. 1-c, 2-d, 3-b, 4-c, 5-b

III-15. 1-a, 2-a, 3-a, 4-b, 5-a, 6-b, 7-b, 8-b

IV. THE CLASSICAL PERIOD

IV-1. Baroque: 1, 2, 5, 7, 8, 11, 12, 15, 19, 20
Classical: 3, 4, 6, 9, 10, 13, 14, 16, 17, 18

IV-2. 1-a, 2-b, 3-a, 4-d, 5-d, 6-b, 7-a, 8-d, 9-b, 10-b

IV-3. 1-exposition, development, recapitulation; 2-introduction; 3-bridge; 4-coda; 5-motives; 6-Ludwig von Köchel, the man who catalogued Mozart's music in the nineteenth century; 7-c, 8-c, 9-a, 10-a, 11-c

IV-4. 1-b, 2-a, 3-b

IV-5. 1-c, 2-a, 3-b, 4-c, 5-d, 6-a, 7-d

IV-6. 1-d, 2-a, 3-d, 4-b, 5-c

IV-7. 1-d, 2-b, 3-a, 4-c, 5-a

IV-8. 1-a, 2-b, 3-c, 4-c, 5-d, 6-b

IV-9. 1-b, 2-b, 3-c, 4-c, 5-a, 6-d

IV-10. 1-Esterházy; 2-London; 3-string quartets, symphonies; 4-*The Seasons, The Creation*; 5-b, 6-d, 7-c

IV-11. 1-d, 2-b, 3-d, 4-a, 5-c, 6-c, 7-a, 8-a, 9-c, 10-c

IV-12. 1-vocal soloists, chorus; 2-musical sketchbooks; 3-*Fidelio*; 4-Napoleon, *Eroica*; 5-classical, romantic; 6-b, 7-d, 8-c, 9-c, 10-b

V. THE ROMANTIC PERIOD

V-1. Classicism: 1, 2, 3, 8, 12, 14, 19, 20

Romanticism: 4, 5, 6, 7, 9, 10, 11, 13, 15, 16, 17, 18

V-2. 1-d, 2-b, 3-d, 4-a, 5-b, 6-French Revolution, Napoleonic Wars; 7-piano; 8-subscription; 9-New York Philharmonic; 10-Chicago, Cleveland, Boston, Oberlin, Philadelphia

V-3. 1-lied; 2-strophic; 3-through-composed; 4-Johann Wolfgang von Goethe, Heinrich Heine; 5-introduction, postlude, piano

V-4. 1-d, 2-a, 3-d, 4-b, 5-c, 6-c

V-5. 1-d, 2-d, 3-d, 4-b, 5-d

V-6. 1-d, 2-b, 3-d, 4-b, 5-a

V-7. 1-d, 2-d, 3-a, 4-a; 5-étude; 6-nocturne; 7-polonaise; 8-polonaises, mazurkas

V-8   1-a, 2-d, 3-d, 4-b, 5-c, 6-d, 7-b, 8-b, 9-a

V-9. 1-a, 2-b, 3-d, 4-c, 5-b

V-10. 1-e, 2-c, 3-d, 4-e, 5-b, 6-a, 7-e, 8-b, 9-b, 10-a, 11-d, 12-c, 13-a, 14-b, 15-b

V-11. 1-b, 2-d, 3-d, 4-d, 5-a, 6-c, 7-c, 8-a, 9-c, 10-a

V-12. 1-b, 2-c, 3-c, 4-b, 5-a, 6-a, 7-d

V-13. 1-d, 2-b, 3-a, 4-b, 5-c, 6-d

V-14. 1-b, 2-b, 3-b, 4-d, 5-b

V-15. 1-d, 2-b, 3-d, 4-c, 5-d, 6-c

V-16. 1-d, 2-b, 3-c, 4-d, 5-d, 6-c, 7-d, 8-a, 9-b, 10-d

V-17. 1-d, 2-c, 3-b, 4-d, 5-d, 6-c, 7-d, 8-a, 9-b, 10-b

V-18. 1-b, 2-d, 3-d, 4-b, 5-a, 6-b, 7-d, 8-b, 9-d, 10-c

VI. THE TWENTIETH CENTURY AND BEYOND

VI-1. 1-d, 2-d, 3-b, 4-b, 5-d, 6-d, 7-d, 8-a, 9-c, 10-d

VI-2. 1-b, 2-b, 3-a, 4-c, 5-a, 6-b, 7-b

VI-3. 1-light, color, atmosphere; 2-Claude Debussy; 3-*Impression: Sunrise*; 4-musical, sonorous; 5-Paul Verlaine; 6-a, 7-c, 8-d, 9-a, 10-a

VI-4. 1-a, 2-b, 3-d, 4-c, 5-d, 6-a, 7-d, 8-d, 9-c

VI-5. 1-d, 2-a, 3-a, 4-c, 5-a, 6-b

VI-6. 1-a, 2-b, 3-c, 4-c, 5-c, 6-c, 7-a, 8-c, 9-d, 10-d

VI-7. 1-c, 2-b, 3-c, 4-d, 5-d, 6-b, 7-a, 8-b, 9-b, 10-b

VI-8. 1-d, 2-b, 3-b, 4-b, 5-b, 6-c

VI-9. 1-a, 2-d, 3-a, 4-a

VI-10. 1-a, 2-c, 3-d, 4-a, 5-c

VI-11. 1-b, 2-d, 3-b, 4-b, 5-d, 6-d

VI-12. 1-b, 2-d, 3-a, 4-c, 5-d, 6-c, 7-b, 8-a

VI-13. 1-a, 2-c, 3-b, 4-d, 5-d, 6-c, 7-d

VI-14. 1-a, 2-b, 3-d, 4-a, 5-d, 6-a

VI-15. 1-d, 2-a, 3-d, 4-a, 5-d, 6-b, 7-b, 8-c, 9-a

VI-16. 1-c, 2-b, 3-b, 4-c, 5-d, 6-c, 7-c

VI-17. 1-c, 2-c, 3-d, 4-c, 5-d, 6-b, 7-b, 8-a, 9-b

VI-18. 1-c, 2-a, 3-a, 4-a, 5-d, 6-b, 7-a, 8-d, 9-b, 10-d, 11-b, 12-d, 13-a, 14-a, 15-c, 16-c, 17-a, 18-a, 19-c, 20-a

VI-19. 1-a, 2-c, 3-f, 4-d, 5-d, 6-e, 7-b, 8-d, 9-c, 10-d, 11-b, 12-b, 13-b, 14-d, 15-b, 16-c, 17-b

VI-20. 1-b, 2-e, 3-g, 4-a, 5-h, 6-c, 7-d, 8-f, 9-c, 10-d, 11-a, 12-a, 13-d, 14-d, 15-b, 16-d

VII. NONWESTERN MUSIC

VII-1. 1-a, 2-d, 3-c, 4-c, 5-b, 6-a, 7-d, 8-c

VII-2. 1-d, 2-a, 3-a, 4-b, 5-b, 6-b, 7-b, 8-d

VII-3. 1-g, 2-f, 3-e, 4-j, 5-b, 6-h, 7-d, 8-i, 9-a, 10-c

CW00321671

To Bob
— with love on your 33rd birthday —
— when Tom came to roost!

LAND
OF THE
EAGLE

LAND OF THE EAGLE

A NATURAL HISTORY OF NORTH AMERICA

ROBERT McCRACKEN PECK

BBC BOOKS

FRONTISPIECE *Bald eagles at Chilkat River, Alaska*
ENDPAPERS *Fall colors in Appalachian woodlands*

Copyright © Robert McCracken Peck 1990

Maps by Line & Line

Index by Richard Raper

Published by BBC Books
a division of BBC Enterprises Limited
Woodlands, 80 Wood Lane, London W12 OTT

First published 1990

ISBN 0 563 20858 9

Set in 11/14 pt Sabon
and printed and bound in England by
Butler and Tanner Limited, Frome and London
Colour separations by Technik Limited, Berkhamsted
Jacket printed by Belmont Press, Northampton

CONTENTS

Page 6 · LIST OF MAPS AND PICTURE CREDITS
Page 7 · ACKNOWLEDGEMENTS
Page 9 · INTRODUCTION

Page 15
THE GREAT ENCOUNTER
THE · ATLANTIC · COAST

Page 51
CONFRONTING THE WILDERNESS
CANADA · AND · THE · GREAT · NORTH · WOODS

Page 89
CONQUERING THE SWAMPS
FLORIDA · AND · THE · SOUTHEAST

Page 119
ACROSS THE SEA OF GRASS
THE · PRAIRIES · AND · GREAT · PLAINS

Page 151
INTO THE SHINING MOUNTAINS
THE · ROCKIES

Page 187
LIVING ON THE EDGE
THE · DESERT · SOUTHWEST

Page 211
THE FIRST AND LAST FRONTIER
ALASKA · AND · THE · PACIFIC · NORTHWEST

Page 245
SEARCHING FOR PARADISE
CALIFORNIA · AND · THE · PACIFIC · COAST

Page 275 · NOTES
Page 282 · SELECTED BIBLIOGRAPHY
Page 283 · INDEX

LIST OF MAPS

Page 10 · North America
Page 12 · Distribution of Indigenous Peoples at the
Time of first European Contact
Page 17 · The Eastern Seaboard
Page 73 · The Exploration of Eastern Canada
and Alaska
Page 83 · North America in 1700
Page 125 · Prairie Regions in the USA and Canada
Page 135 · North America in 1803
Page 156 · The Exploration of the West

PICTURE CREDITS

Academy of Natural Sciences, Philadelphia, page 139 (top right); American Philosophical Society, page 139 (top left); Amon Carter Museum, Fort Worth, Texas, page 129 (top); Ardea, pages 81 (top, I. Beames), 99 (top, F. Gohier), 113 (bottom left, M. Grosnick), 174 (W. Weisser), 175 (S. Roberts), 226 (both, M. Grosnick) & 263 (K. Fink); Barnaby's Picture Library, page 171 (top, Southwest Color/Carlos Elmer); Howard Blakemore, page 199; Bridgeman Art Library, pages 131 (bottom) and 288; British Museum, pages 26 (top left, Fotomas; centre right, Michael Holford; rest, Bridgeman Art Library); British Museum/Natural History, pages 53, 93 (bottom left & right), 148 & 166; Alan & Sandy Carey, pages 19, 137 (top), 176 & 248; Cleveland Museum of Natural History, page 221 (top); Bruce Coleman, front & back endpapers (J. Shaw), pages 14 (M. Price), 45 (W. Lankinen), 67 (B. & C. Calhoun), 122 (G. Ahrens), 128 (L. Stone), 129 (bottom left, D. Overcash; centre, R. Carr; right, J. Shaw), 132 (J. Foott), 136 (J. Foott), 160–161 (J. Foott), 178–179 (N. Devore), 184 (M. Fogden), 220 (S. Krasemann) & 238 (S. Krasemann); DRK Photo, pages 21 (W. Lankinen), 64 (J. Johnson), 69 (S. Nielsen), 94 (D. Perrine), 99 (bottom, C. Lockwood), 113 (bottom right, L. Lipsky), 116–117 (J. Eastcott & Y. Momatiuk), 127 (bottom, D. Cavagnaro), 137 (bottom right, S. Trimble), 144–145 (J. Brandenburg), 168 (bottom right, R. Trine), 182–183 (P. O'Hara), 196 (top, T. Bean; bottom right, S. Krasemann), 203 (top, T. Wiewandt), 206–207 (L. Ulrich), 230–231 (S. Krasemann), 233 (top, S. Krasemann), 236 (S. Krasemann) & 252 (top, S. Krasemann); ET Archive, pages 40, 104 (bottom) & 131 (top left); First Light, pages 55 (S. Homer), 63 (bottom, W. Wegner), 76 (B. Milne) & 81 (bottom left, A. Kuhnigk); Jeff Foott, pages 2, 90 (top), 101, 171 (bottom left), 202, 203 (bottom), 217 & 250; Thomas Gilcrease Institute of American History & Art, Tulsa, Oklahoma, pages 63 (top) & 165; Robert Harding, pages 168 (top, J. Gardey), 244 & 254; Grant Heilman, pages 8, 42–43 (L. Lefever), 210, 264–265 & 272; Hunt Institute for Botanical Documentation (Torner Collection of Sessé & Mociño Biological Illustration), Carnegie Mellon University, Pittsburgh, page 252 (bottom); Hutchison Library, page 93 (top, Dr N. Smith); Frans Lanting, pages 36–37 & 218; William S. Lea, pages 32, 34 & 107 (top); Thomas Mangelsen, page 85 (top); Museum of Fine Arts, Boston (M. & M. Karolik Collection), page 256 (top); NHPA, pages 35 (J. Shaw), 58–59 (J. Shaw), 80 (S. Krasemann), 96 (both, S. Krasemann), 121 (J. Shaw) & 171 (bottom right, J. Shaw); Pat O'Hara, pages 46, 150, 192 (bottom) & 242; Oxford Scientific Films, pages 23 (Animals Animals/B. Kent), 74–75 (S. Osolinski), 78–79 (T. Ulrich), 81 (bottom right, T. Martin), 98 (Animals Animals/Z. Leszczynski), 104 (top, Animals Animals/Z. Leszczynski), 127 (top, W. Shattil & B. Rozinski), 137 (bottom left, S. Osolinski), 158 (top, Animals Animals/R. Richardson), 189 (S. Osolinski), 193 (S. Osolinski), 196 (bottom left, Animals Animals/Z. Leszczynski) & 213 (top left, R. Tyrrell; top right, F. Schneidermeyer); Photographers/Aspen, pages 85 (bottom, D. Hiser), 86 (D. Hiser), 107 (bottom, D. Hiser), 118 (N. Devore), 139 (bottom, D. Hiser), 154–155 (N. Devore) & 168 (bottom left, N. Devore); Photo Researchers, pages 39 (P. & T. Leeson), 50 (D. Guravich), 113 (top, J. Lepore), 158 (bottom, P. & T. Leeson) & 190 (Van Nostrand); Planet Earth Pictures, page 90 (bottom, D. Perrine); Mike Potts, pages 215 & 229; Royal Library, Windsor Castle © 1989, Her Majesty the Queen, pages 110 (top & bottom centre) & 213 (bottom); Smithsonian Institution, Washington, pages 131 (top right, Bridgeman Art Library) & 221 (bottom); Spectrum Colour Library, pages 246, 256 (bottom) & 270 (D. & J. Heaton); Tony Stone Worldwide, pages 88 (Click/Chicago), 192 (top, P. Degginger) & 268–269 (T. Mackie); University of California, Bancroft Library, page 261; University of Pennsylvania Museum, page 233 (bottom); Zefa, page 186; Zoological Society of London, pages 110 (bottom left & right).

ACKNOWLEDGEMENTS

I would like to begin my acknowledgements with special thanks to two individuals who have been essential to the creation of this book. Peter Crawford, Executive Producer of the BBC television series *Land of the Eagle* was the one who first suggested that I write this companion volume. His conceptual role in developing the series and his perceptive suggestions regarding the book have been central to its creation. Also, Professor Charles A. Miller, who generously took time from his busy teaching, research and writing schedule to review the manuscript for content and editorial style. His encouragement and professional advice at each stage of the book's development has been of inestimable value.

Martha Caute of BBC Books and David Wolff of WNET have both been involved with every aspect of this project and to them I am deeply indebted. I also wish to thank Sheila Ableman, designer Linda Blakemore, picture researcher Jennifer Fry, copy-editor Judy Maxwell, and the many individuals behind the scenes at the BBC, WNET, and Macmillan.

In the Natural History Unit of the BBC I would especially like to thank producers Ned Kelly, Steve Nicholls, Paul Reddish, and Sue Western, as well as Vicky Brennand, Clare Flegg and Di Williams who worked with Peter Crawford in developing the series which this book complements. George Page, David Heeley and their colleagues at WNET were responsible for making the series available to American viewers. To them I am also most grateful.

To all of my colleagues at the Academy of Natural Sciences of Philadelphia I am greatly indebted for assistance and support. I would like to thank especially Christine Bush whose countless hours of research, typing, perceptive suggestions, and personal enthusiasm made the preparation of the manuscript a pleasure. Other individuals within the Academy who were extremely generous of their time and knowledge were: Don Azuma, Art Bogan, Genie Bohlke, Ted Daeschler, Margaret Fischer, David Frodin, Frank Gill, Bill Gagliardi, Skip Glenn, John Guarnaccia, Richard Horwitz, Regina Kilimnik, Frank Mattiacci, Jamie Newlin, Dan Otte, Mark Robbins, Linda Rossi, Bill Saul, Ernie Schuyler, Carol Spawn, and Keith Thomson.

Others who provided valuable information and assistance were Richard Ellis, Janet Evans, Joseph Ewan, Jay and Ellen Hass, Pamela Hearne, Paul Meyer, Roger Pasquier, Tony Paul, Lynn Rogers, Dian Stallings, Jessica Thomson, Linda Thomson, Perot and Susie Walker, Greg Wilker, and the many scholars whose books and articles I consulted in the course of my research.

For their careful and meticulous review of manuscripts and suggestions regarding content, emphasis, and style, I am deeply indebted to: T. Peter Bennett, Jocelyn Kelley, Bernard Fontana, J. I. Merritt, Arthur Perkins, Cindy Price, Stanley Senner, Carol Spawn, Keith Thomson, and David Traxel.

Finally, I wish to thank my friends and family for their encouragement and support throughout.

Robert McCracken Peck

INTRODUCTION

On a warm spring day in 1832 the American artist George Catlin left a bustling frontier trading fort in what is now South Dakota and walked to a small tree-crowned hill nearby. In every direction the soft green of the prairie grasses stretched to the horizon. Meadowlarks, recently returned from a winter in Texas, sang in the morning sunlight. Bees moved noisily between the myriad of prairie flowers. A mosquito or two whined in the artist's ear. A gentle breeze brought with it the smell of earth and grass and morning dew.

Catlin seated himself comfortably and after savoring the air's morning freshness, unfolded a map of North America from the pocket of his loose leather jacket. With a paint-stained finger, he slowly traced his route west from Philadelphia, recalling the various stops he had made along the way. He found his place at Fort Pierre, and then scanned the map for the few other outposts of white settlement noted in the western third of the country – Fort Union, Fort Mandan, and Fort Laramie. He hoped eventually to spend time in these places, and among the native peoples whose lands they dotted. Catlin had come to the West expressly to see the Indians and to document their free and wild way of life. But this morning his mind was on even bigger things.

Catlin had set out to create what he called a 'reverie' or internal vision of the continent that would place his experience in a broader geographical and historical context:

> *Excluding my thoughts from every other object in the world, I soon succeeded in producing the desired illusion. This little chart over which I bent was seen in all its parts, as nothing but the green and vivid reality. I was lifted up upon an imaginary pair of wings, which easily raised and held me floating in the open air, from whence I could behold beneath me the Pacific and the Atlantic Oceans – the great cities of the East, and the mighty rivers. I could see the blue chain of the great lakes at the North – the Rocky*

USSR

ARCTIC OCEAN

ICELAND

GREENLAND

BEAUFORT SEA

Barrow

BERING SEA

North Slope
Brooks Range
Prudhoe Bay

Banks I

Devon I

BAFFIN BAY

Central Plateau Area
Alaska
Yukon R

Aleutian Range

Anchorage

Mackenzie Mtns

Victoria I

Baffin I

Gulf of Alaska

Great Bear Lake

Southampton I

Hudson's Strait

Juneau

ROCKY MOUNTAINS

Great Slave Lake

HUDSON'S BAY

Labrador

Coastal Mtns

Peace R

Athabasca R

Churchill

LAURENTIAN SHIELD

Newfound-land

Queen Charlotte I

Nelson R

Laurentian Mtns

Gulf of St Lawrence

Edmonton

N Saskatchewan R

L. Winnipeg

Albany R

Fraser R

S Saskatchewan R

Regina

Quebec

Halifax

Vancouver I

Cascade Range

Winnipeg

St Lawrence R

Vancouver

Missouri R

L. Superior

Nova Scotia

Seattle

Duluth

Montreal

Connecticut R

Portland

Bitterroot Range

Columbia R
Blue Mtns

Ottawa

Niagara Falls

Boston

ROCKY MOUNTAINS

Yellowstone R

Big Horn Mtns

St Paul

L. Huron

L. Ontario

Snake R

Absaroka Range

Minneapolis

L. Michigan

Buffalo

Hudson R

New York

SIERRA NEVADA

Great Salt Lake

Platte R

Chicago

Detroit

L. Erie

Philadelphia

Salt Lake City

Denver

Missouri R

Omaha

Cleveland

Baltimore

San Francisco

GREAT BASIN

COASTAL RANGE

Colorado R

GREAT PLAINS

Mississippi R

Illinois R

St Louis

Ohio R

Pittsburg

Cincinatti

Allegheny Mtns

Washington DC

Grand Canyon

San Juan Mtns

Arkansas R

Kansas City

APPALACHIAN MOUNTAINS

Smoky/Blue Ridge Mtns

Los Angeles

Mojave Desert

Santa Fe

Canadian R

Charleston

ATLANTIC OCEAN

Colorado Plateau

Memphis

San Diego

Phoenix

Sacramento Mtns

Red R

Atlanta

Alabama R

Sonoran Desert

Gila R

El Paso

Rio Grande

Colorado R

Dallas

Natchez

Tampa

Lower (Baja) California

Gulf of California

Chihuahua Desert

San Antonio

Houston

New Orleans

Miami

BAHAMAS

Everglades

DOMINICAN REPUBLIC

Tropic of Cancer

Sierra Madre Occidental

Monterrey

GULF OF MEXICO

CUBA

PACIFIC OCEAN

Sierra Madre Oriental

JAMAICA

HAITI

Canada

Mexico City

MEXICO

CARIBBEAN SEA

USA

0   250   500   750   1000 Miles

Mountains, and beneath them and near their base, the vast and almost boundless plains of grass which were speckled with the bands of grazing buffaloes!

As Catlin pursued his aerial view of earth, he imagined the globe spinning beneath him, but found nothing comparable to the 'Western wilds of my own country'. Here 'myriad herds of buffaloes' and other wild game roamed at leisure and dozens of Indian tribes, as yet relatively unaffected by the influences of white traders from the eastern half of the continent, pursued a life romantics sometimes compared to man before the fall.

Catlin found immense satisfaction in his pastoral vision of the continent, but when his thoughts spun forward through time, he foresaw a very different and far less idyllic America. With uncanny prescience he imagined the buffaloes, symbols of the continent's wild abundance, 'wheeling about in vast columns and herds' then scattering to seek refuge from violent destruction at the hands of man:

Some lay dead and others were pawing the earth for a hiding place – some were sinking down and dying, gushing out their life's blood in deep drawn sighs – and others were contending in furious battle for the life they possessed and the ground that they stood upon.

Unless some action was taken to prevent it, warned Catlin, North America might one day lose not only the buffalo, but many of the continent's other wild resources to the 'insatiable avarice' of its people.

The technology of recent decades has enabled us to see Planet Earth from space much as Catlin imagined it more than a century and a half ago. Many of Catlin's fears have been realized. As he predicted, large sections of the country have been inalterably changed by 'the deadly axe and the desolating hands of cultivating man'. But happily, some of his dreams have been fulfilled as well. In millions of acres of protected land in the United States and Canada some of the continent's most beautiful places and the wildlife they contain have been 'preserved in their pristine beauty and wildness', just as the visionary artist had hoped.

The duality of Catlin's vision of North America lies at the heart of *Land of the Eagle*. Like George Catlin, we can step back from the continent to see its many facets through the perspectives of time and space. Drawing on firsthand descriptions from native Americans, early European explorers, naturalists, artists, writers and pioneers, and moving from east to west, as most European settlers first saw the land, we examine eight general regions from the Atlantic Ocean to the Bering Sea, describing them as they were perceived and altered by different human populations.

From its first 'discovery' by the seafaring nations of Western Europe, the New World was the subject more of speculation and wishful thinking than of accurate understanding. London's *Moderate Intelligencer*, for example, assured would-be emigrants to North America in 1649 that they could be 'plentifully

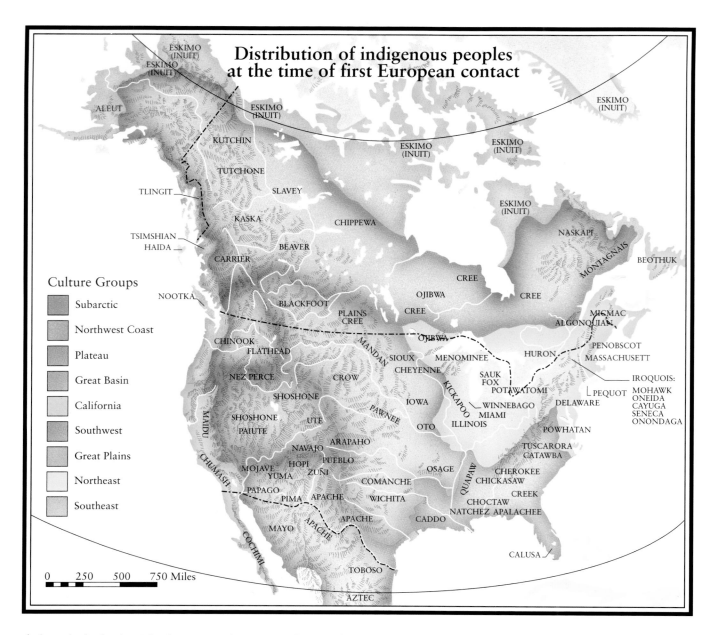

Distribution of indigenous peoples at the time of first European contact

Culture Groups

- Subarctic
- Northwest Coast
- Plateau
- Great Basin
- California
- Southwest
- Great Plains
- Northeast
- Southeast

0 250 500 750 Miles

fed and clothed with the natural Commodities of the Country which fall into your hands without labour or toyle'. So it must have appeared to those reporting back to Europe on the appearance of the continent and the way its people lived. To those who actually settled in North America, however, the nature of the continent proved quite different. Until they could adopt new ways of living or reshape the country in the image of home, European colonists found North America anything but paradisiacal. Extreme temperatures, seemingly endless forests, stony soil, unfamiliar animals, poisonous plants, and stubbornly independent natives made survival in the new land a far cry from the 'delightful recreation' promised in the London press.

As Spanish, French, British, Dutch, Scandinavian, Russian, and other settlers arrived in various parts of North America, each brought different traditions of land and resource management. Unlike the continent's indigenous people who saw themselves as an integral part of the natural world, many Europeans considered nature a force to be subdued, exploited, or destroyed. The amalgamated people who became the new 'Americans' thus created an environmental ethic quite at odds with that of the indigenous people whose lands they occupied. Once European colonies were established in North America, a series of environmental changes were set in motion that continue to the present day.

George Catlin accurately predicted that many of the continent's native people, like the buffalo 'joint and original tenants of the soil', were doomed by the advance of Western 'civilization'. Disease, dislocation and genocide reduced the continent's indigenous tribes to scattered bands of refugees in their own land. Some of the New World's wildlife suffered the same fate. The nineteenth and early twentieth centuries saw a rash of man-induced extinctions, yet the vast majority of native species were resilient enough to resist or adapt to the profound changes in the land created by the rapid imposition of Old World values and attitudes.

Beavers, bears, herons, alligators, bison, bighorn sheep, hummingbirds, warblers, whales, and sea otters each tell stories of survival that are as varied as the species themselves. None has been unaffected by man's presence. Many have played central roles in the cultural and commercial development of the continent. The survival of these and countless other wild species from the coniferous forests of the Canadian North to the sawgrass fields of the Everglades, from the scorching sands of the Desert Southwest to the fog-shrouded coast of Alaska, remind us of the power and durability of a natural world in which humans are but relatively recent arrivals.

Within months of George Catlin's hilltop reverie in the Great Plains, the French traveler Alexis de Tocqueville described the America he saw east of the Mississippi. There were fewer Indians in the East, and a surprising amount of development – 'it is more difficult than one thinks to find the wilderness', he noted, 'the forests fall, the swamps dry up....' – but parts of the land he saw were excitingly virginal in spirit, if not in fact. The continent, de Tocqueville observed in 1831, 'presents, as it did in the primeval time, rivers that rise from never failing sources, green and moist solitudes, and limitless fields which the plowshare of the husbandman has never turned.' For all its changes, North America still possesses much of the wild heritage that both Catlin and de Tocqueville described. Perhaps with a better understanding of the land and its wildlife and how we have treated both in the past, we will be better able to preserve what is left for the centuries to come.

THE GREAT ENCOUNTER
THE · ATLANTIC · COAST

The summers are short in Newfoundland. They are short for the wild flowers, short for the insects, and shorter still for the birds. At the end of each year's nesting, some time in mid to late September, the birds begin to gather for the long flight south. Some travel overland to the Gulf of Mexico, then on to the verdant coast of Venezuela. Others take the more direct but riskier route over water, some 5000 miles non-stop over Cape Cod and Bermuda to the northern Antilles and beyond. They fly in their millions by day and night, some up to 90 hours without rest. It is a vast migration, and an incredible feat of navigation and endurance which still astonishes the people who study it.

Christopher Columbus was no ornithologist, but he was an observer of birds, and he knew enough to surmise that where small birds flew, there must be land for roosting. It was a simple conclusion which would help to change the course of history.

In early October, 1492, Columbus needed something – anything – to boost the flagging hopes of his Enterprise of the Indies, an audacious scheme for reaching the Orient by sailing west from Spain. Neither he nor his crew of 90 men had seen land since leaving the Canary Islands a month before. Most believed they never would. Provisions were low, spirits were lower and some men were talking of mutiny.

As thoughts turned eastward and eyes strained west (there was to be a cash reward for the first to see land), Columbus and his men began to notice signs of life. They had seen birds before – throughout their crossing ocean-going shearwaters and petrels had raised false hopes of landfall – but these birds were different. They were smaller land-birds, moving south-west in flocks of thousands. The ships, the *Niña*, *Pinta* and *Santa María*, were redirected to follow them. All night long the men heard birds passing overhead and saw their tiny forms silhouetted against the moon.

Within a few days the sailors of the *Niña* fished aboard the branch of a blossoming tree which appeared to float in from the west. The *Pinta*'s crew found other fragments of land vegetation and signs of human life, 'a little stick, fashioned, as it appeared, with iron'. That night, at sunset, the ships turned west again. In the early morning hours of 12 October, a shout from the *Pinta*'s forecastle and a celebratory blast from her cannon marked the long-awaited first sight of land.

That the course of Columbus's voyage was twice altered in response to signs of American nature was fortunate for him, and significant in light of all that was to follow. Had he not redirected his crew after encountering the flocks of fall migrants, the ships would have been caught by the current of the Gulf Stream and been carried north into the treacherous coastal waters of mainland North America. Had he not headed west again on the night of 11 October, his fleet would have taken an equally dangerous course into the reef-studded waters of the Bahamas. In either case, he and his ships might well have been lost, or so severely damaged as to prevent their return to Spain.

As it was, the changes in direction brought Columbus and his men to a safe landing on the eastern edge of the Bahama chain, roughly 100 miles southeast of Florida. There Columbus officially laid claim to the new land in the name of his royal Spanish patrons, Ferdinand and Isabella.

Like so many interactions between the Old World and the New that would follow, Columbus's great 'discovery' was riddled with false assumptions and misunderstandings. The islands he had stumbled upon were not the East Indies as he believed. Nor were the people he encountered already living there 'Indians', though it is a name that has endured. Few of the riches he had hoped to secure – spices, silk or possibly gold – materialized. His subsequent attempts to colonize ended in disaster. Although the New World failed to fulfill Columbus's personal expectations, his encounter with it set in motion a series of interactions between cultures and the environment that would irreversibly alter the natural world and man's place in it.

Columbus was not the first European to reach the New World. Maps, manuscripts, and archeological remains in Newfoundland and on the northeast coast of North America confirm that as early as AD 1000, Viking explorers had found their way to the continent from Europe. Irish, Basque, and Breton fishermen also may have crossed the Atlantic to exploit the resources of the New World long before Columbus made his epic journey. But as many of these men were illiterate, or preferred to keep the location of their bountiful harvest secret, their New World discoveries were little noted at home. Columbus's reports, in contrast, were carried directly to the royal court of Spain. His widely publicized accounts of natural wealth sparked a frenzy of competitive exploration and exploitation of the Americas by the increasingly ambitious powers of Western Europe.

Though new to European eyes, North America had been inhabited by people for more than 20 000 years. In the course of this time, like humans everywhere, the native Americans had shaped and modified the land to their own purposes. Using simple but effective stone tools and controlled burning, indigenous tribes

The Eastern Seaboard

Lake Superior

Stadacona

Fort Richelieu

Hochelaga

St John R

Nova Scotia

Lac Iroquois

La Grande Rivière R

Lake Huron

St Laurent R

Lake Ontario

Fort Orange

Fort Nassau

Niagara Falls

Lake Erie

Lake Michigan

Mississipi R

Agamenticus

Gloucester

Salem

Boston

Plymouth

Windsor

Hartford

Providence

Newport

Newhaven

New Amsterdam

Breuckelen

Susquehanna R

Fort Beversrede

Fort Christina

Fort Nassau

Providence

St Mary's

James R

Jamestown

Chesapeake Bay

Roanoke I

Illinois R

Ohio R

Missouri R

De Soto d. 1542

APPALACHIAN MOUNTAINS

Mississipi R

	Columbus 1492-3
	De León 1513
	Verrazzano 1523
	Narváez and De Vaca 1527-8
	De Soto 1539-42
	Champlain 1609-15
	La Salle 1680-2

Colonies 1650:

English

French

Dutch

Spanish

Swedish

0   100   200   300   400 Miles

ATLANTIC OCEAN

Fort Caroline

St Augustine

Narváez d. 1528

Tampa Bay

Florida

North & South Bimini

Lake Okeechobee

GULF OF MEXICO

Dry Tortugas

Florida Keys

BAHAMAS

Havana

CUBA

HISPANIOLA

PUERTO RICO

GREATER ANTILLES

JAMAICA

CARIBBEAN SEA

LESSER ANTILLES

had long since cleared parts of the eastern forest for agriculture. The resulting patchwork of garden plots, abandoned fields, and woodlands had, in turn, increased habitat diversity for wildlife, thus adding to the variety and quantity of game available. Far from a virgin and primeval wilderness as many believed, North America was an already transformed landscape when Europeans first reached its shores.

Columbus assumed that the people he encountered in the Caribbean and later on the North American continent were Asians, living on the far eastern fringes of the Orient. In a sense he was correct, but the 'Indians' he discovered were far removed from their Asian origins in both distance and time.

When humans first crossed the Bering Strait from Asia to what is now Alaska, snow and ice may well have covered most of the northern third of North America. Sea levels were lower then by as much as 410 feet, and a land bridge up to 1000 miles wide made the crossing possible. From the north-west tip of the continent, the first rugged nomads, and others who followed, divided and moved slowly south and east.

The land they found was a land in transition. The last great ice cap, which had once covered present-day Canada, New England, New York, and much of the American midwest in depths up to a mile thick, was in the process of receding, slowly releasing its grip on a scraped and scoured continent. At its southern edge, amid glacial till and raging rivers of snow melt and gravel, new generations of pioneering plants sprouted, pushing north from the botanical refuges in which they had lived out the millennia of the ice age. Behind the plants came countless species of insects, birds, and mammals, flourishing on the newly available range. Some had preceded human hunters across the Bering land bridge from Asia. Other animals had crossed the isthmus of Panama from the south. A third group had evolved on the continent and were in the process of dispersing to other parts of the world by moving in the opposite direction.

The highly varied environmental conditions present in North America during the slow retreat of the ice age made the continent an unusually rich habitat for mammals. There were at least ten species of native horse, seven species of bison, four species of elephant, and several kinds of rhinoceros and wild pig. Also present were badgers, wolverines, otters, muskrats, weasels, deer, skunks, rabbits, seals, and a host of other animals, including three from South America, the porcupine, opossum and armadillo. Some of these species adapted to the warming climate and flourished. They are with us still, looking more or less as they did some 10 000 to 20 000 years ago. Many others could not tolerate the rapid change of climate or the increased pressure of humans and became extinct.

By the end of the ice age almost 200 species of Pleistocene mammals had vanished from North America, including bear-sized beavers, giant ground sloths, lions, and saber-toothed cats. Equal or greater numbers of reptiles, amphibians, and insects may also have disappeared by this time. A small number of species struck an environmental compromise either by following the receding ice sheets north or by finding habitat refuges that continued to approximate ice-age conditions. The musk ox, caribou and polar bear are among the largest species

Echoed by its own reflection a young muskrat feeds and grooms in the shallows of a quiet pond. Like its larger relative the beaver, the muskrat is an aquatic species that comes to land only when it must gather food. It was prized for its fur and flesh by Indians and Europeans alike.

that followed this course. The White Mountain butterfly is one of the smallest. As the climate warmed and the great ice sheet withdrew, this fragile insect sought the cooler temperatures in which it had evolved either by following the receding ice sheet or by moving high into the mountains that jutted from its original range. This ice-age relic survives today in three widely dispersed locations – Labrador; New Hampshire's Mount Washington, the highest peak in the eastern United States; and a comparable peak in the Rocky Mountains of Colorado – which provide similar climates separated by thousands of miles of warmer, recently evolved habitat.

Among the most adaptable species were humans. As they moved down from Alaska and multiplied over the millennia, they made places for themselves in each of North America's varied environments. Some crossed the isthmus of Panama and continued to expand into South America. On the connecting land bridge between the continents, and in the southwest corner of North America, they eventually created the great Inca, Maya, and Aztec civilizations. Others moved east and were well established along the Atlantic coast at least 10 000 years before Columbus claimed the New World for Spain.

The new European arrivals knew none of this history, nor could they appreciate that it was almost as old as their own post-glacial existence. Flushed with the excitement of discovering this land for themselves, Europeans tried to define the New World and its inhabitants in terms fellow Europeans could understand. Their characterizations, like their experiences, ran to extremes. Some found 'a waste and howling wilderness where none inhabited but hellish fiends, and brutish men'. Others saw 'the fairest, fruitfullest and pleasantest [land] of all the worlde' inhabited by 'well shapen and proportioned ... gentill, curtious', and noble people. All agreed that North America, whether heaven or hell on earth, offered natural bounty on a previously unimaginable scale.

The abundance of wildlife that had sustained the first Americans and so impressed Old World explorers can be experienced in almost any part of North America today. The huge flocks of migrating songbirds that guided Columbus to safe harbor still crowd the eastern flyway each fall. Those species that take the overland route are most easily seen massing at geographical points of concentration on their southern journey. Cape May, New Jersey, a peninsula guarding the mouth of Delaware Bay, is such a point.

Cape May acts as the narrow neck in an hourglass for southern migrants. On a cool, foggy morning in early October, the oaks, maples and sassafras trees on Cape May Point swarm with warblers, thrushes, sparrows, flycatchers, kinglets, juncos, and dozens of other birds all waiting for the winds of a northern cold front to help them move on over the Bay. For a day or two, or until the weather shifts, they feed voraciously on seeds, berries, and insects to help replenish their energy reserves and build strength for the long trip ahead. Once across the Bay the flocks will disperse again, broadening on their flight south, until they reach a suitable wintering habitat. If they are flying on to Central America, as many do, they will briefly concentrate in Florida or along the Gulf of Mexico before making the flight across the Caribbean. Still others, though

A Cape May warbler at the peak of breeding plumage searches for insects among the flowering branches of a fruit tree. Though named for Cape May, New Jersey, this bird is seen there only on migration between its wintering grounds in the Caribbean and the coniferous forests of Canada, New England, and the Great Lakes region where it nests.

many fewer, will travel farther, wintering in the rainforests of South America before returning for another breeding season in the north.

Habitats available for wildlife have been drastically reduced and altered by human settlement patterns over the past 500 years. Surprisingly, these settlements have done little to change the migration patterns of non-resident species. Even the sprawl of New York City has not changed the seasonal movements that occurred before human settlement of any kind. As many as 100 species of birds may pass through central Manhattan in a single May morning. In recent years a total of 270 different bird species have been recorded in New York's Central Park. This means that more than a third of all the species of North American birds can be found, at least temporarily, in the heart of one of the largest metropolitan areas in the world.

Not far away, on the Atlantic shores of New Jersey and Delaware, millions of migrating shorebirds – sandpipers, turnstones, plovers, and sanderlings – meet each spring with millions of breeding horseshoe crabs. The birds are on their way north from the desert coast of Chile and pampas of Argentina to their breeding grounds above the Arctic Circle. Evolution has timed the birds' arrival to coincide with the crabs' breeding. The birds break their 6000 mile journey each May to gorge on the rich, granular crab eggs, sometimes doubling their weight in just 14 days. One estimate puts the number of eggs consumed by sanderlings alone at six billion in a two-week period. The crabs, for their part, spawn with abandon, a single crab laying up to 80 000 eggs. So despite the staggering toll, this ancient life form persists, as it has for 300 million years, long before the evolution of the birds.

In many of the great rivers up and down the East Coast of North America, shad, sturgeon, herring, and striped bass still make their annual breeding runs past the oil refineries and international ports to the quieter waters inland. Following a period of pollution-related decline, their numbers and diversity have begun to increase as water quality has improved. While there have been significant losses of wildlife in the past two centuries, recent efforts to preserve critical habitats, regulate game harvests, ban toxic pesticides and control pollution of all kinds have helped to moderate man's negative impact on the wild abundance of the continent. In some cases, wild populations have begun to return to earlier levels.

The account of Jean Ribaut, who tried to establish a French colony in North America in 1562, gives us some idea of what the continent looked like at the time of first European contact, though he often appears to have been left speechless by the enormity of what he saw. He viewed the new land 'with an unspeakable pleasure', described the 'aboundaunce of fische' as 'increadeble', and marvelled that there were 'havens, rivers, and islands of suche fruitefullness as cannot with tonge be expressed'.

Limits of vocabulary notwithstanding, Ribaut's record of his travels, *The Whole and True Discovery of Terra Florida* (1563) provides one of the first attempts at an inventory of North American wildlife. The new land, Ribaut said, abounded in

In a mating ritual more than 300 million years old, horseshoe crabs gather on the same Atlantic beaches every spring to mate and spawn. Female crabs lay up to 80 000 eggs each, supporting with their fecundity hundreds of thousands of migrating shorebirds. The birds make use of the nutritious crab eggs to sustain long flights north to their own breeding grounds in Newfoundland, Labrador, and the High Arctic.

> *honney, veneson, wildfoule, forrestes, woods of all sortes, palme trees, cipers, ceders, bayes, the hiest, greatest, and fairest vynes in all the wourld with grapes accordingly, which naturally and without man's help and tryming growe to the top of okes and other trees that be of a wonderfull greatness and height.*

Grapes had also been noticed and admired by the Vikings four centuries before, giving rise to their name for the continent – Vineland or Vinland.

Among the animals Ribaut encountered during his brief coastal wanderings in what is now North Carolina were

> *herons, corleux [curlew], bitters [bitterns], mallardes, egertes, woodcockes, and all other kinde of smale birdes, with hartes, hyndes, buckes, wild swyne, and sondery other wild beastes as we perceved well bothe then by there foteing [foot-prints] there and also afterwardes in other places by ther crye and brayeng which we herde in the night tyme.*

Ribaut's reports of plants, birds and mammals in 'mervelus numbre [and] a great dele fairer and better' than those of Europe attracted considerable interest in England. His listing of other 'precyous comodyties', including 'gold, silver, pearls [and] turquoise', attracted even more. His vivid descriptions of Florida as a place that 'lacketh nothing' and where 'in a shorte tyme great and precyous comodyties might be found' were heard and heeded. It was not long before the English decided to take a direct hand in securing some of the New World's bounty for themselves.

John Cabot, sailing from Bristol, had explored the coast of Labrador, Newfoundland, Nova Scotia, and New England in 1497. Despite this early claim to the continent the English were relative latecomers in settling North America. It was another 85 years before England was willing and able to establish a colony in the New World.

The first settlement efforts, sponsored by Humphrey Gilbert and his half-brother, Walter Raleigh, were motivated by an unusual mix of financial and social concerns. In requesting permission of Queen Elizabeth to exploit the resources of America with a colony, Gilbert pointed to the

> *divers very rich countries, both civil and others, ... where there are to be found great abundance of gold, silver, precious stones, cloth of gold, silks, all manner of spices, grocery wares, and other kinds of merchandise of an inestimable price which both the Spaniard and Portugal, through the length of their journeys, cannot well attain unto.*

It was a polite way of saying that he intended to relieve the Spanish and Portuguese of their New World bounty either by competition or force. Gilbert further proposed to 'inhabit some part of those countries, and settle there such needy people of our country, which now trouble the commonwealth, and through want here at home are forced to commit outrageous offences, whereby they are daily consumed with the gallows'.

Whether swayed by Gilbert's promise to transport criminals from England, or by his commercial proposals, the Queen authorized him 'to inhabit and possess at his choice all remote and heathen lands not in actual possession of any Christian Prince'.

Gilbert's attempts at colonization ended when he and his men were lost at sea on a return from Newfoundland in 1583. But his plan to establish a North American base for England was continued by Walter Raleigh, who quickly renegotiated his half-brother's charter for exploration and settlement. In a document dated 25 March 1584, Raleigh, like Gilbert, was granted permission to colonize any land in North America not already claimed by another European power. Scant mention was made of the indigenous people. In this primarily commercial enterprise, they were classed with the wildlife as just another resource or hazard to be exploited or overcome. Other settlement schemes would view the Indians as a religious challenge.

Raleigh, who never visited North America, sent a voyage of reconnaissance which returned with glowing reports of an island on the outer banks of what is today North Carolina. Called Roanoke after the tribe of Algonquian Indians who lived there, the island had been seen 60 years before by Giovanni Verrazzano when the Italian navigator was exploring the New World for France. He proclaimed it 'a new land never before seen by any man, ancient or modern' consisting of 'many fair fields and plains, as pleasant and delectable to behold as it is possible to imagine ... It is abundant with many animals – stags, deer, hares, adapted and convenient for every pleasure of the hunt'.

Raleigh's scouts, Philip Amadas and Arthur Barlowe, confirmed Verrazzano's sanguine view of Roanoke, though corrected his misperception of its unoccupied status. It may have been that the Indian inhabitants of the island were away or in hiding at the time of Verrazzano's visit, or that he simply did not remember to report them. In either case, it was a significant omission, for the Indians would play a critical role in the successes and failures of the continent's first English colony.

On the basis of Barlowe's positive reports, and with the Queen's enthusiastic support, Raleigh sent five ships with 108 would-be colonists to Roanoke Island in the spring of 1585. The settlers were warmly received by the Indians, whom they described as 'very handsome and goodly people, and in their behaviour as mannerly, and civil, as any of Europe'. Sadly, the Indians' gracious behaviour was not returned. The settlers took the hospitality for granted and, eased by the false security of the natives' largess, failed to make adequate provision for themselves. Instead they focused their energies on a fruitless search for gold.

As the year progressed and the settlers' demands for food increased, the once cordial relations between natives and newcomers deteriorated. By winter, the English were desperate and starving. When they resorted to violence, forcibly taking from the Indians the crops they themselves had not seen fit to plant and the game they could not find, the Indians fought back. By the following spring, full-scale warfare seemed inevitable and the bewildered, beleaguered colonists retreated to England.

Despite this debacle, Raleigh persisted in his hope of gaining a foothold in the New World. The next year he sent a second expedition under the direction of John White, a veteran of the first attempt who Raleigh believed might bring valuable experience to the venture. White had another important attribute. As he had proven on a previous North American expedition with Martin Frobisher, White was an accomplished artist. It was Raleigh's hope that with drawings of Virginia by White and scientific descriptions of the new land by a respected Oxford scholar named Thomas Hariot who had also participated in the first colonizing effort, he could attract investors and volunteer settlers to his colony.

John White stayed at Roanoke for only a month before he was prevailed upon to return to England to seek additional supplies. In that short time he added to the number of paintings he had made on the earlier trip. Together with Jacques Le Moyne de Morgues' drawings of French discoveries in Florida, John White's illustrations constitute our earliest visual record of life in the New World. His elegantly rendered fruits, vegetables, birds, insects, fish, and turtles reveal the eye of an observant naturalist. His drawings of Indian life, soon engraved and published by Theodore de Bry, provided Europeans with the first truly informative and appealing view of North America's indigenous population.

White's evocative vision of Virginia was published in 1590 with an accompanying text by Thomas Hariot and proved an immediate success. Editions soon appeared in Latin, French and German. At least 17 printings of the book appeared in the 30 years between its first publication and 1620, when the Pilgrims left for American shores.

As Walter Raleigh had hoped, White's illustrations and Hariot's text gave a glowing account of prosperity in the New World. There, amid 'temperate and wholesome ayre' and the 'fertile soyle', Hariot found all manner of useful 'commodities' from minerals, 'Beastes', 'Foule' and 'Fishe' to timber, an especially scarce and valuable material in England at the time. Hariot particularly admired the cedar with 'wood good for Seelings, Chests, Boxes, Bedsteeds, Lutes, Virginals, and many things els', and the white pine or 'Rakiok' as the Indians called it, with 'timber being great, tal, straight, soft, light, & yet tough enough I think (besides other uses) to be fit also for masts of ships'. He also described the sassafras, 'a wood of the most pleasant and sweet smell and of rare virtues in medicine for the cure of many diseases'. For further reference on its miraculous healing powers, Hariot pointed readers to Nicholas Monardes' 1574 publication, *Joyfull Newes Out of the Newe Founde Worlde*, in which that author, a 'physician of Seville', declared the sassafras to be the ultimate remedy for everything from headaches, colds and constipation to malaria and syphilis. It is not surprising that such a panacea would become a natural product of tremendous commercial value to the European colonists. For a period in the seventeenth century, sassafras exceeded all other North American products in export value.

Despite these and the many other valuable resources Hariot described, the second Roanoke colony was no more successful than the first. John White's return to Virginia was delayed for three years while his supply ships were drafted

As a member of Sir Walter Raleigh's Roanoke Colony in Virginia between 1585 and 1587, John White made paintings of the Indians and wildlife of the region. His watercolors show (clockwise) the Indian town of Secota (Secoton), a box turtle, Indians fishing with weirs, spears and nets, fish cooking over an open fire and a fish popular for eating known as a grunt.

into naval service to defend Britain against the Spanish Armada. When he finally reached Virginia in 1590, White found that the colony he had hoped to relieve was deserted. No trace of the 91 men, 17 women and 10 children was ever found, save for the word CROATEAN – the name of a local Indian tribe and a nearby island – carved in the bark of a tree. The repeated failures of Raleigh's Roanoke colony may be attributed to bad planning, poor leadership, and difficult communications but beneath these solvable problems lay some basic and profound misunderstandings about both the Indians and the newly claimed land which would affect English settlement in North America for decades to come.

In his report to Raleigh on the settlement prospects at Roanoke, Arthur Barlowe described the native population as living 'after the manner of the Golden Age'. 'The earth bringeth foorth all things in abundance', he rejoiced, 'as in the first creation, without toile or labour.' From the viewpoint of the English visitors, this observation is quite understandable. During his brief reconnaissance of the island, Barlowe and his shipmates had been entertained by the Indians 'with all love and kindness, and with as much bounty, after their manner, as they could possibly devise'. Deer, rabbits, fish, corn (maize), cucumbers, squash, beans, peas, nuts, and other provisions, all in seemingly endless supply, were brought to the English, as if offerings to gods. It was bounty on a scale known only to the highest levels of contemporary English society.

Barlowe and his companions had reached Roanoke at the height of the summer harvest, and, as honored guests, had been given all the Indians could offer. The unimaginable scale of the Indians' generosity caused Barlowe to assume that the food had emerged 'without toile or labour' even to the Indians. This misunderstanding, reinforced by other Eden-like descriptions of the New World, raised colonial expectations that could never be fulfilled.

Only with heavy investment and continuous re-supply from home, was a permanent English settlement finally established in Jamestown, Virginia, in the spring of 1607. This colony consisted of a cluster of fortified shelters built on the bank of a large, navigable river which one colonist enthusiastically described as teeming with 'sturgeons and other sweet fish as no man's fortune has ever possessed the like'. The river, named James by the colonists in honor of their king, emptied into 'a very goodly Bay', which the Indians called Chesapeake.

Chesapeake Bay, the largest and richest estuary in North America, was indeed an ideal place to establish a colony. Its natural bounty, well known to the Indians, astonished the English and gave them much hope. In his *Generall Historie of Virginia, New England & The Summer Isles*, published in 1624, Captain John Smith, a member and eventual governor of the colony, extolled the Jamestown area as:

a country that may have the prerogative over the most pleasant places knowne, for large and pleasant navigable Rivers heaven & earth never agreed better to frame a place for man's habitation; were it fully manured and inhabited by industrious people. Here are mountaines, hils, plaines, valleyes, rivers, and brookes, all running most pleasantly into a faire Bay, compassed but for the mouth, with fruitfull and delightsome land. ... In sommer no place affordeth more plentie of Sturgeon, nor in winter more abundance of foule.

Smith was an enthusiastic naturalist who based most of his descriptions on first-hand experience. From his own account he was also an accomplished fisherman, once catching 68 sturgeon with a single draw of his net. Considering that some species of this fish can grow up to 14 feet in length, it is not surprising that the colonists sometimes had 'more of it than could be devoured by dog and man'. Smith assured his patrons, a group of merchant investors based in London and Plymouth, that there was financial gain to be had from this bounty. 'Roes of the said sturgeon will make caviar', he wrote, 'and caviar well conditioned is worth £40 per 100 pound weight.'

The fresh waters of the James, the rich brackish estuary, and the salty Chesapeake Bay supported many other kinds of fish as well. There were enough in spring and summer, Smith noted, 'that with hookes those that would take paines had sufficient'. Reflecting a perspective more mercantile than scientific, Smith grouped all water-borne food together without biological distinction. 'Of fish', he wrote, 'we were best acquainted with Sturgeon, Grampus, Porpus, Seales, Stingraies, whose tailes are very dangerous.' His list went on to include:

Bretts, Mullets, white Salmonds, Trowts, Soles, Plaice, Herrings, Conyfish, Rockfish, Eeles, Lampreys, Catfish, Shades, Pearch of three sorts, Crabs, Shrimps, Crevises, Oysters, Cocles, and Muscles. But the most strange fish is a small one, so like the picture of St George his Dragon, as possible can be, except his legs and wings, and the Toadefish, which will swell till it be like to burst, when it commeth into the ayre.

The ideal conditions for marine life, which attracted so many different fish to Chesapeake Bay, began to emerge more than 15 000 years ago. As the climate warmed and the ice sheets around the globe gave up their hold on the land, the ocean absorbed the melt water and began to rise. From 15 000 years ago until 5000 years ago, the sea rose more than 325 vertical feet. For every foot it rose, it advanced 1700 feet laterally across the exposed North American continental shelf. Slowly at first, then more rapidly, the sea invaded low-lying coastal areas at an average rate of 50 feet a year.

Along the fast-shrinking shore of Virginia, the ocean followed the incised valley created by the Susquehanna River farther and farther inland until, 10 000 years ago, its salty waters reached the mouth of today's Chesapeake Bay. The climate continued to warm and the ocean continued to rise, penetrating the basin of the Susquehanna and its tributaries until it reached the present coastline around the Bay. Then, with most of the ice sheets melted, the rate of the sea level's rise slowed and the shoaling by sedimentation came nearly into balance with the rise of the sea.

Only a few land plants could survive the invasion of the salty water, even in its diluted, brackish form. One such plant was cord grass, which thrives on the harsh conditions doled out by the sea and its tides. A large, coarse, well-rooted plant with leaves up to 5 feet high and an inch wide, cord grass anchors the coastal marshlands and acts as a giant filter, absorbing and dissipating the energy of each tide. As the sea water moves among the grass stalks, it slows and drops its rich load of sediments. The sediments, in turn, build the level of the marsh floor which helps the marsh keep pace with the still-rising level of the sea. The process concentrates tremendous amounts of organic material in the marsh, making it a sort of biological reservoir and nursery. The salt marsh serves as the base of an immense, interconnected web of life, that at one time or another affects up to 70 per cent of the fishes along the Atlantic coast. It also supports North America's richest concentration of shellfish, a staple of the human population in John Smith's time and today.

'Oysters there be in whole banks and beds', observed one of Smith's companions. 'I have seen some thirteen inches in length.' Oysters are still one of the Bay's greatest resources. Blue crabs too inhabit the Bay, tens of thousands of them gathering in summer months to mate. This is a two or three day process during which the female crab sheds her exoskeleton under the protective embrace of a male. The fertilized female will not cast her eggs until the following spring, by which time she is once again ready to breed. The Indians, who understood these cycles, collected the crabs at their most plentiful – and vulnerable – time, eating the soft-shelled females whole. Soft-shelled crabs, fried, boiled or steamed, are still a popular regional speciality.

To reap the Chesapeake's harvest, the Indians employed a wide-range of fishing techniques. They collected the breeding shellfish with baited lines and hand nets. For small fish and schools of migrants, they built weirs across the rivers. For larger fish, they used spears or arrows. At night they fished from canoes with torches, the light attracting various species within range of their spears and nets.

The Jamestown colonists watched and emulated the Indians, sometimes with great success. But theirs was a slow learning process, for the species were unfamiliar to them. On one fishing trip, Captain John Smith was seriously wounded by the slashing barb of a stingray. As recounted by one of his party, the accident occurred when the captain 'spyed many fishes lurking in the reeds', and began spearing them with his sword.

> [He] set us all a fishing in that manner: thus we tooke more in one houre than we could eate in a day. But it chansed our Captaine taking a fish from his sword (not knowing her condition) being much of the fashion of a Thornback, but a long tayle like a ryding rodde, whereon the middest is a most poysoned sting, of two or three inches long, bearded like a saw on each side, which she strucke into the wrest of his arme neere an inch and a halfe: no bloud nor wound was seene, but a little blew spot, but the tormet was instantly so extreame, that in foure houres had so swolen his hand, arme and shoulder, we all with much sorrow concluded his funerall, and prepared his grave in an Island by, as himselfe directed: yet it pleased God by a

precious oyle Doctor Russell at the first applyed to it when he sounded it with probe (ere night) his tormenting paine was so well asswaged that he eate of the fish to his supper, which gave no lesse joy and content to us then ease to himselfe.

John Smith's painful encounter with the stingray was but a hint of more serious problems to come. Deceived by the abundance of seafood and wild game during the spring and summer months, and preoccupied with internal bickering, the Jamestown colonists failed to make adequate provision for the leaner winter season. Few of the 104 men who made up the colony knew anything about farming. They relied instead on the Indians to provide them with food, just as Roanoke's colonists had done.

The Indians, for their part, knew how to vary their habits to cope with the seasonal fluctuations of game. Smith noted:

In March and Aprill they live much upon their fishing wires and feed on fish, Turkies, and Squirrels. In May and June they plant their fields, and live most of Acornes, Walnuts, and fish. But to amend their dyet, some disperse themselves in small companies, and live upon fish, beasts, crabs, oysters, land Tortoises, strawberries, mulberries, and such like. In June, July, and August, they feed upon the rootes of Tocknough berries, fish, and greene wheat. It is strange to see how their bodies alter with their dyet, even as the deere & wilde beasts they seeme fat and leane, strong and weake. Powhatan their great King, and some others that are provident, rost their fish and flesh upon hurdles as before is expressed, and keepe it till scarce times.

Afterward, when he wrote his account of life in Jamestown, Smith understood what 'scarce times' could be like, but during that first summer in Virginia the colonists still believed the New World's bounty was endless. The corn and other crops they had not grown themselves they planned to buy from the Indians for 'trifles'. When the trifle market was flooded or the Indians declined to trade, the colonists 'let fly [their] muskets' and simply took what they needed by force.

By late September, Virginia's stifling summer heat gives way to cooler weather. The hardwood forests beyond the coast sparkle with orange and gold. White-tailed deer, fattened by the summer's harvest, begin to herd for mating. The bucks are sporting new antlers, still covered with a thin membrane of velvet. By October their horns are hardened and free of skin, ready to aid in the age-old sparring rituals that help to determine dominance in the herds.

In John Smith's time, the eastern forests also resounded with the clash of larger antlers. The eastern elk, a relic of the ice age, ranged from the Pacific to the Atlantic coast until habitat destruction and human pressures forced it to extinction in the nineteenth century. Less common but also present in the eastern forests was the wood bison, relative of the far more numerous buffalo of the Great Plains. The last bison recorded east of the Appalachians was killed in Buffalo Cross Roads, Pennsylvania, in 1801.

In his inventory of wildlife, Smith described several other mammals of special

interest to the colonists. One was the racoon, a dextrous omnivore that the Indians called 'Aroughcun'. Smith described it as 'much like a badger [in appearance], but useth to live on trees as squirrels doe'. Later explorers would find this adaptable species living in temperate forests throughout the continent. Some declared the racoon's meat 'as good as lamb'. Another mammal of note was the flying squirrel, so named by the English 'because spreading their leggs from whence to either shoulder runs a Flappe or Fynne much like a Batt's wing, and so stretching the largenesse of their skyns . . . they have beene seene to make a pretty flight from one tree to another sometimes 30 or 40 yardes'. A third and even more novel discovery was the opossum, North America's only marsupial. 'An Opassom hath a head like a Swine, and a taile like a Rat, and is of the bignesse of a Cat,' wrote Smith. 'Under her belly shee hath a bagge, wherein she lodgeth, carrieth, and suckleth her young.'

The Jamestown colonists harvested all of these, and whatever other wild game they could, but as they had now alienated even the most friendly Indians, it was dangerous for them to venture far from the safety of their fort. As the season progressed, the temperatures continued to drop and the bright autumn foliage scattered in the wind, the colonists began to recognize how ill prepared they were to face the winter. Then, like manna from heaven, migrating waterfowl began to alight on the Bay and gather in the Chesapeake's protected inlets. They came by the thousands to escape the colder weather farther north, and to feed on the roots and tubers of the cord grass and other marsh plants. John Smith chronicled the windfall, making an inventory of the waterfowl and other birds that had miraculously appeared. 'In winter', he wrote, 'there are great plentie of Swans, Cranes, gray and white with blacke wings, Herons, Geese, Brants, Ducke, Wigeon, Dotterell, Oxeies, Parrats, and Pigeons. Of all those sorts great abundance, and some other strange kinds, to us unknowne by name.'

The birds' arrival, though a welcome reprieve from early winter shortages, could not compensate indefinitely for the colony's failure to grow, harvest, and store adequate provisions. As winter tightened its grip on the Bay and its tributaries, the settlers found themselves increasingly desperate for food. One of the colonists wrote:

The river which was wont before this time of the year to be plentiful had not now a fish to be seen in it, and albeit we laboured and hauled our net twenty times day and night yet we took not so much as would content half the fishermen. . . . So excessive are the frosts that one night the river froze over, almost from bank to bank. There died from the frost some fish in the river which when taken were very good.

Despite brief periods of plenty, the Jamestown colony's first year was calamitous. The seasonal swings of temperature – far more extreme than in Europe – and the region's unfamiliar cycles of life confused and all but defeated the settlers. Buffeted by disease, chronic food shortages and Indian hostility, Jamestown's population was decimated: from 104 on their arrival in June 1607 to 38 by January of the following year. 'Our men were destroyed with cruell diseases as

With still-growing antlers sheathed in a coat of velvet, a white-tailed deer feeds on a summer field's rich vegetation in preparation for the autumn rut. Buckskins became an early staple in trade between Indians and whites. The relatively stable value of the skins provided colonial merchants with a consistent unit of exchange, the name of which continues in today's slang for the US dollar – 'buck'.

LEFT *An intelligent and highly adaptable species, the racoon has learned to co-exist successfully with humans despite its popularity as a food, fur and game animal. Its English name derives from the Algonquian 'Aroughcun', and means literally 'he who scratches with his hands'.*

RIGHT *Another New World creature which caused much interest abroad was the opossum, one of the most primitive and ancient of living mammals and North America's only marsupial. It was accurately described in 1528 as an 'animal with a pocket on its belly in which it carries its young until they know how to seek food'. Later observers noted its ability to feign death or 'play possum' when threatened.*

OVERLEAF *Snow geese by the thousands gather each winter on Chesapeake Bay to feed on cord grass and glean from mechanically-harvested cornfields nearby. In summer they breed on the shores of Hudson's Bay and also in the water-laced tundra of the Arctic.*

Swellings, Fluxes, Burning Fevers, and warres', wrote one of the survivors, 'but for the most part they died of meere famine.'

Fortunately for the colonists, their isolation was only temporary. At six- to twelve-month intervals, ships from home resupplied the settlement and replenished the population, bringing women to Jamestown for the first time in 1608. Despite such help, the colonists' inability to adapt to the land brought repeated failure. Year after year, the seasonal changes caught them ill prepared. During the winter of 1609–10, the so-called 'starving time', the colony's population dropped from 500 to 60. There were even incidents of cannibalism.

Jamestown seemed doomed to follow Roanoke colony into oblivion. Then, in 1613, John Rolfe – one of the few surviving original settlers and husband to the Indian princess Pocohantas – began cultivating a plant he had seen grown and used ceremonially by native Americans. The local Indians called it *uppowoc*. In the Spanish West Indies, where Rolfe had obtained his seeds, it was known as tobacco.

Cured leaves from this New World novelty had been seen and smoked in Spain as early as 1558, but it was Sir Walter Raleigh, with samples from Roanoke, who popularized tobacco among the aristocracy of England. Rolfe's first shipments of the plant to London brought lucrative returns. Soon Jamestown's main street was plowed to fill the demand for tobacco, and the rush for profit was on. The few colonists engaged in agriculture were hard pressed to feed the colony and, at the same time, satisfy Europe's new craving for tobacco. Then, in 1619, another change came to Jamestown. 'About the last of August', recorded John Rolfe, 'there came to Virginia a Dutchman of Warre that sold us twenty Negers.' Thus, a year before the Pilgrims landed at Plymouth Rock, the seeds for slavery, America's plantation system, and the continent's first commercial monoculture, were sown together in Jamestown.

As worldwide demand for tobacco grew, more and more English colonists came to Virginia to cultivate the magic weed. The Indians watched with mystified amusement a people who could not adequately feed themselves struggling to grow a plant they could not eat. To native Americans, tobacco was a sacred herb smoked only at times of great importance, to seal agreements, or to carry their prayers to the spirit world. To the colonists, the plant was a prayer fulfilled: a cash crop to redeem their hopes of New World fortune.

The clash of cultures, begun at first contact, was moving on apace. Despite their superior numbers, the coastal Indians rapidly lost ground. Many were killed by the English in the increasingly violent conflicts over food and land. Many more died from European diseases – typhoid, smallpox, tuberculosis and others – to which they had no immunity. Those who survived eventually left their coastal homeland and their age-old ways for new lives in the country's vast interior.

For a while, the tribes living further inland were unaffected by European settlements. The Cherokee, for example, who inhabited the Great Smoky Mountains of the southern Appalachian range, were buffered from the first English settlers by the coastal Algonquians and some 200 miles of intervening forest.

The smallest and most widely distributed of North America's bears, the black bear held a special place in the mythology of many Indian tribes. European settlers compared the flavor of its meat to pork and valued its grease as a cure for baldness and 'rheumatic complaints'.

America's Indian tribes performed rituals in which they could demonstrate their respect for nature. In 1564–5 Jacques Le Moyne de Morgues described and drew a ceremony (left) in which the stuffed skin of a deer was decorated with garlands and offered to the gods to ensure future prosperity. In the hunting scene (above), Le Moyne shows Indian hunters disguised with deer skins stalking their wild quarry.

The Smokies anchor the southern end of the Appalachians, a 200-million-year-old mountain chain which runs parallel to the Atlantic coast. They rise from the flat, southern coastal plain and rolling foothills – the Piedmont – to elevations of over 6000 feet and include some of the highest peaks in eastern North America.

The Cherokee have an explanation for the Smokies. They say that in the beginning, all living things dwelt in the sky. There was no earth at that time, only a vast body of water that was both fresh and salty. As the sky became overcrowded, the people and animals there sent a water beetle into the ocean to seek land. The beetle swam to the bottom and brought up some mud which immediately began to grow. Eventually it became what we now call the earth. While the land was still soft and pliable, a great buzzard, grandfather of all buzzards, was sent down from heaven to dry the soft earth with the beating of his wings. As he flew over Cherokee country, the bird became tired, sinking so close to the surface that his wings struck the soft earth and formed ridges, mountains and valleys.

Like other woodland tribes, the Cherokee mixed a wide array of agricultural activities with the seasonal harvesting of wild game and other native foods. Their location was ideal for such a harvest, because the southern Appalachians contain the greatest botanical diversity in North America. The Great Smokies occupy only about 800 square miles, but in that small area grow more species of trees than in all of Europe. Europe has 85 species of native trees, while the Great Smokies have 131. The Smokies' inhabitants include 200 different kinds of birds – almost half the total for all of Britain – 50 species of fur-bearing animals, and 80 species of fish. There are also 2000 species of fungi, 1300 flowering plants, 350 mosses and liverworts, 230 lichens, and more species of insect than anyone has managed to count.

The explanation for the Smokies' great diversity of life, like so much of the natural history of North America, can be found in the climatic changes of the ice age. While most of the northern half of the Appalachian ridge was covered with ice and snow during the four successive ice-sheet invasions, the southern end of that great chain was spared. This meant that the plants already living in the Smokies, augmented by many northern refugees, could go on evolving with relatively little interruption. Unlike the lowlands, the range of elevation of the mountains made it possible for species to adjust their living conditions by moving higher and lower as the climate warmed and cooled.

Ecologists have estimated that 6.5 feet in elevation is the rough climatic and ecological equivalent of 1 mile in latitude. Thus, the Smokies, with 6000 feet of elevation, contain almost as many varieties of habitat as all of the land from Atlanta, Georgia, to Montreal. Like the plants, many of the animals in the Smokies have strong biological preferences for specific altitudes and habitats. A few move seasonally between these habitats instead of migrating north or south each spring and fall. The slate-colored junco is a sparrow-sized bird which winters in the foothills of the Smokies and flies some 1000 miles north each spring to nest in the evergreen forests of New England and Canada. The Carolina

OVERLEAF The Great Smoky Mountains at the southern end of the Appalachians created a formidable barrier to the western migration of early colonists. 'It was a pleasing tho' dreadful sight to see the Mountains and Hills as if piled one upon another', wrote a traveler in 1671. Today's Appalachians are actually the eroded remnants of much larger mountains that emerged some 200 million years ago.

41

junco, a barely distinguishable subspecies, migrates to a comparable breeding ground simply by moving higher into the mountains. The time saved by the Carolina junco in its altitudinal migration permits it to breed more frequently than its far-flying cousin. While the northern race can usually only manage one brood of young before beginning its long flight south, the Carolina junco will often parent three broods per summer.

The Cherokee understood the principle of altitudinal migration, focusing their winter activities in the warmer lowland valleys and then moving up into the mountains with the coming of spring. To the Cherokee, as to native groups throughout the continent, wild plants were an essential part of a balanced culinary and medicinal diet. The Cherokee used more than 300 different species of plant, many of which were as important spiritually as nutritionally.

In the Cherokee world all things were – and continued to be – imbued with spiritual properties deserving respect. Mammals were especially powerful because their spirits were the keepers of disease. They could be killed for food only if their spirits had agreed to the sacrifice in advance and voluntarily gave themselves to the hunter. If a deer, squirrel, opossum or any other mammal was killed without its permission, or if it believed that a human hunter had behaved in a wanton, careless, or disrespectful manner, the mammal could inflict punishment on that person by unleashing the specific disease it had under its control. To counter the illness the Cherokee would turn to the plant world, calling on the spirits of appropriate species to remedy their plight. Many of the plants they used still bear English translations of the common names the Cherokee gave them: deer ear, deer skin, deer eye, deer tongue, etc.

While some members of the tribe combed the mountains for wild plants and animals, others, usually the women, cared for extensive garden plots that they had cleared near their villages in the valley bottoms. With the help of tools fashioned from wood, stone and animal bone, they cultivated and mounded the soil, planting together corn, beans and squash – 'the three sisters' of the Indian world. When the plants emerged, the corn grew straight and tall, providing a support pole for the climbing beans. The squash plant trailed down the mounds, its large leaves shading the soil, slowing evaporation, and discouraging weed growth. The nitrogen-fixing roots of the leguminous beans helped to restore nutrients to the soil, thereby strengthening the other crops and prolonging the fertility of the garden plots.

Even more important to the Cherokee and the many other tribes who cultivated 'the three sisters' was that eaten together, with one or two other food supplements, they provided a perfectly balanced diet. To this was added the wild game of the region. Judging from archeological sites and continuing Cherokee practice, the most popular species were deer, elk (wapiti), bear, fox, wolf, squirrel, racoon, opossum, beaver, otter, fish of various kinds, ruffed grouse and turkey.

Cherokee villages generally consisted of log dwellings roofed with bark, clustered near a central town house or *rotunda* in which important tribal ceremonies took place. There elaborate dances were performed, recreating the

RIGHT One bird species which substitutes altitudinal migration for long-distance flights each spring and autumn is the junco. Different races of the bird can be found throughout the continent.

OVERLEAF More than 1400 species of trees and flowering plants create in the Smoky Mountains the greatest botanical diversity in North America. Until they were forcibly removed from the region in the nineteenth century, the Cherokee Indians were an integral part of this environment, augmenting the wild foods they gathered there with crops of their own. To the Cherokee, the animals, plants, stream water, and even the stones were imbued with spirits. 'When we speak of the land', explained a Cherokee leader, 'we are speaking of something truly sacred.'

feats of hunting or wartime prowess. In the racoon and beaver dances, the Cherokee re-enacted the killing and skinning of the animals in ritualized hunts. In the buffalo dance, men and women impersonated the bulls and cows of their woodland quarry with masks, robes and realistic movements. In the bear dance, they honored the Eighth Clan of the Cherokee, for in their mythology the bear had once been human.

In 1540, Hernando de Soto became the first European to invade the Cherokee's domain when he and 600 conquistadores traveled north from Florida in search of gold. Despite the remarkable appearance De Soto's armored foot soldiers and cavalry must have made, their impact appears to have been minimal, for no mention of their visit was recorded in the oral history of the tribe.

Unlike the Spanish, the first English colonists rarely ventured far from their coastal forts. Thomas Hariot's record of Roanoke only mentions the country's unexplored interior and hints at the extended settlements of the Cherokee:

> *Sometimes we made journeys further into the mainland. There we found the soil richer, the trees taller, the ground firmer, and the topsoil deeper. We saw there more and larger fields and finer grass, as good as any in England. In some places the ground was high, rocky, and hilly, fruits grew plentifully, beasts lived in greater abundance, the country was more thickly populated, the towns and houses larger, and the communities better ruled.*

In the early days of contact, the Cherokee managed to keep the best that the Europeans had to offer without losing their own identity or sense of worth. Their trade with Europeans grew quickly. Between 1708 and 1735, the number of furs the Cherokees provided for their English trading partners jumped from 50 000 to 1 000 000 annually. Yet even as the tribe enjoyed the benefits of its new prosperity, the price of Old World contact was growing in unexpected ways. The Cherokee found that the spirits of the plant world could not protect them from European diseases. Nor could the rugged terrain of their homeland defeat the acquisitive nature of the expanding white population. In the last decade of the eighteenth century, the Cherokee chief Dragging Canoe expressed his concern over the state of English-Cherokee relations:

> *We had hoped that the white men would not be willing to travel beyond the mountains. . . . Finally the whole country which the Cherokee and their fathers have so long occupied, will be demanded, and the remnant of Ani-Yun Wiya, the Real People, once so great and formidable, will be compelled to seek refuge in some distant wilderness.*

Dragging Canoe's warning was sadly prophetic. Despite their conversion to Christianity, development of an alphabet, and adoption of a constitution based on that of the United States, most of the Cherokee were eventually driven from their homeland to reservations west of the Mississippi. The tribe's forced relocation in the late 1830s, an experience known as the Trail of Tears, is one of the saddest stories in the long history of white-Indian relations. In departing from the southern Appalachians, the Cherokee were leaving not just the richest woodlands of North America but also a part of themselves, for, as one Cherokee leader explained:

> We Cherokee cannot separate our place on Earth from our lives in it, nor from our vision and meaning as people. From childhood we are taught that the animals and even the trees and plants that we share a place with are our brothers and sisters. So when we speak of land we are not speaking of property, territory, or even the piece of ground upon which our houses sit and our crops are grown. We are speaking of something truly sacred.

The Cherokee called the land 'Eloheh'. To them the same word means history, culture and religion.

Other tribes also held the view that the land did not belong to them, they belonged to the land. It was a concept so alien to Europeans that they failed to recognize its existence let alone comprehend its significance. Most of the new arrivals viewed the land as something to be possessed, controlled and transformed. They saw the Indians' semi-nomadic lifestyle as shiftless, and their lack of defined ownership as a sign of primitive barbarism. Only with active management, they believed, could nature be made truly productive. So they set about reshaping the land in Europe's image: trees were felled, fences built, and the land cultivated to Old World specifications.

While commercial interests drove many of the early colonies, religion soon added to the complex mix of motivations for New World settlement. The Pilgrims, who moved from England to New England by way of Holland to escape religious persecution, were as quick as any settlers to impose their own views on the new land and its people. They saw Indians as savages, their religion as devil worship, and their relationship with the land as ungodly. The Pilgrims worshipped a god who taught that man was superior to nature, not part of it.

The idyllic notion of North America as paradise, which had so misguided the colonists at Roanoke and Jamestown, was replaced by a harsher if more realistic perspective in New England. 'I will not tell you that you may smell the corn fields before you see the land', wrote a Massachusetts colonist in 1628.

> Neither must men think that corn doth grow naturally, (or on trees), nor will the deer come when they are called, or stand still and look on a man until he shot him, not knowing a man from a beast; nor the fish leap into the kettle, nor on the dry land, neither are they so plentiful, that you may dip them up in baskets, nor take cod in nets to make a voyage, which is no truer than that the fowls will present themselves to you with spits through them.

To many New England colonists, the path to prosperity on earth and in heaven was the same. It involved transforming the 'remote rocky, barren, bushy, wild-woody wilderness' of North America into a 'second England'. With hard work and prayer, the Puritans believed they could fulfill God's biblical command to subdue the earth. In so doing, they would also recreate a comforting, understandable piece of home in a hostile and alien land.

Theirs was a pattern of settlement that would eventually prevail in much of North America. Varied natural habitats, which had been maintained and successfully utilized by generations of Indians, were replaced by the colonists' tidier, if less productive, fields. Native diversity gave way to imported mono-cultures. Wild game was displaced by domestic livestock. Communal use and collective effort were replaced by private enterprise.

As transplanted Europeans proclaimed their progress in 'reducing the land to fruitful subjection', and turning 'one of the most Hideous, boundless and unknown Wildernesses in the world ... to a well-ordered Commonwealth', the continent's first inhabitants saw the changes from a very different perspective. A Narragansett chief named Miantonomo summarized the impact of early New England colonists on the land from a native point of view when he spoke to a tribal gathering in 1642:

> *You know our fathers had plenty of deer and skins. Our plains were full of deer, as also our woods, and of turkies, and our coves full of fish and fowl. But these English having gotten our land, they with scythes cut down the grass, and with axes fell the trees; their cows and horses eat the grass, and their hogs spoil our clam banks, and we shall all be starved.*

CONFRONTING THE WILDERNESS

CANADA · AND · THE · GREAT · NORTH · WOODS

You can follow your nose to the Newfoundland coast in springtime. If the fog is in, and it usually is, the smells of nesting seabirds help mark the junction of land and sea. Cormorants, puffins, murres, gulls and other marine birds flock in countless thousands to the fractured shoreline each May to breed. Their squawks, chirps, creaks, and roars are audible for almost as far as the pungent odor of their nests.

Jacques Cartier and the 120 sailors who traveled with him from France must have been cheered by the great colonies' sounds and smells as they dodged the late spring icebergs of the North Atlantic. The year was 1534 and Cartier, a 43-year-old Breton navigator on orders from the French King Francis I, was setting out on the first of three exploratory trips to the new-found land of North America. On earlier fishing trips to the area, Cartier had learned the value of Canada's seabirds, not just as beacons to land, but also as valuable sources of food. He wasted no time directing his ships to a nesting island known for its ready supply of meat and eggs. On one sixteenth-century map, it was called Puanto (stinking), but Cartier gave it a more pleasant name: the Island of Birds. The island, he wrote,

> was encompassed by a cordon of loose ice, split up into cakes. In spite of this belt (of ice) our two long-boats were sent off to the island to procure some of the birds, whose numbers are so great as to be incredible, unless one has seen them; for although the island is about a league in circumference, it is so exceeding full of birds that one would think they had been stowed there. In the air and round about are an hundred times as many more as on the island itself. Some of these birds are as large as geese, being black and white with a beak like a crow's. . . . There were other white ones larger still that keep apart from the rest in a portion of the island, and are very ugly to attack; for they bite like dogs.

The first birds Cartier described were probably guillemots or murres, the second he mentioned were the much larger gannets. The French sailors considered these and any other seabirds they could catch fair game for food; but Cartier and his men were most eager to harvest the largest of the island's species, a lumbering, penguin-like bird called the great auk. 'Some of these birds', wrote Cartier, 'are as large as geese, being black and white with a beak like a crow's. They are always in the water, not being able to fly in the air, inasmuch as they have only small wings about the size of half one's hand. ... And these birds are so fat that it is marvellous. ... Our two long-boats were laden with them, as with stones, in less than half an hour.'

The great auk, North America's only flightless bird, would be sought out by European seamen for the next 300 years, for its meat was both plentiful and good. It was found in such numbers along the Newfoundland coast that it was even used as a navigational aid.

During his visits to the Island of Birds, Cartier observed a bear 'as big as a calf and as white as a swan' swimming 14 leagues 'from the mainland in order to feed on these birds'. It was a polar bear, an immensely powerful creature found in Arctic climates around the globe. The Eskimo, who knew its wide-ranging habits, called it *pihoqahiaq*, the ever-wandering one. Indeed, single bears have been found to travel up to 700 miles per year, feeding on ringed seals in the winter, and on nesting birds, mice, and even grass during the summer months. The one Cartier spotted swimming to the island and later gorging on auks was itself consumed by the hungry French sailors. 'His flesh was as good to eat as that of a two-year-old heifer', noted Cartier with pleasure.

Except for occasional raids by polar bears and small parties of Eskimo hunters, the insular nesting habits of the great auks had always protected the birds from predators during their vulnerable times of breeding. With the arrival of European fishing boats in the sixteenth century, however, the birds began to suffer a decline that accelerated as contact increased. French, English and Portuguese ships would sometimes rely completely on Newfoundland's great auk colonies to provision their trans-Atlantic trips with meat, eggs and oil. In the eighteenth century, the birds were also killed for feathers to stuff cushions and trim hats in Paris and London. By the middle of the nineteenth century, the once abundant seabird had been clubbed to extinction.

Aside from the deep bays, 'marvellous' auks, and good fishing, Cartier could find little to recommend Newfoundland's rugged coast. He entered and explored the Gulf of St Lawrence in the hope of finding a passage to the Orient. Instead he found endless miles of bleak and forbidding shoreline. 'Were the soil as good as the harbors, it would be fine', he remarked, but it was composed of 'stones and frightful rocks and uneven places ... on this entire northern coast I saw not one cartload of earth, though I landed in many places. Except for [a few areas] there is nothing but moss and stunted shrubs. To conclude, I am inclined to regard this land as the one God gave to Cain'.

Cartier did see wildlife – walruses, foxes, more bears, and seals – but found little to excite his interest. Then, one warm July evening as his ships lay at anchor

OVERLEAF A colony of nesting gannets, Cape Mary's Island, Newfoundland. When Jacques Cartier saw such colonies in 1534 he declared 'all the ships of France might load a cargo of them without once perceiving that any had been removed'.

The great auks (below) were once so abundant on the North Atlantic coast that European fishing fleets could depend on them to supply enough fresh meat and eggs to provision their return. North America's only flightless bird, it was hunted to extinction by the middle of the nineteenth century. The Labrador duck (right) suffered a similar fate. John James Audubon painted both for publication in The Birds of America during a trip to Labrador in 1833.

off the Gaspé Peninsula, he spied a flotilla of birch-bark canoes approaching his ships. Aboard were Micmac warriors 'making divers signs of joy' and holding up furs as a sign they wanted to trade. The next day, Cartier 'sent two men ashore to deal with them, bringing knives and other cutlery and a red cap to give their chief'.

Although Breton fishermen had been trading trinkets for furs with local tribes for some time, Cartier's transactions with the Micmacs and later the Hurons may be said to mark the official start of the French fur trade. It was a commercial enterprise that would help to shape the economy and ecology of Canada for centuries to come.

The barren coastal areas noted by Canada's early explorers gave no hint of the rich forest lands that dominate the country's inland regions. There, beneath towering canopies of pine, spruce and maple, in a land shaped by the power of water and ice, European traders would find natural bounty beyond all expectation. Cartier did not see the inland forests on his first trip: he found no easy route to the interior and was afraid to leave the safety of his ships. But he bought enough furs and food products from the Micmacs to know that there was something more interesting beyond the coast than auks and rocky ballast.

In his report to the King of France, Cartier told of a great river leading west from the gulf he had discovered. Although he had not seen the river himself, the Indians had assured him – and he assured his patrons – of its existence. Spurred by this news and further reports of silver and gold, the King and one of his wealthy ministers sent Cartier back the next year to find and explore this great western waterway, wherever it led. All hoped that it might prove to be the elusive Northwest Passage to India.

With the help of two Huron guides who had accompanied him to France after the first trip, Cartier and his men had no difficulty finding and sailing up the St Lawrence River as far as the guides' home village, Stadacona, the site of present-day Quebec City. From there the expedition journeyed up river to the fortified Huron town of Hochelaga, where the Europeans were met and showered with gifts by a joyful crowd of over 1000 people. All night long, as the crew waited cautiously aboard their ships, the Hurons 'remained on the river bank, keeping fires burning, dancing, and calling out "guyase", which is their term for a joyful welcome'. On the following day, with others of his party and 20 sailors armed with pikes, Cartier marched through an impressive oak grove and past fields of ripening corn and other grain to the circular wooden citadel which protected a village of some 50 bark dwellings. There the Frenchmen were greeted by local officials with whom they exchanged gifts.

In his *Brief Recit* (1545) recounting the details of his trip, Cartier described the Hurons and their customs. He noted that their most precious possessions were white wampum beads, called 'esnoguy', made from the shells of river clams. He was told that the clams were cultivated by submerging in the river the lacerated bodies of dead criminals or enemies of the tribe. Within a few days, the desired clams, attracted to the corpses, worked their way into deep cuts in the thighs and buttocks of the human bait. Later they were extracted

and their shells were shaped into beads for use as currency and decoration.

Cartier dispensed less gruesome presents – pewter rings and small religious figures made of tin. He then entertained his hosts with an impromptu concert of trumpets and other instruments, which evinced 'a marvellous joy' among the natives. Next, he climbed the hill overlooking Hochelaga to get his bearings and to admire the spectacular scenery.

The land, he declared, was 'the finest and most excellent one could find anywhere, being everywhere full of oaks as beautiful as in any forest in France, underneath which the ground lay covered with acorns'. Beside the oaks, then reddening in the October frosts, were maples, ablaze with red, yellow and orange leaves; aspens, their shimmering foliage a brilliant gold; towering yellow birch; and mountain ashes, laden with scarlet berries. The brilliance of this autumnal display, set off by the dark green needles of spruce, pine and fir, was unlike anything Cartier had seen at home. A unique mix of climatic and soil conditions make the seasonal pigment changes in the leaves of some northern American trees more intense than any others in the world.

Nor were the trees the only plants vying for Cartier's attention. At his feet were tufts of golden interrupted fern, the maroon leaves and bright red fruit of bunchberry, and evergreen partridgeberry trailing over the forest floor. In open spaces, chest-high goldenrod and violet asters nodded in the breeze. Cartier must have been dazzled by the spectacle of foliage and flower, but in the record he focused on topography. 'We had a view of the land for more than thirty leagues round about', he noted. To the southeast, well beyond the shining ribbon of the St Lawrence, he could see the northern slopes of the Adirondacks and the Green Mountains of New England. To the northeast lay the Gulf of St Lawrence and the Laurentian Hills running to the east and west beside the river. 'Between these ranges', wrote Cartier, 'lies the finest land it is possible to see, being arable, level and flat.' On descending the mountain, he remarked on the wonderful vantage it afforded. So striking a feature deserved a special name, and so he called it Mont Royal. The mountain and the French post that was later established at Hochelaga have been called Montreal ever since.

If he did not know it before, Cartier realized after his climb that he had reached the farthest point on the river his ships could take him. His hopes of journeying on to the Orient were blocked by a forbidding set of rapids, visible from the summit of Mont Royal. Robert Cavalier, Sieur de La Salle, who shared Cartier's dream of an inland water route to Asia, would later name the rapids 'Sault La Chine' (the Chinese rapids). A compressed version of the name, Lachine, is still in use today.

While disappointed, Cartier was not discouraged. Perhaps there were other sources of wealth to be discovered in the area. Besides, with winter fast approaching and his own provisions running low, Cartier was reluctant to take on the North Atlantic. He and his men decided to wait for spring in what Europeans were beginning to call New France. The Hurons called the place *Canata*, their word for lodge. The French would soften the 't' to 'd' and apply the term to all that they saw.

Cartier's experiences during the winter of 1535–6 gave him a first-hand understanding of the new land. Most unexpected was the harshness of the climate. Within a month of their arrival, the long Canadian winter began and Cartier noted its severity with surprise. 'All of our beverages froze in their casks', he wrote, 'and on board our ships, below hatches as on deck, lay four fingers breadth of ice.' Accustomed to the moderating influence of the Gulf Stream, Europeans found the extremes of temperature in North America one of the greatest differences between the New World and the Old. The Indian trade goods which Cartier had put aside for future profit took on new value for the thinly clad French. The heavy fur pelts of beaver, lynx and marten, themselves an adaptation to climate, suddenly became more practical than decorative.

Clothes were not the only life-saving resources that Cartier and his men obtained from the Hurons. Part way through the winter, despite the relative abundance of fresh food, scurvy attacked the Indians and the ice-bound explorers alike. By mid-February, Cartier reports, 50 of the Indians were dead and 'out of the 110 men that we were, not ten were well enough to help the others, a thing pitiful to see'. Then, 'God in His holy grace took pity on us, and sent us knowledge of a remedy'. It was, in fact, the Indians who provided the remedy – a tea brewed from the native arbor-vitae or white cedar, a hardy northern evergreen with highly aromatic foliage and bark. 'After this medicine was found and proved to be true', wrote Cartier,

OVERLEAF A blaze of maple foliage marks the end of another growing season in the northern woods. To native Americans these trees were an important food source, for until the importation of honey bees from Europe in the seventeenth century maple sugar was a primary source of sweetening. Tapped in early spring, before its leaves return, a mature sugar maple can provide up to 32 gallons of sap, enough to produce a gallon of syrup or about 5 pounds of sugar.

> there was such strife about it, who should be first to take it, that they were ready to kill one another, so that a tree as big as any Oake in France was spoiled and lopped bare, and occupied all in five or six daies, and it wrought so wel, that if all the phisicians of Mountpelier and Lovaine had bene there with all the drugs of Alexandria, they would not have done so much in one yere, as that tree did in six dayes, for it did so prevaile, that as many as used of it, by the grace of God recovered their health.

Cartier later carried seedlings of the arbor-vitae back to France, where it may have been the first American plant from north of Mexico to be introduced to European cultivation.

Among the other North American trees to inspire admiration among Europeans was one from which natural sweetness could be obtained. 'There is in some parts of New England', wrote the English chemist Robert Boyle in 1663, 'a kind of tree ... whose juice that weeps out of its incisions, if it be permitted slowly to exhale away the superfluous moisture, doth congeal into a sweet and saccharin substance, and the like was confirmed to me by the agent of the great and populous colony of Massachusetts.' Until imported European honeybees escaped from cultivation and naturalized in the New World, syrup from the sugar maple was the Indians' only source of natural sweetness. They often used it for flavoring their corn puddings and the meat of wild game. Cartier undoubtedly saw maple sugar being produced during the spring thaws of 1536, though he may have wondered, at first, just what the activity was all about.

The trees give no outward sign of it, but sometime in late February or early

March, when the great horned owls begin their mating calls and the skunk cabbages first poke their tips above the snow, the sap of the maple begins its surge from the roots to the leafless canopy. Daily cycles of freezing and thawing help to create the pressure that pumps the nutritious liquid up through the hair-fine tubes of the living wood. At just this time, the Indians would make a cut in the tree and there insert a small reed or spile of hollow sumac. The sap, interrupted in its upward flow, would run down the spile and collect in a bark bowl or bucket. This the harvesters would empty into a larger vessel of elm bark or the hollowed-out trunk of a tree.

The sweetness in the sugar maple makes up only 2–6 per cent of its sap, so a great deal of reduction is required to produce useful syrup. A mature sugar maple just over 100 feet in height, with a 3-foot girth can produce up to 32 gallons of sap each season. But this will yield no more than a gallon of syrup or about 5 pounds of sugar. Since the Indians had no metal pots until after their contact with Europeans, the long boiling periods that are used today to reduce the sap to syrup were impossible to sustain. Instead, the Indians achieved roughly the same effect by dropping heated stones into the buckets, or allowing the syrup to freeze and periodically skimming the ice from its surface.

Beet and cane sugar were scarce and expensive commodities in Europe and in the American colonies well into the eighteenth century, so maple syrup was much appreciated and soon became a valuable trade item. Eventually, white settlers learned how to tap trees and distill their own syrup, creating an industry that is still flourishing in certain parts of North America. The sugar maple's durable, fine-grained wood, brilliant autumnal display, and remarkable sap production have made it one of North America's most popular and valuable hardwoods. The stylized maple leaf that emblazons Canada's flag today is a fair indication of the tree's continuing natural, cultural, and economic significance.

When Cartier left his Huron hosts and headed for home in May 1536, the leaves had emerged on the maples and the trees' red-winged seeds were just beginning to form. Though frustrated in his hope of finding a gateway to the Orient, Cartier had nevertheless discovered a navigable entrance into the continent that would, in time, prove even more important to France.

Cartier hoped that the French court might wish to continue its search for the Northwest Passage, but a series of bloody civil wars between French Huguenots (Calvinists) and Roman Catholics dampened official enthusiasm and support for such exploration. Of more immediate interest to the King and his ministers were the rapidly developing French-American fisheries and fur trade.

Between the Atlantic deep and the fog-bound northern coast of North America – Newfoundland, Nova Scotia and New England – Europeans had discovered rich and productive fishing grounds unmatched by any at home. In a 37 000 square mile area known as the Grand Banks, the cold polar seas moving south meet the warmer seas of the North Atlantic above a raised, marine plateau. As deep waters rich in nutrients are forced to the surface by the land shelf, they are warmed by the sun and their productivity increases. The juncture of currents at the Grand Banks forms a three-dimensional marine meadow of plankton and other single-celled organisms, where fishes by the millions congregate to feed and breed.

Long before the Europeans arrived, North American fishermen used the Grand Banks as part of their seasonal cycle of harvest, making short forays from the coast to gather what fish they needed. They ate some of their fresh catch at once, and preserved the rest by sun drying, smoking, or salting it at temporary camp sites along the coast.

No one knows for sure when European fishermen first crossed the Atlantic to join native Americans in gathering this rich concentration of sea life. Breton, Norman, Basque, Portuguese, Norse, Irish and English partisans have each claimed precedence in reaching the Grand Banks. Probably all should take credit for pioneering in this risky but lucrative trade. The earliest documented fishing voyage to the Grand Banks was made by French sailors in 1504, but there were certainly others much earlier. Though they often failed to record it themselves, we know that European fishermen were regularly exploiting the New World's bounty decades before Columbus's epic voyage. Portugal's harvest of fish from North American waters was so great by 1506 that the Portuguese king imposed a 10 per cent import duty on the catch to protect local fishermen from the unfair advantage enjoyed by those willing to take their boats to the Grand Banks.

The focus of much of the early fishing was cod, a large family of cold-water fishes including haddock, pollack and hake that had been overfished in European waters. So abundant were the cod along the northern coast of North America that fishermen found the sea 'paved' with them, and there were reports of French boats sinking under the weight of their harvest. In those early times it was not uncommon to find Atlantic cod weighing up to 200 pounds. But 300 years of intensive fishing have reduced both the number and size of cod living along the North American coast. Today a 10-pound cod is more typical, and their schools no longer impede boat traffic as was once reported. Though still an important resource, the cod are no longer the 'unexhaustible manna' they were once perceived to be.

A French writer named Louis-Armand Baron de Lahontan, who visited the French-Canadian fishing village of Placentia in 1684, described the Grand Bank fisheries of the time:

Commonly, there comes thirty or forty Ships from France to Placentia every year, and sometimes sixty. Some come with intent to fish, and others have no other design than to truck with the Inhabitants, who live in the Summer time on the other side of the Fort. The ground upon which their Houses stand, is call'd La grande Grave, for in effect, they have nothing but Gravel to spread their Cod-fish upon, in order to have 'em dry'd by the Sun after they are salted. The Inhabitants and the French Fishermen, send their Sloops every day two Leagues off the Port to pursue the Fishery; and sometimes the Sloops return so over-loaded, that they are in a manner bury'd in the Water. You cannot imagine how deep they sink, and 'tis impossible you should believe it, unless you saw it. The Fishery commences in the beginning of

June, and its at an end about the middle of August. In the Harbour they catch a little sort of a fish, which they put upon their Hooks as a bait for the Cod.

'Placentia', Lahontan concluded, 'bears neither Corn nor Rie, nor Pease, for the Soil is good for nothing; not to mention, that if it were as good and as fertile as any in Canada, yet no body would give themselves the trouble to cultivate it; for one Man earns more in Cod-fishing in one Summer, than ten would do in the way of Agriculture.'

A second business more lucrative than farming, to which the French devoted increasing attention, was the fur trade. This is almost certainly the 'truck with the Inhabitants' that Lahontan referred to in his account of Placentia. Cartier had seen the eagerness with which the Micmac and Huron would exchange pelts, sometimes the very clothes off their backs, for 'hatchets, knives, paternoster beads and other merchandise'. 'They bartered all they had', he recalled, 'to such an extent that all went back naked without anything on them; and they made signs to us that they would return on the morrow with more furs.' Return they did, not just for Cartier, but for any other Europeans willing to trade.

The English and Dutch would later establish a lucrative commerce in skins with the Iroquois and their sister tribes, but the French were the first to purchase peltry on a large scale. Their principal trading partners were the Hurons and Algonquians, two allied groups who were already engaged in intertribal trading before the arrival of the Europeans. The French would also eventually establish a strong trading relationship with the Ottawa, a tribe whose name derives from the Algonquian word for trade, and means literally 'he buys'. A more accurate title in the years after European contact might well have been 'he sells', for the Ottawa would sell the French countless thousands of pelts in the years to come.

Like the Iroquois to the south and the Ottawa to the west, the Hurons were primarily farmers of corn, beans and squash, but their strategic location at the northern limits of viable corn cultivation put them in an advantageous position for trade. With hard work each summer, the women of the tribe could produce small amounts of surplus corn and other crops, which the men could exchange for meat, fish and furs with the hunting and gathering tribes further north. With a long tradition of trading behind them, the Hurons saw the French in practical terms, not as invading enemies or visiting gods, but as new trading partners. Before other tribes could become involved, the Hurons placed themselves in the strategic middle ground between competing tribal groups and the eager, even generous, newcomers from Europe.

The French, for their part, found the Hurons bright, enterprising, friendly, and skillfully diplomatic – in short, ideal trading partners. It was a mutually advantageous arrangement. As with all good trading agreements, each side was convinced it was getting the better part of the deal. The French provided hardware – axes, hatchets, knives, metal pots, and other things that could be manufactured and purchased cheaply at home. The Indians provided life-sustaining game and produce, and profit-producing pelts. As trading grew more

Among the earliest visual records of the French-Canadian fur trade are those attributed to Louis Nicolas, a Jesuit priest who worked between 1664 and 1678. Clearly recognizable in his drawing of fur-bearers (right) are an otter (with fish), a buck-toothed beaver, and a seal. The classically-posed Illinois chief (far right) is shown with a ceremonial pipe of peace or 'calumet'. Tobacco was obtained by trade with other Indian tribes or from Europeans in exchange for furs. Long admired for the warmth and softness of its fur, the beaver was the single most important animal in the development of commerce in the New World, fostering extensive exploration of North America and heated competition between European powers. The beaver was also admired for its skills as a natural engineer. Its intricately constructed dams and lodges, like this one in Banff National Park (right), led some early explorers to attribute human characteristics to the species.

sophisticated and European trade goods lost their status, if not their practicality, among the Indians, other items of barter, including guns and alcohol, entered the market. Salt-water and freshwater shell wampum also came to play an increasingly important role as an inter-culture currency.

Though pelts of almost every fur-bearing animal were sought by European traders, the one in greatest demand was the beaver's. This large aquatic rodent had once ranged throughout the British Isles and Europe, but by the end of the thirteenth century it had been trapped and hunted to extinction in England, and close to it on the Continent. In North America the situation was quite different. A low density of humans with no previous interest in commercial exploitation of furs, and an intricate network of streams and rivers and lakes, created ideal conditions for the beaver to flourish. And flourish it did, not just in northern waters, but throughout the continent. When Europeans first reached American shores, virtually every lake, pond, and river in North America showed some evidence of beaver activity.

Though somewhat awkward on land, the beaver is a master of the water. Webbed hind feet and a thick, paddle-shaped tail give it both maneuverability and strength. They also serve the beaver as indispensable tools of engineering. After extolling the virtues of its fur, early describers of the beaver invariably focused on its skills as a natural engineer. Some attributed great intelligence and even human characteristics to the species, pointing to its intricately constructed dams and lodges as evidence of a superior intellect. One eighteenth-century naturalist, who never actually saw an American beaver lodge, suggested that the structure was designed with as many aesthetic considerations as practical ones: 'The window which looks out upon the water', wrote the Comte de Buffon, 'serves [the beaver] as a balcony for the enjoyment of the air, or to bathe during the greater part of the day.' Such fanciful notions aside, the animal's dwelling places and dams are impressive feats of engineering.

Made of intricately woven sticks, branches and reeds cut expressly for the purpose, the beaver dam is usually anchored to stream-side boulders or growing trees, and reinforced with heavy stones brought by the animals to the site. Once constructed, the dam is packed with mud to provide added strength and to create a water-tight seal. Each dam has the highest point at the middle and then tapers to the sides. This form protects the integrity of the structure in case of flooding by shunting the force of the water to the edges. In the event of damage, it is easier for the beavers to repair a leak at the ends where the water pressure is weakest.

The beaver was saved from extinction in the nineteenth century by a fortunate change in European fashion. It has since returned in healthy numbers to the quiet waterways of the United States and Canada.

Depending on their size and location, the dams are built cooperatively by one or more families and are often maintained for decades, even centuries, by successive generations of beavers. The height, thickness, and length of the structures differ widely. There are stories of some dams reaching a length of more than half a mile. The largest currently on record, on the Jefferson River in Montana, is 2240 feet long.

The beavers have a purpose in building their dams, of course: it is to raise the water level upstream and so create a secure, protected place from which to make nightly feeding forays ashore. The dams also provide a suitable lodge site in which a pair of beavers, mated for life, can raise their annual litter of up to eight kits. A large colony may have many such lodges, one per family, in each of which as many as a dozen beavers can overwinter.

Beavers are alert and active even through the coldest months, but most of their activity then takes place indoors. Their lodges are constructed with sufficient space to house animals and food alike. Additional food supplies are anchored under water near the entrance to the lodge. As long as their dam is kept in good repair and the water level in the pond remains constant, the wintering beavers are protected from both predators and cold by underwater entrances and a thick insulating roof of branches and mud.

The beaver is second only to man in manipulating its own environment. Its extensive clearing and flooding activities inevitably affect a whole range of other species. As the beavers cut down trees to use for construction or food, the forest openings provide opportunities for new pioneering plants to emerge, including the birch and aspen favored by beavers. These, in turn, provide an ideal nesting habitat for forest-edge birds, as well as browse for deer, elk (wapiti) and moose (elk), and cover for smaller animals.

The flooded edges of the beaver's pond form a second distinctive habitat, a home for muskrats, red-winged blackbirds, wading birds of various kinds, and a complex community of water-loving plants. Finally, the pond itself creates a new refuge for wildlife. The fish that inhabit the beaver's reservoir are of no interest to the beaver, which is a strict vegetarian, but they support many of the other animals that take up residence in or near the pond, such as ospreys, king-fishers, herons, egrets, otters and mink. On a smaller scale, a myriad other water-dependent creatures benefit from the beaver's self-serving activity: mosquitoes, dragonflies, water spiders, frogs, toads, newts, turtles, and hundreds of other species. By slowing and spreading the water of streams, the beavers also con-tribute to flood control and help to reduce soil erosion.

Abandoned and drained ponds, which became increasingly common as beavers were trapped for European trade, are almost as productive as active ones. Good exposure from the sun and decades, sometimes centuries, of silt sediment trapped by the dams make old pond bottoms excellent for terrestrial plants and animals. The old pond sites were sometimes turned to croplands by Indians or European settlers with gratifying results. When too remote for human cultivation, the sites would go through a natural succession of growth, support-ing, in turn, a wide range of native species.

Cranberries and blueberries, both of which thrive on the boggy soil and sunlight associated with the filling ponds, were extremely important sources of food for native Americans. They were fruits unknown in Europe, and so especially valued by Europeans. Samuel de Champlain found the blueberries of Canada among the country's most plentiful and delicious natural foods. They are, he wrote, 'a small fruit, very good to eat ... and in such plenty that it is marvellous. These people who live there dry these fruits for their winter supply, just as we do plums in France for Lent'. Black bears and scores of wild birds

RIGHT 'God seems to have wanted to give these frightful regions something in its season to serve for refreshment to man,' remarked the French explorer Samuel de Champlain when he found blueberries growing on the Ottawa River in 1615. Long a staple of the Indians' diet, the berries soon became a popular food for European settlers as well.

OVERLEAF The white or paper birch, like the blueberry, thrives in open stream-side settings. Native Americans used its waterproof bark in the construction of durable, lightweight canoes.

also consume vast quantities of blueberries. In summer bears can subsist entirely on them, a single animal consuming up to 10 000 berries or 15 pounds per day.

Another plant which often exploits the open habitat of an abandoned beaver pond is the white or paper birch. Its strong but pliable waterproof bark was used by native Americans to make containers, megaphone-like moose calls, and even wigwam shelters. Its most important use, however, was in transportation. Stretched on a frame of white cedar, stitched with the thread-like roots of the tamarack (another beaver-field resident) and caulked with the resin of white pine or balsam, birch bark was the essential component in one of North America's most important inventions, the birch-bark canoe. Light, durable, and entirely waterproof, these graceful craft enabled the Indians, and later the Europeans, to travel long distances through the same waterways that supported the beaver, muskrat, otter and mink.

In winter the white birch contributed to another form of transportation originating in North America. Birch or white ash forms, stitched with the sinew of deer, caribou or moose, were used for snowshoes. Equipped with canoes and snowshoes, Indian hunters could – and did – travel to virtually every part of the northern woods year round.

In the early years of the fur trade, beaver pelts, like the skins of other fur-bearers, were sold in Europe for their warmth and decorative qualities. As supplies increased the beaver fur was put to more general use, particularly in the manufacture of felt hats. For felt even inferior summer pelts could be used, thereby permitting a year-round harvest.

The demand for beaver fur was by no means restricted to France, nor was the supply restricted to Canada. The Dutch West Indies Company, which in 1625 had established New Amsterdam (later to become New York City) on Manhattan Island, covered its original investment in its first year with a cargo of 7246 beaver, 675 otter, and unnumbered quantities of mink, muskrat and wild cat skins, all harvested from the upper Hudson River valley. Similarly, within a few years of its founding, the Plymouth colony shipped 12 150 pounds of beaver and 1156 otter skins to England to help repay its sponsors for the cost of supporting the colony.

With various European groups vying for control of the fur trade, distinctively different attitudes toward the land and its inhabitants began to emerge. Most of the English colonists, concentrating in settlements along the Atlantic coast, had come to America to escape civil or religious persecution at home. They were committed to settling and to reshaping the land according to their own blueprint of paradise. They believed that what could not be used for food, shelter, clothing, or profit should be improved or eliminated. The seventeenth-century New England clergyman, Cotton Mather, summarized this view when he pronounced that 'what is not useful is vicious'. As often as not, such opinions applied to Indians as well as wildlife. With the exception of William Penn's Quaker-dominated Pennsylvania, English colonies often tried to 'civilize', Christianize, exclude, or eliminate native Americans whose religious beliefs they found objectionable and whose lifestyles they did not understand.

Unlike the British, who sought to establish permanent settlements, the French viewed their North American outposts essentially as bases of convenience for commerce. Untroubled by the logistical and political difficulties of managing large settlements, the French devoted their efforts to reaching into the forests of Canada to extract the seemingly endless bounty they contained. Beginning in 1609, Samuel de Champlain made extensive trips inland from the Gulf of St Lawrence, eventually establishing a French trading monopoly that extended all the way to the Great Lakes.

The men and women who occupied the scattered fishing camps and trading posts of New France had come for profit, not to create a new self-sufficient homeland. They were opportunists who saw no shame in obtaining food and other necessities from the Indians. Some French merchants, like the English, chose to wait in the relative safety of their posts for the Indians to bring furs to them. Others preferred a more active role in the fur trade. These French-Canadian *coureurs de bois* and *voyageurs* learned trapping techniques, canoe construction, wood lore, camp craft, and much more from the Indians, often accompanying them on long canoe journeys and sharing their semi-nomadic lifestyles for months, even years, at a time. The intermingling of races that inevitably resulted from such prolonged contact was readily accepted by the French. Samuel de Champlain had envisioned such relations when he told the Indians 'our young men will marry your daughters, and we shall be one people'. Of four recorded marriages in Quebec between 1604 and 1627, two were between French men and Indian women. There must have been countless other interracial relationships not recorded.

The arrival of French Jesuit missionaries in the early seventeenth century brought another set of attitudes toward the New World and its people. Issues of theology and social conduct aside, the French missionaries and the traders had serious differences on how best to achieve their often conflicting goals. Chrétien Le Clercq identified the most important difference as that involving settlement. The greatest obstacle to the missionaries' work, he observed, came from 'the gentlemen of the company, who, to monopolize trade, did not wish the country to be settled, and did not even wish us to make the Indian sedentary, without which nothing can be done for the salvation of these heathen'. Le Clercq went on to comment bitterly that while the traders 'were very zealous for their trade ... they care little to deserve God's blessing by contributing to the interest of his glory'.

The Catholic French king was sympathetic to Le Clercq's frustration and supportive of the missionaries' efforts to spread the faith while stabilizing the population, both Indian and European, but he saw even more important strategic reasons for encouraging French settlement in Canada. The French government viewed with alarm the growing Spanish and English presence in North America. Only by increasing its own presence on the continent could France hope to maintain a prominent role in world politics and commerce. The king tried to encourage settlement in Canada by making it a condition for securing trading monopolies there. But time after time promises of settlement were ignored and by 1660, there were only 3000 French residents in Canada. More than that number of English colonists had settled in Massachusetts in a single year.

The high degree of mobility required by those involved with the fur trade was one reason for the dearth of French settlement in Canada. The country's rugged topography was another. Champlain, the first European to explore Canada's interior, observed that 'All the countrie which I saw, was nothing but mountaines, the most part of rockes covered with woods of fir trees, cypresses, and birch trees, the soyle very unpleasante, where I found not a league of plaine countrey'. In the farmlands of Europe, rocky soil was a local phenomenon. In Canada, would-be farmers found it far more extensive. The Canadian shield, a geological formation 1 864 000 square miles in size, extends in a large ellipse across the upper tier of North America from the Atlantic to the Arctic Ocean. While only about one tenth of the shield is actually exposed, it lies very close to the surface through most of its range. It was scraped and scoured by successive glaciers during the ice age. What little soil there is above it has accumulated in the last 10 000 years. Even in forests of great height, the soil is often only a few inches deep. For the shallow-rooted conifers − hemlock, spruce and balsam − that dominate the northern forests, this was sufficient. For Europeans trying to plow and plant, it was not.

When the value of North American furs took a temporary drop in the 1660s, many French settlers talked of giving up the hardships of their New World posts and returning to France. To prevent the loss of so important a base, King Louis XIV raised the status of New France to a royal province, complete with its own administrator or *intendant* to coordinate settlement activities. The first man to hold the post, Jean Baptiste Talan, arranged to have forts built along the St Lawrence River and the southern shores of Lake Ontario in order to protect New France from the increasingly hostile and well-armed Iroquois. He then broadened the economic base of the colony by establishing local industries, such as weaving and shipbuilding. Finally, he undertook a serious recruitment campaign to attract settlers to Canada. This included encouraging young couples to have as many children as possible by offering free grants of 100 acres of land to every father of 12 or more. The scheme was so successful that some men petitioned for − and received − grants of 200 acres for their productivity. One may wonder whether so much land would have been claimed if the same offer had been made to women!

Despite such efforts, Talan's progress in increasing and consolidating settlements in Canada was painfully slow. In addition to poor soil, a cold climate, and a commercial base that encouraged mobility, Talan found another major obstacle to his settlement efforts − the geographical configuration of the land itself. Further south, the Appalachian Mountains had served to concentrate European settlement along the Atlantic coast by providing a formidable barrier to all westward expansion. In Canada, by contrast, the St Lawrence River and its many tributaries provided relatively easy, if not always safe, access to and from the continent's heartland. Many would-be settlers felt threatened by the proximity of so much wilderness and all that it implied.

Other new arrivals reacted in the opposite way to the openness of Canada's terrain. Glad to be free of the confines of Europe, they were irresistibly drawn to the seemingly limitless potential of the untamed wilderness. These men – and in a few rare cases women – rejected the restrictions of organized settlements and forged off into the unknown interior.

The two French explorers who best exemplified this adventurous, anti-settlement spirit were Pierre Esprit Radisson and his partner, Médard Chovart Sieur des Groseilliers. This extraordinary pair of *coureurs de bois* explored vast regions of the Canadian interior between Lake Superior and Hudson's Bay in the 1650s and 60s. 'The further we sojourned the delighfuller the land was to us', wrote Radisson in idiomatic English. 'I can say that [in] my lifetime I never saw a more incomparable country'. Though their travels were often fraught with dangers and hardship – for a period the two men lived on boiled lichens – Radisson and Groseilliers clearly relished their opportunities to view a country no European had seen before and to do so entirely unencumbered by official direction or restraint. 'We weare Cesars', Radisson reflected in later years, 'being nobody to contradict us.'

The land they covered was a checkerboard of deep evergreen forests and open, sphagnum-matted bogs called muskeg, from the Cree word *Maskeek*. On long summer evenings they watched 1800-pound moose graze on waterweeds in ponds fringed with wildflowers: white 'bogbean' gentian, blue iris, purple-fringed orchis, and a brilliant scarlet lobelia called cardinal flower among the most conspicuous. They slept on fresh-cut balsam boughs still redolent of pitch. At night the long eerie wails and demonic laughter of loons, and the deep rhythmic hooting of the great horned owl, blended with the snores of the *voyageurs*. By day the splash of fish and fishing osprey seemed to echo the splash of their paddles as they plied the rivers between trading posts and trapping grounds.

Radisson and Groseilliers did most of their traveling by water, so their observations of wildlife were usually from a boatman's-eye-view. Paddling through one of the Great Lakes, Radisson admired

> the beauty of the shore of that sweet sea. Here we saw fishes of divers [sorts] some like the sturgeon. ... There are birds [white pelicans] whose bills are two and 20 thumbs long. That bird swallows a whole salmon, keeps it a long time in his bill. We saw alsoe shee goats very bigg [antelope?]. There is an animal somewhat less than a cow whose meat is exceeding good [caribou?]. There is no want of Staggs [deer or moose] nor Buffs [buffalo]. There are so many Tourkeys that the boys throws stoanes att them for their recreation.

It is not always possible to tell which lakes or rivers Radisson is describing, but it is clear from his accounts that his wanderings took him as far as the Great Plains. There he and Groseilliers were among the very first Europeans to see the great herds of buffalo that would so impress later travelers.

For the French, the most important discovery made by Radisson and Groseilliers during their extensive travels was the Mississippi, which Radisson

The Exploration of Eastern Canada and Alaska

SIBERIA

ICELAND

ARCTIC
OCEAN

GREENLAND

Bering Strait

Seward
Peninsula

Bering
Sea

Pribilof I

Brooks Range

Yukon R.

ALASKA

Kuskokwim R.

Big R.

Aleutian Range

Alaska Range

Mt Katmai

Kodiak I.

Gulf
of
Alaska

Kayak I.

Sitka (New Archangel)

Melville
Hills

Victoria
Island

Mackenzie
Mountains

Yukon R.

Great Bear
Lake

Coppermine R.

Back R.

Davis Strait

Foxe
Basin

Baffin
Island

Hudson's Strait

Laird R.

Coastal Mtns

ROCKY MOUNTAINS

Great Slave
Lake

Thelon R.

Southampton
Island

Ungava
Peninsula

Labrador

I of Birds
(Funk I)

Bering
Sea

ALASKA

Aleutian Islands

0   200   400 Miles

L. Athabasca

Peace R.

Reindeer
Lake

Nelson R.

HUDSON'S
BAY

Newfoundland
(Vinland)

Gulf
of
St Lawrence

Cape
Breton I

PACIFIC
OCEAN

Fraser R.

N. Saskatchewan R.

S. Saskatchewan R.

Hayes R.

Severn R.

Laurentian Mtns

St Lawrence R.

Cartier 1534

Cartier 1535-6

Hudson 1610

Groseilliers and
Radisson 1654-63

Bering and
Steller 1741-2

Cook 1776-9

Columbia R.

Cascade Range

Bitterroot
Range

ROCKY MOUNTAINS

L. Winnipeg

L. Manitoba

Assiniboine R.

Red R.

Missouri R.

Lake
Superior

Albany R.

Abitibi R.

Lake
Huron

Quebec
(Stadacona)

Montreal
(Hochelaga)

Grand
Banks

Nova
Scotia

Hay R.

Lake
Michigan

Mississippi R.

Lake
Ontario

Lake
Erie

APPALACHIAN MOUNTAINS

ATLANTIC
OCEAN

0   250   500   750 Miles

*OVERLEAF The
largest body of fresh
water in the world,
Lake Superior has
every appearance of
an ocean and was so
perceived by early
French explorers who
dubbed it a 'fresh-
water sea'.*

described as 'a beautiful River, large, wide, deep, and worthy of comparison they say, with our great River St Lawrence'. The comparison could not have been more apt. The subsequent explorations of Louis Jolliet, Jacques Marquette and Robert de La Salle would confirm the Mississippi's commercial importance by establishing its course from the upper Midwest to the Gulf of Mexico. The travels of these men dramatically expanded France's commercial and political control in North America.

In many respects, Radisson and Groseilliers represent the best of the free, entrepreneurial spirit which set New France apart from its European-American competitors. But their world was already changing. In 1663, when Radisson and Groseilliers fought their way through Iroquois war parties to bring a year's harvest of furs to Montreal, they discovered they were no longer 'Caesars' in an

73

unregulated world. French trade officials, on learning that the two adventurers had gone into the back country without government license, confiscated their entire stock of furs and so wiped out their income for a year. Furious, Radisson and Groseilliers departed Montreal, severing their relations with a government whose cause they had done so much to advance, and placed their knowledge at the disposal of the English crown.

The English, for their part, had been steadily expanding their control over lands to the south. With the Treaty of Breda in 1667, they took New Netherlands from the Dutch and thus secured a virtual monopoly on all of the fur trade south of New France. King Charles II and the merchants of London were eager to expand still further. Radisson and Groseilliers were prepared to show them how they could do so, and where.

Eight hundred miles to the north of the beaver-flooded Laurentian valleys from which the French extracted so much of their wealth lies a very different Canada – a vast expanse of interfingered forest and tundra where snow and ice have hold of the land for nine months of the year. The few trees there are miniature in scale, stunted by poor soils, short growing seasons and punishing winter weather. Though bleak and barren on first appearance, the subarctic tundra is by no means void of life. Dwarf berry-producing shrubs, willows, saxifrages, gentians, poppies, and a variety of arctic grasses, sedges and lichens provide year-round food for ptarmigan, lemming and arctic hare. These animals, in turn, support a small group of predators including the arctic fox and snowy owl. Two larger grazing animals, the barren-ground caribou and the musk ox, also inhabit Canada's far north, often covering vast distances to secure the nutrition they require.

While they live on one of the world's most challenging frontiers, the residents of the tundra are more accurately viewed as refugees than pioneers, for they were the species that moved north in order to remain a part of the ice-age ecosystem with which they evolved. The musk ox, for instance, a distant relative of the bison, once ranged across much of North America. As the great ice sheets retreated, so did the species, eventually finding a permanent home in the high Arctic.

Some caribou remained in North America's more temperate zones well past the time of European contact. When the Pilgrims landed at Plymouth Rock, the woodland caribou still roamed in large migrating herds in New England, the Great Lakes region, and as far west as present-day Washington state. Due to excessive hunting, human pressure and habitat destruction, these herds were greatly reduced in size and number during the eighteenth and nineteenth centuries. Today they are found only in Alberta, Labrador, Newfoundland and the Gaspé Peninsula of Quebec.

The barren-ground caribou, a more mobile race of the species, live in the transition zone between forest and tundra. They migrate up to 1200 miles each year in order to sustain themselves on the limited grazing available. As winter approaches and the snow cover on the tundra becomes compacted and impenetrable, the caribou move south into the spruce and balsam forests where the

LEFT *The barren-ground caribou travels vast distances to find limited grazing in Canada's far north. In spring, huge herds move to their calving grounds northwest of Hudson's Bay. In these areas they are safe from their two main enemies, wolves and humans, but they are tormented by immense numbers of warble flies and mosquitoes. An adult male can lose up to a quart of blood per week to insect pests.*

OVERLEAF *Living relics of the ice age, a herd of musk oxen masses tightly for defense. These distant relatives of the American bison once roamed through much of North America, but as the climate of the continent warmed they moved north with the retreating ice cap.*

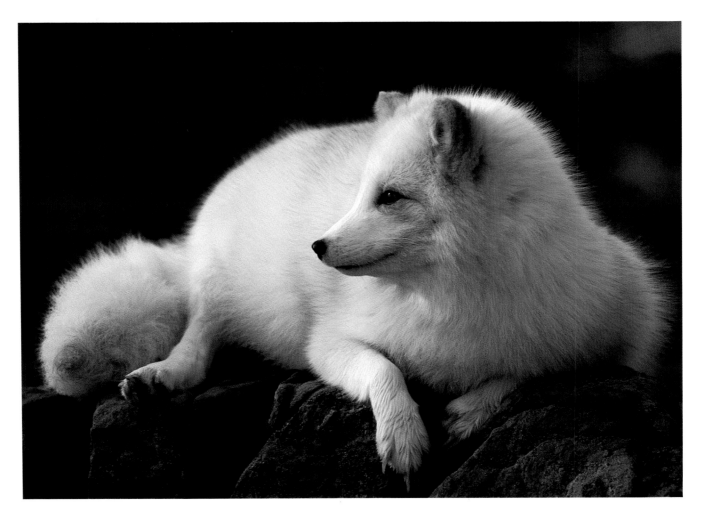

Three permanent residents of the Canadian Arctic – an arctic fox, a rock ptarmigan, and an arctic hare – wear concealing winter coats of pure white. As days lengthen and the snow melts, all three will take on a new camouflage of mottled brown. Meanwhile, hardy plants such as the arctic poppy (left) mark the arrival of the short northern summer.

snow is softer. There, like their woodland relatives, they are able to break through the snow to the lichens and sedges lying protected beneath it. As the days slowly lengthen between February and April, the herds begin their long trip north to the calving grounds. They converge at the tree line in early May, and then push some 300 miles farther at a rate of 15–30 miles per day. Their herd sizes vary from hundreds to tens of thousands, some being so large and spread-out that they have been known to take several weeks to pass a single point.

The caribou calving grounds near the Arctic Circle northwest of Hudson's Bay, are safe from two of the caribou's most serious predators, wolves and humans. But they are filled with warble flies and mosquitoes which emerge by the countless billions just after the calves are born. From then on, the caribou move constantly in their desperate – but largely futile – efforts to escape the thick swarms of insects that can drain up to a quart of blood per animal each week. With the first frosts of August, the herds disperse and begin moving south in small groups. By late September they have converged again for their mass migration back to the forests of the south.

In the past, the caribou herds were often accompanied by nomadic hunters who depended on them for food and clothing. Surplus meat, skins and horns were traded with Indian groups in the warmer and more fertile areas for corn and other agricultural produce which northern tribes could not grow for themselves. In the late seventeenth century, these hunters – mostly Chipewyan and Cree – found new trading partners with entirely new items to trade.

Beginning in 1670, the British established a number of heavily fortified trading posts along the rocky shores of James and Hudson's Bay. The commercial syndicate behind the effort, officially known as The Governor and Company of Adventurers into Hudson's Bay, had been given a charter by King Charles II to find 'a new passage into the South Sea' and to secure trade in furs, minerals, and other valuable commodities in Canada's far north. In the first part of their assignment they would be no more successful than other explorers, but from a commercial point of view, the company would soon fulfill the king's greatest expectations.

While none of the Hudson's Bay Company's original 'adventurers' – a seventeenth-century term for investors or speculators – actually visited the sites of their speculation, they were well apprised of the potential these trading posts held. The sources of their information were none other than the disgruntled Radisson and Groseilliers who, in revenge for their ill-treatment by the French, were only too happy to help the English expand their interests. Thus, adventurers of two sorts combined experience and resources to create what was to become the most powerful fur trading company in the world.

The Hudson's Bay Company's initial domain covered about 1.4 million square miles of North America – all the lands draining into Hudson's Bay. The region was called Rupert's Land in honor of Prince Rupert, a cousin of the king and the first governor of the company. While the company's original trading posts were less than luxurious for their operators, they proved to be ideally

North America in 1700

HUDSON'S
BAY

RUPERT'S LAND

Newfound-
land

Fort Albany 1674 ●

NEW FRANCE

● Québec 1608   Nova
                 Scotia

Sault Ste Marie 1669 ●   Montreal 1642 ●

                    Fort Frontenac 1673 ●   Salem 1630
                                                   Boston 1630

LOUISIANA

Fort Pontchartrain ●   New York 1664
(Detroit) 1701   (New Amsterdam 1626)
                                         ● Philadelphia 1682

Fort Crèvecoeur 1680 ●

                                      THIRTEEN COLONIES

                                         Williamsburg 1699
Cahokia 1698 ●   Jamestown 1607

Santa Fe 1651 ●   ATLANTIC
● Oraibi 1125   OCEAN

                                    Charleston 1672 ●

                    Pensacola 1696 ●   St Augustine 1565
PACIFIC   Florida ●
OCEAN
                         VICE-ROYALTY   BAHAMA IS.
                              OF
                          NEW SPAIN

                              GULF OF
                              MEXICO

                                              CUBA
☐ British possessions

☐ French possessions   HAITI

☐ Spanish possessions   JAMAICA

☐ Areas claimed by British and French

Boston 1630 Date of foundation   Mexico City 1521 ●
                                          (Tenochtitlán 1176)
0   250   500   750   1000 Miles

83

located for trade, drawing skins and furs from a huge area relatively untouched by the Laurentian-based French. As Henry Hudson had predicted in 1610, Canada's great inland sea, Hudson's Bay, and its connecting link to the Atlantic Ocean, Hudson's Strait, provided a ready water route from Canada's northern heartland to the open markets of Europe. Through it, the British were able to import trade goods and export furs more cheaply and in greater quantities than their French competitors to the south. By 1682, additional trading posts had been set up at Rupert River, Albany River, Hayes Island, Fort Nelson, and Fort Severn.

The French, seeing their once unquestioned control of the Canadian fur trade seriously challenged by British interests from both the north and south, decided to expand their efforts in the only direction they could – westward into the Mississippi basin. In 1682 they claimed a huge swath of land from the Great Lakes to the Gulf of Mexico, and named it Louisiana in honor of their king.

For the next 80 years, in a series of regional conflicts that paralleled more serious warfare in Europe, the three major European powers in North America – France, Spain and England – struggled for control of the continent. The Indians, who had once enlisted Europeans as auxiliary troops for themselves, became the pawns of warring European powers.

The Seven Years War, or the French and Indian War as it was known in North America, was the final and most decisive of the European conflicts to affect the political structure of North America. In the Treaty of Paris at the war's conclusion in 1763, France formally relinquished her hold on the New World by turning over to Britain not only her claims to Canada, but also all other French possessions east of the Mississippi River, with the exception of New Orleans, which she deeded to Spain. Spain received all French land west of the Mississippi but, in exchange, was forced to turn over all of her Florida holdings to Britain.

Such paper transactions in a faraway capital would have little immediate effect on the natural history of Canada, for there were only about 60 000 Europeans living in Canada at the time. But the long-term implications were significant, for now English values and policies, not French or Indian, would govern the land.

To the English traders on Hudson's Bay, the extremes of climate were more pressing than the legalities of political control. For nine months out of every twelve, their inland sea and all access to the outside world was locked in ice and snow. Under similar conditions, French traders might have removed to more comfortable quarters, returning to resume business in the spring. The tenacious Hudson's Bay Company traders considered no such option. They were there for the duration, come what may. What came, they soon discovered, were 70-mile-per-hour winds, tons of ice, sleet and snow, long nights, bitter temperatures and, more often than not, marauding bears.

Each autumn, as the days shorten and the temperatures drop, the southern shores of Hudson's Bay are invaded by the great white 'ice bears' of the Arctic north. They are waiting for the winter pack ice on which they will travel out

The snowy owl (right) depends upon lemmings and small birds for winter food. With the arrival of spring, the owl's menu will expand.

A body of water five times larger than the Persian Gulf, Hudson's Bay (below) is locked in ice for almost half of each year.

into the Bay in search of seals. The young males usually arrive first. They wander along the coastline singly or in pairs, warily sparring with each other while they search the exposed rocks for food. As the October snows deepen and the Bay begins to freeze, the larger males arrive, each 8–10 feet long and up to 800 pounds in weight. After a few months of feeding on ringed seals, they can weigh as much as 1400 pounds apiece. By early November as many as 600 male bears may have gathered on a 100-mile stretch of the Hudson's Bay coast. The females, protective of their cubs, wait inland until the Bay is frozen and the males have dispersed. Then they too venture on to the ice to feed. Having waited several months for the opportunity, their appetites are voracious. Some bears have been known to eat up to 100 pounds of seal blubber in a single meal. The carcasses' remains make welcome food for the arctic foxes and ravens that follow.

Captured polar bears had been known in England since the days of Henry VII, when a live specimen from Greenland was presented to the Royal Menagerie. The king was so taken with the creature that he appropriated 'six pense a day to support our White Bear in our Tower of London' and ordered the sheriff of the capital 'to provide a muzzle and iron chain. ... and a long and strong rope to hold him when he [goes] fishing in the Thames'.

The bears of Hudson's Bay wore neither muzzles nor iron chains. To the aboriginal Inuit they represented fellow travelers of the Arctic, sources of food and wisdom. To the English, they were a forceful reminder that treaties, technology and perseverance could help to shape but could never subdue the great northern wilderness of the continent they had decided to make their home.

Through the long shadows of a winter afternoon a pack of wolves treads, single file, in the tracks of its intended prey, probably an injured or aging moose. Family groups of five or six animals often require up to 100 square miles of territory in the sparse northern habitat that serves as a final refuge for these much-maligned (and now endangered) predators.

CONQUERING THE SWAMPS
FLORIDA · AND · THE · SOUTHEAST

A long string of islands the Spanish called *cayos* extends like a comma from the southeastern tip of North America, a terrestrial punctuation suggesting a history and something still to come. Unlike most of the islands that line the Atlantic coast, the Florida Keys are still in the process of growing. They are coral islands built from the fossilized remains of billions of microscopic sea organisms whose progeny continue to thrive in the warm, shallow waters of the Mexican Gulf. The individual organisms that comprise the coral reef live and die attached to the calcified remains of their predecessors, their communal shell-banks building from the ocean floor at rates of up to $3\frac{1}{2}$ feet a century. As the reef grows, its mass deflects and slows the ocean's currents. This causes sediment to collect, adding to the size of the reef. The ocean floor rises, the old coral fossilizes, the new coral grows, more debris gathers, and so on, until, at last, the reef lies just below the water's surface. With the cooling of the earth's climate during successive ice ages, sea levels dropped, and some of Florida's reef was exposed. Plants and other terrestrial organisms invaded its sandy surface and contributed to its growth. When most exposed, the reef extended some 220 miles from the mainland. Then, as the climate warmed and ice sheets melted, it was partially submerged again. The rising ocean cut channels through the reef creating the keys we see today.

Of the thousands of islands that make up the Florida Keys, most are still only a few feet higher than the highest tide. A sea rise of just 18 feet would cover the entire archipelago, from Key Largo to Key West. A few more feet would inundate most of southern Florida. It is this delicate balance of land and water that makes the southeastern tip of the continent scientifically unique and ecologically fragile.

Dig into any part of southern Florida and you will find evidence of the sea. The sandy soil, a mix of fragmented seashells, coral, limestone and leaf litter, lies above a huge limestone shelf that was itself once sea bottom. Dig farther

The brown pelican and green turtle, both inhabitants of the Florida Keys, can be found in coastal areas throughout the Southeast. These and other species were celebrated in the wooden carvings of the Calusa Indians.

and you will probably find fresh water. Like anywhere else on the continent, Florida's permeable soils contain a certain amount of ground water, but what sets this area apart are its artesian springs which draw their water from natural catchment basins hundreds of miles to the north. The water soaks into the ground and is trapped within the interconnected fissures and cavities that honeycomb Florida's limestone bedrock. Then, molecule by molecule, drop by drop, it percolates through this immense limestone filter, clearing itself of impurities and building pressure as it goes. Wherever the water-filled strata are tapped by man (in a well) or by nature (where a stream cuts through the surface), fresh water gushes forth with a clear and steady flow.

Legend has it that a search for a fountain of youth inspired the Spanish discovery of Florida in 1513. If so, the elusive fountain was very likely an artesian spring for there are more of them in Florida than anywhere else on earth. Ever since Columbus's first encounter with the native people of the Caribbean, the Spanish had heard tales that the source of eternal life could be found in a natural fountain on a large island called Bimini, north of Cuba. Given the many other fabulous discoveries in the New World, such stories seemed plausible. But the Spanish were preoccupied by the more immediate and tangible rewards of gold, silver and Indian slaves in the Southern Hemisphere. Few Spaniards bothered to explore north of their Caribbean island bases until 1513, when Juan Ponce de Léon, a former governor of Puerto Rico, set off on a voyage of discovery.

After a few weeks sail from Puerto Rico, Ponce de Léon reached the North American mainland at a point near present-day St Augustine on the Atlantic coast about 325 miles from the southern tip of the peninsula. He named the site of his landfall La Florida because his landing time – 2 April – was in the season of Easter, known in Spain as *Pascua de florida* (the feast of flowers). For the next 250 years, the term would apply to most of southern North America. The original name of Bimini was retained by the Bahamas and later given to a small cluster of islands 70 miles from Florida's eastern shore.

After claiming the new land for himself and Spain, Ponce de Léon proceeded south along the Atlantic coast. He soon encountered a strong, northbound current that 'did not permit the vessels to go forward although they put out all sails'. This was the Gulf Stream, a warm ocean current rising in the Gulf of Mexico, flowing up the East Coast of North America and then across the Atlantic to Europe. It was a discovery of tremendous importance, for it would soon become Spain's principal sea route from the West Indies. This, in turn, would attract some of the earliest French and English coastal settlements, from which enterprising buccaneers could raid Spain's treasure fleet.

Noting the northerly flow of the current, Ponce de Léon's expedition worked through the Gulf Stream and continued its journey south, passing through the Florida Keys and eventually making its way 225 miles up the west coast of the Florida peninsula as far as Tampa Bay. There, with supplies and morale running low due to repeated Indian attacks, the Spaniards decided to head for home. They stopped at a group of small islands, which they named the Dry Tortugas after the green sea turtles (*tortuga* in Spanish) that they found laying eggs on the dry, sandy beaches there. 'In one short time in the night', reported the expedition's chronicler, 'they took ... one hundred and sixty tortoises, and might have taken many more if they had wished. And also they took fourteen seals and there were killed many pelicans and other birds that amounted to five thousand'. Such plentiful wildlife, though useful in resupplying his expedition, was of no interest to Ponce de Léon. He had traveled north for more valuable finds. Instead of bearing youthful elixirs, slaves or gold, he and his men returned to Puerto Rico empty handed and bitterly disappointed, with only scars of Indian skirmish and wrinkles from the tropical sun.

Had Florida's discoverer been able to penetrate the land's interior from either coast, he might well have found one or more of the 300 artesian springs that had given rise to the stories of youthful regeneration. The Calusa Indians, who had blocked Ponce de Léon's inland travel and who would continue to discourage Spanish penetration of southern Florida for another century, were, of course, well acquainted with these miraculous fountains. They revered them not only as an endless source of pure water and year-round food, but as sacred places. The eternal life to which the Indians had alluded was almost certainly spiritual.

Traveling through Florida in the 1770s, the Philadelphia naturalist and writer William Bartram visited several of the area's artesian springs. Like the Calusa, he also perceived a spiritual quality, attributing their freshness, beauty and associated wildlife to the hand of a benevolent Supreme Creator. The largest of the Florida springs that Bartram saw was on the east bank of the Suwannee River where it still issues up to 49 000 gallons of water per minute. 'At noon we approached the admirable Manatee Springs', he wrote in a passage of his famous *Travels*,

> [It] is the product of primitive nature, not to be imitated much less equalled by the united effort of human power and ingenuity! . . .the waters appear of a lucid sea green colour, in some measure owing to the reflection of the leaves above . . .when the waters rush upwards, the surface of the bason immediately over the orifice is greatly swollen or raised a considerable height; and then it is impossible to keep the boat or any other floating vessel over the fountain; but the ebullition quickly subsides, yet, before the surface becomes quite even, the fountain vomits up the waters again, and so on perpetually. . . . The basin and stream [are] continually peopled with pro-digious numbers and variety of fish and other animals, as the alligator and the manate or sea cow, in the winter season; part of a skeleton of one, which the Indians had killed last winter, lay upon the banks of the spring; . . .this bone is esteemed equal to ivory; the flesh of this creature is counted whole-some and pleasant food; the Indians call them by a name which signifies the big beaver.

Christopher Columbus may have been the first European to see and describe the manatee when he noted that the 'mermaids' he had spotted off the coast of Haiti were 'not as beautiful as painted'. Today, greatly reduced in numbers,

Artesian springs such as this may have given rise to early legends about the fountain of youth.

The eighteenth-century naturalist William Bartram painted Florida's colorful inhabitants, including a scarlet snake eating a frog (right) and a purple finch (far right).

these large and gentle sea mammals can still be seen near Haiti and other islands of the Greater Antilles. Though more at home in the warmer waters of the Caribbean, they sometimes gather at Florida's springs in winter to feed on aquatic vegetation and warm themselves in the constant temperatures the springs provide.

While Florida's artesian springs may not be able to prolong human life as the Spanish once hoped, they have probably helped prolong the lives of some present-day manatees by providing safe haven for this now endangered species. They have also helped to preserve the remains of other long-departed visitors to the springs. The dissolved limestone and other minerals absorbed by the spring waters as they pass through the underground aquifers have fossilized the bones of saber-toothed cats, giant ground sloths, camels and other creatures that roamed the continent and drank at the springs some 10 000 years ago. Deep within the recesses of these giant pools, archeologists have also found human remains and some of the earliest examples of the weapons that helped give these early inhabitants the edge over the environment. Most important of these was the atl-atl, a spear-throwing device which dramatically increased man's efficiency in killing large mammals at the end of the ice age.

Ponce de Léon does not record the full range of weaponry used by the Calusa to hasten his departure from southern Florida, but a subsequent Spanish expedition, led by Pánfilo de Narváez in 1528, reported the Indians' proficiency with bows and arrows. Cabeza de Vaca, a member of the expedition who lived to record the events, described this typical exchange in which even the best Spanish armor was useless:

> *We were attacked by many Indians from behind trees who thus covered themselves that we might not get sight of them. . . . They drove their arrows with such effect that they wounded many men and horses. . . . The Indians we had so far seen in Florida are all archers. They go naked, are large of body, and appear at a distance like giants. They are of admirable proportions, very spare and of great activity and strength. The bows they use are as thick as the arm, of eleven or twelve palms in length, which they will discharge at two hundred paces with so great precision that they miss nothing.*

An adult manatee swims with its two calves in the warm and clear spring water of Florida's Crystal River. Columbus may have mistaken these 1300-pound mammals for mermaids. Local Indians considered them 'wholesome and pleasant food', and called them 'big beavers'.

Of the 300 Spanish soldiers and colonists who put ashore near Tampa Bay on Florida's west coast in April 1528, only five lived to tell the story of the disasters that ensued. They had survived Indian attack, shipwreck, injury, starvation, and nearly six years of living as slaves, traders and medicine men among the Indians. After Cabeza de Vaca, three other Spaniards, and a Moorish slave named Estévanico escaped from their Indian captors, they struggled on foot to the nearest Spanish settlements – over 1000 miles away in northern Mexico. Cabeza de Vaca's story, one of the most incredible in the history of New World explorations, provides a fascinating early look at Florida from a European point of view.

Despite the hardships he endured, de Vaca remained an unusually perceptive observer of his surroundings. At first he found the country 'very difficult to travel and wonderful to look upon. In it are vast forests, the trees being

astonishingly high'. After several more weeks of travel, de Vaca paused to describe what he had seen with more precision:

> *The country . . . is for the most part level, the ground of sand and stiff earth. Throughout are immense trees and open woods, in which are walnut, laurel, and another tree called liquid-amber [sweet gum], cedars, savins, evergreen oaks, pines, red-oaks, and palmitos like those of Spain. There are many lakes, great and small, over every part of it; some troublesome of fording, on account of depth and the great number of trees lying throughout them. . . . In this province are many maize fields; and the houses are scattered. . . . There are deer of three kinds, rabbits, hares, bears, lions, and other wild beasts. Among them we saw an animal with a pocket on its belly, in which it carries its young until they know how to seek food, and if it happen that they should be out feeding and any one come near, the mother will not run until she has gathered them in together. The country . . . has fine pastures for herds. Birds are of various kinds. Geese in great numbers. Ducks, mallards, royal-ducks, fly-catchers, night-herons and partridges abound. We saw many falcons, gerfalcons, sparrow-hawks, merlins and numerous other fowl.*

Written in another context de Vaca's descriptions might well have fulfilled Old World fantasies of New World paradise, but told in conjunction with the fiasco of Narváez's expedition, it did little to entice settlement in Florida. His rich list of plants and animals notwithstanding, de Vaca attributed the difficulties of the Narváez expedition to 'the poverty of the land', which he reported left even the Indians in perpetual starvation:

> *Occasionally they kill deer or fish, but the quantity is so small and the famine so great that they eat spiders and the eggs of ants, worms, lizards, salamanders, snakes, and vipers: they eat earth and wood, the dung of deer, and other things that I omit to mention.*

However, Ponce de Léon's failure and de Vaca's bleak report of life in Florida did not convince all Spaniards that this part of the New World would be any less productive than the Inca, Aztec and Maya lands from which they had already extracted great wealth. There were even suggestions that de Vaca and his fellow survivors had seen great treasures, which they would not reveal lest someone else claimed them before they themselves could return to do so.

Hernando de Soto, who had already looted a fortune from the Inca in Peru, was one who still believed there was gold to be had in Florida. After unsuccessfully trying to purchase de Vaca's services as a guide, de Soto set out in May 1539 to lead his own expedition force of 600 men on a gruelling four-year treasure hunt through the southeastern corner of the continent − from western Florida to the southern Appalachians and west across the Mississippi to the Great Plains. Forewarned by de Vaca's account of hardship, de Soto tried to redress the 'poverty of the land' by bringing his own livestock, including a small herd of pigs. By the end of one year the swine had multiplied from a group of 13 to a herd of 300. Despite many escapes and slaughterings, there were over

Immortalized in the lyrics of Stephen Foster's song 'Old Folks at Home', the Suwanee River (above left) winds 250 miles through western Florida from the Okefenokee Swamp in Georgia to the Gulf of Mexico. The battlegrounds, Indian villages and Spanish mission sites that once dotted its shores have long since returned to woodlands. Groves of live oaks (below left) are still common along its thickly forested banks.

During the dry winter months, the water in Florida's Everglades concentrates in deep pools and channels. In the rainy season 3500 square miles of sawgrass are flooded with up to a foot of slowly moving water. Among the Everglades' year-round residents are the poisonous water moccasin or cottonmouth (left) and the alligator snapping turtle (right).

99

1000 by the end of the trip. It is believed that they are the ancestors of the modern razorback hogs living in the southern swamplands today. De Soto's hogs fared better than his men. Half of the 600-man force, including de Soto himself, perished in their futile search for gold.

To the heavily armoured Spanish foot soldiers and cavalry who slogged through the swamps and forests of Florida in one disastrous expedition after another, the land must have seemed a hell on earth. Intense heat, wet, uneven terrain, thick vegetation, mosquitoes, and hostile Indians were just a few of the problems they had to endure. There were also venomous creatures – rattlesnakes, copperheads, water moccasins, scorpions and tarantulas – and rash-producing plants, such as poison ivy, poison sumac, and poison oak. For the Indian inhabitants, Florida was a very different place. The northern region contained fertile forest lands, cleared in many places and well suited to cultivation. The southern wetlands teemed with fish, fowl and other game.

The Calusa were the first people known to have explored the great swath of grass and water that bisects the lower tip of the Florida peninsula. By the time the Spanish began to probe its watery edges, the Calusa had long since learned to live in the area we now call the Everglades. On first appearance it may appear an inhospitable place, but to the Calusa it was a bountiful resource which could be harvested throughout the year.

The weather patterns of southern Florida more closely resemble those of the tropics than the rest of temperate America, for they divide the year into two, not four, seasons. During the wet season, from February to October, up to 50 inches of rain create in the Everglades one of the largest freshwater ecosystems in North America.

If the Everglades can be said to begin anywhere, it is in Lake Okeechobee, a 750-square-mile natural reservoir sitting a third of the way up Florida's peninsula. Shimmering with sunlight and reflected clouds, or lashed by the winds of a summer storm, the lake's surface seems to magnify its already impressive size. Its Seminole name means 'Big Water', an accurate title for although it is relatively shallow – only a few feet deep in places – it is the largest body of fresh water south of the Great Lakes.

The waters that feed Lake Okeechobee come from a chain of smaller lakes to the north by way of the Kissimmee River. As the rainy season saturates the land above it, Lake Okeechobee begins to rise and overflow its shallow banks. This infuses the already saturated swath of grassy swamplands south of the lake with more water than can be absorbed, thus turning the Everglades into an enormous freshwater river which runs slowly south, 100 miles from Lake Okeechobee to the Florida Bay. By midsummer, the flow is more than 50 miles wide, inundating some 3500 square miles of sawgrass and other vegetation with up to a foot of gently moving water.

The origin of the term 'Everglades' is not entirely clear. The earliest Spanish maps fail to record the great grassy river, noting only its outlet, which they call El Laguno del Espíritu Santo. An eighteenth-century surveyor, who may have seen the bright-green sawgrass with its flowing fresh water, described the area

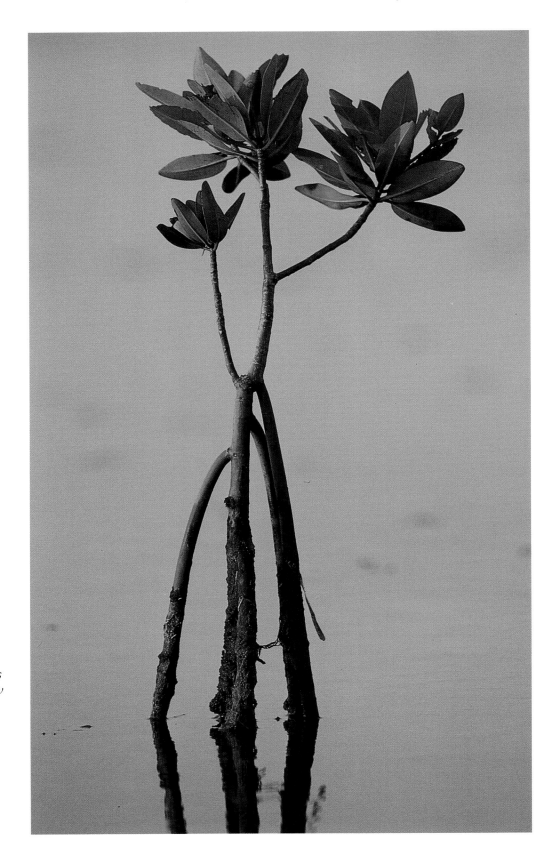

The advance guard in a succession of island-building plants, a young red mangrove establishes a foothold in shallow coastal waters. As debris and sediment catch in the plant's roots, the shoreline will extend and this pioneer, replaced by other species, will move farther into the ocean.

as 'River Glades' which on later maps became 'Ever Glades'. Was it simply a typographical error in transposition or did the new cartographers mean to imply perpetual open spaces of grass? Either term would accurately describe the region. Both came close to the Seminole Indian name for the place, Pa-hay-okee or 'Grassy Water'.

The sawgrass that covers up to 70 per cent of the Everglades, technically a water sedge, has three sharp edges set with fine, serrated teeth of silica that cut like points of glass. The plant grows, flowers and seeds in the rainy season, then dies back each winter as water levels drop. Its 10-foot blades fall and decompose, adding seasonally to the thick interwoven mat of roots and leaf litter that make up the wetland floor. Perched here and there on higher ground are small islands called hammocks, where slightly deeper soil and dryer footing support small stands of bald cypress, palmetto, and other plants. The hammocks, like the seasons, reflect a close tie to the tropics, for almost four fifths of the hammock plant species are also found in the West Indies.

During the November to February dry season, when less than 10 inches of rain falls in the Everglades, the flow of water slows, recedes, and concentrates in pools and channels throughout its course. As the sawgrass and other wetland vegetation dries, it becomes vulnerable to fires, which seasonally sweep the area, their destruction contained by the spider's web of troughs and gullies that remain water-filled throughout the year.

At the end of its long trickling course from Lake Okeechobee to the Mexican Gulf, the Everglades' water enters one of the largest mangrove swamps in the Americas. There, in a tangle of roots and branches, the fresh water of the wetlands meets the salt water of the sea. The mangroves begin above the high tide with a series of hammocks and forests of buttonwood. Although they are classed in a different family of plants, these trees are sometimes called white mangroves because they are such an important part of the mangrove community. Next, at the high tide line, grow the deep-rooted black mangroves, spiking the water from below with bristly organs that help the plants to breathe. The tree's dark green leaves exude salt crystals extracted by the tree from the water, while its roots tint the brackish pools and backwaters brown with tannin. Finally, extending well into the tidal zone, grow the pioneers of this swampland – the red mangroves. Their entwined and interlocking roots nurture and buttress trunks that can reach 7 feet in circumference and stand as high as 80 feet above the water. The roots of the red mangrove, encrusted with oysters and snails, break the force of each incoming wave. As the water recedes, they catch whatever debris the ocean is carrying, and deposit them with their own decaying leaves and any freshwater detritus that has entered the swamp from the inland side. Eventually, the accumulated debris raise the land level enough for the black mangrove to take root. As the coastline grows, the red mangrove moves on, continuing its steady invasion of the sea.

At the time of first Spanish contact, the versatile Calusa Indians ranged through both the Everglades and the mangrove swamps, as well as the higher ground that flanks them. Based in sedentary villages composed of several dozen to several hundred individuals, the Calusa had a highly stratified society with nobles, commoners, and serfs. Unlike most of Florida's other Indians, the Calusa were not agriculturalists, but relied instead on wild plants and animals to support themselves. In the pine forests, the Calusa harvested foot-tall cycads with yellow and orange cone-like flowers. They grated and dried the fleshy roots, and with this flour made bread and a starchy gruel. Local residents now call the plant coontie, or compte. To outsiders it is known as arrowroot, and is used by cooks worldwide for thickening soups and gravy.

The Calusa ate cabbage palm flowers and also its bitter fruits, which one English castaway said tasted like 'nothing else but rotten cheese steeped in tobacco'. More tasty were the wild beach plums, sea grapes, prickly pear cactus, and custard apples. There were also coconuts, bananas, and a wide array of other plants to serve as foods and medicines.

One of the few Europeans to witness the Calusa way of life first-hand was Hernando d'Escalante Fontaneda who, in 1545, survived the shipwreck of a Spanish galleon off the Florida coast. Fontaneda, aged 13, and his older brother were on their way from the island of Cartagena to Spain for schooling when their ship foundered in the Florida Keys. A few members of the stricken ship's crew survived the wreck and the dangerous swim to the mainland only to be killed by the Calusa or lost in the maze of mangrove swamps that lined the shore. Fontaneda was more fortunate. He was captured by the Calusa and adopted as their own. He learned their language, their customs, and their skills of survival in the Florida swamplands during his 17-year stay. At the age of 30, Fontaneda was rescued by French colonists on Florida's upper east coast, and returned to Spain, where he wrote down all he could remember of the extraordinary life he had led.

Fish, he reported, were the most important part of the Calusa diet. Hundreds of varieties, then as now, fed in the mangroves and schooled over the mudflats of the Florida Keys. Some may have been caught in nets and preserved in large holding pools until needed. Others were netted or speared and eaten outright. From freshwater rivers, Fontaneda noted, the Calusa harvested 'quantities of eels, very savoury, and enormous trout. The eels are nearly the size of a man, and as thick as the thigh'.

Another important part of the Calusa diet was made up of shellfish – oysters, clams, crabs, Caribbean lobsters, starfish, sea urchins, and the queen conch. One of the world's largest marine snails, a full-grown queen conch may have a shell more than a foot long and weigh more than 5 pounds. The Calusa extracted the conch's rubbery white meat by cutting a hole in the back of its shell and breaking its strong muscular attachments. They shaped the shells of some into tools and weapons, or used them as weights for their fishing nets. Thousands more they discarded, making shell mounds or middens up to 70 acres in size and 15 feet deep. Recent excavations of the Calusa shell middens and village sites have confirmed the tribe's heavy dependence on seafood. More than 30 species of fish, including sharks and rays, and more than 15 species of mollusk and crustacean have been identified among the archeological remains.

An undisturbed alligator shares its back and a spot of sunlight with a water turtle. Both species depend on external sources of warmth to raise their internal temperatures.

During a visit to Florida in 1565, the French artist Jacques Le Moyne de Morgues witnessed and recorded an alligator hunt by Indians (below).

The Calusa found many other foods to supplement their diet, some of which Fontaneda recorded with disapproval:

The Indians also eat legartos and snakes, and animals like rats which live in the lake, freshwater tortoises, and many other disgusting reptiles which, if we were to continue enumerating, we should never be through.

The most obvious of the 'disgusting reptiles' to which Fontaneda referred were the American crocodile, a now endangered saltwater species which can grow up to 25 feet long, and its more common and slightly smaller freshwater relative, the American alligator, whose name derives from the Spanish *legarto* or lizard. The alligator, like the fish it feeds upon, retreats to the deep water refuges of the Everglades and neighboring cypress swamps in times of drought. In doing so it inadvertently provides a valuable service for other forms of wildlife. By moving back and forth within the Everglades' connected ponds and channels, the alligator actually helps to keep these areas open during critical low-water periods. The resulting alligator holes become gathering points for many other wetland creatures, including egrets, herons, ibises, spoonbills, muskrats, otters and wintering waterfowl.

The Calusa and other Indians within the alligator's range valued the reptile for its meat and leather, but for obvious reasons feared its size and strength. The French artist Jacques Le Moyne de Morgues, who came to Florida in 1564, described and illustrated one Indian tribe's method of killing the alligator:

They take with them a ten-foot pointed pole, and when they come upon the monster – who usually crawls along with open mouth, ready to attack – they push the pole quickly down its throat. The rough tree bark of its sides prevents the pole from slipping out again. Then the beast is turned over on its back and killed by beating it with clubs and piercing its soft belly with arrows.

Working as a team against the alligator, as Le Moyne describes, the Indians were usually successful. One-to-one the odds were considerably less favorable. Francisco Vázquez de Coronado lost one of his men to an alligator while crossing a southern river in June 1542 and the Indians undoubtedly had similar experiences. Le Moyne reported that they lived in constant fear of attack:

The alligators are such a menace that a regular watch has to be kept against them day and night. The Indians guard themselves against these animals just as we guard ourselves from our most dangerous enemies.

Even William Bartram, who generally found wildlife more praiseworthy than loathsome, developed a mistrust and life-long fear of the alligator. No one could blame him after his experience near the St Johns River in northeastern Florida in May, 1774:

The evening was temperately cool and calm. [The alligators] began to roar and appear in uncommon numbers along the shores and in the river. ... I therefore furnished myself with a club for my defence, went on board [my boat], and penetrating the first line of those which surrounded my harbour, they gave way; but being pursued by several very large ones, I kept strickly on the watch, and paddled with all my might towards the entrance of the lagoon, hoping to be sheltered there from the multitude of my assailants; but ere I had half-way reached the place, I was attacked on all sides, several endeavouring to overset the canoe. My situation now became precarious to the last degree: two very large ones attacked me closely, at the same instant, rushing up with their heads and part of their bodies above the water, roaring terribly and belching floods of water over me. They struck their jaws together so close to my ears, as almost to stun me, and I expected every moment to be dragged out of the boat and instantly devoured. . . .

Bartram fled to his campsite pursued by a particularly aggressive bull alligator, which he later dispatched 'by lodging the contents of my gun in his head'.

By the time of Bartram's travels, European disease, slaving and punitive raids by the Spanish had ended the Calusa's control of southern Florida. From a powerful tribe of some 14 000 people in 1692, they had been reduced to a few scattered bands by the middle of the eighteenth century. Remarkably, they managed to keep their social structure and ideology intact to the very end. The only tangible remains of their once flourishing communities are their conch-shell middens and a set of extraordinary masks, implements and carvings unearthed from a peat bog on Marco Island in the Florida Keys in 1885. Exquisitely carved heads of pelicans and sea turtles that were used as floats for fishing nets may have been purely decorative, or may have had significance as totems, clan emblems or even charms designed to help ensure a bigger catch. Other carvings reflect creatures of the mainland: heads of wolves, deer, and alligators, and the full length figure of a kneeling cat. We will probably never know their meaning.

The Calusa were but one of many native groups to suffer at the hands of the Spanish. The conquistadores, steeped in the military practices with which they had successfully ousted the Moors from Spain, treated most of their exploratory incursions of new lands as military conquests. Their inhuman treatment of the Indians was as appallingly brutal as any in the history of warfare. Hernando de Soto, a man 'much given to the sport of hunting Indians', enjoyed throwing his terrified captives to the pack of savage and powerful dogs that accompanied his army to Florida in 1539. When Indians failed to produce the gold he was looking for, De Soto had no compunction about chopping off their hands, feet or heads to encourage better cooperation from their friends and relatives.

While de Soto and others were trying to extract fortunes from Florida's Indians by force, Spain's Catholic missionaries were more peacefully at work on the peninsula attempting to convert the inhabitants to Christianity. By 1635 they had already established some 40 mission stations among the predominantly agricultural Timucua and Apalachee of northern Florida and the Guale of Georgia. More than 30 000 Indians eventually converted and gathered around the mission stations for protection and trade.

'The commodities of this land are more than are yet known to any man,' wrote Sir John Hawkins of Florida in 1565. 'It flourisheth with meadow, pasture ground, with woods of Cedar and Cypress, and other sorts, as better can not be in the world.' Among the wildlife observed by Hawkins were undoubtedly white-tailed deer, seen here enjoying the warmth of the after-noon sun, and turtles.

Yet by 1690 the pressure of slave raids from the British colonies of the Carolinas had led the Spanish to withdraw their northern missions to an area near St Augustine, and by 1705 the entire endeavor had collapsed. Some of the Indian converts fled south, joined at times by Africans escaping slavery on the English colonial plantations. The restructured groups, living in the comparative safety of Florida's swamps, called themselves Ikanivksalgi, 'the people of the peninsula'. To the outside world they became known as Seminoles, which may have come from the Spanish word *cimarrón*, 'runaways', or from a Creek word meaning 'outlander' or 'far from the fires of the old towns'. Certainly all three descriptions applied.

Like the Calusa, whose dwindling numbers they may have absorbed, the Seminoles learned to exploit the wildlife of the swamps and coastline. Conch, fish, turtle, deer, bear, turkey and ducks of various kinds helped to sustain the new arrivals. The Seminoles also brought with them farming practices that the Calusa never knew. They planted corn, peas and beans in any dry places they could find. Indeed, the word 'hammock' is Seminole for 'garden place'. To these traditional crops were added new ones. Limes, lemons and sour oranges, acquired from the Spanish missions, grew wild in the Everglades. Bananas, plantains and manioc soon also contributed to the newcomers' tropical economy.

As the Seminoles accustomed themselves to the new environmental conditions of Florida, the political turmoil in their northern homelands continued. This was principally a result of the region's rapidly expanding plantation system which required a large work force and so indirectly encouraged slave raids on Indian settlements throughout the Southeast.

Rice, introduced to South Carolina from Africa in the 1680s and 90s, and indigo from the West Indies had joined tobacco as important plantation crops. The cultivation of rice required not only a great deal of physical toil but also specialized knowledge of its cultivation. For this reason, black slaves from the rice-growing windward coast of Africa (from Sierra Leone to the Ivory Coast) were preferred. They could be obtained directly from Africa for cash and agricultural produce, or from the West Indies in exchange for Indian slaves. European slave merchants therefore encouraged wars between Indian tribes, surreptitiously providing arms and ammunition to both sides in exchange for prisoners who could then be used immediately or bartered for the desired Africans. A South Carolina census of 1708 shows 1400 Indian slaves and more than four times that number of blacks. Together, the colony's slave populations exceeded that of the free whites, and these large work forces dramatically affected the use of land.

Before European settlement, small groups of semi-nomadic people had ranged over large areas of the Southeast, subsisting on a wide variety of native foods and small, scattered agricultural plots. With the advent of the plantation system, a large number of permanently housed people depended on a smaller variety of foods grown in more concentrated areas. Domesticated livestock, unknown to native Americans, provided a stable source of protein without the need for hunting trips. As trade among the colonies grew more sophisticated and subsistence farming gave way to monocultures, such as rice and tobacco, cash crops paid for what the plantation owners did not grow. A cash economy, in turn, led to increased specialization, the growth of urban centers, and the emergence of a white middle class.

Additional wealth and leisure gave colonists a chance to purchase some of the intellectual and cultural activities being enjoyed by the highest levels of European society; books became more widely available, schools and colleges were established and artists began to find patrons for their skills with pencil and brush.

Natural history, though a topic of growing academic interest in Europe, lagged behind other disciplines in eighteenth-century America. Practical knowledge of American plants for medicinal or agricultural purposes had been valued since the time of earliest settlement, but a more abstract interest in American nature for its own sake was rarely considered or expressed. The first person to make a concerted study of North American natural history was Mark Catesby. He was an English naturalist who came to Virginia in 1712 to visit his sister in Williamsburg, the colony's capital. So pleased was Catesby with life in the colonies that he stayed for seven years. In Virginia and on extended trips west into the Appalachians and south to Jamaica and other Caribbean islands, Catesby indulged his life-long fascination with nature by observing, collecting and sketching the plants and wildlife he encountered.

When he returned to England in 1719, he shared his findings with his family and friends, including a small group of influential amateur naturalists. The group had for years discussed the desirability of sponsoring a comprehensive, scientific survey of the flora and fauna of the Americas. At their urging, and with the support of the Royal Society of London, Catesby returned to America in February 1722 to embark on three years of exploration in the southeastern regions of the continent. Though trained as a botanist, Catesby took care to note every aspect of the country through which he traveled. In his field journals and letters to home, he remarked on everything from bird migration to catastrophic autumn storms. 'About the middle of September here', he reported to one of his patrons, 'fell the greatest flood attended with a Hurricane that has been known since the country was settled. Great numbers of Cattle, Horses, Hogs, and some people were drowned. The Deer were found frequently lodged on high trees.'

Catesby prided himself on gathering his information from firsthand observation, but sometimes his experiences were a bit too close for comfort. On one occasion, the naturalist's breakfast was interrupted by the screams of a servant who had discovered a rattlesnake in his recently vacated bed. Catesby rushed to the bedroom where he saw the snake

actually between the sheets in the very place where I lay, full of ire, biting at everything that approached him. Probably it crept in for warmth in the night, but how long I had the company of the charming bedfellow, I am not able to say.

Cupressus Americana Park 1076

Catesby began his studies in Charleston, South Carolina, where he found very little known about natural history 'except that related to Commerce, such as Rice, Pitch and Tar'. He found equally fruitful grounds for study as he traveled south through Georgia and into Florida. While he focused most of his efforts along the coastal areas where transportation was easiest, he also ventured well into the 'uninhabited parts of the Country' with gratifying results. 'I was much delighted to see Nature differ in these Upper Parts', he wrote after a visit to the foothills of the Smoky Mountains

and to find here abundance of things not to be seen in the lower parts of the Country. This encouraged me to take several Journeys with the Indians higher up the Rivers, towards the Mountains, which afforded not only a succession of new vegetable Appearances, but the most delightful Prospects imaginable, besides the Diversion of Hunting Buffaloes, Bears, Panthers, and other wild Beasts.

In the course of his three years of travel, Catesby collected hundreds of plant specimens, which he sent to England alive in tubs of earth or as study specimens pressed between sheets of absorbent paper. He would later use these plants as models for his illustrations, associating them with the birds, mammals and other creatures he had seen and studied during his various collecting trips.

He returned to England in 1725, and spent the next 20 years producing his landmark book, *The Natural History of Carolina, Florida, and the Bahama Islands*, which he published in sections, 20 plates at a time, from 1731 to 1743. Catesby's *Natural History*, which featured 220 of his own illustrations and a lively text in English and French, was to remain the most comprehensive publication on the natural history of North America for more than 50 years. It is still one of the most pleasing. Among the many plants first described, illustrated or introduced to European cultivation by Mark Catesby are: the catalpa, umbrella tree, pawpaw, dahoon holly, mock orange, pink dogwood, sour black-gum, tupelo gum, pignut, water oak, and palmetto.

Although Mark Catesby never visited the Everglades, he would have recognized most of its wildlife. Much of what he illustrated and described from other parts of the Southeast were common in Florida's swamps. As habitat destruction and hunting pressures increased elsewhere, some species sought refuge, like the Seminoles, in the Everglades that white men seemed to shun.

Then in the nineteenth century, after changing hands from Spanish to English and then back to Spanish, Florida was purchased by the government of the United States. In the 1820s and 30s, Americans promoted settlement in their new territory and the Seminoles were perceived as an obstacle to progress, as obstinate and savage as the land itself. At first they were forced further south to a 7800-square-mile tract where the government promised 'protection against all persons whomsoever and to restrain and prevent all white persons from hunting, settling, and otherwise intruding upon their lands'. But increasing pressure from would-be settlers led to blatant infractions, and soon new treaties were drafted, offering to relocate the Seminoles in Arkansas. When the Seminoles refused to move,

In his pioneering work The Natural History of Carolina, Florida, and the Bahama Islands (1731–43), *the English naturalist Mark Catesby provided the first color plates of North America's wildlife. Several of the birds he illustrated, including the once-plentiful Carolina parakeet (above) and the ivory-billed woodpecker, have become extinct. Other species such as the globe fish and the bullfrog are still common.*

battle lines formed in the shifting sawgrass of the Everglades, and from 1835 to 1842 a bloody war raged through the once quiet swampland. The effort cost 20 000 000 dollars in military expenses and the lives of 1500 American troops. No one knows how many Indian lives were lost. The Seminole who were not killed or sent west by the end of the war stayed on in the Everglades, where their descendants still live.

In the mid-nineteenth century, the wildlife of America, like its indigenous people, suffered from the press of expanding settlement and technological advance. Following the nation's Civil War, an increased demand for building supplies brought on an extensive period of deforestation. At the same time, improvements in railroad transportation and firearm technology fostered by the war made bird shooting and mammal hunting more widely available and effective. To the vanquished Southerners, wild food became even more important than earlier. To Northerners, the booming economy brought increased leisure time and the resources to enjoy it. Thus, the birds and mammals Catesby had described as abundant in the 1720s had grown scarce by the end of the next century. Some would disappear altogether.

In Catesby's day the passenger pigeon, whose massive flocks had fed Cartier, Champlain, and the colonies at Roanoke, Jamestown, and Plymouth, still darkened the sky and 'broke down the limbs of oaks with their weight'. By 1914 they were completely gone, the victims of lumbermen, commercial gunners and casual sportsmen. The Carolina parakeet, once common throughout the Southeast, suffered the same fate a few years later. Its fondness for fruit and its gregarious social behavior doomed it to extermination by the guns of American orchardists. The last wild flocks may well have sought refuge in the cypress swamps bordering the Everglades.

The ivory-billed woodpecker, a more secretive inhabitant of southern swamplands, managed to survive longer. This crow-sized bird with a brilliant red crest was dubbed *carpintero* by the Spanish, who watched it hammering tree trunks in an endless search for ants and termites. 'Nature ... so formed their bills', wrote Catesby, 'that in an hour or two they will raise a bushel of chips.' Human pressures and the increased harvest of trees still in their prime brought a slow but steady decline to the ivory-bill, the largest of the North American woodpeckers. Though a few pairs of a variant of the species still survive in Cuba, the North American ivory-bill no longer hammers, calls or flies in the continent's southern swamps.

In the closing decades of the nineteenth century, many more birds came close to extermination as hundreds of thousands of migratory birds were shot for sport and sale. The shorebirds – plovers, sandpipers and curlews – were especially vulnerable because their habit of gathering in dense flocks made them easy targets. They were salted, packed in barrels, and sent to markets up and down the East Coast. Even songbirds were taken for this purpose. During one week in the spring of 1897, 2600 robins shot in North Carolina were offered for sale in a single shop in Washington, D.C. Many were taken as ornaments, to be stuffed and displayed in Victorian drawing rooms. Some birds were shot as

The purple flowers of swamp coreopsis (above right) surround a stand of yellow trumpet pitcher plants. The tube-shaped leaves of the taller species help this carnivorous plant to trap insects and thereby augment the nutrient deficiencies of the wetland soils in which it grows.

The roseate spoonbill (right) and great blue heron (far right) are among Florida's most conspicuous water birds. Along with other large wading birds, they were once aggressively hunted for their feathers. Both birds are now protected by law.

threats to crops or livestock. Some were simply shot for fun. Since the first European settlements, eastern North America had seen open season on virtually every form of wildlife. As the technology of destruction improved, wildlife diminished still further.

The slaughter took longer to reach the Florida Everglades, but eventually even this secluded sanctuary echoed to the crack of gunfire and the thuds of falling birds. Drawn by the abundance of food and protected habitat, the Everglades had long been the preferred breeding ground of many of North America's most spectacular wading birds: great blue herons, and their rare relatives, the great whites, black- and yellow-crowned night herons, little blue and green herons, white and glossy ibises, great, snowy, and reddish egrets, even the brilliant roseate spoonbills. In breeding time the males of some species, most notably the egrets, grow special display feathers called aigrettes, which are used to attract the attention of females. In the 1870s and 80s they attracted the attention of less welcome suitors – the plume hunters. In a violent and bloody Everglades harvest lasting many years, countless thousands of the birds were killed at breeding time so that their elegant feathers could be used to embellish ladies' hats worldwide. The killing almost extinguished the egrets before public opinion turned against it.

The efforts to stop the killing were led by a Massachusetts conservation group named after John James Audubon, the artist, author and America's first great popularizer of birds. In England there were precedents for such an organization – the Selbourne Society and the Royal Society for the Protection of Birds – but the Massachusetts Audubon Society was North America's first conservation organization devoted to bird preservation. The idea caught on, and within two years there were separate Audubon societies in 15 other states from New York to California. Their combined influence and the work of other conservation groups helped to pass a series of game laws protecting not only the egrets but also shorebirds, waterfowl, songbirds and many other migrating species. In 1903, President Theodore Roosevelt created the first National Wildlife Refuge at Pelican Island, a once threatened breeding colony of brown pelicans just off the eastern coast of Florida.

The dawning of the conservation movement, too late for some species, did help to slow the uncontrolled decimation of others. But America's consumption and destruction of the land itself continued virtually unchecked. Attitudes toward subduing the wilderness, articulated by the first European settlers, were still widespread. Many believed that much of Florida in its natural state was worthless. There was money to be made there, but something first had to be done about improving the inhospitable nature of the peninsula's southern tip. It was time to drain the Everglades.

Calls for such action had been made since before the Civil War, but by 1905 the technology, finances and local sentiment had combined to make it possible. Napoleon Bonaparte Broward, one of many proponents of reclamation, was elected governor of Florida in that year largely on the strength of his pledge to drain the 'worthless swamplands'. He promised to create 'The Empire of the

Everglades' from the Seminoles' 'Grassy Water'. 'Look at Egypt and the Nile. Look at Holland', Broward proclaimed:

> *Shall the sovereign people of Florida …supinely confess that they cannot knock a hole in a wall of coral and let a body of water obey a natural law and seek the level of the sea? To answer yes to such a question is to prove ourselves unworthy of freedom, happiness or prosperity.*

The drive for prosperity began at once, with dredging, digging channels, and dynamiting age-old formations of rock and coral. Miami real estate worth 2 dollars an acre before the undertaking sold for 15 times that amount within a year. Two decades later, in 1927, a road was completed from east to west across the Everglades, from Miami to Naples and on north to Tampa. Combining the names of its termini, developers called it the Tamiami Trail.

Human technology could do much to manipulate the physical features of the Everglades, but it could not control the weather. In 1928 a hurricane similar to the one Catesby had described 200 years before, leveled 2000 houses in Miami and inundated much of southern Florida with water. To prevent future flooding caused by hurricane-driven rains, the Army Corps of Engineers was called in to construct 1500 miles of drainage canals in the Everglades. In rural areas, sugar-cane was planted where sawgrass once grew. As habitats for people and new crops increased, areas for wildlife declined; and the fresh water that supported both was drained away.

Prior to the Everglades' channeling, the fresh water moving south from Lake Okeechobe balanced the invasion of salt water from Florida Bay. By the early 1940s, with the partial drainage of the Everglades, the salt water was working inland at a rate of 235 feet per year, and in periods of drought it was invading at four times that rate. Southern Florida and its development was sowing the seeds for disaster. Then, in 1947, what was left of the Everglades was given national protection. The largest remaining subtropical wilderness in North America, Everglades National Park is not only a refuge for wildlife and a living laboratory for ecological study, it is also a vital safeguard for Florida's future. By helping to hold the ocean's salt water at bay, it preserves fresh water essential for the human populations that once threatened to drain it.

Today the Everglades are again on the verge of destruction. As more and more fresh water is pumped from the ground to supply the municipal and recreational needs of southern Florida, it is replaced by nutrient-rich waters from surrounding agricultural lands. These, in turn, have spawned an explosive growth of plants that were never a part of the Everglades ecosystem. Spreading at a rate of 4 acres a day, new, exotic species of plants are clogging waterways, robbing them of oxygen and crowding out indigenous wildlife. The National Audubon Society estimates that the egrets and other long-legged wading birds that came so close to destruction at the hands of plume hunters have declined in number by 90 per cent since the 1920s. Whether they and the Everglades can survive the pressures of the twenty-first century will depend upon events and decisions well beyond the boundaries of the park.

OVERLEAF Morning mist silhouettes the giant cypress trees that characterize Louisiana's great Atchafalaya Swamp, largest in the Southeast. River channelization and other government-sponsored flood control projects threaten to deny this rich wildlife habitat adequate supplies of fresh water.

ACROSS THE SEA OF GRASS
THE · PRAIRIES · AND · GREAT · PLAINS

The eastern forests of North America were so extensive at the time of first European contact that it is said an ambitious squirrel with an inclination to travel could have passed from the Atlantic coast to the Mississippi River without ever putting paw to ground. No squirrel has ever harbored such ambitions – most pass their lives in a territory a few acres in size – but if one had, its journey would have been much farther than the 800 miles separating the two bodies of water. Forest areas cleared by Indians for agriculture, cut and flooded by beavers, or opened by wildfire, hurricanes, and blight gave many eastern woodlands an open, park-like appearance quite unlike the mass of tangled wilderness commonly imagined.

Such game-rich openings notwithstanding, it was the forests themselves that most impressed Europeans. A seemingly endless supply of tall, strong timber, free to anyone with the strength and will to harvest it, gave new settlers a sense of wealth undreamed of in the timber-poor lands from which they had come. 'A poor servant here that is to possesse but 50 acres of land', wrote one seventeenth-century New Englander, 'may afford to give more wood for Timber and Fire as good as the world yields, than many Noble men in England can afford to do.'

For all the timber harvested to make houses, fences, ships' masts and furniture, and all the woodlands burned to clear land for agriculture, the greatest use of America's forests during the colonial period was for fuel. The Swedish naturalist Peter Kalm, who traveled from Pennsylvania to Quebec in 1749, remarked that 'an incredible amount of wood is really squandered in this country for fuel; day and night all winter, or for nearly half of the year, in all rooms, a fire is kept going'. The average New England household probably consumed as much as an acre of forest or 40 cords of firewood per year. That is a stack of wood roughly 4 feet wide, 4 feet high, and 300 feet long.

As one might expect, the effects of firewood and timber harvests up and down the East Coast were considerable. By the end of the eighteenth century, large portions of the eastern forest had been leveled. 'Our timber trees are greatly reduced, and quite gone in many parts,' lamented George Washington's friend and fellow general, Benjamin Lincoln, shortly after the American Revolution:

> In towns near and bordering on the sea shore, little can now be found within the distance of twenty miles; and it is not uncommon for the builder to send at this day from thirty to forty miles for timber and planks, and the stock fast decreasing, not only from the demand of timber and planks, but from scarcity of other fuel.

Apart from the inconvenience to settlers, the deforestation had a significant effect on wildlife, reducing suitable habitats for many species and improving conditions for others. Among the species of birds to actually gain from the clearing of the land were robins, barn swallows, purple martins, quail and mourning doves. White-tailed deer and cottontail rabbits also benefited, though growing hunting pressures more than offset the advantage for these popular game animals.

As the forests gave way to open fields, a new community of wildflowers began to flourish. Some, like goldenrod, New England aster, common fleabane and black-eyed Susan, were native plants already adapted to open spaces. Many more were alien species imported by accident or design. Most of these are still among North America's most common field flowers, including Queen Anne's lace, ox-eye daisy, yarrow, purple loosestrife, orange hawkweed, sow-thistle, and the ubiquitous dandelion. Another tenacious import, the common plantain, was called 'whiteman's foot' by the Indians, for it seemed to spring up wherever Europeans trod. It now flourishes in open spaces across the continent.

The early cutting of eastern forests had other effects less noticeable at first, but potentially more serious than wildlife and vegetation changes. 'Our Runs dry up apace,' noted an environmentally alert Pennsylvanian homesteader in 1753.

> Several which formerly would turn a fulling Mill, are now scarce sufficient for the Use of a Farm, the Reason of which is this: when the Country was cover'd with Woods & the Swamps with Brush, the Rain that fell was detain'd by these Interruptions.

Reduced vegetation meant reduced groundwater. This, in turn, led to the drying up of streams. The same factors also tended to raise temperatures, increase droughts, and predispose lands to flooding.

Despite these ecological changes, the removal of the forest was seen as a welcome improvement to most transplanted Europeans. It not only fulfilled the biblical command to subdue the earth, it made life seem more secure. Many settlers had felt threatened by North America's woodlands, for such extensive forests had not existed in the Old World for centuries. The newly created pastures and farmlands were closer to the agricultural conditions that first-generation settlers had known at home. Moreover, they permitted the use of

RIGHT The settlers who moved into the Great Plains from the forested lands of the East were overwhelmed by the openness of the prairies and the abundance of wildflowers. Changing patterns of land use have since reduced the number of wildflower species found in many parts of the Midwest.

OVERLEAF Despite English laws which prohibited migration beyond the Appalachians, a steady flow of pioneers pushed west at the end of the French and Indian, or Seven Years' War (1763). The Cumberland Gap, which lies at the juncture of Virginia, Kentucky and Tennessee, was the most popular of several natural breaches in the Appalachians' otherwise formidable physical barrier to western movement.

imported European implements and farming techniques. European settlers were slowly but surely remaking the New World in the image of the Old.

While most colonists looked on their accomplishments with pride, there were some who preferred less settled areas, and others who, as second and third generation Americans or recent arrivals to the continent, sought new land to tame for themselves. These restless spirits looked westward to the forests of the Appalachian frontier. Beyond these they would eventually find another land as different from the eastern woodlands as those woodlands had been from the landscape of Europe.

The first great barrier to their movement was, ironically, the very same geographical feature that had permitted the easy north-south movements of plants and animals during the climatic changes of the ice age. By the mid-eighteenth century, colonists, increasingly hungry for land, found the Appalachian Mountains a frustrating block to western expansion. British policy-makers, on the other hand, viewed the mountain range more positively: it ensured a relatively restricted, natural, easily accessible and defensible concentration of settlements along the Atlantic coast. Florida and Canada, without this geographic barrier, tended to have more widely scattered settlements and never achieved the cohesion of England's mid-Atlantic colonies.

When Great Britain won sovereignty over the eastern half of the previously French-controlled Mississippi Valley at the end of the Seven Years' War (1763), many Anglo-American colonists decided it was time to breach the Appalachians and push West (despite a Parliamentary ban on such migration). What these pioneers encountered at first – in Kentucky, Tennessee, western Pennsylvania, Ohio, and in all the regions just beyond the gaps of the Appalachians – were forested areas quite similar to those they had known back East. Nevertheless, because the lands were new and, despite the Indian presence, perceived as free for the taking, settlers often attached to the territories many of the naively romantic notions that their forebears had attributed to the coastal lands of the New World. In *The Discovery, Settlement and Present State of Kentucke* (1784), for example, John Filson describes the frontier country beyond the Cumberland Gap as a 'land of promise, flowing with milk and honey, a land of brooks of water . . . a land of wheat and barley, and all kinds of fruits', where new settlers would 'eat bread without scarceness and not lack any thing in it'.

Such promotional enthusiasm aside, life was no easier on the trans-Appalachian frontier than it had been along the Atlantic coast a century and a half before. The significant difference was that these settlers were more experienced and so better prepared to take advantage of the resources at hand.

The resources were clearly abundant. In addition to white-tailed deer, hunters found the large browsing mammals that had been eliminated from most lands east of the Appalachians – elk, wood bison, and, in northern areas, moose. There, too, were turkeys 'so over-burthened with fat that they flew with difficulty' and ruffed grouse or partridge which filled the forest with the sound of drumming wings each spring and autumn as they engaged in territorial displays. In wetter ground were woodcock or timber doodles, renowned for their early springtime courtship flights and for the tastiness of their meat. Also present but unwelcome were the large and potentially troublesome predators: the timber wolf and cougar.

The settlers who flowed through the Appalachians and pushed west into the Ohio and Mississippi valleys began to notice changes in the land. The thick deciduous forests of the uplands, boasting walnut trees, chestnuts, sycamores, and oaks 6 feet or more in diameter and hundreds of feet high, gave way to more open terrain. Clearings, confusingly named 'barrens', and meadows carpeted with grasses, wildflowers, wild rye, and wild oats, broke the woodlands with increasing frequency. In the area now known as Illinois, early settlers reported the country 'intersected with a vast number of creeks and streams, and interspersed with prairies of natural meadows, containing from 1000 to 100 000 acres. They are very irregular in figure and are dotted and clumped with trees, like English parks'.

As the settlers established themselves in parts of present-day Indiana, Illinois, and in the lands west of the Mississippi River, they found so much open grassland that trees, not meadows, became the exceptional features worth mentioning in letters and diaries. They had reached the American tallgrass prairie. There, Indian grass, big bluestem and cord grasses of various sorts rose higher than a person on horseback and extended farther than the eye could see.

Beyond the Missouri, at about the 100th meridian, the soil became drier and more sandy. The tallgrass prairie merged with shorter, mixed grasses, including little bluestem, June grass, needle grass, and western wheatgrass 2–4 feet high. Farther west, in parts of what would become Nebraska, Kansas, Montana, Wyoming and Colorado, these midgrasses merged with the shortgrasses. There, buffalo grass and blue grama grass, only a few inches in height, thrived where few other plants could grow. They covered the gently rolling country in a land receiving less than 20 inches of rain a year.

Just how to describe this new terrain was a question at first. French fur trappers probing south and west from the Great Lakes region had called it all prairie, their word for meadow. This term was quickly adopted by Anglo-Americans, but primarily for referring to the tallgrass areas of the east. The midgrass and shortgrass regions closer to the Rockies were described by early explorers as the Great American Desert because of the low rainfall they received. In time they became more generally known as the Great Plains. The terms prairie and plains, therefore, held vegetative or climatic and geographic distinctions for some, while others used them interchangeably.

Whatever they called it, the tallgrass region in the middle of North America came as a shock to those whose lives had been spent in the shadows of the great eastern forests. 'I am at a loss to account for the formation of these extraordinary meadows,' wrote one new arrival. Ecologists are still at a loss to explain them. The prairie appears to have developed at the end of the ice age when the midwestern climate was much drier than it is today. Grasses, which can tolerate the winds of the Midwest and which require less moisture than trees because of their smaller surface area and shorter growing season, were well suited to the

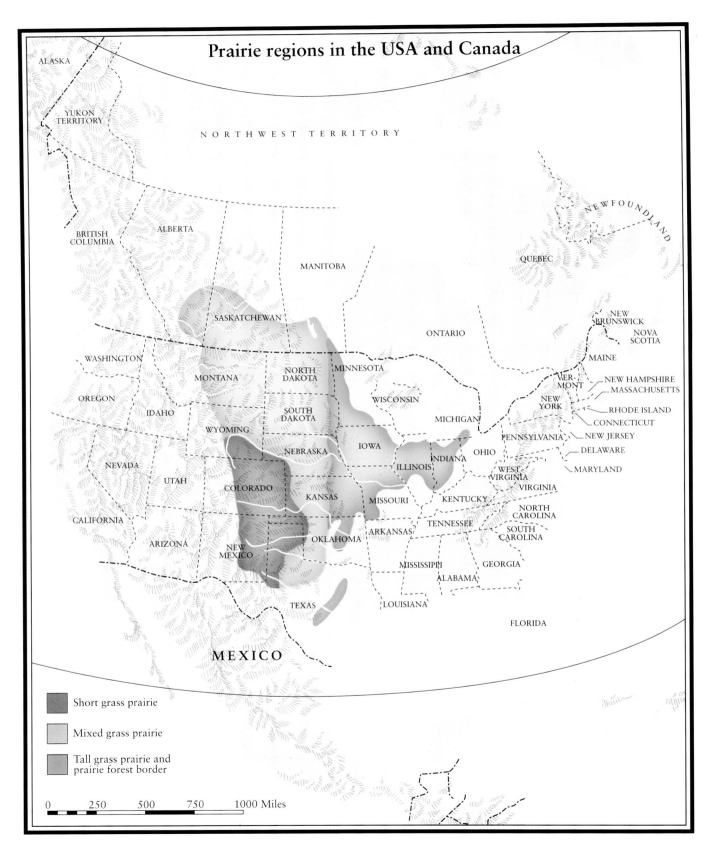

Prairie regions in the USA and Canada

- **Short grass prairie**
- **Mixed grass prairie**
- **Tall grass prairie and prairie forest border**

```
0      250      500      750      1000 Miles
```

post-glacial conditions and invaded the fertile soils of the region. Once the prairie had been established, it may have been maintained by grazing animals and fires set by lightning strikes or people. To some Indians, fires were so closely associated with the prairie that they used the same word for both.

Early travelers wrote of prairie fires that 'obscure the sun, moon, and stars for many days, or until the winter rains descend to quench the fire and purge the thick ropey air, which is seen, tasted, handled and felt'. To prairie settlers they were uncontrollable forces of terrifying power. 'It is a strange and terrible sight to see all the fields a sea of fire,' wrote one Swedish immigrant. 'Quite often the scorching flames sweep everything along in their path – people, cattle, hay, fences. In dry weather with a strong wind the fire will race faster than the speediest horse.'

Of course, a prairie fire was equally devastating to wildlife, sometimes trapping and burning entire herds of buffalo, deer and antelope. Birds of prey often exploited the fires by hovering before their advancing flames and catching small creatures as they fled. Carrion eaters followed the fires, consuming the charred remains of those caught in the conflagration.

When not fearing for their lives, prairie travelers saw in the fires a certain majesty:

> *It is a beautiful sight to see the fire shooting in every direction over these broad expanses of land, which are kindled at a variety of points. The flame at one moment curls along the ground, and seems to lick up its fuel from below, while at the next it tumbles over like the breakers of the sea upon the dried grass, and sweeps it in a wave of fire from the ground.*

The fires moved so quickly that they left the deep-rooted grasses unharmed and the soil enriched with a layer of potash. From this fertile bed burst new growth each spring, setting the prairie ablaze again, this time with orange, yellow, blue, and white blooms: pasque flowers, bird's-foot violets, prairie cat's foot, false dandelion (the 'real' dandelion having come as a stowaway with settlers from Europe), paintbrush, groundplum vetch, upland buttercups, and yellow lousewort. The prairie buzzed with insects too, more than 10 million per acre busily pollinating the sea of blossoms. As the bluestem began to emerge in mid-April, the short spring flowers rushed to complete their blooming before being overshadowed by the grass. Taller plants – daisies, larkspur, purple coneflower, and the foot-high prairie lily – peppered the lush grass well into summer.

Those accustomed to the forests of the East were overwhelmed by the openness of the prairie. 'I was perfectly alone', wrote one traveler:

> *and could see nothing in any direction but sky and grass. ... Not a living thing could I see or hear, except the occasional rising of some prairie fowl, or perhaps a large hawk or eagle wheeling about over my head. In the woods I have often experienced this silence and solitude, but it struck me more forcibly in these boundless meadows.*

Coronado and his men were among the first Europeans to describe the vast prairies where they saw bison, antelope and elk (above). 'Who could believe that 1000 horses and 500 of our cows and more than 5000 rams and ewes and more than 1500 friendly Indians and servants in traveling over these plains would leave no more trace where they had passed than if nothing had been there.'

Although part of the prairies' natural cycle of life, wild fires were terrifying forces for early settlers to overcome. 'No one dares to travel without carrying matches so that if there is a fire he can fight it by building another and in this way save his life,' wrote a nineteenth-century homesteader. In Arthur Tait's picture Life on the Prairie (1862), published by Currier and Ives (above right), three frontiersmen fight fire with fire. The fast-burning flames actually improved growing conditions for many of the prairies' plants, including bluestem grass (left), bird's foot violet (right), goldenrod (center), and Indian paintbrush (far right).

The American writer Washington Irving also tried to explain the solitude of a prairie by contrasting it with the loneliness of the eastern forests. There, he wrote, 'the view is shut in by the trees and the imagination is left to picture some livelier scene beyond. But here we have the immense extent of landscape without a sign of human existence.'

There was other human existence, of course. Native peoples had known and lived on the prairie since the end of the ice age. In the eastern tallgrass prairie, the first white settlers found tribes like the Osage and Pawnee who subsisted, as their eastern relatives had done, on a seasonal mix of agriculture and wild game. Farther west, in the shortgrass region of the Great Plains, lived more nomadic groups like the Comanche, Blackfoot, and Sioux. Some of these peoples had been driven on to the Great Plains by competition from other groups, but most had been drawn there by the abundance of deer, antelope, rabbits, prairie chicken, and other wild game.

By far the most abundant of the large Great Plains species was the American bison or buffalo. At the time of first European contact, these great grazing animals may have numbered more than 50 million. They ranged over 400 000 square miles of grassland from northwestern Canada to northern Mexico and from the eastern prairie of Illinois west to the Rocky Mountains. Some even wandered into the Great Basin beyond. Their closely related relative, the wood bison, lived in smaller numbers between the Mississippi River and the Atlantic coast.

The Spanish were the first Europeans to see the buffalo. When Hernán Cortés and his conquistadores entered the Aztec capital Tenochtitlán (now Mexico City) in 1521, they found captive bulls in Montezuma's royal zoo. A decade later, Cabeza de Vaca encountered wild buffalo in western Florida and Texas, remarking that their flesh was 'finer and fatter' than Spanish beef. But it was Pedro de Castañeda who gave the earliest extended description of the species in his account of Francisco Coronado's 1540 expedition through the American Southwest:

> They have a narrow, short face, the brow two palms across from eye to eye, the eyes sticking out at the side, so that, when they are running, they can see who is following them. They have very long beards, like goats, and when they are running they throw their heads back with the beard dragging on the ground. There is a sort of girdle round the middle of the body. The hair is very woolly, like a sheep's, very fine, and in front of the girdle the hair is very long and rough like a lion's. They have a great hump, larger than a camel's. The horns are short and thick, so that they are not seen much above the hair. In May they change the hair in the middle of the body for a down, which makes perfect lions of them. They rub against the small trees in the little ravines to shed their hair and they continue this until only the down is left, as a snake changes his skin.

Before the horse revolutionized their way of life, the plains Indians hunted the Buffalo on foot with spears and arrows. Disguising themselves with the skins

The close relationship between the Indian and the buffalo was vividly documented by George Catlin in his Buffalo Hunt *and* Buffalo Dance *when he visited the Great Plains in the 1830s. The buffalo illustration in Louis Hennepin's* A New Dictionary of a Vast Country in America *(1698) (above) was almost certainly based on verbal accounts of the species rather than on firsthand observations.*

of antelope or wolves, they would cautiously approach the 2000-pound bulls or 900-pound females at the edge of a herd. If luck was with them, the wind was right, and the buffalo were too absorbed in grazing to notice, the hunters might take their prey by surprise. The risks to the hunters were enormous – a wounded buffalo could easily kill a man – but so were the rewards. A single kill could feed a large family for more than a month.

A somewhat safer but more wasteful method of hunting was to drive buffalo over steep escarpments or 'pishkins' (a Blackfoot word) by setting the prairie ablaze or startling a herd into a stampede. The terrified animals, led by an Indian decoy, would hurtle to their deaths over the edge of the unseen precipice. The Indians then skinned the bison and preserved their meat for lean times when the herds were in another part of the plains. After the arrival of the horse from Spain, some groups became entirely dependent on the buffalo and followed the herds wherever they moved.

To most Americans at the beginning of the nineteenth century, two thirds of whom still lived within 50 miles of the Atlantic coast, vague reports of great open spaces with thundering herds of buffalo seemed very remote indeed. The Great Plains were, in fact, beyond the borders of the United States at the time. While the US government controlled most land east of the Mississippi, the lands west of the great river, once French possessions, had been owned by Spain since the Treaty of Paris in 1763.

In 1801, Napoleon Bonaparte arranged by secret treaty with Spain that France would resume ownership of the Spanish half of its original Louisiana territory. Thus he gained control of more than 800 000 square miles in the middle of the continent. President Thomas Jefferson and the government viewed this acquisition of land with concern. They much preferred having weak Spain as a national neighbor to the powerful and increasingly bellicose France.

An immediate issue was the port city of New Orleans. Since the Mississippi and its tributaries formed the principal route of commerce for America's western regions, New Orleans was considered crucial to national prosperity. For years Spain had granted American citizens free access to the port. In October 1802, the local administrators closed New Orleans to American trade, and Jefferson decided that action of some kind was essential. He authorized the US minister to France, Robert Livingston, and his own special emissary, James Monroe, to meet with Napoleon and his foreign minister, Talleyrand, to discuss a possible American purchase of the city and its port.

At first Napoleon had no interest in the American offer. But as the prospects for war against Britain grew and his hopes for a New World empire foundered in a West Indian slave revolt, he reversed his position with a stunning counter-offer. He suggested that the United States take not only New Orleans but the entire Louisiana territory. Such a transaction would provide France with badly needed funds, remove a potentially troublesome administrative problem, and prevent Britain from seizing North American possessions that France could not defend. The settlement price was 15 million dollars. Thus, in a stroke of New World fortune, and at roughly 3 cents an acre, the United States doubled in size.

At the time of its acquisition, very little was known about the new territory. The few Europeans who had scouted the region were fur traders probing narrow ribbons of land along the largest rivers. Jefferson was determined to find out what he could and to make the American presence known through as much of the new territory as possible.

Even before the successful conclusion of the Louisiana Purchase, Jefferson had asked his private secretary, Meriwether Lewis, to begin planning an expedition of discovery to the West and requested Congress to fund the undertaking. In his written instructions to Lewis, Jefferson charged the 29-year-old Virginian with exploring 'the Missouri river, and such principal streams of it, as by its course and communication with the waters of the Pacific Ocean ... may offer the most direct and practicable water communication across the continent for the purposes of commerce'.

But Lewis's trip was to be more than a search for the elusive Northwest Passage. Jefferson, a passionate naturalist with an extensive knowledge of the natural history of the Southeast, was eager to mount a scientific as well as a political expedition. So he also asked Lewis

to acquire what knowledge you can of ... the soil and face of the country, its growth and vegetable productions ... the animals of the country generally and especially those not known in the US, the remains and accounts of any which may be deemed rare or extinct, the mineral productions ... the dates at which particular plants put forth or lose their flower or leaf, times of appearance of particular birds, reptiles, or insects.

It was no small assignment for a party that would also have to traverse more than 8000 miles of unknown wilderness.

As his co-leader, Lewis selected William Clark, younger brother of the Revolutionary War hero George Rogers Clark (to whom Jefferson had once proposed a similar expedition). Lewis and Clark had become close friends while serving together in the army some years before. The even-tempered, gregarious Clark was a perfect complement to the more intellectual, meticulous, and highly strung Lewis.

On 14 May 1804 the Corps of Discovery, consisting of 26 soldiers, an interpreter-guide, and Clark's black servant, York, left Camp Wood near St Louis where they had spent the winter preparing for the trip. They traveled by keelboat up the Missouri, meeting with Indian leaders, collecting wildlife and plant specimens, and charting the course of the river as they went. By midsummer they were still passing through prairie which Clark described as 'rich, covered with grass from 5 to 8 feet high, interspersed with copses of hazel, plumbs, currents ... raspberries and grapes of different kinds'. Throughout this open country they saw 'immense herds of buffalo, deer, elk, and antelopes ... in every direction', some 'so gentle that we pass near them without appearing to excite any alarm among them'. They also saw wolves both large and small (the smaller ones we now call coyotes) and large hares with ears so long that others would later call them jackass rabbits, or jackrabbits for short.

PREVIOUS PAGES A herd of wild horses or mustangs (from the Spanish mesteño *for stray animal) pick their way through western sagebrush country during a winter storm. Once found throughout North America, the horse became extinct on the continent some 10 000 years ago. When it was reintroduced by the Spaniards, it revolutionized the Indians' way of life.*

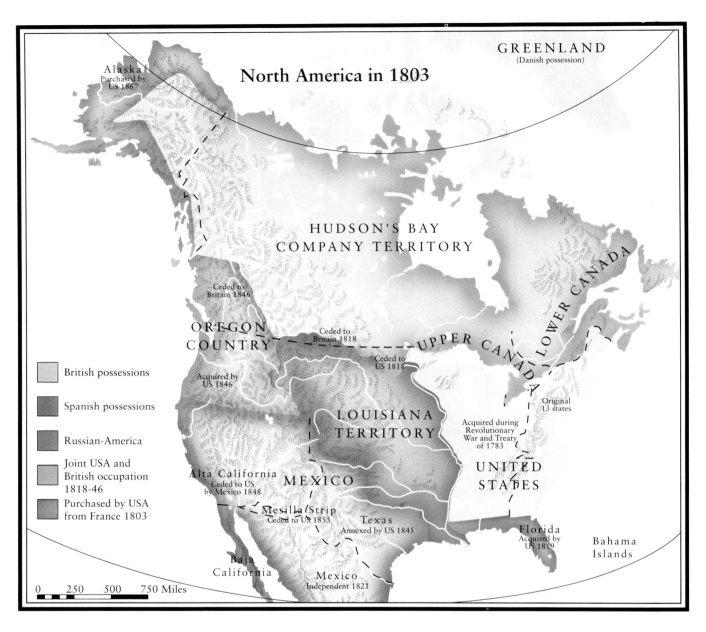

North America in 1803

GREENLAND
(Danish possession)

Alaska
Purchased by
US 1867

HUDSON'S BAY
COMPANY TERRITORY

LOWER CANADA

UPPER CANADA

Ceded to
Britain 1846

OREGON
COUNTRY

Ceded to
Britain 1818

Ceded to
US 1818

Acquired by
US 1846

Original
13 states

LOUISIANA
TERRITORY

Acquired during
Revolutionary
War and Treaty
of 1783

UNITED
STATES

Alta California
Ceded to US
by Mexico 1848

MEXICO

Mesilla Strip
Ceded to US 1853

Texas
Annexed by US 1845

Florida
Acquired by
US 1819

Bahama
Islands

Baja
California

Mexico
Independent 1821

British possessions

Spanish possessions

Russian-America

Joint USA and
British occupation
1818-46

Purchased by USA
from France 1803

0   250   500   750 Miles

One prairie mammal that especially intrigued the explorers was a soft-furred ground squirrel which, as Lewis noted, 'generally associate in large societies placing their burrows near each other and frequently occupy in this manner several hundred acres of land'. Because of their dog-like yelps, French *voyageurs* had named the rodents *petit chiens*. The name was biologically inappropriate – Lewis preferred the more apt 'barking squirrel' – but a portion of it stuck. The societies in which they lived became known as prairie dog towns.

Lewis and Clark decided to capture a prairie dog to send back to Jefferson and had their party spend the better part of a day trying to unearth one of the creatures from its underground warren with picks and shovels. The effort was successful, and Jefferson received a live prairie dog the following spring. It came

LEFT *Despite more than a century of efforts to destroy it, the highly adaptive coyote has actually expanded its range and can be found in wild areas throughout most of North America.*

Lewis and Clark reported large numbers of pronghorn antelope (right) during their travels across the country. Other prairie mammals they described were the black-tailed prairie dog (below) and the jackrabbit (below right).

as part of a large shipment of scientific specimens sent east by the expedition from their winter quarters at Fort Mandan, near present-day Bismarck, North Dakota. In the same shipment were skinned or stuffed specimens of a number of other prairie species as well as four live magpies and a wild prairie chicken. Jefferson displayed many of the trophies in the White House and later at Monticello. The rest, including the live animals that had survived the 4000-mile trip east, he sent to Philadelphia for public exhibition in Charles Willson Peale's museum of natural history.

At the first breakup of winter ice, the explorers continued west by water, passing the mouth of the Yellowstone River and portaging 25 days around the Great Falls of the Missouri. With the help of the local Shoshoni Indians, whose leader's sister, Sacagawea, was one of the expedition's most helpful guides, the expedition crossed over the Continental Divide in a series of arduous climbs through the Bitterroot Mountains in today's Idaho. Once in the Pacific watershed, the party continued by canoe through the spectacular scenery and treacherous rapids of the Clearwater and Snake Rivers to the Columbia, which they followed to the Pacific coast.

Clark recorded the achievement by carving into the bark of an ocean-side pine: 'Capt. William Clark December 3rd, 1805. By land from the U. States in 1804–5.' The gesture may have been intended to parallel a similar inscription made by the Scottish-Canadian fur trader Alexander Mackenzie, who had reached the Pacific by land from Canada in July 1793. Jefferson, Lewis and Clark had all read Mackenzie's account of his journey, and had planned the American expedition, in part, to match the Canadian's accomplishment and thereby counter British claims to the Pacific Northwest.

After wintering near the coast in a fort they named Clatsop after the Indian tribe who lived nearby, the Corps of Discovery retraced its route the following spring. They returned to St Louis at the end of September 1806. In more than 28 months of travel through dangerous and hostile terrain, they had lost but one man (probably to a ruptured appendix) and had experienced only one violent encounter with Indians in which two Indians were killed with no injury to the expedition. While Lewis and Clark had not found an easily navigable route to the Pacific as Jefferson had hoped, they had given the US government a strong position in claiming the lands of the far Northwest for its future use. They had also gathered a storehouse of information about the Louisiana Territory.

Most historians agree that Lewis and Clark's expedition was the most successful ever to explore the American West. Its most regrettable shortcoming was that, except for a few crude field sketches, it left virtually no visual depiction of the territory. Fortunately, a number of highly talented artists visited the Great Plains in succeeding decades to record the natural and cultural qualities of the region before it was forever changed by the impact of white settlement. Among the best-known of these was George Catlin.

Catlin was a painter who gave up a successful career as a portraitist in New York and Philadelphia in order, he said, to rescue 'from oblivion the looks and

In their remarkable journey across the continent, Lewis and Clark kept careful records of everything they saw, from giant herds of bison (below right) to birds, plants, insects and fish. Lewis's illustrated journal (right) is one of eighteen notebooks that survived the rigorous trip. While most of the wildlife that the expedition discovered was already well known to the Indians of the region, much was new to the scientific world. Several species, including Lewis's woodpecker and Clark's crow (now called Clark's nutcracker), were named after the explorers. They were first illustrated (above far right), together with another new species, the western tanager, in Alexander Wilson's American Ornithology *(1811).*

customs of the vanishing races of native man in America'. He traveled to St Louis in 1830 where William Clark, then serving as Superintendent of Indian Affairs for the Upper Louisiana Territory, arranged for him to paint many of the Indian delegations visiting that booming frontier town. Two years later Catlin went deeper into Indian country when he journeyed 2000 miles up the Missouri as far as Fort Union on the maiden voyage of the American Fur Company's steamship *Yellowstone*. For the next four years, he traveled among the plains Indians, visiting and painting the Pawnee, Blackfoot, Crow, Ojibwa, Comanche, and others.

It was George Catlin who first reported the disappearance of western wildlife and who foresaw the loss of Indian cultures at the hands of whites. In an 1832 journal entry, which later appeared in a New York newspaper and in his own book on North American Indians, Catlin proposed the concept of a national park:

> *Nature has nowhere presented more beautiful and lovely scenes, than those of the vast prairies of the West; and of man and beast, no nobler specimens than those who inhabit them – the Indian and the buffalo – joint and original tenants of the soil, and fugitives together from the approach of civilised man; they have fled to the great plains of the West, and there, under an equal doom, they have taken up their last abode, where their race will expire, and their bones will bleach together. . . .*
>
> *This strip of country, which extends from the province of Mexico to Lake Winnipeg in the North, is almost one entire plain of grass, which is, and ever must be, useless to cultivating man. It is here, and here chiefly, that the buffaloes dwell; and with, and hovering about them, live and flourish the tribes of Indians, whom God made for the enjoyment of that fair land and its luxuries.*
>
> *And what a splendid contemplation too, when one imagines them as they might in future be seen (by some great protecting policy of government) preserved in their pristine beauty and wildness, in a magnificent park, where the world could see for ages to come, the native Indian in his classic attire, galloping his wild horse, with sinewy bow, and shield and lance, amid the fleeting herds of elks and buffaloes . . . A nation's Park, containing man and beast, in all the wild freshness of their nature's beauty.*

Forty years after Catlin entered these prophetic observations in his journal, Congress would establish a 2 000 000 acre reserve in Wyoming, Montana, and Idaho, and Catlin would gain his hoped-for preserve – at least for the buffalo – in Yellowstone National Park.

While Catlin and other artists were recording life in the western Great Plains, white settlers were still coming to grips with the tallgrass prairie to the east. At first they settled in the forested bottomlands along the streams and rivers where, in addition to wood for building and fuel, the trees provided a comforting reminder of the forests that had been left behind. 'A settler regards a distance of half a mile from the forest as an intolerable burden,' wrote an English visitor to Illinois in 1833. The first prairie homesteaders were accustomed to clearing fields from forests and continued to do so, assuming that the surrounding grasslands were of such poor soil and so vulnerable to prairie fire that they were not worth the effort it took to plant them. Reflecting this, Illinois timberland in the 1830s was valued over prairie land at a ratio of seven to one, with an acre of forested property bringing about 35 dollars and a comparable amount of prairie selling for 5 dollars.

What the first generation of western pioneers did not realize was that the tallgrass prairie lands were far richer than the forests. Grass debris and ash accumulated over 20 000 years made the region one of the most fertile areas on earth. Once this was recognized, the problem still remained how to break through the interwoven mat of roots that made up the prairie sod. Most eastern plows, the settlers discovered, were ill-suited to the depth and thickness of the western grasses. The heavy, cast-iron plow blades and moldboards that were designed for the light forest soils and rocky fields of New England were almost useless on the prairie. They could not cut deep enough and would not 'scour' to rid themselves of the clinging loam. There were commercial plowmen with massive wheeled plowshares and teams of oxen who would do the job for 10 to 12 dollars an acre, but for most settlers this was an expensive and impractical way of farming.

A great breakthrough came in 1837 when John Deere, an Illinois blacksmith, developed and began to sell a plow specifically designed for prairie use. With its deeper blade and light, tempered-steel moldboard, it cut through the sod and effectively shed the loam. The John Deere plow could be drawn by horses through prairie sod with amazing efficiency and revolutionized prairie living. Midwestern settlers, now named sodbusters, began to leave the security of the forests and establish homesteads in what contemporaries often called the great sea of grass.

Ocean analogies, indeed, were an effective way to describe the prairie. They conjured images that were both evocative and understandable to friends and relatives back East:

> *For miles we saw nothing but a vast prairie of what can compare to nothing else but the ocean itself. The tall grass, interspersed occasionally with fields of corn, looked like the deep sea; it seemed as if we were out of sight of land, for no house, no barn, no tree was visible, and the horizon presented the rolling of waves in the afar-off distance. There were all sorts of flowers – as if the sun were shining upon the gay and dancing waters.*

A *Harper's New Monthly Magazine* reporter even tried to give sensual substance to the nautical imagery:

> *As one stands on the boundless rolling prairies of this country, and looks around him on every side, and sees the interminable reach of slightly undulating soil, clad with golden-rod, fire-weed, and a vast variety of other flowering plants intermixed with prairie-grass, and notices the almost utter*

absence of forest, and catches the onward rush of the fresh, cool southern breeze that sweeps by with a voluminous force, he involuntarily thinks of the wide expanse of the ocean, and snuffs the wind as he would the sea-breeze itself.

As settlers pushed on through the prairie toward the open lands beyond, their wagons, with graceful sweeping lines and white canvas tops, became known as 'prairie schooners'.

But it was not to be all clear sailing for the plainsmen. Fires, food shortages, contagious diseases, and hostile Indians were constant dangers on the prairie frontier. The farther the settlers moved from the forests, the fewer building materials they had to work with. Many built houses from the sod itself. For warmth and cooking the Indians burned bison dung or 'buffalo chips' but the settlers preferred other fuel if they could find it. They often burned 'cats' of twisted prairie grass in special hay-burning stoves. Later, as planted crops replaced native grassland, corncobs became a popular prairie fuel.

In the 1830s and 40s the introduction of steamboats to the Missouri and its tributaries, coupled with relatively low prices for land from the public domain, gave immigration to the prairies a considerable boost. A potato famine in Ireland and concurrent political upheavals and a cholera epidemic in Europe further encouraged the flow of immigration. As the United States grew in population, strength and confidence, cries of 'manifest destiny' accompanied its geographical and political expansion. The annexation of Texas (1845), the acquisition of Oregon (1846), and the securing of California and most of the Southwest by treaty settlement and purchase following the war with Mexico (1846–48) stimulated still more movement across the prairies.

In an effort to keep up with the mobile population, eastern trade centers such as New York, Philadelphia, and Baltimore began to develop transportation systems that could carry goods to the rest of the country more efficiently and cheaply than wagons on often impassable roads. The Baltimore and Ohio Railroad, begun in 1828, was the start of what became a nationwide network of trains. By 1854, the Chicago and Rock Island Railroad had reached the Mississippi, and two years later its many spurs were spreading through Iowa. In 1869, when the first transcontinental line was completed, four midwestern railroads were ready to connect it to the East.

In order to encourage the construction of still more railroads, the US Congress granted several companies an astonishing 174 million acres of public lands, an area greater than New England, New York, Pennsylvania, and Ohio combined. This acreage was used for rights-of-way for the tracks and to sell to the settlers. Proceeds from the land sales were intended to subsidize the cost of railroad construction. Launching aggressive advertising and recruitment campaigns to attract new settlers, the railroads carried their sales efforts not just to eastern states but to Europe as well. England, Ireland, Germany, Sweden, Norway, and Denmark were blanketed with posters, newspaper advertisements, and brochures extolling settlement in the American Midwest.

As the prairies became more crowded, wetlands were drained and native tallgrass was replaced with corn and other grain crops. This meant less habitat for the flocks of migrating waterbirds which once gathered there in great numbers. American avocets, black-necked stilts, snowy and piping plovers, willets, killdeer, spotted and upland sandpipers, long-billed dowitchers, semi-palmate and black-bellied plover, and the now extinct Eskimo curlew were among the birds that suffered from the change.

Thousands of Eskimo curlew used to invade the grasslands each spring. It was an ideal resting and refueling stop for the birds on their 8000-mile flight from the grasslands of Argentina where they wintered to the Arctic tundra where they bred. The curlew, which provided essential food for the Eskimo, became a popular sporting bird for prairie farmers who soon learned the power of a 10-bore gun. 'The slaughter of these poor birds was appalling and almost unbelievable,' wrote one witness of a spring curlew migration in Nebraska. 'Hunters would shoot the birds without mercy until they had literally slaughtered a wagonload of them. ... The compact flocks and tameness of the birds made the slaughter possible, and at each shot usually dozens of birds would fall.'

The Eskimo curlew was once the second most numerous species of wading bird in North America, the lesser golden plover possibly migrating in even larger numbers. Yet the curlew was on the brink of extinction by the close of the nineteenth century. Small groups continued to survive for another 50 years, but the numbers necessary to sustain the species had been lost forever.

The decimation of the Eskimo curlew was paralleled by the even more conspicuous slaughter of the buffalo. To the western plains Indians, the buffalo provided both practical and spiritual sustenance. Its meat was the mainstay of the Indians' diet. Its hide was used for clothing, the construction of portable shelters (tepees), moccasins, shields, water containers, and even basket-shaped boats called bull-boats (which were coincidentally similar in design and construction to the coracles used by ancient Britons). The buffalo's horns were made into spoons and drinking vessels, its sinews into thread, rawhide for rope, and its dung used for fuel. Providing so much to the Indians, the buffalo was, understandably, the object of great veneration both in life and death to many Great Plains tribes.

The coming of the whites to the West, even if only to trade rather than settle, changed the balanced physical and spiritual relationship between man and nature that had long existed in the area. Indians on horseback and armed with guns could kill many more buffalo than they needed. The buffaloes could then be used in trade for items they wanted from the whites. In a journal entry written at Fort Pierre in present-day South Dakota, George Catlin reported the degradation of values that ensued:

When I first arrived at this place, on my way up the river, which was in the month of May, in 1832, and had taken up my lodgings in the Fur Company's Fort, [I was told] that only a few days before I arrived (when an immense herd of buffaloes had showed themselves on the opposite side of the river,

OVERLEAF A lone common tern skims over the surface of a prairie slough. Gouged from the land by retreating glaciers 10 000 to 12 000 years ago, millions of such natural ponds cover a 300 000 square mile region in Alberta, Saskatchewan, Man-itoba, Montana, the Dakotas, Minnesota and Iowa. They provide critical wetland habitat for migrating birds and other wildlife.

almost blackening the plains for a great distance), a party of five or six hundred Sioux Indians on horseback, forded the river about mid-day, and spending a few hours amongst them, recrossed the river at sun-down and came into the Fort with fourteen hundred fresh buffalo tongues, which were thrown down in a mass, and for which they required but a few gallons of whiskey, which was soon demolished, indulging them in a little, and harmless carouse.

This profligate waste of the lives of these noble and useful animals, when, from all that I could learn, not a skin or a pound of the meat (except the tongues), was brought in, fully supports me in the seemingly extravagant predictions that I have made as to their extinction, which I am certain is near at hand.

The slaughter that Catlin recounted gave only a hint of what was to come. In the 1850s and 60s, professional hunters who accompanied the crews building the transcontinental railroad killed thousands of buffalo at a time in order to feed the army of laborers. When the Union Pacific and Central Pacific railroads were finally joined in 1869, still more easterners flowed into the West. Many shot buffalo for sport, while others killed them for their hides, to be sold back East.

The US military actively encouraged the slaughter in the hope of denying the plains Indians a ready source of food. Exterminating the buffalo 'is the only way to bring lasting peace and allow civilization to advance' declared western commander General Philip Henry Sheridan. To Sheridan, the only good buffalo, like the only good Indian, was a dead one. In this case, time was on the general's side. Close to 4 million buffalo were destroyed between 1872 and 1874. In those same years the invention and widespread deployment of barbed wire and the increase of large-scale cattle ranching further disrupted age-old patterns of life for the buffalo that remained, breaking their migration routes and exhausting their once-abundant food supplies.

As the buffalo population plummeted, concerned citizens began to recognize the accuracy of George Catlin's prediction of the species' demise. In 1874, a bill was passed by both houses of Congress to impose a penalty 'on every man, red, white, or black, who might wantonly kill buffaloes'. But the bill was vetoed by President Ulysses S. Grant, who may have agreed with Sheridan and other military men that the Indians of the West could never be subdued until their source of food – and independence – was destroyed. It was another three decades before the US government followed Canada's lead and moved to protect the species by establishing national bison reserves in Oklahoma, western Montana, Wyoming and North Dakota.

Ironically, in 1913, when the buffalo was teetering on the brink of extinction, it was memorialized, along with the American Indian, on a US 5 cent piece or nickel. Only in this guise would the buffalo – or the Indian – ever regain the numbers or dominance they had once enjoyed. By the time the coin was issued, the continent's Great Plains had been transformed from the 'Great American

Desert' to the 'Breadbasket of the World', and there was no longer room for their original inhabitants.

Of the many other Great Plains species to be reduced by agricultural activity, the prairie dogs were among the last. For a while they actually benefited from inadvertent human protection, as ranchers eliminated such real or imagined livestock predators as wolves, coyotes, bobcats, eagles and hawks. Freed of these natural enemies, the prairie dogs flourished, grazing the prairie grasses as their ancestors had done for millennia. With densities of 25 to 80 burrows in a single acre, these sociable rodents covered vast areas of the plains. In 1900 it was estimated that one aggregation of prairie dog 'townships' in Texas extended over 25 000 square miles, and that their 400 million inhabitants were consuming grass sufficient for 1.5 million cattle. Thousands of comparable communities existed throughout the West. Eventually the prairie dogs were seen as unwelcome competition for livestock, and a systematic campaign of poisoning began. The effects were devastating, not only for the prairie dogs, whose numbers were drastically reduced, but for the many other species that depended on them for food and on their excavations for shelter. The burrowing owl, the badger, and the black-footed ferret were among the most severely affected, for each, in its own way, had evolved a dependence on the populous rodent.

While livestock ranchers were introducing cattle to the Great Plains, crop farmers were making changes of their own. The increased mechanization of farming practices allowed larger and larger areas of prairie to be broken for cultivation in the late nineteenth and early twentieth centuries. The related removal of existing windscreens, copses and hedgerows expanded field sizes and increased agricultural efficiency. It also reduced the amount of cover available to wildlife, and it left the land vulnerable to wind erosion. Without windbreaks or the stabilizing network of prairie grass roots, the loosened soil was easily blown away. 'Real estate moved considerably this week,' joked a plains newspaper in 1880, but the subject would be no laughing matter in the years ahead.

News of America's emerging prosperity, coupled with European political and economic instability at the close of the nineteenth century, stimulated unprecedented levels of immigration to the United States. In the 1880s, 675,000 Scandinavians, including one third of the population of Iceland, came to America. Many of them settled in Minnesota and the Dakotas where the climate was similar to that of their homelands and where earlier Scandinavian immigrants could give them a foothold on the new land. Similarly, many German immigrants – a quarter of a million of whom came to the United States in 1882 alone – settled in the Great Plains where friends and relatives had already established communities. Others from around the world were drawn to an agricultural life in the Midwest by the reports of inexpensive land and bountiful harvests being touted by railroad promoters, land speculators, and regional propagandists. The effect of this great influx was to complete the settling of the region which had begun in the 1820s and 30s.

Settlers were told that rain would follow the plow on the prairie, and for a while it appeared to do so. During the second half of the nineteenth century the

Audubon's prophetic picture of an Eskimo curlew looking at its fallen mate. Thousands were shot in the late nineteenth and early twentieth centuries and no living birds have been sighted since 1976. The black-footed ferret (seen below in an illustration by Audubon's son) has also suffered serious decline.

plains enjoyed a period of unusually high precipitation. Then in the years immediately following the First World War, recession, compounded by a period of extremely low rainfall in the northern plains, caused the abandonment of many marginal farms. Of the 70 000 to 80 000 people who had homesteaded between 1909 and 1918 in Montana, for example, 60 000 had left by 1922. A decade later, most of their abandoned acreage was still unprotected by permanent vegetation and the stage was set for disaster. Continued drought and unusually high winds soon removed hundreds of millions of tons of prairie topsoil. During the Dust Bowl days of the 1930s, skies as far east as New York City and Washington DC were darkened by clouds of blowing prairie soil. Ships 300 miles at sea in the Atlantic were coated with the dust of disappearing prairie farms. In little less than a decade, 18 million acres of prairie were turned to desert by the eroding winds. Thousands more farms were abandoned as the Depression worsened. Between 1930 and 1940, American cropland declined from 413 to 399 million acres. This was despite valiant efforts by the Civilian Conservation Corps (established in 1933), the US Soil Conservation Service (established in 1935), and other New Deal agencies, to remedy the conditions that had led to the Dust Bowl disaster.

Today, although parts of the plains superficially resemble the grasslands of old, soils and vegetation have been greatly impoverished. In most cases the grasses are exotic imports. Even where native grasses have been carefully reintroduced, there are generally no more than 30 different species where 200 or more once grew. Some wild prairie habitat does survive, but only in scattered fragments that history and circumstance have spared. In old graveyards, along fence rows and railroad rights-of-way, and in forgotten pockets too rough to till, one can still see patches of the prairie, remnant tidepools of America's great sea of grass.

INTO THE SHINING MOUNTAINS

THE · ROCKIES

From the seemingly endless sea of grass that makes up the western plains, the Rocky Mountains rise so abruptly as to seem a mirage. To many travelers, reaching the Rockies after crossing 1000 miles of ocean prairie was like reaching dry land.

The first American exploring expedition to see the southern expanse of the Rockies mistook the mountains for clouds. It took careful examination by telescope for the explorers to recognize them for the massive peaks they were. The leader of the expedition was a 27-year-old army lieutenant, Zebulon Pike. 'The small blue cloud' on the horizon that had first caught his eye was to become both his lasting memorial and the symbolic, if not actual, destination for many a western traveler in the decades to come: Pike's Peak.

A complex series of geologically related ridges that runs 3000 miles from the Brooks Range in Alaska to the Sierra Madre Oriental in Mexico, the Rocky Mountains comprise the longest mountain chain in the world. They began to emerge from the still-forming continent some 175 million years ago and reached their greatest period of activity about 60 million years ago in an era of upheaval that witnessed the cooling of the climate, the extinction of the dinosaurs, and the rise of mammals to eminence on the planet. Subsequent erosion and uplifting has continued to shape the rugged features we see today. The Rockies' relative instability can be attributed partly to the nearby juncture of two massive global plates which, moving in opposite directions, slide over or past one another creating much heat and pressure, and dramatically affecting the land above. The interaction of the plates, which once contributed to the formation of the Rockies, is now creating seismic and volcanic activity closer to the Pacific coast.

Like the Appalachians, their much older eastern counterparts, the Rockies have served as both barrier and refuge, obstacle and sanctuary to countless life forms. To white travelers in the early nineteenth century, the rugged ranges of the Rockies – which they also called the Stony Mountains, or the Shining

Mountains – appeared to be the last great vertical barrier to be hurdled or bypassed in seeking an overland route to the Pacific. These pioneers had not yet learned of the Sierra Nevada, the Cascade Range, or the Coast Range that lay beyond.

In the years following the Louisiana Purchase, Thomas Jefferson and his western representatives dispatched a number of exploratory expeditions to complement the work of Lewis and Clark and ascertain the topography of the new territory that included the Rocky Mountains. The primary assignment of the explorers was to discover through these mountains the best 'communication' between the Atlantic and Pacific Oceans. The government needed a convenient route across the Continental Divide, the invisible line that separates the waters draining into the Mississippi River and Gulf of Mexico from those draining toward the Pacific. In addition to exploring, these teams were to establish a political, military, and economic presence through as much of the continent as conditions would permit. Zebulon Pike led two such expeditions. The first in 1805 was to find the source of the Mississippi, which he mistakenly thought was Lake Leech in northern Minnesota. The second was to find the headwaters of the Arkansas and Red Rivers, the southwestern boundaries of the Louisiana Territory. It was on this second trip, in November 1806, that Pike saw and explored parts of the southern Rockies.

In the course of their travels, Pike and his men wandered into Spanish territory where they were promptly arrested. Some historians have suggested that Pike's ultimate objective was to gather information about Spanish strength in the area and that he actually provoked the arrest in order to be taken to the Spanish stronghold in Santa Fe. Whatever his purpose, Pike's observation, published a few years after his release from Spanish custody, had two important effects on eastern perceptions of the West.

The first was that the Great Plains were a 'sterile' place 'incapable of cultivation'. Having encountered the massive sand dunes of southern Colorado, Pike asserted that the entire region might some day 'become equally celebrated as the sandy deserts of Africa'. The description caught the imagination of eastern readers and, compounded by similar descriptions from later explorers, helped to create a popular impression that much of the West was a Great American Desert.

At the opposite extreme, Pike's description of the Rockies made them seem far more benign than his own experience actually suggested. Although he and his men trudged through the mountains in midwinter, suffering starvation and severe frostbite (two men lost their feet completely), Pike characterized the mountains in the most positive terms. He described his winter campsite as a 'terrestrial paradise' surrounded by 'great and lofty mountains' and a 'luxuriant vale' inhabited by 'innumerable herds of deer'.

Astoundingly, Pike also claimed to have found the 'best communication between the Atlantic and Pacific oceans ... a grand central reservoir of snows and fountains'. This, he claimed, straddled the Continental Divide and gave birth to five great rivers: four flowing east, the Yellowstone, the Platte, the

Arkansas, and the Rio Grande; and one, the Colorado, flowing west to the Pacific. 'I have no hesitation in asserting', he continued, 'that I can take a position in the mountains from whence I can visit the source of any of those rivers in a day.' Thus Pike suggested that by using his southern route across the continent, all that stood between an enterprising settler and his fortune on the Pacific coast was a land carriage no more difficult than the 'public high ways over the Allegheny Mountains', preceded and followed by convenient river travel on both sides of the Divide.

Pike's promise of easy access to the West – and ultimately the riches of the Orient – seemed to fulfill a dream for the continent dating back to Columbus. However, it was based more on hope and hearsay than on reality. There was, of course, no central reservoir and the Rockies would prove a far more complex and formidable barrier to movement than Pike had realized or was willing to concede.

Just three months before Pike entered the southern Rockies, Lewis and Clark had traversed the northern part of the range. They found their crossing in present-day Idaho anything but the gentle footpath Pike suggested could be found to the south. The Indian trail that Lewis and Clark followed in the Bitterroot Range went over 'emence hills and some of the worst roads that ever horses passed'. From Lemhi Pass on the Continental Divide, the men saw no easy descent to the ocean. Rather, before them lay seemingly endless 'ranges of high mountains still to the west of us with their tops partially covered with snow'. For more than a month, the party struggled through this frozen morass along narrow animal paths, past gaping precipices and over a chaos of wind-blown timber. 'Much fatigued', noted Clark in his journal, 'and horses much more so. . . . Several horses slipped and roled down steep hills which hurt them very much. The one which carried my desk and small trunk turned over and roled down a mountain for 40 yards & lodged against a tree; broke the desk.' That horse miraculously survived, but others were not so lucky, and a number of them were eaten by the starving men. A few days later, staggering through 6 inches of snow, Clark was 'as wet and as cold in every part as I ever was in my life, indeed I was at one time fearful my feet would freeze in the thin mockirsons which I wore'.

After these experiences it is understandable that the Lewis and Clark expedition responded to leaving the Rockies as positively as Pike's men had reacted to reaching them. Sergeant Patrick Gass, a member of the Corps of Discovery, described the party's first view of the level land beyond the mountains in language that others would later use on first sighting the Rockies from the Plains: 'When the discovery was made there was as much joy and rejoicing among the corps, as happens among passengers at sea who have experienced a dangerous protracted voyage, when they first discover land on the long looked-for coast.' For the next 50 years, the Rockies, like the Plains, would be both obstacle and destination, ocean and land, terrestrial paradise and desert.

What was it that made the Rockies so different from and so much harder to negotiate than the Appalachians? First, they were far higher than the eastern

OVERLEAF Sometimes invisible, sometimes conspicuously evident, the Continental Divide is the geographical line which separates North America's Atlantic and Pacific watersheds. Crossing the Great Divide was the literal and figurative high point of many transcontinental journeys.

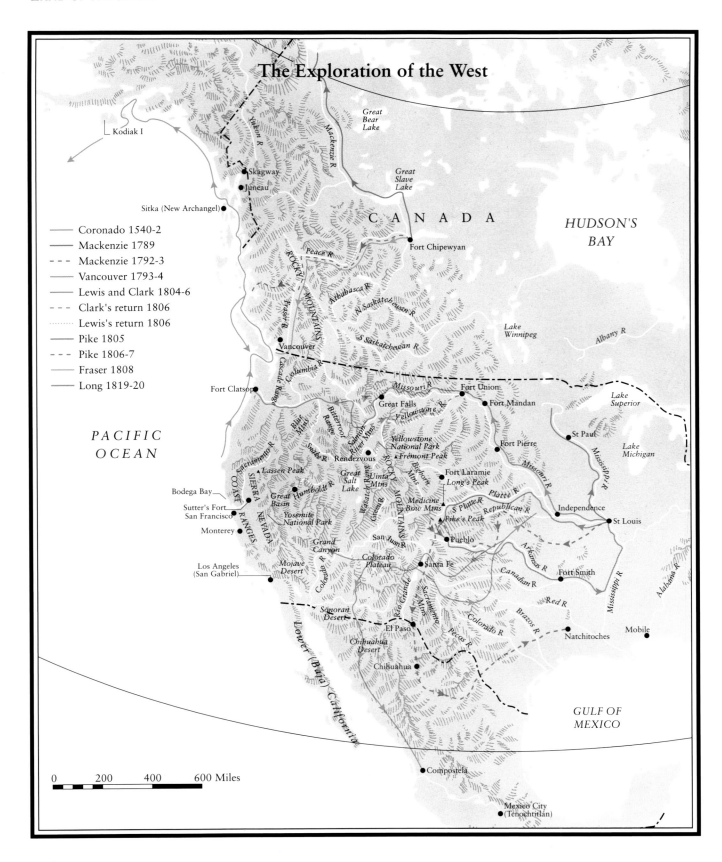

The Exploration of the West

Kodiak I

Skagway
Juneau

Sitka (New Archangel)

Great Bear Lake

Great Slave Lake

Yukon R

Mackenzie R

C A N A D A

Fort Chipewyan

Peace R

Fraser R

ROCKY MOUNTAINS

Athabasca R

N Saskatchewan R

S Saskatchewan R

Vancouver

Cascade Range

Columbia R

HUDSON'S BAY

Lake Winnipeg

Albany R

- —— Coronado 1540-2
- —— Mackenzie 1789
- - - - Mackenzie 1792-3
- —— Vancouver 1793-4
- —— Lewis and Clark 1804-6
- - - - Clark's return 1806
- · · · · Lewis's return 1806
- —— Pike 1805
- - - - Pike 1806-7
- —— Fraser 1808
- —— Long 1819-20

Fort Clatsop

Missouri R

Great Falls

Yellowstone R

Fort Union

Fort Mandan

Lake Superior

St Paul

Lake Michigan

PACIFIC OCEAN

Blue Mtns

Bitterroot Range

Salmon River Mtns

Snake R

Rendezvous

Yellowstone National Park
▲ Frémont Peak

ROCKY MOUNTAINS

Fort Pierre

Missouri R

Sacramento R

Lassen Peak

Humboldt R

Great Salt Lake

Uinta Mtns

Bighorn Mtns

Fort Laramie
Long's Peak

Independence

St Louis

Bodega Bay

Sutter's Fort
San Francisco

Monterey

COAST RANGES

SIERRA NEVADA

Great Basin

Yosemite National Park

Kasatch Range

Green R

Medicine Bow Mtns

S Platte R

Platte R

Republican R

Missouri R

Los Angeles
(San Gabriel)

Mojave Desert

Colorado R

Grand Canyon

Colorado Plateau

San Juan R

San Juan Mts

▲ Pike's Peak

Pueblo

Santa Fe

Arkansas R

Canadian R

Fort Smith

Red R

Mississippi R

Alabama R

Lower (Baja) California

Sonoran Desert

El Paso

Chihuahua Desert

Rio Grande

Sacramento Mts

Pecos R

Colorado R

Brazos R

Natchitoches

Mobile

Chihuahua

GULF OF MEXICO

Compostela

0   200   400   600 Miles

Mexico City
(Tenochtitlán)

mountains, both from base to summit and in altitude above sea level. Fifty-three of the Rockies' peaks rise above 14000 feet and many more are capped with immense snowbanks throughout the year. Most of the Appalachians' peaks are less than a third that height, and snowless except in winter months. Second, the Rockies are much wider than the Appalachians, and far from a single ridge as was originally believed. Third, the Rockies are much rougher. The smoothing effects of erosion, which have mellowed the Appalachians' profile for more than 200 million years, have not yet blunted the harshness of the newer western mountains.

The greater altitude and rougher terrain of the Rockies create a different set of climatic conditions and habitats for plant and animals than those found in the East. One of the mountain species encountered by Lewis and Clark was 'a big horned animal … somewhat larger than the male of the common deer'. The rams of the Rocky Mountain bighorn sheep have massive horns which equal the animal's entire skeleton in weight. The explorers observed that the sheep often descended to lower elevations for grazing, but usually returned to the steepness of the mountains for protection against wolves, coyotes, and other predators. 'The places they generally select to lodge is the crannies or crevices of the rocks in the faces of inaccessible precipices,' wrote Lewis. 'These animals bound from rock to rock and stand apparently in the most careless manner on the sides of precipices of many hundred feet. They are very shy and are quick of both scent and sight.'

The bighorn sheep was included in the seasonal diet of Indian tribes whose hunting grounds stretched into the Rockies. One group living in the Bitterroot's Snake and Salmon River gorges relied on the species so heavily that they came to be known as the Sheepeaters. At times during their expedition, Lewis and his men themselves became sheep-eaters, noting that 'the flesh much resembles mutton though not so strong'. In addition to nourishment, the bighorn provided the Indians with skins and horns which the explorers observed were used in constructing bows.

With the arrival of more lethal hunting technology in the nineteenth century, the sure-footed species lost the protective advantage of their mountain strong-holds. Like so many other animals that had evolved to avoid physical attack, the sheep were unprepared for the long-distance predation made possible by guns. The less cautious ones were killed off immediately, while the rest began to modify their behavior to avoid all contact with humans. When the English sportsman George Ruxton visited the Rockies in 1846, he commented on the animals' wariness:

As they love to resort to the highest and most inaccessible spots, whence a view can readily be had of approaching danger, and particularly as one of the band is always stationed on the most commanding pinnacle of rock as sentinel, whilst the others are feeding, it is no easy matter to get within rifleshot of the cautious animals. When alarmed they ascend still higher up the mountain; halting now and then on some overhanging crag and looking

down at the object which may have frightened them, they again commence their ascent, leaping from point to point and throwing down an avalanche of rocks and stones as they bound up the steep sides of the mountain.

Despite such evasive maneuvers and the rugged nature of the terrain they inhabited, the bighorn sheep were doomed to relentless shooting, first by meat hunters, then by sportsmen. By 1900 the North American bighorn sheep population had been reduced to one tenth of its original size. Several subspecies are now extinct and the remaining sheep live only in protected areas.

Another large mammal that was widespread in the Plains and Rockies in Lewis and Clark's day, but now lives only in refuges and parks, is the grizzly bear. Long a symbol of strength and courage to the Indians, it was also a much-feared competitor for food. A Hudson's Bay Company trader, Henry Kelsey, who traveled extensively in the Canadian Rockies and northern Great Plains, gave us the earliest known account of the grizzly. In his verse-like field notes written in 1691, he described both the fierceness of the bear and the Indian's reverence of it:

And then you have beast of severall kind
The one is a black a Buffillo great
Another is an outgrown Bear wch. is good meat
His skin to gett I have used all ye ways I can
He is mans food & he makes food of man
His hide they would not me it preserve
But said it was a god & they should Starve.

After he had experienced several close calls with injured animals, Meriwether Lewis wrote, 'I must confess that I do not like the gentleman and had rather fight two Indians than one bear.' Though at first confused by the variations in appearance of individual bears, the explorers soon recognized enough similarities to accurately group them as a single species. Lewis described the grizzly in his field notes as 'much more ferocious and formidable' than the smaller black bear. Having been chased up a tree by a grizzly on one occasion and forced to dive into the Missouri River on another, Lewis had good reason to observe that the animal 'will frequently pursue the hunter when wounded. It is astonishing to see the wound they will bear before they can be put to death'. One animal, he reported, 'ran at his usual pace nearly a quarter of a mile, after having been shot through the heart'.

Though multiple musket shots or arrow wounds would eventually kill a bear, the dying animal often wreaked terrible vengeance on its assailants with its own formidable weaponry. Its claws and teeth, both highly prized by Indians as trophies of a courageous struggle, took their toll on many human victims. The history of the American West is strewn with the mangled remains of humans who ventured too close to an aggressive grizzly.

In 1808, Zebulon Pike presented two live grizzly bear cubs to Thomas Jefferson so that the president might see for himself how different the species

LEFT Mountain goats (above), distant relatives of the European chamois, live in the highest and most inaccessible mountains of the American West. Like the more widely distributed bighorn sheep (below), they were first described by Europeans from skins obtained in trade with Indian hunters.

OVERLEAF A grizzly bear sow teaches her two cubs to fish in the clear runoff of a Rocky Mountain stream. Once common through much of the West, the grizzly is now restricted to national parks and protected wilderness areas in the Rockies, northwestern Canada and Alaska.

was from the black bears of the East. These and other specimens returned by Lewis and Clark served as the basis for the first scientific publication on the grizzly which was officially named *Ursus horribilis* or the 'horrible bear' in 1815. Though its common name referred to its grizzled coat, one naturalist suggested changing it to 'grisly' to reflect its violent nature and predatory habits.

The meat of the grizzly was not so highly valued as that of the black bear, being somewhat tougher in texture and stronger in taste. But its fat, or more specifically the oil that could be rendered from the fat, had great food value. A big bear in the right season might provide 30 gallons of oil, which was considered 'better than lard for any culinary purpose' and, when properly prepared, would 'keep good and sweet at any season'.

The black bear, also found in the Rockies, had long been valued as a source of oil. In 1785, the British naturalist Thomas Pennant reported its use in cooking and in treating everything from rheumatic complaints to baldness. 'The fat is of pure white', he reported, 'and has the singular quality of never lying heavy on the stomach, notwithstanding a person drank a quart of it.' To the Indians, the fat also served as an insecticide and muscle relaxant. They 'daub their hands and face with the grease', reported Pennant, 'to prevent them from the bite of musketoes: they also smear their bodies with the oil after excessive exercise. They think, like the Romans of old, that oil supples their joints, and preserves them in full activity.' The Indians may also have believed that by anointing themselves with the oil of so powerful a creature, they would absorb some of its strength and courage as well.

The spiritual affinity to bears felt by native Americans across the continent is reflected in the names they applied to the animals. To the Cree Indians, the grizzly bear was the 'four-legged human' or 'chief's son'. The Sauks called it 'old man'. The Menomini's name for the species meant 'elder brother'. Indians living in the East called the black bear 'grandmother' and 'cousin'. Each had its own legend explaining the close relationship between the bear and its human kin, and each honored the animal with a special ceremony or dance.

The eagle was similarly honored, for to many Indians the eagle was as powerful and important a spiritual presence as the bear. Its 7- to 8-foot wingspan and unchallenged mastery of the air gave it supreme status among creatures of the feathered world. The two North American species, the bald or white-headed eagle and the golden eagle, were equally revered. Their tail feathers, like the claws of the grizzly bear, were worn as badges of achievement, denoting and imparting power. 'With these feathers the natives decorate the stems of their sacred pipes or calumets,' observed Meriwether Lewis.

The natives in every part of the continent who can procure these feathers attach them to their own hair and the mains and tails of their favorite horses by way of ornament. They also decorate their war caps or bonnets with these feathers.

Because of their spiritual importance to the Indians, the tail feathers of an eagle could assume considerable trading value. Two tails, or about 24 feathers, were 'esteemed by the Mandans, Minnetares, Ricares, &c as the full value of a good horse, or gun and accoutrements', according to Lewis. 'With the Great and Little Osages and those nations inhabiting countries where this bird is more rare, the price is even double of that mentioned.'

Since killing the sacred eagle was taboo for many tribes, their feathers were usually obtained from living captive birds. These were either taken as fledglings from the aerie – an extremely dangerous undertaking – or trapped as adults. The German naturalist and explorer Prince Maximilian zu Wied-Neuwied, who traveled to the foothills of the Rockies in 1833, described the process:

> *The birdcatcher lies down at full length in a narrow pit made on purpose, and exactly large enough to hold him. As soon as he has lain down, the pit is covered with brushwood and hay, pieces of meat are laid upon it, and a crow, or some such bird, fastened to it. The eagle, or other bird of prey, is said to descend, and to sit down, in order to eat, on which the birdcatcher seizes it by the legs. I would not believe this had not men worthy of credit given me their word for it.*

Prince Maximilian's report on the eagle came in his account of a 5000-mile journey up the Missouri River and into the Rockies, during which the prince gathered information on the life of the Indians and the wildlife they depended upon. Assisting in this effort was a 24-year-old Swiss artist, Karl Bodmer, whose exquisitely rendered paintings recorded life among many western tribes: Mandan, Blackfoot, Cree, Sioux, Minnetaree, Assiniboin, and Gros Ventres. The two European travelers reached these tribes only a few years before their cultures were irreversibly altered – and in some cases destroyed – by contact with whites.

Many of the villages that Maximilian and Bodmer visited in 1833 were decimated by smallpox just three years later. The semi-agricultural Mandans with whom the visitors spent much of the winter were particularly hard hit. Excellent farmers, traders and artisans with a flair for dramatic dress and ceremony, the Mandans were generally considered the most culturally advanced of all the Plains tribes. After a smallpox infection from an American Fur Company trading party in June 1837, the Mandan were reduced from a tribe of 1500 to little over 100 people in only four months. Within a few years, the Mandan had disappeared entirely. Karl Bodmer's paintings, and those of George Catlin from a few years before, survive as a poignant memorial to this rich but extinguished culture.

Prince Maximilian's access to the Mandans and other tribes was assisted by the rapidly developing commercial activity on the upper Missouri River basin. In the years following Lewis and Clark's expedition, posts had been built there to exploit the rich fur trade of the Rocky Mountain region. Nor was Maximilian the only foreign traveler to take advantage of the new forts and the boat traffic which supported them. Maximilian's countryman and fellow naturalist Frederick Paul Wilhelm, Duke of Württemberg, traveled extensively in the American West between 1820 and 1860. There he amassed a personal collection of American Indian artifacts and natural history specimens that, at the time of his death, was unmatched anywhere in the world.

Another western traveler to witness the Rocky Mountain fur trade and to capture the fast-changing way of life of its participants was Captain William Drummond Stewart. Stewart had served with Wellington in Spain and been decorated for valor at Waterloo. Being the second son of a Scottish baronet, he saw no opportunity to inherit his family's estate, and so set off for America. There he spent the next six years, much of it among the Missouri fur traders and the Indians of the western plains. Unlike Prince Maximillian or Duke Paul, Stewart was not a trained naturalist. He had come to experience the West, not to study it. Nevertheless, in an effort to record his impressions of frontier life, he employed a talented 26-year-old artist, Alfred Jacob Miller, whose paintings survive as a vivid chronicle of the Rocky Mountain fur trade. Stewart met the artist in New Orleans, to which Miller had recently moved from his native Baltimore after two years of art training in Rome and Paris.

In 1837, Miller accompanied Stewart on a trip across the Continental Divide to experience the annual fur trappers' rendezvous. Begun in 1825 on the Green River in present-day Oregon, the rendezvous permitted freelance trappers, the so-called mountain men of the Rockies, to exchange their winter's harvest of pelts for various goods without making the long trip back to the trading posts on the Missouri. The summer gathering was as much a social occasion as an open market for furs. Miller described it in all its colorful glory:

> *At certain specified times, the American Fur Company appoint a Rendezvous for trading with Indians and Trappers, and here they congregate from all quarters. The first day is devoted to 'High Jinks', in which feasting, drinking, and gambling form prominent parts. Sometimes an Indian becomes so excited with 'Fire Water' that he commences 'running a muck'. 'Affairs of honor' are adjusted between rival Trappers – all caused evidently from mixing too much Alcohol with their water. Night closes this scene of revelry and confusion. The following days exhibit the strongest contrast. . . . The Company's great tent is raised; The Indians erect their picturesque white lodges; The accumulated furs are brought forth, and the Company's tent is a besieged and busy place.*

At the heart of the rendezvous was beaver skin, which since the end of the seventeenth century had been one of North America's most important exports. At the time of the Lewis and Clark expedition, the North American fur trade was dominated by the British-owned Hudson's Bay Company (founded in 1670) and its rival the Montreal-based North West Company (founded in 1784). The traders of these companies, like the French *coureurs de bois* before them, traveled widely into the interior of the continent – and in the case of Alexander Mackenzie, all the way to the Pacific coast – to supply the world demand for furs. The managers of these companies watched with dismay as their combined monopoly was threatened by the increasing activities of fur traders from the United States.

Early river travelers depended on hunters for relief from a diet of salt pork and beans. Retrieving their cached supplies was not always a simple matter as the artist Karl Bodmer recorded in his grizzly bear picture of 1833 (above). Fur company forts provided safer and more dependable provisions, serving Indians, trappers and traders alike. Alfred J. Miller painted Fort Laramie during a visit there in 1837.

John Jacob Astor's American Fur Company (1808), the Missouri Fur Company (1809), and the Pacific Fur Company (1810) were among the first of the US groups to challenge the supremacy of the English and French-Canadians in the North American fur trade. Central to the success of the US effort were the independent mountain men whose wanderings these companies supported through the rendezvous system. These were the men who really opened the Rocky Mountains to the outside world.

By the time William Drummond Stewart and Alfred Jacob Miller attended the fur traders' rendezvous in 1837, the heyday of the mountain man – less than three decades old – was already coming to a close. Within a few years, as silk and other materials replaced beaver in the manufacture of fashionable hats, the market that had spawned the exploration of so much of the continent collapsed. Other furbearing animals, including racoon, lynx, mink, marten and otter, continued to be harvested, but the difficulties in trapping these animals and the relatively small return they brought could not justify the hardship associated with living in so inhospitable a place as the Rockies. Moreover, the Indians, who had done much of the trapping, were no longer eager to deal with the white man. Their villages ravaged by white-borne disease and their game in rapid decline, the native Americans now feared and resented their once-welcome trading partners.

Some whites, like Catlin and Stewart, appreciated the Indians and their way of life, and called for their protection and the protection of the wildlife that supported them. But most white Americans of the time, including President Andrew Jackson, saw the Indians' removal as both necessary and inevitable. This view was concisely expressed in 1833 by Timothy Flint, a Massachusetts missionary who, as editor of the *Western Monthly Review*, was an early and vigorous proponent of westward expansion:

Two animals central to the Rocky Mountain fur trade – and to the resulting exploration of the Rockies – were the beaver (above left) and mink (left). They were among the 150 mammals illustrated by John James Audubon and his sons in The Viviparous Quadrupeds of North America *(1845–9).*

> *Either this great continent, in the order of Providence, should have remained in the occupancy of half a million savages, engaged in everlasting conflicts of their peculiar warfare with each other, or it must have become, as it has, the domain of civilized millions. It is in vain to charge upon the latter race results which grew out of the laws of nature, and the universal march of human events. Let the same occupancy of the American wilderness by the municipal European be repeated, if it could be, under the control of the most philanthropic eulogists of the savages, and every reasoning mind will discover that in the gradual ascendancy of the one race, the decline of the other must have been a consequence, and that substantially the same annals would be repeated, as the dark and revolting incidents which we have to record.*

Inevitable or not, the decline of Indian power in the West encouraged more whites to venture into the region. They, in turn, called for increased protection from the Indians who remained. The cycle repeated itself until America's native people were eventually relegated to reservations out of the way of western migration.

'The time between
winter and winter is
very short and the
flowery growth and
blossom of a whole
year are compressed
into two months,'
wrote Isabella Bird in
A Lady's Life in the
Rocky Mountains
(1879). 'The wild-
flowers are gorgeous
and innumerable.'
Bird focused her
attention on Estes
Park in northern
Colorado, but her
descriptions could
just as easily apply to
these Wind River
Range plants in
Wyoming.

Until the 1850s, relatively few whites were eager to settle permanently in the Rockies, but many encountered the mountains while on their way to Oregon and California. As the hopeful homesteaders and, after 1849, gold rushers pushed west on Indian trails that had been mapped by the mountain men, they did so with a growing body of literature about the land through which they journeyed. Travel guides, maps, and dozens of works of popular fiction about the West were available from the 1820s and 30s. In this literature was a great deal of information on the natural history of the area. For the first time in American history, trained naturalists had preceded settlers into the wild.

The scientific exploration that Lewis and Clark had begun was continued by others following the War of 1812. The western river survey of Major Stephen H. Long in 1819–20 was the first expedition sponsored by the government to include trained artists and naturalists and as such set a precedent that would be followed by western expeditions for the rest of the century.

Like Zebulon Pike, whose peak they would climb, Long's expedition first saw the southern Rockies as a mirage. 'For some time we were unable to decide whether what we saw were mountains, or banks of cumulus clouds skirting the horizon, and glittering in the reflected rays of the sun,' reported the trip's chronicler, Edwin James. 'It was only by watching the bright parts, and observing that their form and position remained unaltered, that we were able to satisfy ourselves, they were indeed mountains.' James became the first person on record to climb Pike's Peak and found the mountain a botanist's paradise:

A little above the point where the timber disappears entirely, commences a region of astonishing beauty, and of great interest on account of its productions; the intervals of soil are sometimes extensive, and are covered with a carpet of low but brilliantly flowering alpine plants. Most of these have either matted procumbent stems, or such as including the flower, rarely rise more than an inch in height. In many of them, the flower is the most conspicuous and the largest part of the plant, and in all, the colouring is astonishingly brilliant.

James's botanical collections were some of the very first made in North America above the permanent timberline (the area above which trees will not grow) and were among the most important discoveries of Long's expedition. By revealing the affinity between Rocky Mountain alpine plants and those in alpine and arctic Europe and Asia, they led to a better understanding of North America's geological and climatic past. We now know that some of the plants that grow and bloom above the tree line in the loose gravel and thin air of the Rockies can also be found in the Alps, in Scandinavia, in the Pyrenees, in the Himalayas, in the Altai Mountains of Mongolia, as well as in Greenland, Spitzbergen, and arctic Russia. They are survivors of continental fractures, global climate shifts, and millennia of botanical evolution.

James's climb on Pike's Peak prompted other discoveries as well. In the talus above the tree line he found a small relative of the rabbit, the pika, which he watched drying grass in the sun. He described the animal as 'nearly the size of the common gray squirrel, but shorter and more clumsily formed. . . . In habits and appearance they resemble the prairie dog'. Even more unexpectedly, at the peak's summit he observed a swarm of high-flying insects:

> We were surprised to observe the air in every direction filled with such clouds of grasshoppers, as partially to obscure the day. They had been seen in vast numbers about all the higher parts of the mountain, and many had fallen upon the snow and perished.

The 'grasshoppers' James had seen were almost certainly Rocky Mountain locusts engaged in one of their periodic swarms. Like its African relative, a plague since biblical times, this North American locust massed in huge numbers and, with the help of Rocky Mountain updrafts, moved in cloud-like swarms from Manitoba, Canada, as far south and east as Texas. In his *Standard Natural History* (1884), the American naturalist C.V. Riley gave a vivid account of a locust swarm in the agricultural regions east of the mountains:

> Falling upon a cornfield, the insects convert in a few hours the green and promising acres into a desolate stretch of bare, spindling stalks and stubs. Covering each hill by hundreds; scrambling from row to row like a lot of young, famished pigs, let out to their trough; they sweep clean a field quicker than would a whole herd of hungry steers. Imagine hundreds of square miles covered with such a ravenous horde, and one can get some realization of the picture presented in many parts of the country west of the Mississippi during years of locust invasion. Their flight may be likened to an immense snow-storm, extending from the ground to a height at which our visual organs perceive them only as minute, darting scintillations, leaving the imagination to picture them indefinite distances beyond. In alighting, they circle in myriads about you, beating against everything animate or inanimate; driving into open doors and windows; heaping about your feet and around your buildings, their jaws constantly at work biting and testing all things in seeking what they can devour.

So devastating were the swarms that bounties of 1 dollar for each bushel of insects and 50 cents per gallon of eggs were placed on the locusts in several midwestern states. The Canadian government proposed that its northwestern police and military forces unite in 'a locust vigilance committee' to combat the insect swarms.

Mysteriously, at the end of the nineteenth century the Rocky Mountain locust disappeared completely. Scientists have speculated on the cause of its extinction without reaching a conclusive explanation. Some believe that it required the vegetative disturbance of large herds of buffalo to create a suitable breeding habitat and that the disappearance of the buffalo doomed the locust as well. Others think that the cultivation of the prairie may have caused its demise. Though we will never see their swarming clouds again, scientists may some day unravel the mystery of their behavior and extinction by studying naturally preserved specimens. From Grasshopper Glacier in Montana to the

A conspicuous symbol of the Rocky Mountain West, Pike's Peak serves as home to a number of western mammals, including the rat-sized pika (right) and the larger rockchuck or yellowbelly marmot (far right). A colonial species living in talus slopes and rockslides near the timberline, the pika was admired by early settlers for its habit of cutting, drying and storing large quantities of 'hay' for winter use. The marmot's larger size and fondness for alfalfa has made it unwelcome in many agricultural areas.

summit of Pike's Peak, millions of locusts and other insects still lie frozen in the mountain snows where they fell during flights long ago.

While Edwin James was collecting plants and insects on Pike's Peak, fellow naturalists on Long's expedition, Thomas Say and Titian Peale, were making comparable collections at a lower elevation. Many of the Long expedition's specimens were the first of their kind to reach the nation's growing scientific establishment, then centered in Philadelphia. There they were identified, classified, illustrated, displayed, and usually published within a few years of their collection.

Two other naturalists whose early western discoveries made their way east and into print were Thomas Nuttall and John Kirk Townsend. Nuttall was a somewhat eccentric but highly accomplished English botanist who had collected plants in the Rockies as early as 1811. He had achieved wide acclaim by publishing one of the first botanical texts of the country, *The Genera of North American Plants* (1818), and a field guide to the birds entitled *A Manual of the Ornithology of the United States and Canada* published in two pocket-sized volumes in 1832 and 1834. John Kirk Townsend was a 24-year-old physician and pharmacist with a passion for birds and a knack for writing. In 1834, Nuttall and Townsend made an expedition to the Rockies to collect plants and animals for Philadelphia's Academy of Natural Sciences. Townsend's account of their trip, *Narrative of a Journey Across the Rocky Mountains* (1839), is a classic of American western literature. Riding west to the Rockies from Independence, Missouri, with a trading party of 70 men, 250 horses, a band of missionaries and a large herd of horned cattle, the two naturalists found new species at every turn. 'The road was very uneven and difficult', wrote Townsend, but flanked by 'flowers of every hue':

> *Mr. N. was here in his glory. He rode on ahead and cleared the passages with a trembling hand, looking anxiously back at the approaching party as though he feared it would come ere he had finished and tread his lovely prizes underfoot.*

Townsend too was overwhelmed:

> *I never before saw so great a variety of birds in the same space. All were beautiful and many new to me. My game bag was full and I was loathe to leave. None but a naturalist can appreciate a naturalist's feeling – his delight amounting to ecstasy – when a specimen he has never before seen meets his eye, and the sorrow and grief which he feels when he is compelled to tear himself from a spot abounding with all he has anxiously and unremittingly sought for.*

While crossing the Rockies, Townsend and Nuttall traveled for a while with William Drummond Stewart and Alfred Jacob Miller. In the end, the two naturalists journeyed all the way to Fort Vancouver, a Hudson's Bay Company post on the Pacific coast. There Townsend remained for several years as a physician while Nuttall continued on to Hawaii and California.

Nuttall and Townsend's specimens, both birds and plants, were sent back to Philadelphia. There John James Audubon, completing his massive book on the birds of America, was able to examine them. In 1836 the great artist bought 93 duplicate bird skins from the Academy of Natural Sciences to serve as models for the plates of *The Birds of America*. 'Such beauties! Such rarities! Such Novelties!' he exulted in a letter to a friend. And so they were, among them the sharp-tailed and sage grouse, the dipper, rufous hummingbird, yellow-headed blackbird, mountain bluebird, valley or California quail, and varied thrush. Audubon had a chance to see some of these western birds in the wild during his own trip on the Missouri River in 1842, while collecting specimens for his companion volume on the mammals of North America. Sadly, failing health, logistical difficulties and the threats of Indian attack prevented the ageing naturalist from reaching the Rockies on this, the last great expedition.

By mid-century, published accounts of the Rockies as a sportsman's paradise were drawing increasing numbers of foreign visitors to the mountains. The most extravagant was surely Sir St George Gore, an Irish baronet, who traveled through Colorado, Wyoming and Montana from 1854 to 1857 on a hunting safari unique to the American experience. Gore's baggage train consisted of 21 Red River carts, four 6-mule wagons and two 3-yoke ox wagons, one filled entirely with sporting arms made by England's finest gunsmiths. Included in the entourage were guides, secretaries, cooks, dog tenders (to care for a pack of 50 thoroughbred hunting hounds), and a professional 'fly dresser' who could prepare trout lures on demand. There were over 100 horses, 18 oxen, 3 milk cows, and an unrecorded number of mules. Gore camped under a green and white striped linen tent with comfortable furniture, carpets and a brass bed. His gourmet meals were complemented by French wines and other imported condiments. His three-year hunting trip cost 500 000 dollars and the lives of 2000 buffalo, 1600 elk and deer, and 100 bear.

Most Rocky Mountain sportsmen were far less profligate. They learned in a flood of 'how to' guide books that it was possible to make the trip of a lifetime without spending a lifetime's fortune. In 1853, John Palliser assured his 'brother sportsmen of England and Scotland', that a hunting trip to the Rockies needed only the bare essentials to be a success:

> *Before leaving the settlements, provide yourselves with lead, tobacco, coffee, sugar, salt, needles, one or two dressed skins for making and mending moccasins and with this equipment, you may pass from Independence [Missouri] to the Pacific Ocean.*

Palliser pointed out in a popular account of his own expedition to the upper Missouri (1847–8) that there was much more to be gained by a trip to the Rockies than access to wild game. 'The atmosphere in these regions is extremely healthy and its effect upon the constitution something wonderful,' he declared.

The idea of mountain rejuvenation was one that would be expanded and reinforced by other writers in the years to come. The Rockies, once a wilderness known only to Indians and a handful of rugged mountain men, were beginning

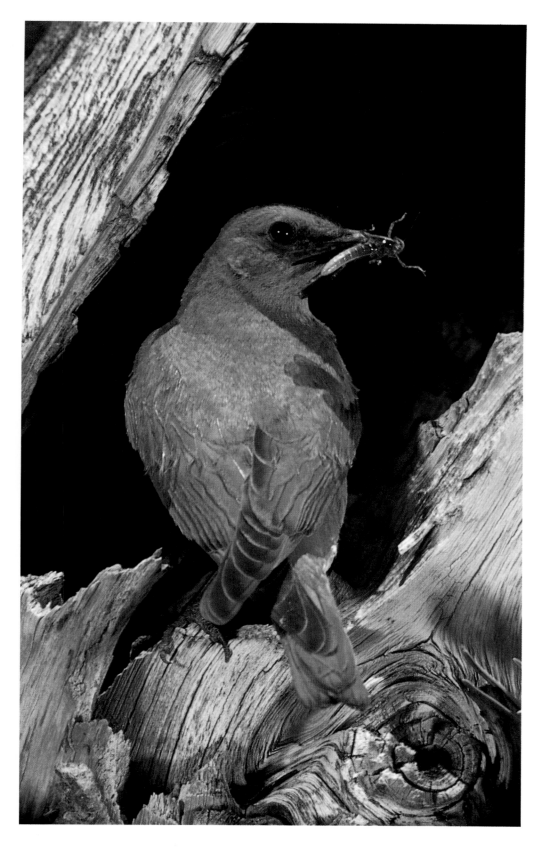

LEFT A male mountain bluebird pauses near its nest in a sun-bleached hollow tree. It is most often found in western mountains between 5000 and 13000 feet.

RIGHT 'The mountains of Europe and Asia recall gods and dryads and the long procession of man,' wrote the Himalayan mountaineer and Arctic explorer T. G. Longstaff after a visit to the Canadian Rockies. 'These empty wilds are peopled only by our bare imagination.' With careful promotion by the Canadian Pacific Railroad, such magnificent peaks as Mt Edith Cavell in Jasper National Park, Alberta, became major tourist destinations within only a few decades of their 'discovery' by government surveyors.

OVERLEAF A lynx pauses at the water's edge in the pink glow of sunrise. These solitary animals can range up to 50 miles in search of snowshoe hare and other small game.

to become a holiday destination for tourists. The dangers that remained in the region provided what one enthusiastic visitor called 'that dash of excitement which is always needed to make any life really perfect'.

Horace Greely, the founder and editor of the influential *New York Tribune* and a strong advocate of western development, was one who helped to depict the mountains as a place for healthful recreation with his appealing description in *An Overland Journey from New York to San Francisco in 1859*:

> *The Rocky Mountains, with their grand aromatic forests, their grassy glades, their frequent springs, and dancing streams of the brightest, sweetest water, their pure, elastic atmosphere, and their unequalled game and fish, are destined to be a favourite resort and home of civilised man. I never visited a region where physical life could be more surely prolonged or fully enjoyed.*

Only one thing was more attractive than the promise of a long, healthy and enjoyable life: gold. By the 1850s the Rockies offered this as well. The tremendous heat and pressure that accompanied the creation of the Rockies had at the same time formed small deposits of gold amid the mountains' metamorphic rocks. Later, these narrow veins of gold were exposed and carried away by mountain streams as small flakes and particles. As the fast current of the streams slowed at the mountain bases, the gold was dropped along with other suspended matter. Lewis, Clark, Pike, Long, and other early explorers failed to notice it, but there were small amounts of gold in the sand and gravel bars of many of the streams that they drank from or followed in the course of their travels.

With the discovery of gold in California in 1848, prospectors began to look more carefully in the streams of the Rockies. Results were disappointing at first, but in 1857 and 1858 several small finds in Colorado, near Pike's Peak and the newly established town of Denver some 70 miles north, raised interest and hope. A financial panic in the East, and aggressive promotion by land speculators and merchants eager to supply prospectors, soon turned a minor discovery into a major rush.

As many as 100 000 Easterners set out for the gold fields of Colorado in the spring of 1859 with 'Pike's Peak or bust' emblazoned on their minds if not their wagons. As the vanguard reached the mountains they quickly overran the mining areas and exhausted the meager supplies of food and shelter available. When thousands more arrived in their wake, a panic swept the makeshift camps and shanty towns that had sprung up along the eastern foothills of the Rockies. Rumors of food riots and looting sent some of the new arrivals home and stopped others midway across the continent. It is estimated that as many as half of those who set out for Pike's Peak turned back before reaching their goal. But the 50 000 who made it were not disappointed. While few struck it rich, most were able to make more from mining and the business that supported it than they might have from manual labor at home. Roughly half stayed on as permanent residents of the Rocky Mountain region.

The initial placer mines (those that collected the gold washed out of the hills) were soon augmented by large-scale excavations and various separation

processes, including smelting. In 1868 the Colorado territory produced more than 2 million dollars worth of gold. In 1871 the figure rose to 3.5 million. Silver soon joined gold as a crucial source of mineral wealth in the southern Rockies.

The intrepid English traveler Isabella Bird, who visited Colorado in 1873, found Denver a bustling place benefiting from its new prosperity and railroad links with east and west. The fast-growing city was successfully catering to the business of residents and tourists alike:

> *Denver is no longer the Denver of Hepworth Dixon [a popular writer of Wild West fiction]. A shooting affray in the street is as rare as in Liverpool, and one no longer sees men dangling to the lamp-posts when one looks out in the morning! It is a busy place, the* entrepôt *and distributing point for an immense district, with good shops, some factories, fair hotels, and the usual deformities and refinements of civilization. Peltry [pelt] shops abound, sportsman, hunter, miner, teamster, emigrant, can be completely rigged out at fifty different stores. At Denver, people who come from the East to try the 'camp cure' now so fashionable, get their outfit of wagon, driver, horses, tent, bedding, and stove, and start for the mountains. Asthmatic people are there in such numbers as to warrant the holding of an 'asthmatic convention' of patients cured and benefited.*

Like many others drawn to the Rockies for their magnificent scenery and wildlife, Isabella Bird was horrified by what was happening to the land:

> *There was mining everywhere along that grand road, with all its destruction and devastation, its digging, burrowing, gulching, and sluicing; and up all along the seemingly inaccessible heights were holes with their roofs log supported, in which solitary and patient men were selling their lives for treasure. Down by the stream, all among the icicles, men were sluicing and washing, and everywhere along the heights were the scars of hardly-passable trails, too steep even for pack-jacks, leading to the holes, and down which the miner packs the ore on his back. Many a heart has been broken for the few finds which have been made along those hill sides. All the ledges are covered with charred stumps, a picture of desolation, where nature had made everything grand and fair.*

The sportsman and writer William A. Baillie-Grohman, who visited the Rockies between 1879 and 1881, characterized the frontier mentality that created such devastation:

> *Reverence for old landmarks and time-hallowed institutions the frontiersman knows not, for there are none of these venerable finger-posts to mature civilization. Nothing on the face of the broad Earth is sacred to him. Nature presents herself as his slave. He digs and delves wherever he fancies; forests are there but to be felled, or, if that process be too slow and laborious, to be set ablaze; mountains are made to be honeycombed by his drills and sluices; rocks and hills exist but to be blasted or to be spirited away by the*

PREVIOUS PAGES *Still carving its way into the Montana landscape, the Missouri River has shaped the human history of the West as profoundly as it has etched the terrain through which it flows. To Lewis and Clark and other explorers, it was an avenue to the Pacific. To American fur traders of the 1830s, it was a seemingly inexhaustible source of peltry and a reliable way to transport it. To the Indians of the region, it was a source of food, a place of commerce, and an important spiritual force.*

powerful jet from the nozzle of his hydraulic tube. Landscape itself is not secure, for eminences may be levelled, lakes laid dry, and the watercourse of rivers may be turned off, as best suits his immediate desires.

While Baillie-Grohman's description was ostensibly about the tamers of the American West, in many respects it accurately captured the prevailing attitudes of people across the continent. For more than two centuries, American immigrants had been successfully 'making something from nothing' and 'forging civilization from wilderness'. Americans prided themselves on their accomplishments and wore their irreverence as a badge of honor. It was therefore difficult, even revolutionary, to suggest that the time had come for restraint and that some wild places were so unusual as to deserve protection from exploitation.

The concept of a national park had been suggested by George Catlin as early as 1833. In the succeeding decades Ralph Waldo Emerson, Henry David Thoreau and other eastern intellectuals picked up the idea and called for preservation of the wild. In the period of rapid industrialization that followed the American Civil War, a national concern for conservation began to take root.

One of the first places that the conservationists focused on was an area of unusual thermal springs and geysers in northwestern Wyoming. A mountain man, trapper and member of the Lewis and Clark expedition, John Colter, may have been the first white man to visit the upper Yellowstone basin in 1807. He reported such bizarre phenomena – boiling hot springs, brilliantly colored mineral deposits, calcified remains of trees – that most people believed he had made them up. Subsequent exploration of the area now known as Colter's Hell revealed that all that Colter had said was true, and that there were many other natural wonders and curiosities to be found in the area. Photographer William Henry Jackson and artist Thomas Moran, accompanying a government survey of 1871, brought back powerful visual evidence of the breathtaking beauty of the region. Their works showed spectacular canyons, waterfalls and thermal pools. A geyser that shot water hundreds of feet in the air with predictable regularity was later named Old Faithful.

In 1872 Congress took up the debate about setting the Yellowstone area aside as a national park to prevent its exploitation by private entrepreneurs. Proponents of the idea assured their colleagues that not only was the area geographically unique, but because it was too high and cold to cultivate, maintaining it as a park would do 'no harm to the material interests' of the nation. After sharp discussion, Congress agreed to preserve what the government's topographer Ferdinand Hayden called 'the beautiful decorations' of the Yellowstone. When President Ulysses S. Grant signed the act designating over 2 million acres as the world's first national park on 1 March 1872, the intention was to protect the 'remarkable curiosities' and 'rare wonders' of the Yellowstone geyser basin from spoilage. Yet in the years to follow, an even greater importance for the park was recognized. By establishing a preserve and 'public pleasuring ground', the United States had also created what one senator in the 1880s called a physical and spiritual 'breathing place for the national lungs'.

OVERLEAF An area of extraordinary thermal activity, the Yellowstone River basin in northwestern Wyoming was set aside as a 'public park or pleasuring ground for the benefit and enjoyment of the people' in 1872. The world's first National Park, Yellowstone was described a decade later as the real and symbolic 'breathing place for the national lungs'.

PAGE 184 Early descriptions of the Mammoth Hot Springs and other 'natural curiosities' in the Yellowstone region were discounted by the rest of the country as tall tales invented by imaginative mountain men. A series of government surveying expeditions following the Civil War made clear that Yellowstone really was a 'wonderland' and an area worth protecting.

Not everyone agreed that Yellowstone Park was a necessary or even a good idea. In 1883, for example, Senator John J. Ingalls of Kansas attacked it as an expensive irrelevancy. 'The best thing the Government could do with Yellowstone National Park', Ingalls contended, 'is to survey it and sell it as other public lands are sold.' A few years later, when railroad interests lobbied Congress for a right-of-way through the park to facilitate mining in the area, the issue of either using the land or preserving it inviolate came to a head. 'Is it true', asked a railroad company spokesman incredulously, 'that the rights and privileges of citizenship, the vast accumulation of property, and the demands of commerce ... are to yield to ... a few sportsmen bent only on the protection of a few buffalo?'

In reply, park defenders argued that there were some things more valuable than commerce. To Representative William McAdoo of New Jersey, Yellowstone was a place where citizens could seek 'in the great West the inspiring sights and mysteries of nature that elevate mankind and bring it closer communion with omniscience'. With a plea for colleagues to 'prefer the beautiful and sublime ... to the heartless mammon and the greed of capital', McAdoo and his forces defeated the railroad application by 107 to 65 votes. The principle of wilderness preservation had prevailed.

LIVING ON THE EDGE
THE · DESERT · SOUTHWEST

When Francisco Vázquez de Coronado with an expeditionary force of 300 Spanish soldiers trudged north from Mexico City in early 1540, he expected to find the fabled Seven Cities of Cíbola brimming with turquoise, silver and gold. What he found instead were extensive tracts of desert and an Indian culture that had been flourishing for as long as his own.

Coronado was not a naturalist, nor did he have any real interest in natural history except as it pertained to food or shelter. The observations of his party had more to do with military matters and extractable wealth. But there were certain things he could not help but notice. While his mind was on glittering dreams of El Dorado, his feet were unavoidably treading over the hot, dry, sun-baked soils of the desert Southwest, one of the most beautiful and biologically complex series of desert habitats on earth.

Coronado or his men actually touched on parts of several different deserts during this exploratory journey, each characterized by a distinctive climate and vegetation. The first he saw was the Sonoran Desert which straddles the Gulf of California (or Sea of Cortés) like a giant wishbone, covering more than 100 000 square miles in northern Mexico, Arizona, eastern California, and southern Nevada. It is a land of searing temperatures – often well over 100 degrees Fahrenheit – and sparse rainfall, in some areas less than 2 inches a year. North of the Sonoran Desert lies the Mojave Desert and, above that, the Great Basin Desert which includes much of the land between the Sierra Nevada and the Rocky Mountains. Both the Mojave and the Great Basin deserts are of higher elevation than the Sonoran and have much colder winters and seasonably sporadic rainfall. Farther east, in northern Mexico, western Texas and southern New Mexico, is the continent's only other true desert, the Chihuahuan Desert, separated from the others by the Continental Divide.

Coronado's chronicler, Pedro de Castañeda, characterized the vegetation in much of the Southwest with a single word, 'spiky'. It was an accurate if overly succinct description of the 100 or so species of cacti which dominate the region. The most conspicuous of the cacti, and the one exclusively associated with the Sonoran Desert, is the saguaro cactus with a bulbous central trunk and four to eight thick uplifted branches. A full-grown saguaro can reach heights of up to 50 feet, and weigh well over 10 tons, 90 per cent of which is water contained in the tissues of the expandable, fleshy trunk. Two other similarly shaped cacti of roughly the same size are the cardon and the hairbrush cactus, the last named for its bristly apple-sized fruit which were used as combs by the Yaqui and Mayo Indians.

The organpipe, senita, pitaya agria, and sina cacti, also residents of the Sonoran Desert, take on a different form. They have clusters of 10 or 20 upright arms which spring from a central base at ground level. When mature, all four species grow taller than a person on horseback.

Castañeda probably intended 'spiky' to describe the overall shapes of these giant desert plants, but it could also have applied to their distinctive surface texture, for most cacti are covered with thorns. 'Thorns', wrote an early Jesuit missionary to the region, 'are surprisingly numerous, and there are many of frightening aspect.' Within a single handspan on an organpipe cactus, the enterprising priest counted no less than 1680 toothpick-sized spines. 'It is easy to see', he concluded, 'that according to my calculations, a single one of these shrubs carries more than a million thorns.'

The thorns of the cactus perform several useful functions for the plant as it tries to conserve water and avoid excessive heat. Without transpiring moisture, they provide a certain amount of daytime shade to the fleshy branches and trunk. They break the desiccating desert winds, thus enveloping the cactus in a thin blanket of still air which helps to reduce evaporation. Finally, they provide protection from the few browsing animals that can survive in this harsh climate. Some thorns, like those of the cholla, actually help the plants to spread to new terrain by snagging themselves into almost anything that brushes against them. One variety is called jumping cholla because its thorns break off in jointed segments so easily that it appears to aggressively seek a host to attach itself to. Its barbed spines are among the most painful to encounter and difficult to extract. When finally dropped by its reluctant carrier, the cholla sprouts roots and begins a new life.

Some animals take advantage of the bristly defenses of the cacti and employ them for their own benefit. The cactus wren, for example, the largest wren in North America, nests almost exclusively in cholla. Using sticks and grass, it constructs a bulky, melon-shaped nest amid the cactus's protective branches. Thrashers and doves are other frequent nesters in the cholla's spiny branches. Mammals, too, employ the formidable defenses of the cholla. Packrats often reinforce the external structure of their nests with a barrier of cholla joints, though just how they manage to carry the spiny sections in their mouths without getting pricked is still a mystery. Protected by the spines of one cactus, the packrat lives on the flesh of another cactus, the saguaro. The saguaro is poisonous to many animals, but the packrat has evolved ways of overcoming its toxins

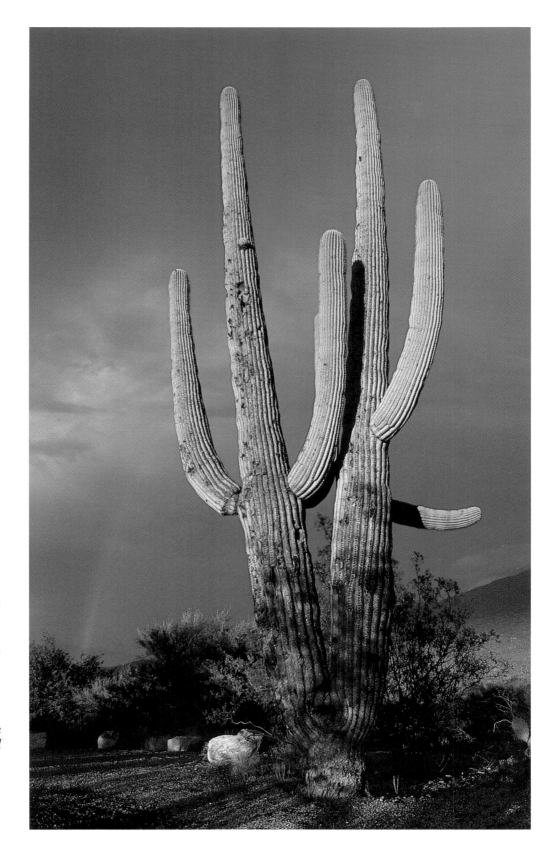

Its huge trunk ready to store the water of a passing storm, a saguaro cactus glows in the sunlight of an Arizona afternoon. A full grown saguaro such as this can absorb and hold up to a ton of water, enabling the plant to grow and flower even in times of prolonged drought. Its root-lined catchment basin may extend more than 40 feet from the plant.

and will often make tunnels inside the huge structures without fatally harming the cactus.

Another species to make use of the saguaro is the Gila woodpecker. A yellow-bellied bird with a brilliant red crown patch, it excavates nesting cavities in the trunks of the largest cacti. Like the other birds that use these plants for nesting, it is virtually invulnerable from predation when inside the plant. Abandoned woodpecker holes may subsequently serve as the homes of elf owls, flycatchers, purple martins and other cavity-nesting species.

Biologists have identified seven distinctive zones of vegetation within the Sonoran Desert, but to Coronado and Castañeda it was all 'wilderness'. Only when they reached the higher elevations of the so-called 'cold' desert, north and east of the Gila River, did they note a significant change. There, piñon pine began to replace the saguaro cactus and mesquite bushes grew to tree height. After five months of exhausting travel, the flagging conquistadores took the changes in vegetation as welcome evidence that they were approaching more conventionally fertile land. They were encouraged by an occasional river or spring seep supporting plants that were familiar to them – 'grass like that of Castile', watercress, pennyroyal and wild marjoram. Most of all they welcomed increasing signs of human activity for it meant they might soon reach the golden cities of their dreams.

The Zuni Indians had been observing the Spaniards' movements from afar, and signalled one another of the Europeans' approach with fires, 'a method of communication as good as we could have devised ourselves', Coronado observed. Unfortunately, communication between the Zuni and the Spaniards was not so effective. The two groups soon came to blows when Coronado demanded entrance to the first of Cíbola's seven cities. 'It is a village of about two hundred warriors, three and four stories high with the houses small and having only a few rooms,' wrote Castañeda. 'There are haciendas in New Spain which make a better appearance at a distance.' It was not quite what Coronado had expected. Nor was access as easy as he had hoped. His arrival at the village walls brought a hail of stones and arrows. 'For myself', he wrote,

they knocked me down to the ground twice with countless great stones which they threw down from above, and if I had not been protected by the very good headpiece which I wore, I think that the outcome would have been bad for me.

Eventually, despite the numerical superiority of the Zuni, the Spaniards' technology carried the day and the conquistadores took the town. Though bitterly disappointed by the lack of gold in Cíbola or any of the other villages they captured, the Spanish were grateful for, and intrigued by, the abundance of food they found in the communal granaries of each. How was it, they wondered, that the Indians were able to wrest so bountiful a harvest from so harsh a land?

The answer is one that goes back thousands of years. While the various groups living in the Southwest were always adept at harvesting the natural

An immature Gila woodpecker peers from its nest hole as an adult male arrives with one of dozens of meals its brood requires each day. The woodpecker carves its nesting site a year in advance in order to give the cactus flesh time to scar and harden into a suitable cavity. When abandoned, the valuable excavation may be used by other birds.

The name and soft, fuzzy appearance of the teddy bear cholla (above) are deceptive. Its thorns are so sharp that the slightest brush against them can be painful. Despite such protection, the peccary and other desert mammals somehow manage to eat the delicate flowers of these and other cholla (left) without injury. A barrel cactus (right) blooms in the wake of a late winter storm.

resources of the area – fruits from the saguaro cactus and prickly pear, seeds from the mesquite, nuts from the piñon pine, hearts from the agave – they knew that the irregularity and paucity of rain made for highly erratic harvests. To augment the naturally occurring foods, therefore, the Indians began to grow crops of their own, such as corn, beans, onions, and peas, the seeds for many of which they obtained in trade with native groups from other parts of the hemisphere.

The agricultural tribes, some of whom lived in southern Arizona long before the arrival of the Spaniards, are known to have cultivated 19 different domesticated plants and over 30 native species. In addition, they knew and had names for 275 different species of wild plants, 40 of which were substantial food sources. Among these tribes was the Papago, or 'bean-eating people', now known as the Tohono O'odham.

At the heart of the Papago agronomy was the tepary bean, a squat, hardy plant which manages to overcome drought by maturing rapidly and by sending roots as deep as 6 feet into the sandy Sonoran soil. Similarly, the Papago corn and yellow-coated squashes produce bountiful yields with less than 5 inches of rainfall per year.

One of the Papagos' secrets was that they laid their fields so as to maximize the available water. They cut burrows in the desert at points where flash floods would slow and soak into the soil. They connected washes and built ditches so that rains in the hills would irrigate their thirsty plants up to 10 miles away. Prehistoric Indians in the Sonoran Desert built irrigation canals as sophisticated as any in Europe, Asia or Africa.

The first Spanish explorers had a grudging respect for the Indians whose towns or pueblos they invaded. 'These people are very intelligent', Castañeda reported:

> They wear long robes of feathers and of the skins of hares, and cotton blankets. ... They do not have chiefs as in New Spain, but are ruled by a council of the oldest men. They have priests who preach to them whom they call papás. These are the elders. ... They tell them how they are to live, and I believe that they give certain commandments for them to keep, for there is no drunkenness among them nor sodomy nor sacrifices, neither do they eat human flesh, nor steal, but they are usually at work.

The Indians' admirable behavior and a coincidence of custom – 'They make the cross as a sign of peace' – convinced Coronado that these people were ripe for Christianity. And so, for the next 300 years, Franciscan and Jesuit missionaries devoted their lives to converting the Indians to a new religion and a European way of life.

Settling along the green river valleys, the priests expanded the Indians' farming areas, adding new crops to those that the native Americans already grew. The results were sometimes quite remarkable. 'I am in a most fertile country', reported Eusebio Francisco Kino, a widely traveled and highly revered Jesuit missionary:

There are already very rich and abundant fields, plantings and crops of wheat, maize, frijoles, chickpeas, beans, lentils, bastard chickpeas, etc. There are good gardens, and in them vineyards for wine for masses, with cane-brakes of sweet cane for syrup and panocha, and, with the favor of heaven, before long for sugar. There are many Castilian fruit trees, such as fig trees, quinces, oranges, pomegranates, peaches, apricots, pear trees, apples, mulberries, pecans, prickly pears, etc., with all sorts of garden stuff, such as cabbages, leeks, garlic, watermelons, white cabbage, lettuce, onions, anise, pepper, mustard, mint, Castilian roses, white lilies, etc., with very good timber for all kinds of building, such as pine, ash, cypress, walnut, china trees, mesquite, alders, poplar, willow, tamarind, etc.

While Jesuit mission lands rarely contained all of the crops Father Kino described in this probably amalgamated account, they were verdant paradises compared to the desert that surrounded them. Building on a base of indigenous agriculture, the missionaries created oases of European civilization with which they kept at bay the threatening and dangerous world beyond.

'Hot countries are particularly plagued by poisonous animals,' observed an apprehensive priest. 'In Sonora they are so numerous that it can almost be said that hidden murderers sit under every stone.' One hazard was the Gila monster:

There is a four-footed kind of lizard ... which is very poisonous and has a stumpy tail and markings of various colors. It is claimed that there is no other cure for its bite than to cut away the affected part immediately. It runs fast after its prey and seems to draw its victim to it with its deadly breath, swallowing it whole as does the buyo [boa constrictor], according to Father Gumilla. Someone once told me he had seen an escorpian [Gila monster] with half a rabbit in its mouth, having already swallowed the other half.

The Gila monster and its close relative, the beaded lizard of Mexico, are the only poisonous lizards in the world. While rarely fast-moving, and incapable of attracting victims with its 'deadly breath' as legend held, the Gila monster does have a potent and potentially fatal venom which enters a wound through the grooved teeth of its powerful jaw. Fortunately for the Spanish, the Gila monster is more interested in its usual prey of small rodents, bird eggs, and insects than in humans, and it spends as much as 95 per cent of its time underground, away from the desiccating heat of the sun.

The Jesuits who traveled through the Southwest in the first half of the eighteenth century knew of no cure for the Gila monster's bite: 'he who is thus poisoned will be a corpse in a few hours,' reported one. However they did offer an unusual – and totally useless – treatment for the poison of another of the desert's venomous reptiles, the rattlesnake:

The most common and efficacious remedy consists of securing the head of the snake between two sticks, keeping the head in such a position that the snake cannot bite. Then the tail is held firmly and stretched out so that the snake cannot coil. The victim of the snakebite then bites the snake. At this

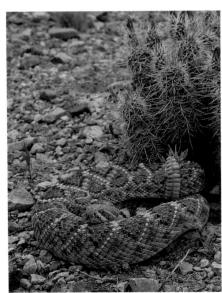

point something truly remarkable happens. The patient does not swell, but the snake does, monstrously so, until it bursts.

Other missionaries noted that thanks to 'the benign foresight of the Creator', rattlesnakes 'reveal their own presence and, as it were, warn persons against misfortune' with the shaking of their horny tails. To the Jesuits this was perhaps the only useful attribute they possessed. In both practical terms and according to holy scripture, the snake embodied for them everything that was evil.

To the Hopi Indians of northeastern Arizona, the rattlesnake had a very different meaning. Because of its shape and quick movement, the Indians associated it with both lightning and rushing water. Thus it became a powerful symbol of life and fertility, and is still incorporated into a yearly religious ceremony petitioning the gods for rain to nourish the Hopi's desert crops.

Each August, after many days of preparation, black and red painted snake priests emerge from holy enclosures called *kivas*, which are dug into the ground so that the priests can commune with positive underworld spirits. As their fellow antelope priests chant, the snake priests reach into an altar in the central plaza of the village where as many as 60 bull snakes, gopher snakes and rattlesnakes have been gathered from the wild. Each of the priests in turn puts a snake in his mouth and then dances ceremoniously around the plaza while a second priest distracts and soothes the writhing serpent with a feathered stick. In the end, the snakes are released back in the wild to the north, east, south and west. They carry the message to the spirits that the Hopi still practice their traditional ways of life, and they petition those deities who control the rains to assist in watering the summer crops.

Unlike the Plains Indians, to whom warfare became an important part of life, the Hopi focused their energies on religious activities, community life, and the struggle of desert survival. Perhaps the difficulty of eking a living from the land made the time and disruption of warfare undesirable, or their religious convictions made it repugnant. In any case their pacific ways were reflected in their own name for themselves, *Hopitu Shinumu*, 'the peaceful people'.

Until the introduction of horses from Spain, the inhospitable nature of the desert helped to buffer the Hopi from conflict with most other indigenous people. Their life was remarkably stable, with village sites lasting for many hundreds of years. The town of Oraibi, for example, which served as the unofficial capital of the Hopi until 1906, was first settled in AD 1125. Predating many European cities, including Berlin, Stockholm, Liverpool and Vienna, and the Aztec capital of Tenochtitlán (Mexico City), Oraibi is almost certainly the oldest continuously inhabited town in North America.

Such stability, based on the integral link between deeply rooted religious beliefs and highly efficient agricultural practices, made the Hopi less open to Christianity and other European practices than the Spaniards had hoped. For more than a century the Spaniards tried, sometimes ruthlessly, to convert, 'civilize', and subjugate the Hopi and other Indians of the Southwest, until the oppressed tribes rose up in the great Pueblo Revolt of 1680. In a well-coordinated

Their arrival suspended in time in an Indian pictograph (above left), Spanish conquistadores and missionaries brought lasting changes to the Desert Southwest in the form of horses, livestock and new religious beliefs.

'Hot countries are particularly plagued by poisonous animals,' observed an early missionary. The Gila monster (far left) and the diamondback rattlesnake (left) to which he referred, represented positive spiritual forces to the Indians of the region.

series of attacks, the Indians killed most of the Spanish missionaries and drove the rest from the area, thus regaining their independence. But this lasted little more than a decade. Then, driven by a continuing interest in mineral resources and a wish to resecure political control of the area, the Spanish began a second period of conquest. Spanish control of New Mexico continued until the time of Mexican independence, more than a century later.

Spanish settlement in the Southwest had several important environmental impacts on the region. It gave rise to the large herds of cattle and flocks of domestic sheep and goats that would eventually dominate the grasslands of the Great Basin and drastically overgraze the deserts of the Southwest. The sheep and goats not only affected the land but also changed the Hopi's and Navajo's traditional weaving from agave and yucca fibers and cotton to wool. The fragile desert ecology had not supported large grazing animals before and was soon altered by the pounding hooves and widely foraging livestock. The thorns of the cactus helped to protect some of the native vegetation, but many of the less-protected plants were consumed and, in some cases, extinguished.

By far the greatest long-term environmental impact to the continent as a whole, however, derived from the Spaniards' introduction of the horse. Ironically it was the horse that would also compromise their own activities by providing the Apache, Comanche and other warlike tribes with the means to terrorize and ultimately destroy many of the Spaniards' isolated mission outposts.

When they first brought horses to the New World, the Spaniards were actually reintroducing a family of mammals that had flourished in the Americas long before the ice age. Exactly why the several species of North American horse became extinct some 8000 to 10000 years ago is still a mystery. The conquistadores originally obtained their horses from the invading Moors of North Africa, and brought the animals to America as a means of transport. They soon found them to be of great psychological advantage as well. 'Horses are the most necessary things in the new countries,' reported Pedro de Castañeda after his return from Coronado's expedition. 'They frighten the enemy most.'

The first reaction of the Indians was to kill the unfamiliar animals. However, they quickly learned to ride them, their equestrian skill often surpassing that of the whites. The Spanish tried to prevent the Indians from obtaining horses, but it was inevitable that some would escape from Coronado's herd of 1000 and that during subsequent settlements still more would be stolen. The Pueblo Revolt of 1680 appears to have put the greatest number of horses into Indian hands.

Horses spread quickly among Indian groups after the Revolt, dramatically changing the Indians' way of life and their relationship with the land. From their introduction in the Southwest, they were traded northward along the west slopes of the Rocky Mountains and from there east into the Great Plains. The Shoshone, Crow and Blackfoot of the northern Rockies had obtained horses by the late seventeenth century, long before they had even encountered Europeans. By 1690 horses had reached the Red River to the east of the Rockies, and by 1719 two villages of the Wichita in present-day Oklahoma possessed a herd of 300 animals.

Montezuma's Castle in Arizona (with which the Aztec chief had no connection) dates from about AD 1100. From a natural sinkhole 7 miles away, ancient farmers irrigated crops by day, then climbed ladders to this 5-storeyed, 20-room cliff dwelling. The building was declared a National Monument in 1906.

While Indians to the north and east were adjusting their lives to the increased mobility afforded by the horses, tribes of the Southwest, such as the Zuni, Hopi, Pima, and Papago, continued the quiet agricultural existence they had known since long before the arrival of whites. The missionaries, who had learned much about desert agronomy from the Indians – and depended upon them for the planting and harvesting of crops – were nevertheless exasperated by the Indians' attitudes toward the land. As the German Jesuit, Ignaz Pfefferkorn, wrote:

> *Sonorans are sworn enemies of all work and exertion, unless it is associated either with the greatest necessity or with their pleasure. They till and sow a piece of land so small that it yields them hardly as much maize as they need to subsist. And if they could get food more easily, they would not perform even this meager labor. Hunting, though it is laborious and difficult, is nevertheless the common practice of the Sonorans, partly because it is a pleasure which conforms to their inclination. But even in hunting they do not overlook their comfort. ... The missionary, of course, expended all conceivable effort to effect an improvement in these and in other horrible customs of the Sonorans by introducing a Christian mode of life. In some cases the end was realized through zealous admonitions, but in most cases little could be accomplished.*

While some of the Indians' reluctance to labor in a European mold was undoubtedly conscious resistance to European servitude, their slower pace of life and subsistence-level harvest was actually a sensible adaptation to desert living. When Pfefferkorn observed with derision that 'the behavior of a Sonoran is little different from the manner of living of an unreasoning brute', he was unwittingly complimenting the Indians on their ability to adjust their expenditure of energy to the conditions of the environment.

The secret of survival for all desert species, plant and animal, involves retaining moisture and reducing or avoiding extremes of temperature. Many desert-living mammals spend the hot daylight hours drowsing in burrows excavated in soft sand and gravel, or in nests built of branches and twigs. These not only keep them safe from daytime predators, but also enable the mammals to conserve precious body moisture by avoiding unnecessary activity and remaining in a cool and relatively moist environment. Similarly the 'lazy' Indians preferred their grassy shelters to the blazing heat of the mission fields.

Lizards, snakes, turtles and other reptiles require external sources of heat to become active, and so tend to sleep by night, seek shelter during the hottest part of the day, and feed during the morning and evening hours. Their low metabolism and thick body coverings of skin and scales help to reduce moisture loss. In colder desert areas, some reptiles and mammals lower their energy and moisture demands by hibernating during the harshest winter months. In hot southern deserts, other species achieve similar results through aestivation, the summertime equivalent of hibernation.

Like its animals, the desert's plants adapt to hot and dry conditions. Some have short periods of dormancy that are the botanical equivalent of hibernation or aestivation. The ocotillo or coachwhip plant grows and sheds its leaves in response to periodic rainfall. When there is sufficient water in the soil to stimulate leaf growth, it sprouts leaves. As moisture evaporates and the land begins to dry, it just as promptly drops them. In temperate climates deciduous trees and shrubs undergo this cycle annually, but the ocotillo may grow and shed more than half a dozen sets of leaves in a single year.

For most cactus plants, the food-producing process of photosynthesis takes place in the green fleshy trunks and branches so that there are no leaves to grow or shed. Their response to rain is to produce a fine network of special 'rain roots' whose growth is stimulated by the moisture in the soil. When the rain has passed and the plant has gathered all of the water it can, the extra roots shrivel and the root system returns to the minimum network needed to hold the often top-heavy cactus in place.

Some of the plants that weather the desert's long periods of drought and heat engage in chemical warfare as a way of improving their chances of survival. The common desert brittlebush, for example, keeps potential competitors at bay by poisoning the soil around it with a growth-retarding toxin in its fallen leaves. The desert guayule or rubber plant excretes a toxic substance that prevents germination of its own seeds too close to the parent plant.

While the desert's botanical drought-resisters struggle to survive the vagaries of intermittent rainfall, another group of plants practice drought evasion. They avoid the need for moisture conservation altogether by responding quickly to the brief periods of moisture that do occur. California's Death Valley is a scorched landscape 280 feet below sea level where ground temperatures can reach 190 degrees Fahrenheit and rainfall averages less than 2 inches a year. Some 600 species of plants have been identified there, but, as in the other deserts of the Southwest, most of them are nowhere to be seen for much of the year. Then with the proper set of weather conditions an astonishing display of spring blooms appears. Poppies, primroses, lilies, orchids, sunflowers, and scores of other annuals rush to maturity in less than two months. Unlike the perennial drought-resisters, these so-called ephemerals have no need for extensive root systems, water-storage mechanisms or specially adapted foliage. They put all their energy into rapid growth and reproduction.

The late winter rains also trigger the emergence of countless species of insects which help fertilize the plants and provide food for migrating and resident birds. Some birds, like the Costa's hummingbird, engage in the fertilizing process directly as they fly from flower to flower gorging on the sweet, nutritious nectar.

The attention of the earliest Spanish explorers and missionaries was clearly on other things for they made little mention of the spectacular beauty of the blooming deserts. Nevertheless, the periodic lushness of this hostile land may have convinced them that, if properly irrigated, the desert could support crops and livestock. With little prospect of easy mineral wealth, the Spaniards substituted cattle as financial incentives for settling the dry lands of northern New Spain. While the Jesuits worked to convert Indians to Christianity in the northwestern part of the region and the Franciscans struggled on a similar

Desert plants must adjust constantly to changing climatic conditions. When winter rains have been generous, California poppies, seen here with Joshua trees (*above*), brittlebush (*right*) and the ocotillo or coachwhip plant (*left*) respond with profusions of bloom. If the rains do not come, the plants will reduce or eliminate their investment in reproduction.

mission as far east as Texas, secular Spaniards established large ranches through-out the area. On many of them Indians provided enforced labor. Thus, ironically, Indians became America's first cowboys under the tutelage of Spanish caballeros.

Using the old Aztec capital of Tenochtitlán as its New World base, the Spanish government established an arc of colonial outposts from the fog-shrouded bay at San Francisco to the fertile fields of eastern Texas. For almost 200 years these settlements remained isolated from all but occasional contact with the outside world. The primary responsibility of the Spanish soldiers assigned to the area was to protect mission settlements from attack by Apache, Comanche and Pawnee raiders. By 1767, when the Spanish monarch expelled the Jesuits from the region of northwestern New Spain, mining and ranching activities had become sufficiently important to require the continued presence of the Spanish military.

In the early nineteenth century, a new threat to Spanish authority emerged. The United States government began to probe the edges of its recently acquired Louisiana Territory, and the Spanish government responded with alarm. Additional soldiers were rushed to the frontier to discourage any commercial, political, or military initiatives from the ambitious North Americans. In 1806, a Spanish force based in Santa Fe intercepted Zebulon Pike's exploratory expedition to the southern Rockies as soon as it crossed out of United States territory. Subsequent incursions by American traders and mountain men were treated even more harshly, and soldiers from the Spanish *presidios* or garrisons confiscated trade goods and imprisoned the American trespassers.

In the fall of 1821, conditions suddenly changed. Among the first to hear the news was a party of merchants from the American frontier hamlet of Franklin, Missouri, struggling along the Arkansas River and over the 7800-foot Raton Pass on the border of today's New Mexico and Colorado. Encountering a group of Spanish-speaking soldiers and expecting immediate arrest, the Americans were astounded when the soldiers greeted them 'with hospitable disposition and friendly feelings'. Mexico had declared its independence from Spain and welcomed trade with the United States. Hurrying on to Santa Fe, William Becknell, leader of the trading party, exchanged his goods for huge profits in Mexican silver. In spring he returned with a wagon train of merchandise, this time crossing the Cimarron Desert instead of the Raton Pass. It was a grueling journey, which his men survived only by drinking the liquid stomach contents of a freshly killed buffalo, but it established a passable trade route to Santa Fe.

The Santa Fe Trail, running 800 miles from Independence, Missouri, to New Mexico's provincial capital, became one of the most important and profitable routes in the American West. The returns for those willing to make the trip were impressive even by frontier standards – up to 400 per cent profit on a load of goods – and for a while American caravans averaged business of 130 000 dollars each season. But the risks were great as well. In addition to the punishing terrain, well-armed Indian raiders posed constant threats to individual merchants. Only by traveling in large wagon trains could the traders hope to make the journey unscathed. In 1824 the United States Congress appropriated

20 000 dollars to buy peace from the tribes along the trail – a hopeless task – and an additional 10 000 dollars to mark and improve the highway. In 1829 soldiers were assigned to escort the caravans, the beginning of a major United States military presence in the area that would eventually position the United States to wrest most of the Southwest away from Mexico.

In the decades following the Mexican War, the United States government spent much of its time and military budget in the Southwest trying to map and assess the value of the land it had acquired and to defend its new citizens against Indian attack. In 1849, 1000 soldiers, one seventh of the entire United States Army, were assigned to New Mexico. By 1859 there were twice that number stationed in 16 military outposts.

Like everyone else, the army had difficulty dealing with the harshness of the desert. One of the most unusual experiments to counter the scarcity of water and grazing land began in 1856. With the backing of the chief surveyor of the Mexican boundary, John Bartell, and the Secretary of War, Jefferson Davis, 75 dromedaries were imported from North Africa to serve in a United States Camel Corps. The first caravan of camels left their base at Camp Verde, Texas, northwest of San Antonio in the spring of 1857. They trekked west across New Mexico and Arizona and on to California. Turkish, Greek and Armenian drivers, imported with the camels, complemented the US Army engineers and Navy personnel who made up the odd party. After a disorganized start, the animals' performance on the four-month journey was deemed a success. A favorable report was sent to Washington and an additional 1000 camels were requested from the War Department. But Congress, having appropriated 30 000 dollars for the experimental program, was skeptical and denied additional funding. For the next few years camels continued to be used by survey teams in the Southwest, where they were preferred over mules for long-distance travel. In consort with other animals, however, they were a problem, for, as one participant reported, the camels 'frightened horses and mules and caused several accidents'.

During the Civil War, the government's dromedaries were dispersed. Some of the animals hauled freight near Los Angeles. Some were shipped to Victoria, British Columbia, where they helped with road construction. Still others escaped or were released from their stables in Texas and allowed to wander freely through the deserts of the Southwest. Like the feral Spanish horses or mustangs (from the Spanish *mesteño* or stray animal) that naturalized in the western plains, the released camels represented a reintroduction of a mammal type that had once existed through much of North America. But unlike the horse, the camel never successfully re-established a wild population.

Of the many geographic surveys of the Southwest conducted in the nineteenth century, the most memorable was that led by a one-armed veteran of the Civil War named John Wesley Powell. He became the first person on record to successfully lead an expedition through the Grand Canyon of the Colorado. For more than three months, Powell and nine volunteers braved the tumultuous rapids of the last completely unknown river in the United States.

The Grand Canyon was first seen and described for European eyes by a

OVERLEAF 'We are but pigmies running up and down the sands or lost among the boulders,' observed John Wesley Powell in describing the Grand Canyon. The 2000 square miles inside the canyon's rim remained unknown terrain until Powell and a small party of men traveled through it in 1869. Formal mapping of the canyon was only completed in 1971.

detachment of Coronado's men in 1540, though their brief account of the mile deep, 18-mile wide gorge hardly does justice to its magnificence. Confused by its immense scale, they at first believed the river at its base to be 6 feet across, but recalculated its dimensions after three of their party climbed part way down toward it. 'It was impossible to descend' all the way to the bottom of the canyon, they reported, 'on account of the great difficulties which they found.'

While the Spaniards saw the canyon as an obstacle to progress, Powell saw it as an opportunity. By exploring the Colorado River he hoped to advance the cause of science and forward his own career. He was admirably successful in accomplishing both. With his harrowing Grand Canyon journey, Powell not only achieved international fame and a rewarding life as the government's most influential geographer, but, more importantly, he unlocked the mysteries of the Colorado and the geography of the Great Basin region through which it flows.

Armed with firsthand observations from his Colorado River trip of 1869 and a more detailed exploration of the river in 1871, Powell developed theories about stratigraphy and river erosion that had applications well beyond an understanding of the dramatic topography of the Grand Canyon itself. The Colorado River, he theorized, was like a great saw which cut through the Colorado plateau as it uplifted over time:

> The upheaval was not marked by a great convulsion, for the lifting of the rocks was so slow that the rains removed the sandstones almost as fast as they came up. The mountains were not thrust up as peaks, but a great block was slowly lifted, and from this the mountains were carved by the clouds. ... We speak of mountains forming clouds about their tops; the clouds have formed the mountains. Lift a district of granite, or marble, into their region, and they gather about it, and hurl their storms against it, beating the rocks into sands, and then they carry them out into the sea, carving out cañóns, gulches, and valleys, and leaving plateaus and mountains embossed on the surface.

Powell had identified and delineated the three great processes of geologic formation in a single wonder of nature: uplift, erosion, and sedimentation. His work formed the basis for the new science of physiography.

Fascinated by the power of water, not only as a force for erosion, but as a determining factor in human settlement, Powell followed his Grand Canyon triumph by devoting the rest of his professional career to studying issues of precipitation in the American West. In his landmark *Report on the Lands of the Arid Region of the United States* (1878), he shocked proponents of American expansionism by declaring that 'more than four-tenths of the whole country excluding Alaska' was arid land – that is, received less than 20 inches of rain per year – and was naturally ill-suited to farming. He asserted that in all the terrain from the middle of the Great Plains to the Pacific coast, 'only a small portion of the country is irrigable' and therefore salvageable for agriculture. Most of the rest he divided into lands more or less suitable for pasturage or for 'the growth of timber necessary to the mining, manufacturing, and agricultural industries of the country'. Highly controversial at the time, these observations flew in the face of the promotional propaganda that railroad companies, land speculators, and overly zealous politicians had been distributing at home and abroad. 'The rain follows the plow,' they argued, convinced that all that was needed to reclaim the West was the same Yankee initiative that had made lands east of the Mississippi so productive.

Gloomy descriptions of a Great American Desert had been heard before. Zebulon Pike had called the plains east of the Rockies 'sterile' and 'incapable of cultivation'. Stephen Long had declared the same area 'almost wholly unfit for cultivation, and of course uninhabitable by a people depending on agriculture for their subsistence'. But Powell steered a course between the extremes. He undercut the sanguine claims of the promoters, many of whom had never seen the land they were promoting. At the same time he debunked the Great American Desert myth which had been based on brief impressions rather than long-term hydrographic studies. Powell fully recognized the existence of true desert, but he saw there were marginal areas that could be made productive.

Envisioning large-scale irrigation for these areas, Powell represented a new scientific approach to the country's natural resources. He also presaged the important role that government would take in managing the Southwest.

> To a great extent, the redemption of all these lands will require extensive and comprehensive plans, for the execution of which aggregated capital or cooperative labor will be necessary. Here, individual farmers, being poor men, cannot undertake the task. For its accomplishment a wise prevision, embodied in carefully considered legislation, is necessary.

In advocating that the government finance the irrigation of arid regions, Powell was actually suggesting a method of cooperative land use that the agricultural Indians of the desert Southwest had undertaken more than 1000 years before.

Though highly ambitious by the standards of the 1870s, Powell's proposals for western irrigation were modest in the light of subsequent developments. Nor could he have foreseen the many non-agricultural uses to which the limited western water supplies would be put. Many of the booming 'sun belt' cities of the twentieth century Southwest have long since exhausted the available surface water and now pump water from rapidly diminishing natural reservoirs deep beneath the ground. Other cities draw water from the Colorado River and more distant watersheds to supply their increasing needs. Crops grow where Pike, Long and even Powell would never have imagined they could. Between golf courses, private lawns and swimming pools, the American deserts have literally come to 'blossom as a rose'.

The dramatic influx of humans to the American Southwest since the Second World War has created pressures on the deserts that these harsh but fragile habitats are not prepared to endure. As rivers are diverted to irrigation, wild habitats are lost. As cattle invade the patchy grasslands, vegetation is irreparably destroyed. As vacationers ravage the country with dirt bikes and 'all-terrain vehicles', ecological relationships that have taken millennia to evolve are flattened, torn or pulverised.

THE FIRST AND LAST FRONTIER

ALASKA · AND · THE · PACIFIC · NORTHWEST

No two habitats could be more different than the Sonoran Desert of northern Mexico and the rain-drenched spruce forests of southeastern Alaska. Yet each year one of the continent's smallest birds, the rufous hummingbird, makes a 4000-mile round trip between the two. Flying over the parched sands, prickly pear, and saguaro cactus of Sonora from its mountainous wintering grounds flanking the desert, the tiny bird flies north through California and the Rocky Mountain foothills to the fog-shrouded coast of the northern Pacific. There, in a land that can receive up to 200 inches of rain a year – 100 times that of the Sonoran Desert – the rufous hummingbird builds its lichen-covered nest, lays two pearl-sized white eggs, and raises its young.

Offshore currents and weather patterns affect the contrasting climates at both ends of the bird's migration route. High-pressure areas off the Mexican coast tend to deflect moisture-laden air away from the deserts of the Southwest. In contrast, in southern Alaska a warm water current coming north and east from Japan carries water-saturated air to shore. Blocked from progressing farther inland by a chain of coastal mountains, the water is dropped almost at once as rain or snow.

Generally, the moderating effects of the ocean keep the temperatures of southeastern Alaska, coastal British Columbia and northern Washington state relatively warm throughout the year. This warmth, combined with the constant supply of moisture, makes the Pacific Northwest one of the lushest botanical habitats in North America. There, in towering forests of western hemlock and sitka spruce, the rufous hummingbirds feed on the nectar from the blossoms of the salmonberry, blueberry, huckleberry and rusty menziesia.

For all of their lushness, Alaska's coastal forests are surprisingly limited in botanical diversity. This is because they are relatively young and have not had the time to develop the wide range of species variation enjoyed by their tropical counterparts. Until 10 000 to 15 000 years ago, most of Alaska was covered with ice. The coastal forests are even younger than that. Many have emerged from retreating glaciers within the past few thousand years and some only within the last century.

A short distance from the coast, on the north side of the Alaska Range, climatic conditions are entirely different. Lying in the rain shadow of the mountains and lacking the moderating effects of the Japan current, Alaska's Central Plateau has only a tenth of the precipitation found along the ocean, and its temperature can register from 50 to 75 degrees Fahrenheit below zero for days on end during the long arctic winter. Farther north lies the Brooks Range, 600 miles east to west and 150 miles wide, and above it the North Slope, a semi-frozen desert that extends 250 miles north to the Arctic Ocean.

The northern two-thirds of Alaska is a cold and forbidding but wildly beautiful place. Its vegetation consists of sparse forests of black and white spruce, birch, aspen, and poplar, and vast areas of tundra – from Russian, Lapp and Finnish words for land without trees – covered by lichens, mosses, grasses, small flowering plants and stunted willow and birch. Caribou, moose, and grizzly bear are the largest mammals of the Central Plateau and North Slope, while a distinctive race of bighorn sheep called Dall's sheep roam Alaska's interior mountain ranges.

It was along the forested southern coast in July, 1741, that the Danish-born navigator Vitus Bering and the German-born naturalist George Steller became the first Europeans to see America's northwestern shore. The two men were engaged in a comprehensive survey of Russia's eastern provinces begun in 1724 by Czar Peter the Great. Bering had come close to Alaska on an earlier expedition in which he had surveyed the eastern coast of Siberia and discovered the sea that now bears his name. On this, his second trip, Bering wished to locate the western coast of the New World. But, concerned for the safety of his ship and crew, he was eager to return home without exploring the land itself.

Steller, by contrast, had an intense desire to establish his reputation as a naturalist by examining as much of Alaska's flora and fauna as he could. When the party's ship, the *St Peter*, stopped for water on the island of St Elias (today called Kayak Island), Steller seized the opportunity to go ashore. Accompanied by a Cossack assistant, he set off to explore 'the very thick and dark' coastal forest. For several hours the two men collected all of the plants and animals they could. In this briefest of intervals they discovered 10 species of birds including a crested blue bird with a raucous call. Steller recorded the find in his journal:

> Good luck, thanks to my huntsman, placed in my hands a single specimen, of which I remember to have seen a likeness painted in lively colors and described in the newest account of the birds and plants of the Carolinas published in French and English. ... This bird proved to me that we were really in America.

Steller was recalling the blue jay of eastern North America illustrated in Mark Catesby's multi-volume *Natural History of Carolina, Florida and the Bahama*

A rufous hummingbird (right) feeds at an Indian paintbrush during the 2000-mile flight to its Alaskan nesting ground. The less brilliant but no less conspicuous Steller's jay (far right) was the first Alaskan bird to be described by George Steller during a visit to the region in 1741. When he saw the then unknown species, Steller was reminded of the blue jay illustrated in The Natural History of Carolina, Florida and the Bahama Islands *by Mark Catesby (below right).*

OVERLEAF A rare moment of calm in the Aleutian Islands, a 1700-mile-long archipelago separating the North Pacific from the Bering Sea. Russian fur traders or pro-myshlenniki found the islands a rich source of revenue in furs. As otters, seals and other marine mammals declined in numbers locally, the promyshlenniki pursued them in waters closer to the Alaskan mainland. Russian activity eventually extended all the way to California.

Smilax lævis, Salicis folio non
serrato, baccis Nigris

Islands. The distinctive western species that Steller had found was later named *Cyanocitta stelleri*, Steller's jay. The only crested jay that lives west of the Rocky Mountains, it is still found commonly in coniferous forests from Alaska to Mexico.

Steller sent word to Bering requesting additional men to help him collect more specimens, but the captain refused. Alarmed by deteriorating weather conditions, Bering ordered all personnel back to the ship at once and they weighed anchor early the next morning. Steller was bitterly disappointed. 'The time here spent in investigation bears an arithmetical ratio to the time used in fitting out,' he fumed in his journal. 'Ten years the preparation for this great undertaking lasted, and ten hours were devoted to the work itself.'

For the next four months the *St Peter* sailed slowly west toward Kamchatka, making occasional landfalls along the Alaska Peninsula and Aleutian Islands. As the winter progressed, heavy gales and a debilitating outbreak of scurvy aboard ship caused Bering to seek anchorage on an island that would later bear his name. In the process, the ship was driven aground and wrecked. Within two weeks Bering himself had died of disease, and nearly all of the crew had become seriously ill. Only Steller, who had consistently added anti-scorbutic plants to his diet, avoided scurvy. Until his fellow voyagers agreed to follow his example, the disease continued to rage and the ships' company fell from 78 to 46 men.

Steller made the most of his winter stranded on Bering Island by observing and collecting the wildlife that abounded there. Off the eastern shore he saw immense flocks of black, white and brown diving ducks, later named Steller's eiders. On the rocky coastline he found a large and almost flightless species of cormorant weighing as much as 14 pounds apiece 'so that one single bird was sufficient for three starving men'. Within 100 years the species, the Pallas's cormorant, had been hunted to extinction. The world's museums have only four skins of this once-abundant species and Steller's is the only scientifically accurate description of the bird from life.

Of greater interest to the shipwrecked party were the Steller's sea cows, large mammals that traveled 'like cattle' in herds just off the coast. 'This matchless creature, which is so suitable for eating, is without doubt far and away the best of all the creatures I have described,' exclaimed a member of the expedition:

The sea-cows we caught here weighed from 6000 ... to 8000 pounds, so that one sea cow provided us with food for the whole company of almost fifty men for more than fourteen days ... I can in very truth say that none of us properly recovered until we began eating them.

Steller's detailed descriptions of the sea cow give some idea why this gentle creature, like the Pallas's cormorant, was doomed to extinction at the hands of humans within only a few decades of its discovery:

They are most innocent and harmless in their manners, and most strongly attached to one another. When one is hooked, the whole herd will attempt its rescue: some will strive to overset the boat by going beneath it; others

will fling themselves on the rope of the hook and press it down in order to break it; and others again will make the utmost efforts to force the instrument out of its wounded companion.

Their conjugal affection is most exemplary: a male, after using all its endeavors to release its mate which had been stuck, pursued it to the very edge of the water; no blows could force it away. As long as the deceased female continued in the water, he persisted in his attendance; and even for three days after she was drawn on shore, and even cut up and carried away, was observed to remain, as if in expectation of her return.

Steller provided the first descriptions of several other mammals during his stay on Bering Island. The most important of these was the sea otter, which served as another welcome source of food for the stranded expedition. Steller reported that over 700 were killed and eaten between the party's arrival on the island in November 1741 and its return to the Russian mainland in a reconstructed boat the following August: 'This animal deserves from us all the greatest reverence, as for more than six months it served us almost exclusively as food and at the same time as a medicine for the scurvy-stricken.' Though Steller found the adult otters 'fairly good to eat' and the young as 'dainty as suckling lamb', it was the richness of their fur rather than the taste of their meat that would shape the future of the region.

While seals, whales, and other sea mammals conserve their warm body temperatures with thick layers of fat or blubber, sea otters depend solely on fur to insulate against the cold water of the North Pacific. The soft, thick pelts of the sea otters, many measuring up to 6 feet in length, convinced Bering's men that they had discovered a resource of enormous value. They were so eager to carry the skins back to Kamchatka that Steller was forced to abandon many of his precious scientific specimens to make room for peltry on the party's small escape boat.

In the months and years following the Bering expedition, a number of its members returned to Bering Island and the Aleutian chain to collect more of the highly prized pelts. The profits they realized could be considerable, as one of the expedition's members explained a few years after his return:

In Kamchatka, sea otter skins sell for 15, 20, and 25 rubles apiece. Often they are bartered again down by the frontier with China for Chinese goods worth 50, 60, or 70 rubles, and I have been told that from China the skins are sent to the country of the Great Mogul where they are sold for high prices, such skins being reputedly the height of fashion.

In their search for sea otter furs, the independent Russian traders, called *promyshlenniki*, traveled widely through the storm-lashed Aleutian archipelago and along the fog-shrouded coast of Alaska. There they encountered the highly efficient seafaring people for whom the region was named, the Aleuts, and their close relatives, the Eskimos.

The Eskimos are believed to have been the last migrants from Asia to have

LEFT *During his stranding on Bering Island in the winter of 1741–2, George Steller discovered a number of marine mammals, including a species of sea lion that now bears his name. Steller and his fellow castaways managed to capture some of the animals 'and thought the flesh of the young very savory'. Long esteemed by the Aleuts for their skin and oil, the Steller's sea lions were quick to avoid human predators. 'The males have a terrible aspect', reported Steller, 'yet they take to flight on the first appearance of a human creature.'*

PREVIOUS PAGES *Using its chest as a table, a sea otter enjoys a meal of abalone. This gregarious and playful furbearer was the focus of relentless hunting in the eighteenth and nineteenth centuries. After a close brush with extinction, it has begun to return to protected habitats along the Pacific coast.*

arrived in North America, coming by water some 2500 years ago, after the land bridge across the Bering Strait had resubmerged. They have thus fished, hunted and lived among Alaska's islands and along its northern shores for as long as Romans have been in Rome and considerably longer than the French have been in France. Despite their common Asiatic origins, the Eskimos are unrelated to the Indians of North America who preceded them to the continent by as much as 40 000 years. The name Eskimo may have come from an Algonquian word meaning 'raw-meat-eaters', which the Eskimos sometimes were, or from a term applied by early French missionaries from Canada meaning 'the excommunicated'. Although it is the term still applied to the group by anthropologists, the Eskimos' own name for themselves is *Inuit*, The People.

For the first 20 years of Russian fur trading in America, the czarist government imposed no rules governing the treatment of indigenous people. Officials in St Petersburg were only concerned with securing the *yasak*, a 10 per cent royal tax on furs. Recognizing the Aleuts' superior knowledge of the area and unsurpassed skill at hunting, the *promyshlenniki* turned to them – or, more accurately, turned on them – for the furs they desired. They would rob and pillage an Aleut village, take its women hostage, and demand ransom from the men in the form of peltry. The Aleuts had no firearms and so were at the mercy of the Russian seamen, and no mercy was shown. If the Aleut hunters failed to produce the furs, the hostages were raped and murdered. If furs were supplied, the Russian seamen would take them without compensation (along with anything else they wanted, including the women) and depart until the next season.

Sea otters were the principal focus of the traders' attention. The species had no instinctive fear of humans, having been hunted little before, and were therefore extremely vulnerable. Scattered groups, each of several hundred, lived in shallow coastal waters from Kamchatka to Alaska, and as far south as Baja California. They were found near thick beds of Pacific kelp where they could hunt for mussels, abalone and other shellfish while hiding from their natural enemies, the sea lions, sharks, and killer whales. Like all otters they were active and playful, often feeding while floating on their backs. 'Nothing can be more beautiful than one of these animals when seen swimming,' wrote a nineteenth-century American sailor:

especially when on the lookout for any object. At such times it raises its head quite above the surface, and the contrast between the shining black and white [face markings that appear in some individuals], together with the sharp ears and a long tuft of hair rising from the middle of its forehead, which look like three small horns, render it quite a novel and attractive object.

Because sea otter populations were socially gregarious and lived in geographically restricted areas, they were soon exterminated in the western Aleutians by the *promyshlenniki* and their Aleut conscripts. By the 1760s, the commercial Russian fleets were searching the eastern Aleutians and the Alaskan coast for otter colonies not yet exploited.

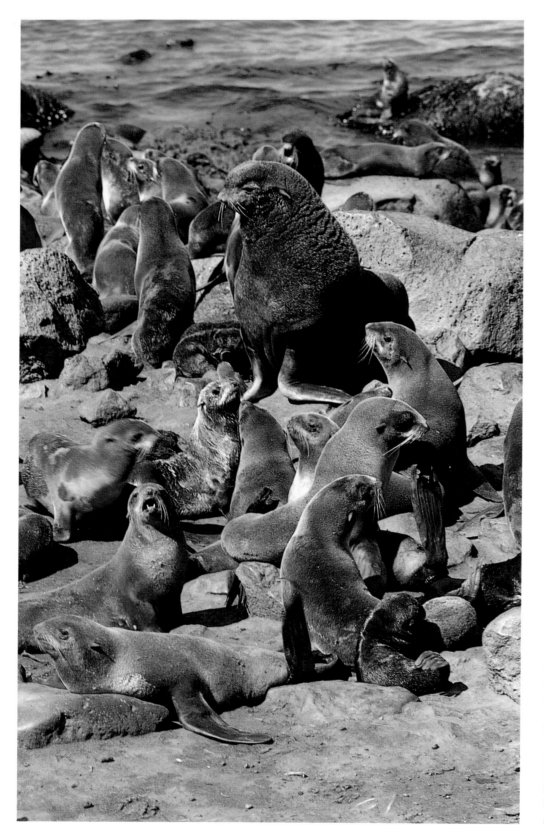

Henry Wood Elliott, a US treasury agent stationed in the Pribilof Islands, recorded Aleutian hunters killing humpback whales with poison-tipped darts (right) and roping fur seals (above right) on behalf of European traders. Such pelagic sealing was banned by international treaty in 1911. Fur seal breeding grounds on the Pribilofs and elsewhere (left) are now carefully managed to ensure the survival of this once endangered species.

The arrival of the fur traders in new areas caused much excitement and fear among the natives, as is revealed by the recollections of an Aleut from Koniag:

I was a boy of 9 or 10, for they already had me now in a baidarka [kayak] when the first Russian ship, a two master, arrived. . . . When we saw the ship far off, we believed it was a giant whale and curiosity drove us to examine it more closely. We went out in baidarkas, but soon saw that it was not a whale, but a strange monster, never seen before, which we feared and whose stench made us sick. The people on board wore buttons on their clothes, we thought they were squids, but when we saw that they took fire into their mouth and blew out smoke – we knew nothing of tobacco – we could only believe that they were devils.

The Russians' brutal behaviour toward the Aleuts confirmed their devilish first impression and belatedly sparked native resistance. On the island of Umnak in 1761, the enraged inhabitants attacked a party of poorly armed Russian traders, killing many and causing the rest to flee. The following year they destroyed a number of Russian ships. The uprising was enough to regain the Aleuts five years of independence during which they returned to their traditional subsistence-level hunting and fishing. But the ultimate cost of this period of freedom was high. In 1766 the Russians retaliated with a privately funded armada and army of mercenary troops. The sailors and soldiers systematically attacked and destroyed Aleut villages, killing or enslaving resisters. It is estimated that at least 3000 natives were executed during the short but devastating 'war', and within a few months the Aleuts were entirely under Russian control. Forced by their Russian overlords, they reluctantly resumed the pursuit of the otters – considered distant relatives by the Aleuts – until only a few of the animals remained alive.

As otter supplies diminished, the Russian traders sought other sources of fur. One animal that had interested them since its first description by George Steller and the other survivors of the Bering expedition was the northern fur seal. Its pelt was second in quality only to that of the otter. The seal was generally found and hunted at sea, a task that proved difficult even for the Aleuts in the maneuverable kayaks. Then, in 1786, Gavril Pribilof discovered the principal breeding and calving site of the northern fur seal – a cluster of islands in the Bering Sea that would eventually bear his name. There, from May to August, up to 2.5 million animals gathered to bear their young and breed for the following year. It was the largest concentration of sea mammals in the world and, for the Russians, a commercial gold mine.

From 1786 on, during the breeding season, large groups of seals were herded to convenient places on the islands. They were then dispatched with club blows to the head, skinned, and loaded aboard ships for the lucrative China trade. Hundreds of thousands were killed each year until supply far outweighed demand. So excessive was the killing that in 1803 one company destroyed seven years' harvest of pelts when the skins rotted in their warehouses after being held back to avoid glutting an over-saturated market.

Russian activity in what it considered Russian America quickly attracted the attention of other European powers. Spain claimed the entire Pacific rim of North America, and so viewed Russia's forays as an intrusion on its own territory. In 1774 and again in the following year, the Spanish crown sent expeditions north from Mexico to assess the extent of Russian activity and lay the foundation for Spanish missionary work through which it hoped eventually to gain political control of the region. Juan Pérez, leader of the 1774 expedition, was specifically instructed

> *to attract the numerous Indians to the desirable vassalage of His Majesty, to spread the light of the gospel, to bring the spiritual conquest that may remove them from the shadows of idolatry, and to teach them the road to eternal salvation.*

Further instructions specified that under no circumstances was there to be any removal of the Indians' property without their expressed approval. The officers were to prevent such incidents so that the Indians would welcome Spanish settlers in the future. So eager for friendly relations were the Spaniards that their men were forbidden from engaging in any hostilities, even if provoked. In every way different from the Russian approach to the area, it was also a marked change from the Spaniards' earlier policies toward North American Indians. It reflected Spain's recognition that it would never be able to control the region through force of arms.

Pérez's expedition did not reach as far as Aleut or Eskimo territory. The people they encountered were the Nootka, Haida, and Tlingit Indians who inhabited the coastal areas from northern California to southeastern Alaska. Both Pérez and his second officer, Estéban José Martínez, formed positive impressions of these people, finding them 'very docile since they give away their skins even before they are paid'. By the following year, however, conditions had changed dramatically. Possibly Russian *promyshlenniki*, raiding the coast south of the Aleutians, had contacted the Indians and changed their attitudes towards whites. Perhaps the Spaniards simply had the bad luck to encounter a hostile village. In any case, near present-day Point Grenville on the Washington coast, seven Spanish seamen under the command of Juan Francisco de la Bodega were massacred when they landed to obtain water. Following royal instructions, and in a rare European reaction to native Americans, the Spaniards restrained their urge for retaliation to this and similar acts of hostility. When they finally gave up their claim to the region in 1795, the Spaniards could thus point to a history of unusually fair and peaceful relations with the indigenous people of the North-west.

In 1778, several years after the first Spanish expeditions to the area, Captain James Cook carefully charted the Alaskan coast for Britain and thereby made his expedition the one with more lasting impact. Cook had been secretly charged by the British admiralty 'to find out a Northern passage by Sea from the Pacific to the Atlantic Ocean' and to explore 'such Rivers or Inlets as may appear to be of a considerable extent and pointing towards Hudson's or Baffin's Bay'. It was the search for the Northwest Passage that for centuries had prompted exploration in the opposite direction, from eastern North America. Cook, and later his countryman and shipmate George Vancouver, was no more successful than others in locating the non-existent passage. Even without the easy water access the British had hoped to find, however, Cook's exploration of the Pacific helped to open the area to increased commercial activity. Cook's crew discovered that an otter pelt purchased from Indian hunters for trinkets or sixpence sold for more than 100 pounds sterling in China. With such profits available, it is not surprising that traders were quick to move in. In 1786 alone, nine British vessels were present from Copper Island to Prince William Sound, giving a fair indication of Britain's commercial interest in the area.

By the early nineteenth century, Spain was incapable of defending any claims to the Pacific. Even waters closer to its bases of strength were subject to intrusion by other nations. Among Spain's increasingly troublesome maritime competitors was the United States, whose naval superiority was described by the Russian artist Louis Choris in 1816:

> Two hundred and fifty American ships from Boston, New York, and elsewhere, came to the coast every year. Half of them engage in smuggling with enormous profit. No point for landing goods along the entire Spanish-American coast bathed by the Pacific Ocean, from Chile to California, is neglected. It often happens that Spanish warships give chase to American vessels, but these, being equipped with much sail, having large crews, and having moreover, arms with which to defend themselves, are rarely caught.

Having gained access to the rest of the Pacific coast, it was inevitable that American sailors would press north to engage in the lucrative fur trade. What they discovered in the process excited them even more and would draw many other American vessels to Alaskan waters in the decades to come: whales.

North America's native people living along the coast on both sides of the continent benefited from the proximity of these largest of sea mammals. Some harvested them when, by chance, sick or injured whales beached themselves, or feeding whales ventured too close to shore. Other native Americans, including the Aleuts and Eskimos, actively hunted the giant creatures at sea, a daring and extremely dangerous activity which continues in some parts of Alaska today.

When Europeans first came to eastern North America they found many whales close to shore and easy to capture. These were hunted by the thousands, primarily for their meat and oil. When coastal species grew scarce, whalers turned to different species which required much more difficult methods of hunting, and long and dangerous sea voyages. It was, therefore, especially gratifying to whalers entering the North Pacific in the early nineteenth century to discover a new supply of the whale species they most coveted – the right whale. This had been so named by British and American seamen because it was slow swimming and easy to kill, floated when dead, produced plentiful oil and bone, and was, therefore, the *right* whale to capture.

A second, closely related species, also seasonally abundant in the Bering Sea, was the somewhat larger bowhead whale which possessed all of the same desirable qualities. Both species of whales filter small food organisms from the ocean water with fibrous, sieve-like bony plates called baleen, attached to their upper jaws. In the eighteenth and nineteenth centuries, baleen was eagerly sought as a commercial product because it combined strength and flexibility. It was used in ladies' corsets and shirt hoops, in the ribs of umbrellas and parasols, and for fishing rods, ramrods, and buggy whips. (It was also useful for disciplining uncooperative children who were said to receive a 'whaling' when whipped with these resilient rods.) Even the fringes of the baleen were employed as stuffing for upholstered furniture. At the peak of its demand in the late nineteenth century, the 1.5 tons of baleen harvested from a single bowhead whale could pay for the cost of an entire whaling expedition.

Equally lucrative was the oil rendered from the whale's blubber. Up to 80 barrels – more than 2000 gallons – could be retrieved from a single bowhead. It was used for everything from home lighting and machinery lubrication to the manufacture of rope, paint and soap. Before the discovery of petroleum in Pennsylvania in 1859, and for many years thereafter, whale oil was considered as essential as we now consider the petroleum that replaced it. Finding a new supply of whales for harvest was, therefore, of the greatest significance to the economy of the United States.

The presence of American whalers in the Pacific Northwest had another important advantage for the United States. It helped to bolster the government's claims to the area which it had been trying to establish almost from the moment of independence from Britain. The first American party on record to visit the disputed region was led by a Boston sea captain named Robert Gray. He showed the stars and stripes in Nootka Sound, Vancouver Island, in 1788 during America's first circumnavigation of the world. Four years later, Gray returned to the Pacific Northwest and explored the San Rogue, which he renamed the Columbia River after his ship. Several other American ships visited the area in the 1790s. As representatives of the US government, Lewis and Clark formally reinforced the nation's claim to the region with their overland arrival on the Washington coast in 1805. Finally, John Jacob Astor's Pacific Fur Company post, Astoria, established in March 1811 at the mouth of the Columbia River, provided a settled if short-lived American presence in the area.

Britain's claims were almost as strong, however. Its ships, under Cook, Vancouver, and others, had charted the coast. Traders from the Hudson's Bay Company and the North West Company, following the pioneering travels of Alexander Mackenzie, Simon Fraser and David Thompson, dominated most of the land-based fur trade in the region during the first few decades of the nineteenth century. The Russians, meanwhile, had reinforced their 1741 declaration of sovereignty over Russian America with the establishment of permanent trading posts on Kodiak Island (1784), at Yakutat (1787), Sitka (1799) and as far south as Bodega Bay in northern California in 1812.

Rather than attempt to settle by arms or by treaty the issue of who should or should not fish, trade or hunt in the area, the US government preferred to let

Its summit perpetually covered with snow, Alaska's Mt McKinley rises 20 320 feet above sea level and higher above the surrounding country than any other mountain in the world. Among the large mammals that inhabit its slopes are Dall's sheep, a close relative of the Rocky Mountain bighorn. Here a bachelor herd enjoys a brief rest between periods of feeding.

entrepreneurs decide the future of the region. When the Russian government asked Washington to curtail the activities of its whaling and hunting parties in Alaska, the US State Department innocently replied: 'We cannot prevent our citizens from going out of the country; if they then create disturbances in your territory, it is up to you to defend it.' The Russian-American Company, chartered by the crown like its British counterpart, the Hudson's Bay Company, was impotent to resist US expansion.

Writing to his chancellor in 1867, the Russian Ambassador to the United States, Baron de Stoeckl, recounted the history that eventually brought about US control of Russian America:

> However spacious the regions of the United States Federation may be, they do not seem extensive enough for the feverish activity and spirit of enterprise of the Americans. They look upon that continent as their patrimony. Their destiny ('our manifest destiny', as they call it) is forever to expand ... with as much perseverance as success.

Dissatisfied with the price of holding Alaska, and fearful of its possible loss to Britain (with which it had recently fought a costly war in the Crimea), Imperial Russia decided to sell the 586 400 square mile territory to the United States in 1867. The asking price was just over 7 million dollars, or 2 cents an acre, an even cheaper price than Jefferson had paid for the Louisiana Territory 64 years before.

It was undoubtedly the greatest real estate bargain of all time. Alaska is more than two and a half times the size of France, or bigger than Texas, Florida, New York, Wisconsin, and California put together. The state has more than 3 million lakes, 33 000 miles of coastline, and 12 major rivers. It also contains 14 of the highest peaks in North America, including the tallest, Mt McKinley (or Denali as it is known by the Athapaskan natives) at 20 320 feet.

At the time of the transaction, much of the United States was just recovering from the trauma and expense of its Civil War and the public was scarcely interested in acquiring a seemingly worthless tract of ice and snow to the northwest, regardless of its impressive statistics and low price. Nevertheless Congress went through with the purchase, while President Andrew Johnson and Secretary of State William Henry Seward, who promoted it in the national interest, received the criticism. The land they acquired was widely ridiculed as 'Seward's icebox', 'Johnson's polar bear garden', and 'a dreary waste of glaciers, icebergs ... and walruses'.

Pejoratives aside, the descriptions were reasonably accurate. Today about 30 000 square miles of Alaska, roughly 5 per cent of the state's total area, are covered by active, moving glaciers. Many of these are fed by the same moist air that drenches the southeastern coast with rain. In the highest elevations, the Chugach, St Elias, and Wrangell Mountains, this moisture turns to snow and collects in huge fields. These eventually compress to ice and, with gravity's help, move toward lower ground. In Glacier Bay and elsewhere along the southeastern shore of Alaska, walls of ice 150 feet high flow directly into the ocean.

OVERLEAF Their brown coats resembling sand, a herd of walruses line the shores of Alaska's Round Island. The species migrate with the advance and retreat of the Arctic ice pack. To the native peoples of the Bering Strait, the walrus provided a reliable source of meat. Its blubber was used as fuel for cooking and for lighting, its hide was used to cover boat frames, and its ivory tusks and bones provided raw material for innumerable items from harpoons to ornaments.

Many of these coastal glaciers are now receding, leaving in their wake not only icebergs that have calved from the mother flow, but, more permanently, a complex arrangement of inlets, fjords and bays.

The Brooks Range, some 500 miles to the north of Glacier Bay, contains U-shaped valley glaciers, and a large number of cirque glaciers, which are bowl-shaped depressions filled with ice and snow. Even in lands not covered by active glaciers, there is permafrost – soil, gravel or rock that has remained at a temperature below freezing for two years or more. It is a condition that prevails over 85 per cent of Alaska at varying depths and ages. The Eskimo community of Barrow on Alaska's North Slope lives on permafrost 1300 feet thick and several thousand years old.

The permafrost, combined with other environmental conditions, restricts much of Alaska's interior vegetation to grasses, sedges, and low, scrubby trees and shrubs. By preventing rainwater and surface melt from soaking into the ground, it creates ideal habitat for water-breeding insects, and for the waterfowl and wading birds that migrate here by the millions each spring to nest and raise their young. Some of the swans that fed the first English colonists in Virginia and Massachusetts were undoubtedly born in the tundra of Alaska. Seventy thousand of them from throughout North America still fly here each summer, along with 12 million ducks, 1 million geese, and as many as 400 million other birds. So rich are the avian food and nesting resources throughout Alaska that birds converge on the area from every one of the world's continents: wagtails from Asia, wheatears from Africa, loons from northern Europe, China and Japan, arctic terns from South America and Antarctica, and godwits from Australia. Though much of it is frozen, 'Seward's icebox' is packed with living things.

Some critics of Alaska's purchase derisively dubbed the land 'Walrussia', and in doing so, unwittingly identified what would become one of the region's most important commercial resources. By 1869, two-thirds of the North Pacific bowhead whale population had been killed and walruses replaced them as the principal focus of commercial activity in northwestern waters.

The most valuable attributes of the walrus were its 3-foot-long ivory tusks (actually oversized upper canine teeth) and its huge quantity of body fat which could be rendered into oil. The fat, of course, helps to insulate the warm-blooded walrus from the frigid waters of the Arctic. The tusks serve purposes that are less well understood. The creature's scientific name, *Odobenidae*, comes from the Greek and means literally 'those that walk with their teeth'. Walruses do sometimes pull themselves onto ice floes in this way, and they will also hook themselves to the ice for stability when sleeping. It was once believed that walruses used their tusks to dislodge clams, sea snails and other shellfish from the ocean floor for food, but recent studies have shown that such feeding is accomplished with the animals' powerful lips and tongue. That the tusks can be used effectively as offensive and defensive weapons is readily apparent to anyone who ventures too close.

Walrus hunters discovered that the 13-foot-long bulls, weighing up to 3500

pounds each, were not to be taken lightly. 'They are harmless, unless provoked', wrote Thomas Pennant:

> *but when wounded, or attacked grow very fierce, and are very vindictive. ... They will sometimes attempt to fasten their teeth on the boats, with an intent to sink them, or rise in numbers under them to overset them; at the same time they show all marks of rage, by roaring in a dreadful manner, and gnashing their teeth with great violence.*

Little wonder, then, that the walrus hunters preferred to kill their prey from a safe distance. When the animals defended themselves against polar bears or Eskimo hunters who traditionally used only knives or spears and arrows, the walruses were extremely effective. Against rifles they were hopelessly vulnerable:

> *At the first sound of the rifle they all raise their heads, and if one has been wounded and goes into the water the rest all follow; but if the shot has been effective, they soon drop their heads and go to sleep again. This is repeated a few times, until they become so accustomed to the firing that they take no notice of it. Then they are approached within a few feet and dispatched as fast as the guns can be loaded and fired.*

At times the gunners fired so rapidly that their rifles became too hot to hold. They would then drop the rifles into the water on a lanyard to cool while they went on shooting with others.

The inevitable decline in walruses and whales reduced profits for the Russian, American and Canadian companies involved in the trade, but the consequences for the Eskimo were far more serious. Captain Frederick A. Barker explained these in a letter to a New Bedford newspaper:

> *The natives of the entire Arctic shores ... are almost entirely dependent on the walrus for their food, clothing, boats, and dwellings. Twenty years ago whales were plenty and easily caught, but the whales have been destroyed, so that now the natives seldom get a whale.... Several captains lately ... have told me that they saw the natives 30 or 40 miles from land, on the ice, trying to catch a walrus to eat, and were living on the carcasses of those the whalemen had killed.... Should I ever come to the Arctic Ocean again I will never catch another walrus, for these poor people along the coast have nothing else to live upon.*

'Fully one third of the [human] population of St Lawrence Bay perished the past winter [1879] for want of food', reported another captain who predicted that 'like the dodo', the walrus would soon 'be extinct; then God help the natives of this whole northern country; all must perish'.

The indigenous people in southeastern Alaska, British Columbia and Washington fared much better in their contacts with whites than the more northerly Aleuts and Eskimos. The Tlingit, Haida, and other Indian groups of the region were fierce warriors and shrewd traders. They made handsome profits as middlemen between the landlocked Athapaskan people, who had beaver, moose and

PREVIOUS PAGES
Their lines of contact revealed by gravelly moraines, several glaciers snake their way from the St Elias and Wrangell Mountains to Glacier Bay on Alaska's southern coast. More than 5500 square miles of glaciers flow from the St Elias Mountains, one of the continent's most concentrated areas of glacial activity.

The Tlingit Indians, comprising fourteen tribal groups, occupied most of the Alaskan panhandle at the time of first European contact. Although many of the Tlingit's cultural traditions were irreversibly altered by European trade, their strong religious beliefs and unrivaled skills at carving persisted well into the nineteenth century, as the ceremonial raven helmet (right) reveals. Modern totem poles (above) continue to include stylized depictions of wildlife from the region.

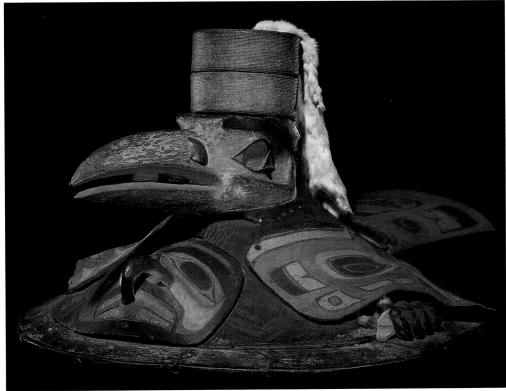

caribou skins to sell, and the eager European buyers, who plied their shores with increasing frequency in the late eighteenth and nineteenth centuries.

The Northwest Coast peoples had developed a highly sophisticated culture ranking with that of the Pueblos of the Southwest. Without either agriculture or pottery, they relied on locally available food and excelled in the art of wood carving. Alone among the highest cultures of the New World, the Northwest Coast Indian cultures were not influenced by the civilizations of Central America. Their ultimate affinities were still with northeastern Asia from which they had migrated thousands of years earlier. In their large coastal communities, related families lived together in gabled plank houses with elaborately carved and painted posts and doors. Their stratified societies were almost European in class structure, containing nobles, commoners and slaves. Among the exceptionally powerful chiefs of the Haida tribe in the Queen Charlotte Islands, there was even an embryonic royalty.

Most of the Northwest Coast Indians divided themselves into two major clans represented by ravens and wolves, animals that had strong religious significance. These, in turn, were divided into smaller groups based on matri-lineal descent. Each had its own crest, symbolically representing some part of nature: sun, moon, big dipper, eagle, owl, whale, salmon, frog, beaver, bear, petrel, and sea lion. Traditionally carved on the corner posts of their houses, the crests later evolved into the famous totem poles of the nineteenth century after the introduction of metal tools to the Indian communities made carving on such a large-scale possible.

Each of the animals or other natural forces represented in the carvings fitted into the complex mythology of the Indians. Of all these the raven was perhaps the most important, for it was the creature credited with bringing water to the earth, as an ancient Tlingit legend explains:

In all the world there was no fresh water save for a single spring that belonged to Petrel the seabird, who watched it carefully, building his house over the water so that he could guard it even while he slept. One day, Raven thought, How fine it would be if there were fresh water all over the earth. Then people could drink, and salmon would have a place to swim to. So Raven preened his feathers, which were then snow white, and set off to visit Petrel and steal his fresh water. But Petrel was wary and would not leave Raven alone by the spring for even a moment, try as Raven might to lure his host away. Finally, while Petrel slept, Raven took some mud and covered his host with it. Then he cried out: Oh, poor friend, you are covered with dirt. Petrel awoke and saw that this was true and rushed outside to clean himself. Left alone, Raven jumped to the spring and began gulping the fresh water. It was nearly gone when Petrel returned. Now Raven, to make his escape, flew toward the smoke-hole [in the roof of the petrel's lodge], and Petrel in anger cried out to his smoke-hole spirits: Grab him, hold him! The smoke-hole spirits did so, but Raven wriggled free, though not before the bird's white feathers were covered with black soot. While flying, Raven tried to clean his feathers, but his beak was filled with the water he had stolen, and each time he opened it some liquid spilled to earth. From these splashes came the rivers, lakes and glaciers. As for Raven, he never could get clean and remains sooty-black to this very day.

Fresh water, so important in this story, was central to the lives of Indian groups throughout the Northwest for from it came salmon and most of the other resources on which their economy was based.

Five different species of salmon – chinook, chum, coho, pink and sockeye – ascend the rivers of the Northwest each year to spawn. They were easily captured in weirs and traps, or speared with harpoons and gaffs, then smoked, salted, or dried for future use. The Scottish naturalist David Douglas, who made extensive plant-collecting trips in what would later become Washington state, Oregon and British Columbia in the 1820s, gave an excellent account of salmon fishing he observed on the Columbia River about 200 miles from the ocean:

> *This being the fishing season, the natives are numerous on the banks of the river; they come several hundred miles to their favourite fishing grounds. At the Rapids an almost incredible number of salmon are caught. They are taken in the following manner; before the water rises on the approach of summer, small channels are made among the stones and rocks, 2 feet broad and running out into various branches, over which is placed a platform for the person to stand. Several channels are made, some higher, some lower, so as to suit the water as it falls or rises. A scoop net or net fastened round a hoop at the end of a long pole, 12 to 15 feet, is all that is used; the person stands on the extremity of the stage or platform and places his net at the top of the channel, which is always made to fit it exactly, and it is carried down with the current. The poor salmon, coming up his smooth and agreeable road as he conceives it to be, thrusts himself in the net and is immediately thrown on the stage; the handle or pole of the net is tied to the platform by a rope lest the pressure of water or strength of the fish should snatch it out of the hands of the fisher.*

Douglas measured two of the netted salmon and found them each over $3\frac{1}{2}$ feet in length and weighing about 35 pounds. 'Both were purchased for two inches of tobacco (one half ounce), value twopence, or one penny each,' he noted in his journal. 'How little the value from that in England where the same quantity would cost three or four pounds.'

Salmon were not the only large fish available to the Indians of the Northwest, nor the only ones enjoyed by Douglas in the course of his travels. While visiting a Chinook chief named Cockqua, who was 'exceedingly fond of all the chiefs that came from King George', Douglas was shown

> *to one of his large canoes in which lay a sturgeon ten feet long, three at the thickest part in circumference, weighing probably from 400 to 500 lb., [and asked] to choose what part should be cooked for me. I gave him the preference as to knowledge about the savoury mouthfuls, which he took as a great*

compliment. In justice to my Indian friend … he afforded me the most comfortable meal I had had for a considerable time before, from the spine and head of the fish.

Douglas learned of other 'savoury mouthfuls' from the Indians, including camas root, cranberries, blueberries, currants, and the Saskatoon berry. He carefully collected these and other plants on behalf of the Royal Horticultural Society and, with the help of the Hudson's Bay Company, shipped them back to Britain for cultivation. In all, Douglas is credited with introducing 254 North American plants to European cultivation. Among his most important discoveries from the Northwest were the sitka spruce, the lodgepole pine, the silver, noble, white and lowland fir, and, of course, the magnificent Douglas fir that bears his name.

Douglas was one of the few naturalists to penetrate the region before the middle of the nineteenth century. Then, in 1859, sponsored by the Smithsonian Institution, a gifted young naturalist named Robert Kennicott began a five-year collecting expedition in Canada's Northwest Territories, British Columbia and Alaska. Enlisting the help of Hudson's Bay Company traders, the 24-year-old Kennicott traveled from Hudson Bay to the Yukon and west, gathering for scientific study everything from birds and eggs to snow fleas. Kennicott died of heart failure at the age of 30 while still surveying Alaska's unknown interior. But, cherishing 'the opportunity to be the first naturalist in this unknown region', he achieved immortality through the names of dozens of species of plant and animal. Even a glacier and a river bear the naturalist's name. Equally important, Kennicott's contributions helped convince the US Congress that Alaska was worth the 7.2 million dollar price tag set by the Russian government in 1867.

Working with information furnished by Kennicott, Charles Sumner, chairman of the Foreign Relations Committee, extolled the virtues of Russian America in a three-hour speech before the US Senate. It was Sumner who brought into common use the Aleut name for the region, Alaska, meaning the mainland, peninsula, or 'great land'. Pointing out the resources that would soon play an important role in the development of the territory, he cited fisheries 'which, in waters superabundant with animal life beyond any of the globe, seem to promise a new commerce', forests 'waiting for the axe', and mineral resources 'among which are coal and copper, if not iron, silver, lead, and gold'.

The minerals provided the lure which drew tens of thousands of people into Alaska before the century's close. A gold rush in 1897–8 saw some 15 000 people choke Skagway and other coastal towns in a mad scramble to reach the gold-producing rivers of Canada's Yukon Territory. A second rush a few years later brought 20 000 prospectors to the Seward Peninsula in western Alaska where gold nuggets had been found on a beach near Nome. In both cases more money was made by merchants supplying food and supplies at exorbitantly inflated prices than was made from gold. Nevertheless, both rushes were widely reported by the world press, and brought unprecedented attention to 'Seward's icebox' and the resources it contained.

The shallow glacier-etched ponds of Canada's Yukon Territory and Alaska's Central Plateau are a haven for millions of breeding birds each summer. Despite limited amounts of precipitation, the region's permanently frozen subsoil keeps moisture on the surface. This creates a rich wetland habitat which attracts migrants from as far away as Europe, Australia and Japan.

Jack London, Rex Beach and Robert W. Service captured the romantic elements of the gold rush era in their best-selling novels and poems. Their writings forever imprinted the names of the land on their readers' imagination, with Dawson, Whitehorse, Skagway, and the Klondike and Yukon Rivers becoming as familiar as battlefields in a distant war. To armchair adventurers, the exploitation of the land and the testing of those who worked it became an exciting extension of Charles Darwin's biological theories as applied to commerce and social activity. Robert Service made the analogy clear in 'The Law of the Yukon':

> This is the Law of the Yukon, that only the Strong shall thrive;
> That surely the Weak shall perish, and only the Fit survive.
> Dissolute, damned and despairful, crippled and palsied and slain,
> This is the Will of the Yukon – Lo, how she makes it plain!

America had found a new proving ground. Those who had grown up with stories of their forebears conquering the American wilderness had been given the chance of one last frontier experience. Young men who had missed fighting in the 'splendid little war' with Spain in 1898 could test their manhood in Alaska. Newcomers to the United States or anyone down on their luck could dream of instant fortune in the frozen north. All it took, they were told by the steamship companies and land speculators, was a ticket of passage from San Francisco or Seattle, a grubstake to get started, and the gumption to do what needed to be done.

The feverish excitement of the times was captured in the opening stanzas of Service's poem, 'The Trail of Ninety-Eight':

> Gold! We leapt from our benches. Gold! We sprang from our stools.
> Gold! We wheeled in the furrow, fired with the faith of fools.
> Fearless, unfound, unfitted, far from the night and the cold,
> Heard we the clarion summons, followed the master-lure – Gold!
>
> Men from the sands of the Sunland; men from the woods of the West;
> Men from the farms and the cities, into the Northland we pressed.
> Graybeards and striplings and women, good men and bad men and bold,
> Leaving our homes and our loved ones, crying exultantly – Gold!

Once the site of North America's largest volcanic eruption, the 40-square-mile Valley of Ten Thousand Smokes in Katmai National Park no longer resembles the massed steam engines described by geologist Robert Griggs in 1916. It is nevertheless sufficiently barren to have served NASA astronauts as a training ground for lunar exploration.

The exploitation of Alaska's mineral wealth was paralleled by the continuing slaughter of the sea mammals in the northeastern Pacific. Ever since the United States had taken possession of the breeding grounds of the fur seals, British, Russian, Canadian, and, later, Japanese companies had increased their efforts at harvesting the mammals at sea, beyond the legal control of US government regulations. This pelagic or open-sea sealing was an extremely inefficient and wasteful form of harvest. As many as nine out of ten seals killed by the pelagic hunters sank before their bodies could be recovered for skinning. Thus, for every 100 000 skins to reach London furriers, as many as a million seals had probably been killed at sea.

Through the tireless efforts of Henry Wood Elliott, a retired US treasury agent once assigned to the Pribilof Islands, the American public was made aware of the wasteful killing and warned of the impending extinction of the species. For more than a decade Elliott campaigned to stop the pelagic sealing until, in December 1911, the US Senate finally ratified the world's first treaty for the protection of wildlife. In the agreement, the five world powers involved pledged to give up hunting the seals at sea in exchange for a share of the revenue from the animals' strictly regulated harvest on the Pribilof Island breeding grounds, after a five-year moratorium to allow the herds to recover their numbers. In an amendment to the treaty, the five countries further agreed to end forever all hunting of the nearly extinct sea otter.

While the pelagic seal treaty was little noticed by anyone outside conservation circles and the affected industry, an event which took place in the following year drew world attention back to Alaska. At Mt Katmai near the base of the Alaska Peninsula occurred the greatest geologic cataclysm of modern times. For two and a half days, 33 million tons of rock exploded from the earth, depositing a layer of ash and pumice, 300 feet deep in places, over an area of more than 40 square miles.

Kodiak, situated 100 miles away from the blast, reported snow-like drifts of ash and pumice up to 12 feet deep. Roofs collapsed, and the town was evacuated. In all, more than 7 cubic miles of debris from the explosion rose 25 miles into the stratosphere to be carried by winds around the northern half of the globe. Night skies glowed eerily over North America, Europe and Asia, while sunsets and sunrises took on an added brilliance. Solar radiation was reduced by as much as 10 per cent, lowering global temperatures by an average of 1.8 degrees Fahrenheit.

It was three years before any organized attempt was made to explore the area of the eruption. Then, in a series of expeditions sponsored by the National Geographic Society, Dr Robert F. Griggs and his colleagues tried to piece together the story of the explosion. In 1916 they discovered the 40-square-mile Valley of Ten Thousand Smokes:

> The whole valley as far as the eye could reach was full of hundreds, no thousands – literally, tens of thousands – of smokes curling up from its fissured floor. It was as though all the steam engines in the world, assembled together, had popped their safety valves at once and were letting off surplus steam in concert.

The area became a National Monument in 1917 and was expanded and upgraded to National Park status in 1980. Today in the $4\frac{1}{4}$ million acre Mt Katmai National Park and Preserve most of the 'smokes' have extinguished as the volcanic activity beneath the surface has subsided. What remains is a pink pumice-strewn desert, so bleak and other-worldly that it has been used as a training ground for NASA astronauts preparing for trips to the moon.

The explosion and collapse of Katmai – and the simultaneous creation of a new volcano named Novarupta a few miles away – was the largest in a continuing series of tectonic activities to affect the Pacific Northwest. Like the 1912 explosion, the Alaskan Good Friday earthquake of 1964 and the eruption of Mt St Helens in Washington state in 1980 were caused by a combination of faulting and subduction. All of the region's seismic activity results from the dense North Pacific sea floor moving slowly under the lighter continental crust of western North America and southern Alaska. The friction of this movement creates deep-seated earthquakes and sends fingers of molten rock to the surface creating the many volcanos, including the Aleutian Islands that spike the North Pacific coast.

A far less violent geologic process in northern Alaska has had consequences that are almost as dramatic as the volcanic events of the south. Slowly and steadily over the past 200 million years, the accumulation of marine sediments in the waters just off the northern coast has extended Alaska's shoreline into the Arctic Ocean, creating the North Slope. Heat and pressure within these deposits have created ideal conditions for the production of oil.

The history of the region has been characterized by economic booms and busts, and petroleum has figured prominently in the most recent cycle. The discovery of oil on Alaska's North Slope in 1969 led to the construction of an 800-mile pipeline from Prudhoe Bay to Port Valdez in Prince William Sound. The pipeline, the economic effect of the oil boom and the environmental impact of the disastrous *Exxon Valdez* oil spill of 1989, have all had incalculable consequences on the wildlife and the people of Alaska.

Massive lumbering operations in southeastern Alaska, British Columbia, Washington and Oregon have also had a profound impact on the region. While providing jobs for native Americans and Old World immigrants alike, the logging of the Northwest's old-growth forests has upset the complex natural communities that depended upon them, destroying the ecological balance of the region and threatening age-old cycles of life on which humans themselves have depended for more than 40 000 years.

Despite this activity, there are still enormous tracts of land, sea and coast that are as wild and pristine as they were when Bering made his voyage in 1741. Alaska has more area set aside for wildlife than anywhere else in North America, and more designated wilderness per capita than anywhere else on earth. Although large parts of the state were protected from commercial exploitation as early as 1918, it was the Alaska National Interest Lands Conservation Act of 1980 that broke all records for land preservation. In setting aside more than 100 million acres of wilderness – a land area larger than the state of California – the US Congress and President Jimmy Carter reasserted North America's role as a world leader in conservation. At the same time, they recognized the importance of the region's cultural history by permitting the continued use of the land and its wildlife by indigenous peoples.

In debating the pros and cons of what was widely billed as the conservation vote of the century, legislators came to recognize what Henry Gannett, Chief Geographer of the United States, had concluded after his own survey of Alaska 80 years before:

OVERLEAF *Warm, moisture-laden air from the Pacific Ocean encourages year-round plant growth in the rain-forests of the Pacific Northwest. Although 85–90 per cent of the old-growth forests of the region have been cut, hundreds of thousands of acres continue to be harvested each year, much of it for export to Japan.*

There are resources in Alaska that far exceed our ability to calculate them. There is one other asset of the Territory not yet enumerated – imponderable and difficult to appraise, yet one of the chief assets of Alaska, if not the greatest. This is the scenery. There are glaciers, mountains, and fjords elsewhere, but nowhere else on earth is there such abundance and magnificence of mountain, fjord and glacier scenery. For thousands of miles the coast is a continuous panorama. For the one Yosemite of California, Alaska has hundreds. The mountains and glaciers of the Cascade Range are duplicated and a thousand-fold exceeded in Alaska. The Alaska coast is to become the show-place of the earth, and pilgrims, not only from the United States, but from far beyond the seas, will throng in endless procession to see it. Its grandeur is more valuable than the gold or the fish or the timber, for it will never be exhausted. This value, measured by direct returns in money received from tourists, will be enormous; measured by health and pleasure, it will be incalculable.

Gannett closed his remarks with 'a word of caution' for the endless procession of pilgrims who he thought would visit Alaska:

If you are old, go by all means; but if you are young, stay away until you grow older. The scenery of Alaska is so much grander than anything else of the kind in the world that, once beheld, all other scenery becomes flat and insipid. It is not well to dull one's capacity for such enjoyment by seeing the finest first.

SEARCHING FOR PARADISE

CALIFORNIA · AND · THE · PACIFIC · COAST

Seven miles from downtown Los Angeles, beside the restless roar of Wilshire Boulevard, lies a silent piece of California's complex past. It is not a preserved Spanish mission or a gold sluicer's cabin, the location for some Hollywood epic, or a monument to someone's glory. It is a 23-acre park that was once a pool of water with an unusual tar-like bottom. Beneath its now mostly dry surface lies the telescoped record of 40 000 years.

Chumash and Gabrielino Indians knew of the Rancho La Brea Tar Pits thousands of years before the first Spanish missionaries, Russian fur traders, or Yankee gold rushers set foot on Californian soil. They found its sticky black pitch useful for caulking their plank canoes, water-sealing their reed baskets, repairing broken tools, and securing decorative shell inlays to ceremonial and household items. They also knew its dangers. More than a few were trapped in the adhesive grip of the pits while trying to collect the tar. Perhaps they saw animals similarly trapped. Certainly, they would have seen carcasses fouling the pond's waters, filling the air with the stench of decaying flesh. The gathering of vultures, crows and other carrion-eaters must have marked it as something sacred – or evil – a place to be treated with caution and respect. What none of them could have known was that this curious bog contained a record of North American life extending back to the closing phases of the last great ice age.

In 1792, 11 years after the founding of Los Angeles, a visitor to the tar pit lake at Rancho La Brea reported that in hot weather animals had been seen to sink into the pond:

> and when they tried to escape they were unable to do so because their feet were stuck and the lake swallowed them. After many years, their bones have come up through the holes, as if petrified.

Excavations of the site, most of them since 1900, have revealed among those petrifications the fossilized remains of virtually everything that grew, walked,

ran, hopped, flew or crawled across southern California between 4000 and 40 000 years ago. Preserved there were single-celled plants called diatoms, flower pollen, seeds, leaves, pieces of wood, clam and snail shells, insects and spiders, fish, frogs and toads, snakes and turtles, birds and mammals – in all more than 420 species of animal and 140 species of plant.

Like the North Slope of Alaska, much of California's Pacific coastal plain once lay beneath the ocean where marine deposits set the stage for future petroleum production. At the onset of the last ice age, the sea retreated, exposing an extensive flat plain in southern California between the receding edge of the ocean and the coastal Santa Monica, and the San Bernardino Mountains. Subsequent stream erosion deposited additional sediments from the mountains and etched the plain into its current configuration. Meanwhile oil, forming in large reservoirs beneath the ground, here and there seeped upward through porous layers of stone and through faults and fissures in the earth's crust. Sometimes it came up beneath the sea. Early travelers along the southern California coast noted that the ocean water was 'often covered with an iridescent film of oil which finds its way to the surface over an extent of at least twenty miles'. At Rancho La Brea and other inland sites, the oil had no chance to dissipate and instead concentrated. The lighter petroleum portion evaporated, leaving behind shallow, sticky pools of natural asphalt.

From the pollen and other botanical remains captured and preserved in the La Brea deposits, it is known that California's post-glacial climate was considerably cooler and more moist than the area is today. It also supported a much larger and more diverse mammal population. The pits show that there were once mammoths and mastodons there, some standing over 12 feet tall and weighing as much as 10 000 pounds. The mastodon family, distantly related to today's elephants, originated in Africa and spread to Europe and Asia about 20 million years ago, reaching North America some 15 million years ago. Another group of mammals trapped at La Brea and extinguished some 10 000 years ago were the ground sloths. One species stood over 6 feet high and weighed 3500 pounds. The ground sloths are believed to have originated in South America and migrated north 7 or 8 million years ago. The pits also contain the remains of native horses and tapirs, peccaries, camels, llamas, musk oxen, a long-horned bison, bears, lions, saber-toothed cats, and a host of smaller creatures.

Of all the animals preserved at La Brea, an unusually high proportion were carnivores – wolves, foxes, weasels, coyotes, and a variety of cats. There were also more than 20 species of eagles, hawks and falcons. This does not mean that there were more meat-eaters when the pits were active but rather that these were the animals most often caught as they came to scavenge other species already ensnared in the sticky tar. Democratically lethal under warm, summer conditions, the tar pits could be equally dangerous to birds and mammals, predators and prey, weak and strong. One group of animals not represented in the La Brea deposits are the dinosaurs. They had disappeared from the continent about 65 million years earlier, while the Los Angeles area was still well under the surface of the sea.

A fiberglass mammoth mired in tar recreates a scene of tragedy (or good fortune for paleontologists) at the La Brea Tar Pits. Over one million mammal fossils representing at least 59 different species have been recovered from the asphalt deposits at La Brea since excavations began there in 1901.

Of the many
carnivores whose
remains are pre-
served in the La Brea
Tar Pits, the bobcat
(above) and kit fox
(left) have remained
virtually unchanged
in 40 000 years.

Climate and vegetative changes probably contributed to the extinction of most of the larger mammals preserved at Rancho La Brea. The region's first human inhabitants undoubtedly speeded the process. By contrast, many of the smaller species survived both environmental and human pressures, and can be found living throughout most of southern California today. They would probably inhabit Los Angeles itself if they could. The mammals that survived that earlier age include foxes, skunks, badgers, coyotes, weasels, bobcats, rabbits, shrews, and bats.

Of the 135 bird species found at La Brea, only 19 are now extinct. The bald and golden eagle, prairie falcon, peregrine falcon, kestrel, burrowing owl, common flicker, western meadowlark and common raven are among the birds trapped thousands of years ago that are still found throughout the West. All seven species of lizard, nine varieties of snake and five kinds of toad and frog found at La Brea still occur in southern California.

The continuing viability of ancient species is nowhere more dramatically revealed than in the Sierra Nevada or 'snowy range', 200 miles inland from the coast. Here, not just species, but individual organisms date back thousands of years. The Sierra Nevada parallels the Pacific Ocean from the cactus flats of the Mojave Desert to Lassen Peak, 400 miles farther north. On the western slopes of the range, at altitudes of 5000 to 8000 feet, grow some of the largest and oldest of all living organisms, the giant sequoia or California Big Trees.

The Big Trees are well named for they are immense by any standard. Their trunks average 25 feet in diameter with many reaching diameters of 30 to 32 feet. One individual tree, the General Grant, has a base diameter of 40.3 feet and a circumference of 107.6 feet. Another, the General Sherman, is presumed to be the world's largest living thing. It weighs an estimated 6167 tons and any one of its limbs is larger than most of the trees in the Rocky Mountains.

As impressive as their size is the longevity of the remaining sequoias. Their annual growth rings put their age at well over 4000 years. Most were growing when the Palace of Minos was built at Knossos and when the first stones were set up at Stonehenge. The trees were already flourishing when Buddha preached his sermons, when Jesus Christ was crucified, and when Mohammed dictated the Koran.

The giant sequoia's coastal relatives, the California redwoods, are not quite as old, though most of them had already sprouted when Hannibal was taking his elephants over the Alps. The trees were brought to European attention in 1769 by the first Spanish exploration of the Californian coast. The expedition's chronicler, Father Juan Crespi, reported traveling through

plains and low hills, well forested with very high trees of a red color, not known to us. They have a very different leaf from cedars, and although the wood resembles cedar somewhat in color, it is very different and has not the same odor. ... In this region there is a great abundance of these trees and because none of the expedition recognizes them they are named red-wood (palo colorado) from their color.

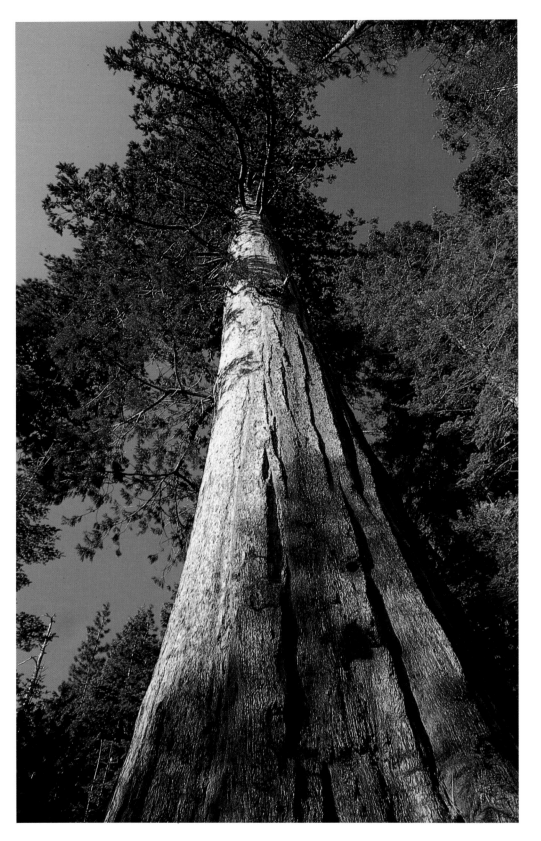

Their age surpassed
only by California's
bristlecone pine, the
giant sequoias or
California Big Trees
are among the
world's oldest and
largest living organ-
isms. Their remark-
able longevity may
be partly attributed
to the tannin that
impregnates their
bark and heartwood,
giving them their rich
red color and making
them resistant to
attacks of insects or
fungi. Though once
more widely dis-
tributed, the Big
Trees are found
today growing only
on the western slopes
of the Sierra Nevada.
Their close relative,
the California red-
woods, grow at
lower elevations
closer to the coast.

The trees were seen and recorded by many subsequent expeditions, but the first complete botanical description came from Archibald Menzies, a Scottish botanist who accompanied George Vancouver's 1791–94 expedition to the Pacific Northwest. Menzies' countryman, David Douglas, also reported the redwoods during his visit to California in 1831. By the time the tree was introduced to cultivation in Britain by Karl T. Hartweg in 1876, therefore, it had more than a century of attention in the literature of California.

The giant sequoias of the Sierra Nevada, by contrast, were not recognized and publicized until the California gold strikes of 1848 drew miners – and newspaper reporters – into the mountains where the Big Trees lived. An English publisher who was there at the time noted that following an 1852 discovery of the trees by a hunter named Augustus Dowd:

> the trumpet-tongued press proclaimed the wonder to all sections of the state, and to all parts of the world, and the lovers of the marvelous began first to doubt, then to believe, and afterwards to flock to see with their own eyes the objects of which they had heard so much.

The immediate response to the discovery of the sequoias was commercial exploitation. Tourists were shown the remarkable trees for a fee. Hotels were built and other amusements developed to entertain visitors. Five men took 22 days to cut one Big Tree and remove 50 feet of its bark. This was shipped to San Francisco, then by way of Cape Horn to New York, where it was reassembled for view in the racquet court of the Union Club on Broadway. Another entrepreneur arranged to strip the bark of an even larger specimen and have it sent to London for display in the Crystal Palace. There it astounded visitors from 1857 until it caught fire and burned in 1866.

Not everyone was pleased by such commercial use. In a letter to the editor of the widely read *Gleason's Pictorial*, one Californian protested the stripping as 'a cruel idea' and a 'perfect desecration':

> In Europe such a natural production would have been cherished and protected by law; but in this money-making-go-ahead community ... the purchaser chops it down and ships it off for a shilling show. We hope that no one will conceive the idea of purchasing Niagara Falls for the same purpose.

The giant sequoia, like its coastal relative, was named for the Cherokee who invented the first Indian alphabet. Sequoia himself never saw the trees, nor had anything to do with them, but then neither did the other men who at one time or another were honored by scientific names applied to the Big Tree: the Duke of Wellington and George Washington. Since 1939, the scientific world has given each of the trees a genus of its own: *Sequoiadendron giganteum*, the Sierra Big Tree, and *Sequoia sempervirens*, the 'everliving' California redwood.

Because of its proximity to the Bering land bridge, California was one of the first areas in North America to receive permanent human populations. It is hard to say exactly when nomadic hunters found their way to California from their ancestral homelands in Asia, but they are believed to have established themselves

In the closing decades of the eighteenth century, Spain augmented her commercial, religious and military interest in California with a major scientific study of the Pacific coast (above). An exploring expedition under the command of Martin de Sessé y Lacasta and José Mariano Mociño brought to Spain hundreds of natural history specimens and drawings, including the handsome blue crab (left).

along the coast between 50 000 and 35 000 years ago. The temperate coastal climate and an abundance of wild food encouraged a shift from strictly hunting to more generalized food-gathering activities. The environment also supported large numbers of people. Before European contact with the New World, nearly a third of all the Indians in North America north of Mexico lived in California. The region's topography, with two parallel mountain chains running north and south, desert areas in the south and east, and an ocean in the west, tended to hold populations in California and isolate them from indigenous groups elsewhere.

As well as a high density of population, there was a wide variety of cultural groups, with over 300 different languages or dialects spoken in California at the time of first Spanish contact. Despite this, there appears to have been little conflict among the inhabitants because natural resources were adequate for all. Salmon filled the northern rivers through most of the summer. Shellfish, sea mammals, and coastal fisheries provided a year-round source of food for groups near the ocean. A variety of seeds, among them acorns, pine nuts and mesquite beans, grew in the valleys and on the hillsides in virtually every Indian territory. These were harvested and ground into flour, the acorns first having been leached of their bitter tannic acid. Surplus grains were stored in baskets on platforms out of reach of rodents. Wild berries and fruits of many kinds were gathered and dried for winter use. Wild game, from birds and small rodents to bear, elk and deer, were widely available as, in earlier times, were the other large herbivores whose fossil remains are preserved at La Brea.

Groups related by bloodline or marriage lived in villages of 100 to 500 people, called *rancherias* by the Spanish. According to the demands of the seasons – the maturing of plants, the fattening of animals, the migrations of fish – the people of each *rancheria* moved in a set pattern through a carefully delineated block of territory. Unlike the tribal groups of eastern North America who shared languages and had developed inter-tribal trade relations and military alliances, the Californian tribes were self-sufficient and independent of one another, thus inhibiting coordinated resistance to European invaders. Having lived in relative peace among themselves for millennia, they were not experienced fighters and were therefore slow to combat Spanish domination when it came.

Spain first explored the southern (Baja) and northern (Alta) coast of California in the 1540s but, finding little of commercial interest, did not attempt to settle the area at the time. Instead, the Spanish concentrated their energies on the more accessible southeastern and southwestern parts of the continent. Despite an English claim to Alta California by Sir Francis Drake in 1579, Spain was not able, or did not feel it necessary, to defend its territorial claims for almost two centuries. Then, beginning in the 1760s, perceived threats of Russian expansion and the personal ambitions of Jóse Gálvez, Visitador General of New Spain, led to the establishment of a string of settlements along the Californian coast. Since Spain could not induce large numbers of its own people to settle in North America, its strategy for controlling the land was to Christianize the Indians and use them as proxies for the mother country.

At the heart of the Spanish system of geographic, economic, military, and

social control were the missions. Manned by two or more priests and a handful of soldiers, and backed by a string of *presidios* or military barracks, the missions were generally set up near Indian *rancherias*. At first they were simple, non-threatening compounds, which, with the lure of free food, bright trinkets, and the wonders of music and pageantry, attracted the natives to resettle nearby. As the missions grew in size and property, the neophytes or novices, as the Christianized Indians were called, were pressed into service to grow grapes, grain and other crops, and to herd cattle and sheep for the Jesuit or Franciscan fathers. Under the control of the Catholic Church, the Spanish developed a plantation system in California not unlike that of the American Southeast.

Life in the missions proved less than a blessing for the Indians. Once integrated into the mission system, the neophytes were trapped by economic dependence, and some were even held by force. Their work grew increasingly difficult and time-consuming. Instead of their rich, varied indigenous diet, they came to subsist on a daily ration of a starchy cereal soup called *atole*. Housed in crowded facilities with poor sanitary conditions, the novices weakened and became highly susceptible to European diseases.

When reports of Spanish cruelty to Indian workers – including whipping, mutilation, branding, hobbling, and even execution – made their way back to Madrid, the actions were rationalized by the missionaries as part of the process of civilization. 'It is evident that a nation which is barbarous, ferocious and ignorant requires more frequent punishment than a nation which is cultured, educated and of gentle and moderate customs,' explained one California mission priest. Historical evidence suggests that his characterizations of the two cultures might more accurately have been reversed.

There was some Indian resistance to the mission system. However, by the time conditions warranted a response, most of the Indians were too weak and disorganized to defend themselves. There was, therefore, no uprising in California like the Pueblo Revolt in the Southwest. When Indians tried to avoid conflict by fleeing the most oppressive missions, there was nowhere for them to go. Their own *rancherias* were long since abandoned and in other missions they were quickly recognized as escapees, flogged, and put in irons until they could be returned. Once back at the mission from which they had fled, they suffered further punishment.

After Mexico gained independence from Spain in 1821, the Spanish were expelled from California and the new Mexican authorities began to secularize the missions. The action was not as altruistic as it first appeared, nor did it work to the advantage of the indigenous Californians. Instead of the mission lands reverting to the Indians from whom they had been taken, they were turned into extensive private ranches owned by the administrators whose task it had been to dismantle the holdings of the Church. Though the Indians were legally liberated from religious servitude, their new position was no better than the old. Many had come to rely on the missions for food, shelter and protection. Suddenly turned out, they had the fabric of neither the Spanish nor their own culture to support them. 'I am very old', lamented one dispossessed neophyte:

An extensive network of mission settlements, including Santa Inez north of Santa Barbara, helped Spain to maintain political control of California without a large commitment of money or troops. Spanish influences in architecture can still be seen in many parts of California.

The California gold rush drew countless thousands of miners to the Sierra Nevada in the 1840s and 50s. Gold washing, as shown in this painting of the Calaveras River, though environmentally disastrous at the time, had only limited long-term consequences. California's vineyards (left) have made a more lasting impact on the economy and the ecology of the region.

*My people were once around me like the sands of the shore ... many ...
many. They have all passed away. They have died like the grass ... I am a
Christian Indian, I am all that is left of my people. I am alone.*

The Indians who tried to reconstitute their tribal organizations and return to
subsistence life in the wild soon found themselves in conflict with white land
owners, and many were systematically hunted and destroyed.

When the United States government assumed jurisdiction over California in
February 1848 under the Treaty of Guadalupe Hidalgo, its own record of Indian
abuse was little better than that of the Spanish, Russians or Mexicans. Perhaps
given some time, new policies might have been developed, but circumstances
would not afford this luxury. Unbeknown to the signers of the treaty, gold had
been discovered in California just nine days before it was ceded to the United
States. Almost overnight the greatest mining rush in history was underway.
Before it subsided, 100 000 people had converged on the Pacific coast, further
displacing the region's indigenous people and transforming California from a
half-tamed wilderness to a settled commonwealth.

The rush began when gold nuggets were found near a saw mill owned by
the Swiss-born John A. Sutter, on the American River, a tributary of the
Sacramento River. After a brief period of skepticism, local Californians decided
the reports of gold were real and they rushed, en masse, to the American River
and into the foothills of the Sierra Nevada through which it flowed. By May
1848, San Francisco was a virtual ghost town, all but a few of its 800 residents
having taken to the hills. By July the same was true of every town and hamlet
in north-central and southern California. In the ports of Monterey and San
Francisco, ships rode empty at anchor, their crews having abandoned them for
the hope of land-based fortunes in the Sierra Nevada. A San Francisco editor,
announcing the suspension of his paper because of lack of readers, wrote:

> *The whole country, from San Francisco to Los Angeles, and from the sea
> shore to the base of the Sierra Nevadas, resounds with the sordid cry of
> 'gold!, GOLD!, GOLD!' While the field is left half planted, the house half
> built, and everything neglected but the manufacture of shovels and pickaxes.*

The mineral treasure that sparked the rush was created some 150 million
years ago when two of the earth's crustal plates grated over one another near
the Pacific coast. Later, a huge block of the continental plate was further crushed
and tilted, creating part of the Sierra Nevada. Liquids and gases rose from deep
within the earth, carrying with them minerals that penetrated cracks in the
mountains and formed veins of copper, tungsten, silver and gold. By 1848, at
altitudes of 1000 to 2700 feet, the remains of these eroded veins appeared as a
120-mile-long string of gold-impregnated quartz pockets in a belt up to 2 miles
wide. The miners called this the mother lode, mistakenly believing it to be the
edge of a single gigantic mass of gold. The stream sediment or placer gold they
found at the Sierra's base came from bits of the metal that had been eroded
from the pockets in the so-called mother lode.

Word of California's treasure spread first to the Sandwich Islands (now called Hawaii) and then around Cape Horn to the East Coast. By August 1848, the *New York Herald* had printed a letter describing the find and reporting that prospectors were making 30 dollars a day, more than ten times the salary of the average daily worker in the East. In December, President James K. Polk confirmed the reports of gold by devoting a section of his State of the Union message to the Californian discoveries. 'The accounts of the abundance of gold in that territory', said the President, 'are of such an extraordinary character as would scarcely command belief were they not corroborated by the authentic reports of officers in the public service.'

The formerly reticent Eastern press now jumped on the story: 'The Eldorado of the old Spaniards is discovered at last.' Newspaper headlines proclaimed: 'We are on the brink of the Age of Gold,' 'Now have the dreams of Cortez and Pizarro become realised.' Merchants across the country scrambled to provide future prospectors with tents, picks, shovels, washpans (for panning gold dust from the streams), and other basic equipment, while manufacturers grew wealthy producing the needed supplies. A New York clothier named Levi Strauss made his reputation, and his fortune, producing durable blue jeans for California's gold rushers.

Daguerreotype operators in newly opened photographic studios recorded the hopeful images of young men from Boston to Savannah, and Chicago to St Paul, who were leaving home to seek their fortunes in the gold fields. Even musicians leaped on the band wagon with such timely compositions as 'The Gold Digger's Waltz' and 'The Sacramento Gallup'. Everywhere the country rejoiced in the prospects of new prosperity as departing gold rushers sang their own national anthem of economic optimism:

> *Oh Susannah, don't you cry for me*
> *I'm gone to California with my wash-bowl on my knee.*

The environmental consequences of California's gold rush were almost as enormous as the social and economic ones. As tens of thousands of miners invaded the Sierra Nevada, shanty towns sprang up where forests of live and blue oak, or of ponderosa and sugar pine had grown undisturbed for centuries. Stream banks once lined with lupin, shooting star, larkspur, and wild geranium were rubbed raw by prospectors' boots, while the stream beds themselves were destroyed by the endless panning, digging, damming and sluicing of the 'forty-niners'.

Within a few years, commercial mining operations cut and blasted into gold-bearing veins, slashing bare the hillsides and turning pristine mountain streams into open troughs of silt and sludge. Mountain forests were cleared for fuel and for the timber needed in mining operations. Streamlife was destroyed. Birds and animals were shot on sight as the hungry miners tried to augment their limited food supplies. Huge areas of California, primarily along the Sacramento and San Joaquin River drainages, were wasted in the frenzied rush for wealth. 'A sense of more than depression confronts the traveler who takes this desolation to heart,' wrote a California visitor at the time. 'It is much the same impression left by the scorched earth found in the wake of a passing army.'

As the number of miners mushroomed and mining techniques grew more sophisticated – and more environmentally damaging – the amount of gold extracted increased from 10 million ounces in 1849 to 81 million in 1852. California changed from a backwater of the old Spanish Empire with a non-Indian population of 15 000 (in 1848) to a bristling cosmopolitan territory of 224 435 non-Indians (in 1852). Many were newcomers to America. In 1853, half of San Francisco's 50 000 residents had been born abroad, including Germans, French, Irish, Spanish Americans and Chinese. Only 8000 were women and only 3000 children. Yet despite the area's unusual demographics, there were enough US citizens in California in 1850 for it to qualify for statehood.

The tens of thousands of Americans who had recently arrived in California had reached the Golden State by gruelling overland travel, or by expensive and uncomfortable ocean voyages around Cape Horn, or to and from the Isthmus of Panama by clipper ship. Whichever way they had come, and no matter their luck in the gold fields, few relished the prospect of retracing their route. Besides, California was, in the words of one of the first overland arrivals, 'a land of sunshine and plenty' and a pleasant place to start a new life. 'If a man were to ask of God a climate', wrote an early West Coast enthusiast, 'he would ask just such one as that of California.'

Another major advantage for long-term settlement was the ready availability of fertile land. 'Lying on this coast . . . with a climate nowhere on earth surpassed, was a vast area of country almost literally without house or inhabitant,' wrote a veteran of California's early years of statehood:

> On account of the productiveness of the soil, this area was fitted to become the home of millions of people. Most of it could be given to the plow almost without cutting down a tree or removing a stone, but it was land asleep. . . . Under its covering of thickly blooming flowers – white, pink, blue, purple, and yellow, all tiny but beautiful things – are concealed possibilities of production so great that I dare not express the facts in the case, lest the reader's incredulity shall break out in words I should not care to hear.

Encouraged by land speculators' glowing accounts of California's potential, many new arrivals turned from gold prospecting to farming, ultimately trans-forming the state into the nation's leader in agricultural production. By the mid-1850s, the Los Angeles area was already exporting large quantities of grain, and an annual half million gallons of sweet wine and brandy produced from the hardy stock of mission grapes, originally cultivated by the Franciscan fathers and their Indian converts. Reported in one promotional brochure as a paradise 'too heterogeneous for easy description', southern California was a land of enormous agricultural possibilities:

> Los Angeles County alone has far more variety in soil, climate, and scenery than is usually found in an area many times as large in the East; and it would

not be far from the truth to say that its variety of actual products is as great as that in all the States bordering on the Atlantic.

In fact, some of the claims made about the area were reminiscent of those that had been made for eastern North America three centuries before. As with earlier land promotions, newcomers were assured of easy success, regardless of their abilities or previous experience. Some promoters even represented existing skills as liabilities in their efforts to attract non-farmers to southern California:

It is said that our best fruit-growers and tillers of the soil are those who had totally different employments before coming here. 'It is better to come in ignorance', say many, 'and learn all new than to try to put in practice the principles of agriculture already learned.'

Another fertile region was to be found further inland in the Sacramento and San Joaquin Valleys, which together form the state's great Central Valley. In the 1860s and 70s, large areas of this region were transformed from native prairie habitat supporting populations of tule elk and antelope to wheat farms producing agricultural gold for California.

Meanwhile, within a 100-mile arc of San Francisco, a transplanted East was beginning to evolve. 'Substantial private dwellings, well-fenced fields, broad patches of vineyard and fruit orchards, alternate with grainfields, extending as far as the eye can search,' wrote a resident of the 1850s. Frame houses with broad verandas and brightly painted shutters resembled their contemporaries in Ohio and Illinois, though their colorful gardens with palm trees and exotic vines brought from Asia or Australia lent them a luxurious, almost tropical air.

San Francisco itself grew rapidly from the sleepy town of 1848 to a city of 25 000 by the end of 1850, and double that number by 1853. Though periodically shaken by earthquakes and gutted by fire six times in three years, the city was rebuilt more lavishly after each conflagration. Building materials which could not be found close at hand were imported: Douglas fir from Washington state's Puget Sound, redwood from Oregon and California's north coast, granite from China, and sandstone from Australia. 'San Francisco', marveled the *New York Tribune* correspondent Bayard Taylor in the summer of 1850, 'seemed to have accomplished in a day the growth of half a century.'

By 1853, there were 537 saloons, 160 hotels and 66 restaurants selling wild game from the interior and seabird eggs collected on the Farallon Islands. San Francisco could also boast a growing number of theatres, a circus, a zoo, and even a mercantile library association. In the library's collection was a copy of John James Audubon's *The Birds of America*, containing 435 hand-colored plates with life-sized depictions of 1065 individual birds. The book so inspired one San Francisco resident that, after seeing it, he devoted the rest of his life to observing and painting the birds of the Pacific slope.

Andrew Jackson Grayson had received no formal training in either art or science, but his interest in these subjects dated back to his Louisiana childhood and school days in St Louis. Having made a comfortable fortune in real estate

Inspired by a San Francisco library's copy of Audubon's The Birds of America, *Andrew Jackson Grayson gave up a successful business career in 1853 to paint the birds of the Pacific Slope. His water-color of orioles must have given him special pleasure for this subspecies had been named Grayson's oriole in his honor.*

and merchandise in San Francisco during the boom years of the gold rush, Grayson found himself in a position to pursue his avocational interest. In 1856, he contacted the Smithsonian Institution for advice and offered his services as a collector. Grayson was gratified to learn that, while previous expeditions had done some collecting along the Pacific coast, the national museum had very little information about the birds of the state's interior. The Smithsonian's Assistant Secretary, Spencer Fullerton Baird, accepted Grayson's offer to collect and urged him to send him specimens 'of the very commonest kinds' of birds. 'As many species, two of a kind, as we can get will be welcomed, as we have a constant drain on our duplicates to supply other museums.' Recognizing Grayson's still modest talents as an artist, Baird tactfully stressed the importance of gathering information and specimens rather than painting:

> You could readily become known in the scientific world as the Audubon of the West; the truest merit of this man was not in his drawings, but in his masterly delineations of the habits and peculiarities – the life of American birds.

From his first contact with the Smithsonian until his death in 1869, Grayson systematically observed, described, collected and illustrated the birds of California and Mexico, providing the first scientific accounts of many western species. The opportunities for collecting were great indeed, as one of Grayson's journal entries from a visit to the Tulare Plains in central California reveals:

> We reached the main Kern River by noon. ... Our encampment here was beautiful, and one of plenty. I could not describe the innumerable quantity of water fowl and the large herds of elk. ... Such a noise, of a clear, cool morning when the air is bracing and the sun just peeping over the distant snow-capped mountains of the Sierra. Your ears are confused with the many sounds of the fowls: the quacking of the mallard, the soft, delicate whistle of the bald pate and teal, the underground-like notes of the rail or marsh hen, the flute-like notes of the wild goose and brant, the wild ranting of the heron – not to forget the bugle-like notes of the whooping [sandhill] crane and the swan. These and a thousand other birds mingling their songs together create that indescribable sensation of pleasure that can only be felt by one fond of nature in its wildest and most beautiful forms.

Some birds were not so noisy or easy to find. The California condor, North America's largest bird, was already quite rare when Baird wrote to Grayson with a special request in 1856:

> Our great desideratum ... is the egg of the California Vulture. No specimen is extant in our eastern collections. If you can get anyone to collect and send some, I will dispose of them to the best advantage. No other species is in such demand. I have no doubt I could get 8 or 10 dollars each, for half a dozen.

In his reply, Grayson noted the disappearance of the giant scavenger which once soared on 4-foot wings through most of the Coast Range from Baja California

RIGHT *The 9-foot wingspan of the California condor once carried North America's largest bird throughout the state's coastal ranges. Habitat destruction, poisoned bait and illegal shooting have brought this magnificent bird to the edge of extinction. The last three wild condors were taken into protective custody in 1986 and are now part of a captive breeding program aimed at one day restoring the species to its original habitat.*

OVERLEAF *The highest point in the continental US outside of Alaska, California's Mt Whitney lies at the southern end of the Sierra Nevada Range. It was named in 1864 for Harvard professor Josiah Whitney, who had served as chief of the California State Geological Survey since 1860. At the age of 41, Whitney was charged with the overwhelming task of mapping 1200 miles of uncharted coastline and some of the most varied topography in North America.*

to the Columbia River. 'In the early days of California history', he wrote, 'it was more frequently met with than now. Being of a cautious and shy disposition, the rapid settlement of the country has partially driven it off to more secluded localities.'

The species had actually been in decline since long before the arrival of Europeans, the fossil record suggesting that the species spanned the continent before the last ice age. However, there is no doubt that human pressures have dramatically affected its viability over the past century and a half. Habitat loss, hunting, and poisoning had so reduced the condor population by 1986 that only three birds remained in the wild. These were captured in a last-ditch effort to save the species from extinction. In time, through a carefully controlled captive breeding program, it is hoped that wild condors will be reintroduced to the wild and that once again they will soar through California's sky.

While Grayson was doing his part for the Smithsonian's ornithological collections, other, more professionally trained scientists were undertaking the daunting task of surveying the Pacific coast state. 'I have found that the state of California is a prodigiously large place,' wrote Josiah Whitney, the first director of the State Geological Survey, as he took up the task in 1860. 'It is as big as Great Britain, Belgium, Hanover, and Bavaria put together!' Not just the size of the state – over 158 000 square miles – but the scale of its features overwhelmed the scientists charged with its delineation. It had 1200 miles of uncharted coastline, one of the nation's largest continuous mountain chains, and a top-ography and climate of unmatched extremes. Between San Francisco and the Sacramento Valley, temperatures characteristically vary by 50 degrees in as many miles. Between the Sonoran Desert in the southeast and the coastal rainforest in the northwest corner of the state, annual rainfall ranges from less than 2 inches to over 100 inches. Mt Whitney, at 14 501 feet high the tallest mountain south of Alaska, stands only 60 miles from Death Valley, 280 feet below sea level. This remarkable variety creates in California some of the greatest biological complexity in the continent. As one nineteenth-century scientist put it, 'there is from end to end of California scarcely a commonplace mile.'

California afforded an unprecedented opportunity to study virtually every kind of habitat the continent could offer. It also afforded the opportunity to use and abuse these environments without restraint. Patterns of land use that had begun on the Atlantic coast two centuries before repeated themselves in California with accelerated speed. Those who objected to the exploitation of public resources for private gain faced the task of convincing Californians to become the exception to America's environmental history, to reject rather than embrace the extractive culture that had characterized the nation's development to date.

The most significant spokesman for wilderness preservation was John Muir, a Scottish-born farmer and inventor with a passionate love of nature. Muir had begun his wilderness wanderings in 1867 with a 1000-mile walk from Louisville, Kentucky to the Gulf of Mexico. 'My plan was simply to push on in a general southward direction by the wildest, leafiest, and least trodden way I could find, promising the greatest extent of virgin forest,' he explained in a book about the trip. From the Florida Keys he sailed to Havana, intending to travel on to South America to continue his explorations. Deteriorating health and lack of suitable transport south directed him instead to New York City where he felt 'completely lost in the vast throngs of people, the noise of the streets, and the immense size of the buildings. Often I thought I would like to explore the city', he claimed, 'if, like a lot of wild hills and valleys, it was clear of inhabitants.'

The wild hills and valleys Muir decided to explore instead were those of California, to which he sailed in the spring of 1868:

Arriving by the Panama steamer, I stopped one day in San Francisco, and then inquired for the nearest way out of town. 'But where do you want to go?' asked the man to whom I had applied for this important information. 'To any place that is wild,' I said.

Muir set off on foot for the Yosemite Valley, 150 miles east of San Francisco:

It was the bloom-time of the year over the lowlands and coast ranges; the landscapes of the Santa Clara Valley were fairly drenched with sunshine, all the air was quivering with the songs of the meadow-larks, and the hills were so covered with flowers that they seemed to be painted.

Crossing the Coast Range, Muir found the Central Valley to be 'a lake of pure sunshine, forty or fifty miles wide, five hundred miles long ... a vast golden flower-bed'. From its eastern edge 'rose the mighty Sierra, miles in height, and so gloriously colored and so radiant it seemed not clothed with light, but wholly composed of it, like the wall of some celestial city'. Muir's destination was a glacial valley nearly a mile deep, 7 miles long, and more than a mile wide.

Although seen by a party of mountain men traveling east to west in 1833, the Yosemite Valley rested in obscurity to all but its Indian inhabitants (from whom the valley takes its name) and a handful of hunters until 1851. Then a volunteer militia, the Mariposa Battalion, explored the area while trying to redress a bloody Indian raid on a nearby trading post for miners. The soldiers' reports of Yosemite's natural wonders soon brought it to the attention of others, who eventually secured its permanent protection as a state park.

In 1860, the federal government ceded to the State of California Yosemite Valley and the adjoining Mariposa Grove of Big Trees 'for public use, resort, and recreation ... for all time'. This marked the beginning of government involvement in land protection which led ultimately to the National Park system. Important as the transfer was in establishing a precedent for government protection of wilderness, it was not entirely successful in saving Yosemite from commercial exploitation by private interests. As John Muir grew to know the region, he realized that without further control, overgrazing by sheep and overcutting of trees by aggressive timber interests would eventually destroy the area that others had worked so hard to save.

The son of a dogmatic Calvinist, Muir had been given a strong religious view of the world during childhood. After moving to Portage, Wisconsin from Dunbar, Scotland at the age of 11, the focus of Muir's religious thoughts had

OVERLEAF A field of California poppies. Early travelers in California's Central Valley were overwhelmed by the wildflowers they found there. In the spring of 1868 John Muir described the area as 'a vast golden flowerbed' drenched with sunshine and 'quivering' with bird song. While much of the region has been turned to agriculture, some areas still fulfill Muir's description.

267

shifted from scripture, which he had memorized, to nature, which he could explore and describe himself. He saw wilderness as a place of divine beauty and a source of great spiritual power, and he championed its protection with religious zeal. Like his transcendentalist contemporaries in the East, Muir considered natural objects 'the terrestrial manifestations of God', and looked upon nature as a 'window opening into heaven, a mirror reflecting the Creator'.

Muir's boundless enthusiasm for nature was combined with a personality which attracted many visitors to his Yosemite home. 'In the wilderness', recalled a contemporary, 'Muir looked like John the Baptist as portrayed in bronze by Donatello.' And Muir was happy to play the part. 'John the Baptist was not more eager to get all of his fellow sinners into the Jordan than I to baptize all [of] mine in the beauty of God's Mountains,' he explained. In his articles on behalf of the wilderness, he often employed religious metaphor, for Muir was a proselytizer who saw his battle against the despoiling of nature as a holy way. 'The money-changers [are] in the temple,' he proclaimed when pointing to the political influence of sheep owners and the damage their flocks had done in the vicinity of the park. 'As sheep advance', he explained, 'flowers, vegetation, grass, soil, plenty, and poetry vanish.' He called the sheep 'hoofed locusts' and lobbied for their ejection from Yosemite.

On the commercial cutting of sequoias, Muir was equally indignant:

> Through all the wonderful, eventful centuries since Christ's time – and long before that – God has cared for these trees, saved them from drought, disease, avalanches, and a thousand straining, levelling tempests and floods; but he cannot save them from fools – only Uncle Sam can do that.

Through articles in America's leading newspapers and magazines, including *Century, Harper's Weekly, Scribner's Monthly, Atlantic Monthly* and *Overland Monthly*, Muir pleaded for wilderness protection to an audience that, since the Civil War, had grown increasingly interested in America's wild heritage.

Eastern writers, such as Ralph Waldo Emerson and Henry David Thoreau, had been calling for forest preservation since the 1840s. Even such apostles of progress as Horace Greely, after a visit to Europe in 1851, charged Americans 'to spare, preserve and cherish some portion of your primitive forest'. By the late nineteenth century, it appeared that some were ready to heed this advice.

Real estate developers, miners, sheep owners and timber barons dismissed Muir and his fellow conservationists as misguided 'nature lovers' who were inhibiting the progress of the nation. Putting aside the spiritual arguments of the preservationists, the timber lobby argued that wood was necessary to built the West: 'The broad, fertile plains to the west of us *must* be peopled. Farms *must* be cultivated, fenced, and supplied with buildings; cities *must* be built, and rivers bridged and navigated.' For all of this, they reasoned, trees needed to be cut. It was the 'manifest destiny' argument with an ecological twist. When asked about the rapid decline of forests across the country, their answer was a question: 'Must we stop the growth of this Great West, that we may save a forest or two? *Can* we stop it? No, no; as long as we need lumber let us have it.'

An eloquent defender of wilderness everywhere, John Muir was especially attracted to the Sierra Nevada. He spent much of his life working to protect the Yosemite Valley from commercial exploitation. 'Mountain parks are useful not only as fountains of timber and irrigation rivers,' he wrote, 'but as fountains of life.' Muir considered that Yosemite's streams and mountains were 'the terrestrial manifestations of God'.

'What if the supply [of pine] is exhausted?' asked George Kaime rhetorically in an article in the *Western Monthly Magazine*. Surely another source of timber would be found:

> *What necessary article ever became scarce that we did not find something to replace it? Where firewood is limited, we have coal; and who regrets the discovery of the 'black diamonds?' We once taxed our eyesight by the use of whale oil as an illuminator, but there was a prospect of being denied even that, for the wholesale slaughter of the monsters of the deep was fast thinning their ranks. There was a call for a substitute. Gas first came to relieve the pressing demand for light-giving material. Then the very earth was tapped and made to yield, in copious streams, the very substance so much needed. Thus it will be with our pine forests. When they are gone, there will be a substitute given us.*

For the first time in American history such allegedly practical arguments were countered effectively with callings to other values. While Muir admitted that some trees 'had to make way for orchards and cornfields', he pointed out equally compelling arguments for the protection of the most beautiful areas:

> *Thousands of tired, nerve-shaken, over-civlilized people are beginning to find out that going to the mountains is going home, that wilderness is a necessity; and that mountain parks are useful not only as fountains of timber and irrigation rivers, but as fountains of life.*

John Muir was not only an impassioned spokesman for a conservation ethic then gaining public support, he was an effective politician as well, enlisting influential figures in his crusade for government protection of wild lands. An aging Emerson accepted his invitation to 'worship with Nature in the high temples of the great Sierra Crown beyond our holy Yosemite'. He befriended railroad magnate Edward Henry Harriman and *Century* magazine editor Robert Underwood Johnson. He even worked his magic on President Theodore Roosevelt, who declared after camping out with Muir in Yosemite in 1903 that he had 'the grandest day of my life!' With such opinion-shapers on his side, Muir was able to build an ever-larger public constituency for conservation. He influenced the establishment of six national parks – Yosemite (expanded in 1890 and taken back from state control in 1906), Sequoia, Mt Rainier, Crater Lake, Glacier, and Mesa Verde – and a dozen National Monuments, including two that would later become national parks: Grand Canyon and Olympic.

As well as being an environmental politician, Muir was also a realist. He knew that the hard-won fights to preserve park land would need continuing public support. So, in 1892, with like-minded conservationists in California, he helped to establish the Sierra Club, an organization committed to 'explore, enjoy and protect the nation's scenic resources'.

Great as it may have been, the political influence of Muir and of the Sierra Club was not always successful. In 1913, after a 12-year crusade by Muir to prevent it, the US Congress agreed to allow the city of San Francisco to dam the

A sweet legacy of Spanish conquest, California's citrus crops now play a major part in the state's economy. The Valencia orange was introduced to New World cultivation in the sixteenth century, but the fruit did not reach California for more than 200 years. The first commercial grove in California was planted in 1841.

Hetch Hetchy valley within Yosemite National Park in order to provide water for the city's growing needs. To Muir, it was the ultimate desecration of sacred land. 'That anyone would try to destroy such a place [as Hetch Hetchy] seems incredible, but sad experience shows that there are people good enough and bad enough for anything,' wrote Muir in 1912:

> These temple destroyers, devotees of ravaging commercialism, seem to have a perfect contempt for Nature, and, instead of lifting their eyes to the God of the mountains, lift them to the Almighty Dollar.
>
> Dam Hetch Hetchy! As well dam for water-tanks the people's cathedrals and churches, for no holier temple has ever been consecrated by the heart of man.

John Muir's attitudes toward the High Sierra, which continue to echo in conservation battles, were close to the attitudes of America's first inhabitants. The following counsel to Muir's civilization-worn contemporaries might have been said by an Indian medicine man to his people on the eve of Columbus's fateful voyage. 'Climb the mountains and get their good tidings,' wrote Muir:

> Nature's peace will flow into you as sunshine flows into trees. The winds will blow their own freshness into you and the storms their energy while cares will drop off like autumn leaves.

John Muir's campaign for wildlife and land protection was both timely and timeless; regional in focus and global in scope. 'When we try to pick out anything by itself', he wrote, 'we find it hitched to everything else in the universe.' Despite its geographical isolation, within Muir's lifetime California became connected both physically – by land and sea, telegraph (in 1861) and rail (in 1869) – and culturally to the larger world beyond its borders. In many respects it was and continues to be a physical and philosophical microcosm of North America. The biological diversity and abundance of the state reflects the bounty of the continent, while issues of natural resource use and abuse, exploitation and preservation, echo those of the United States as a whole.

In the span of just two human lives, California has gone from a wild land of woods and meadows to the most populous state in the nation. It has pioneered the field of land preservation, and destroyed some of the most beautiful land on earth. It has set the country's highest standards for air and water quality while choking on its own exhaust. It has led the world in creating a philosophical reverence for nature, while having an economy dependent on the permanent destruction of fragile habitats through mining, water diversion, lumbering, offshore drilling and land development.

As elsewhere, the complex environmental issues of California are linked to the economic and social concerns of a state and a nation whose material appetite threatens to exceed the land's ability to support it. California's environmental history has condensed to a century the changes that took much longer to transform the East. Today its mix of visionary policies and disastrous practices reveal the environmental paradox of North America itself.

NOTES

Full reference, and author's name in **bold**, given at first mention only.

INTRODUCTION

p. 9 'Excluding my thoughts ... they stood upon.' George **Catlin** *North American Indians: Being Letters and Notes on Their Manners, Customs, and Conditions, Written During Eight Years' Travel Amongst the Wildest Tribes in North America. 1832–1839*, 2 vols. (London, 1880), vol. 1, pp. 288–95

p. 11 'plentifully fed ...' Quoted in Thomas R. **Cox** et al., *This Well-Wooded Land: Americans and Their Forests from Colonial Times to the Present* (Lincoln: University of Nebraska Press, 1985), p. 6

p. 12 'delightful recreation' Ibid.

p. 13 'presents, as it did ...' Alexis **de Tocqueville**, *Democracy in America*, Philips Bradley (ed.) (New York: Knopf, 1945), pp. 290–2.

THE GREAT ENCOUNTER

p. 15 'As thoughts turned ... moon.' Columbus's journal, quoted in Peter **Matthiessen**, *Wildlife in America* (New York: Viking Press, 1959), p. 10

p. 16 '"a little stick ... "' Captain Pinzón, quoted in John **Bakeless**, *The Eyes of Discovery* (Philadelphia: J. B. Lippincott Co., 1950), p. 10

p. 20 '"a waste ... "' This often-cited quotation is from Michael Wigglesworth. See Roderick **Nash**, *Wilderness and the American Mind* (New Haven: Yale Univ. Press, 1967), p. 36; or Paul **Brooks**, *Speaking for Nature* (Boston: Houghton Mifflin Co., 1980), p. 253

p. 20 '"the fairest ... curtious"' Jean **Ribaut**, *The Whole and True Discovery of Terra Florida* (London, 1563) quoted in Stefan **Lorant** (ed.), *The New World: The First Pictures of America* (New York: Duell, Sloan & Pearce, 1946), p. 7

p. 22 '"with an unspeakable ... expressed."' Ibid.

p. 24 '"honney, veneson ... ;"' Ibid. Ribaut's reference to honey must be wishful thinking, for honeybees were not native to North America. The first documented introduction of the species from Europe is 1621

p. 24 'These grapes....' Matthiessen, *Wildlife in America*, p. 25

p. 24 '"herons, corleux ... "' Ribaut quoted in Lorant, p. 7

p. 24 '"mervelus numbre ... and better"' Ibid., p. 7

p. 24 '"precyous ... turquoise"' Ibid., pp. 7, 10

p. 24 '"lacketh nothing ... be found"' Ibid., p. 7

p. 24 '"divers very rich ... gallows."' **Humphrey Gilbert**, *Discourse to Prove a Passage by the Northwest to Cathaia and the East Indies* (1574), quoted in Lorant, p. 123

p. 25 '"to inhabit and ... "' Lorant, p. 123

p. 25 '"a new land ... the hunt."'

p. 25 '"very handsome and ... "' Samuel Eliot **Morison**, *The European Discovery of America: The Northern Voyages* (New York: Oxford Univ. Press, 1971), p. 624

p. 27 '"temperate and ... fertile soyle"' T. Hariot, quoted in Lorant, p. 276

p. 27 '"commodities ... masts of ships."' Ibid., p. 236, 256

p. 27 '"a wood of the ... "' Ibid., p. 236

p. 27 'For further reference ... syphilis.' Donald Culross **Peattie**, *A Natural History of Trees of Eastern and Central North America* (Boston: Houghton Mifflin Co., 1946), pp. 294–5

p. 28 '"after the manner ... "' Barlow quoted in Morison, *The European Discovery of America*, p. 625

p. 28 '"The earth bringeth ... labour."' Ibid., p. 625

p. 28 '"with all love ... "' Ibid.

p. 28 '"sturgeons and ... "' Letter from the Council in Virginia to the Council in England, 1607, quoted in James **Wharton**, *The Bounty of Chesapeake* (Charlottesville: University Press of Virginia, 1957)

p. 28 '"a very goodly Bay"' **John Smith**, *The Generall Historie of Virginia, New England & The Summer Isles*, fac. ed. (Glasgow: Univ. of Glasgow Press; London: Macmillan & Co., 1907), p. 44

p. 28 '"a country that ... "' Ibid., pp. 44–7

p. 29 'From his own ... his net.' Ibid., p. 47

p. 29 '"more of it ... "' John Smith, quoted in Bakeless, p. 195

p. 29 '"Roes of ... weight."' Lord de la Warr, 1610, quoted in Wharton

p. 29 '"that with hookes ... "' John Smith, p. 48

p. 29 '"Of fish ... the ayre."' Ibid., pp. 57–8

p. 29 'The ideal conditions ... 50 feet a year.' J. R. **Schubel**, *The Living Chesapeake* (Baltimore: Johns Hopkins Univ. Press, 1981), pp. 4–5, 21

p. 29 'Along the fast ... rise of the sea.' Ibid., pp. 4–5

p. 29 'Only a few land ... Atlantic coast.' Ibid., p. 18

p. 30 '"Oysters ... in length"' William Strachey, quoted in Wharton

p. 30 '"spyed many ... to himselfe."' John Smith, pp. 122–3

p. 31 '"In March ... "' Ibid., pp. 64–5

p. 31 '"trifles"' Lorant, p. 238; and William **Cronon**, *Changes in the Land: Indians,*

Colonists and the Ecology of New England (New York: Hill and Wang, 1983), p. 83

p. 31 '"let fly muskets"' John Smith, p. 93

p. 33 '"much like a badger ... "' Ibid., p. 56

p. 33 '"as good as lamb"' Raphe Hamor, quoted in Bakeless, p. 187

p. 33 '"because spreading ... "' John Smith, p. 56

p. 33 '"An Opassom ... her young."' Ibid.

p. 33 '"In winter, there ... "' Ibid., p. 57

p. 33 '"The river which ... "' William Strachey, quoted in Wharton

p. 33 '"Our men ... meere famine."' George Percy, quoted in Edward **Arber** (ed.), *Travels and Works of John Smith* (Edinburgh: 1910)

p. 38 '"starving time"' Robert **Ferris**, *Explorers and Settlers* (Wash. D C: National Park Service, 1968), p. 102. Confirmed by Dian Stallings, US Park Service, Jamestown, Virg. 8/15/89

p. 38 '"About the last ... Negers."' A.L. **Higginbotham**, *In the Matter of Color* (New York: Oxford Univ. Press, 1978), p. 20

p. 41 'The Cherokee have ... ' Edward **Abbey**, *Appalachian Wilderness: The Great Smoky Mountains* (New York: Ballantine Books, 1973), p. 24

p. 41 'The Great Smokies ... have 131.' Edwin W. **Teale**, *North with the Spring* (New York: Dodd, Mead & Co., 1957), p. 188

p. 41 'The Smokies' inhabitants ... to count.' Arthur **Stupka**, *Notes on the Birds of Great Smoky Mountain National Park* (Knoxville: Univ. of Tennessee Press, 1963) and Teale, p. 188

p. 41 'Thus, the Smokies ... to Montreal.' Teale, p. 188 and Robert E. **Ricklefs**, *Ecology* (Newton, Mass.: Chiron Press, 1973), p. 43

p. 44 'In the Cherokee world ... deer tongue, etc.' Wilcomb E. **Washburn** (ed.), *Handbook of North American Indians: History of Indian-White Relations* (Wash., D C: Smithsonian Inst. Press, 1988), p. 418

p. 44 'While some members ... the Indian world.' Margaret **Visser**, *Much Depends on Dinner* (New York: Collier Books, 1986), p. 31

p. 44 'Judging from archeological ... and turkey.' Gordon R. **Willey**, *An Introduction to American Archeology* (Englewood Cliffs, N J: Prentice-Hall, 1966), p. 254

p. 47 '"Sometimes we made ... "' T. Hariot, quoted in Lorant, p. 273

p. 47 '"We had hoped ...'"' Abraham Wood, quoted in Grace Steele **Woodward**, *The Cherokees* (Norman: Univ. of Oklahoma Press, 1963), p. 22

p. 48 '"We Cherokee ... "' Jimmie Durham in testimony before a congressional committee, quoted in J. Donald

Hughes, *American Indian Ecology* (El Paso: Texas Western Press, 1983)

p. 48 ' "I will not . . . through them." ' Christopher Levett, quoted in Cronon, p. 34

p. 48 ' "remote rocky . . . second England." ' Edward Johnson, 1653, quoted in Cronon, p. 5

p. 49 ' "reducing the . . ." ' Nash, *Wilderness and the American Mind*, p. 27

p. 49 ' "one of the most Hideous . . ." ' Edward Johnson, 1653, in Ibid., p. 37

p. 49 ' "You know our . . ." ' Miantonomo, quoted in Cronon, p. 162

CONFRONTING THE WILDERNESS

p. 51 'the Island of Birds' Morison, *The European Discovery of America*, p. 346. Today known as Funk Island

p. 51 ' "was encompassed . . ." ' H. P. **Biggar** (ed.), *The Voyages of Jacques Cartier* (Ottawa: Public Archives of Canada, 1924)

p. 52 ' "Some of these birds are . . ." ' Ibid.

p. 52 ' "as big . . . these birds." ' Ibid.

p. 52 ' "His flesh . . ." ' Cartier, quoted in Bakeless, p. 104

p. 52 ' "Were the soil . . . to Cain." ' Cartier, quoted in Morison, *The European Discovery of America*, p. 354

p. 54 ' "making divers . . ." ' Ibid., p. 370

p. 54 ' "sent two men . . ." ' Ibid., p. 370

p. 54 ' "remained on . . ." ' Ibid., p. 413

p. 54 'He noted that . . . and decoration.' Ibid., p. 414

p. 56 ' "a marvelous joy" ' Ibid.

p. 56 ' "the finest . . ." ' Cartier, quoted in Bakeless, p. 112

p. 56 ' "We had a view . . ." ' Ibid., p. 113

p. 56 ' "Between these ranges lies . . ." ' Ibid.

p. 56 'On descending . . . ever since.' Morison, *The European Discovery of America*, p. 143

p. 56 ' "Sault La Chine" ' Ibid., p. 415

p. 57 ' "All of our . . . of ice." ' Ibid., p. 418

p. 57 ' "out of the 110 . . ." ' Ibid., p. 419; and Richard **Hakluyt**, *The Principal Navigations* (1600), p. 73

p. 57 ' "God in His . . ." ' Morison, *The European Discovery of America*, p. 419

p. 57 ' "After this . . . their health." ' Hakluyt, pp. 76–7

p. 57 'Cartier later . . . cultivation' Peattie, *A Natural History of Trees of Eastern and Central North America*, p. 67

p. 57 ' "There is in . . . Massachusetts." ' Robert Boyle, quoted in. Ibid., p. 457

p. 60 'The sweetness . . . its surface.' Ibid., p. 458

p. 61 'The earliest documented . . . much earlier.' Morison, *The European Discovery of America*, p. 225

p. 61 'So abundant . . . their harvest.' Baron de **Lahontan**, *New Voyages to North America* (London, 1703) ed. by Reuben G. **Thwaites**, 2 vols (Chicago: A. C. McClurg & Co., 1905), pp. 337, 401

p. 61 'impede boat traffic' Reporting John Mason, an English fishing skipper, in Farley **Mowat**, *Sea of Slaughter* (New York: Bantam Books, 1984)

p. 61 ' "unexhaustible manna" ' Reporting Nicolas Denys in Ibid.

p. 61–2 ' "Commonly, there . . ." ' Lahontan, quoted in Thwaites, vol. 1, p. 336

p. 62 ' "Placentia bears . . ." ' Ibid., vol. 1, p. 338

p. 62 ' "hatchets, knives . . ." ' Morison, *The European Discovery of America*, p. 370

p. 62 ' "They bartered . . . more furs." ' Biggar (ed.), *The Voyages of Cartier*

p. 62 'Like the Iroquois . . . further north.' Bruce G. **Trigger** (ed.), *Handbook of North American Indians: Northeast* (Wash. DC: Smithsonian Inst. Press, 1978) p. 602

p. 62 'With a long . . . from Europe.' Brian M. **Fagan**, *Clash of Cultures* (New York: W. H. Freeman & Co., 1984), p. 196

p. 62 'The French . . . currency.' Cronon, p. 95

p. 65 'This large aquatic . . . Continent.' Karl **von Frisch**, *Animal Architecture* (New York: Van Nostrand Reinhold Co., 1974), p. 267

p. 65 ' "The window . . . of the day." ' Buffon, quoted in Matthiessen, p. 80

p. 65 'There are stories . . . half a mile.' Percy **Knauth**, *The North Woods* (New York: Time-Life Books, 1972), p. 86

p. 66 'The largest currently . . . long.' von Frisch, p. 274

p. 66 ' "a small fruit . . ." ' H. P. **Biggar** (ed.), *The Works of Samuel Champlain* (Toronto: The Champlain Society, 1929), p. 38

p. 68 'In summer months . . . per day.' From a study on black bear feeding behavior by Lynn Rogers and Greg Wilder, US Forest Service, Ely, Minnesota

p. 68 'The Dutch West . . . Hudson River valley.' Howard P. **Brokaw** (ed.), *Wildlife and America* (Wash., DC: Council on Envir. Quality), 1978, p. 9

p. 68 'Similarly, within . . . colony.' Samuel Eliot **Morison**, *William Bradford of Plymouth Plantation, 1620–1647* (New York: Alfred A. Knopf Inc., 1977), cited in Brokaw, p. 4

p. 68 ' "what is not . . ." ' Cotton Mather, quoted in Robert **Elman**, *First in the Field: America's Pioneering Naturalists* (New York: Mason/Charter, 1977), p. 6

p. 70 ' "our young men . . ." ' Samuel Champlain, quoted in Washburn (ed.), p. 24

p. 70 'Of four recorded . . . women.' Ibid.

p. 70 ' "the gentlemen of . . ." ' Ibid.

p. 70 ' "were very zealous . . ." ' Ibid.

p. 71 'More than that . . . single year.' *The Conquest of North America* (Garden City, NY: Doubleday & Co., 1971), p. 291

p. 71 ' "All the countrie . . ." ' Biggar (ed.), *The Works of Samuel Champlain*, p. 42

p. 71 'The Canadian shield . . . Arctic Ocean.' Knauth, p. 50

p. 72 ' "The further . . . country." ' Radisson quoted in Bakeless, p. 153

p. 72 ' "We weare Cesars being . . ." ' Ibid., p. 155

p. 72 ' "the beauty of . . ." ' Ibid., p. 153

p. 73 ' "a beautiful River . . ." ' Ibid., p. 152

p. 82 'They converge . . . per day.' Robin **Baker** (ed.), *The Mystery of Migration* (New York: Viking Press, 1981), p. 206

p. 82 'Their herd sizes . . . point.' Ronald M. **Nowak**, *Walker's Mammals of the World*, 4th edn., vol. 2 (Baltimore: Johns Hopkins Univ. Press, 1983), p. 1224

p. 82 'the thick swarms . . . each week.' George W. **Calef**, 'Numbers beyond counting, miles beyond measure', *Audubon Magazine* (July 1976), p. 54

p. 82 ' "a new passage . . ." ' Helen **Delpar** (ed.), *The Discoverers* (New York: McGraw-Hill Books, 1980), p. 98

p. 82 'The Hudson's Bay . . . Hudson's Bay.' Howard R. **Lamar**, *The Readers' Encyclopedia of the American West* (New York: Harper & Row, 1977), p. 520

p. 84 'The Seven Years . . . to Britain.' *The Conquest of North America*, p. 315

p. 84 'Each autumn . . . Hudson's Bay coast.' Fred **Bruemmer**, 'Two weeks in a polar bear prison', *Audubon Magazine* (Nov. 1981), p. 30

p. 87 ' "six pence . . . Thames." ' Thomas **Pennant**, *Arctic Zoology* (London, 1742), vol. I, p. 65

CONQUERING THE SWAMPS

p. 89 'The individual organisms . . . a century.' Bill **Thomas**, *The Island* (New York: W. W. Norton & Co., 1980), p. 88

p. 91 'Legend has it . . . else on earth.' Archie **Carr**, "All the way down upon the Suwannee River," *Audubon Magazine* (March 1983), p. 7

p. 91 ' "did not permit . . ." ' Marjory S. **Douglas**, *The Everglades: River of Grass* (New York: Rinehart & Co., 1947), p. 102

p. 92 ' "In one short . . . thousand." ' Herrera, quoted in Douglas, pp. 104–5

p. 92 'The largest of the . . . minute.' Robert McCracken **Peck** (ed.), *Bartram Heritage Report* (Wash. DC and Atlanta: US Dept. of the Interior and Bartram Trail Conference, 1978), pp. 11–31

p. 92 ' "At noon . . . big beaver." ' Bartram quoted in Robert McCracken **Peck** (ed.), *William Bartram's Travels* (Salt Lake City: Peregrine Smith, Inc., 1980), pp. 145–6

p. 95 ' "We were attacked . . ." ' de Vaca, quoted in Frederick W. **Hodge** (ed.), *Spanish Explorers in the Southern United States: 1528–1543* (New York: Charles Scribner's Sons, 1907), pp. 31–2

p. 95 ' "very difficult . . ." ' Ibid., p. 27

p. 97 ' "The country . . ." ' Ibid., pp. 29–30

p. 97 ' "Occasionally they kill . . ." ' *The Conquest of North America*, p. 203

p. 97 'Forewarned by . . . swamplands today.' Matthiessen, p. 41; and Bakeless, p. 47

p. 102 'The mangroves begin ... invasion of the sea.' Victor E. **Shelford**, *The Ecology of North America* (Urbana: Univ. of Illinois Press, 1978), p. 480–2

p. 103 '"nothing else ... "' Jonathan Dickinson, quoted in Douglas, p. 178

p. 103 'One of the world's ... 5 pounds.' Peter **Wood**, *Caribbean Isles* (New York: Time-Life Books, 1975), p. 23

p. 103 'The Calusa extracted ... archaeological remains.' William H. **Marquardt**, 'Politics and production Among the Calusa of South Florida,' in Tim Ingold, et al. (eds), *Hunters and Gatherers: History of Evolution and Social Change* (New York: Berg, 1988), p. 164

p. 105 '"They take ... "' Le Moyne, quoted in Lorant, p. 87

p. 105 'Francisco Vázquez ... June 1542' Hodge, p. 378

p. 105 '"The alligators ... "' Le Moyne, quoted in Lorant, p. 87

p. 105 '"The evening ... "' Bartram, quoted in Peck, *William Bartram's Travels*, pp. 75–6

p. 106 '"by lodging ... "' Ibid., p. 77

p. 106 'By the time ... the very end.' William H. **Marquardt**, 'The Calusa Social Formation in Protohistoric South Florida' in T. C. **Patterson** and C. W. **Gailey** (eds.), *Power Relations and State Formation* (Wash., D C: American Anthro. Assoc., 1987), pp. 108–11

p. 106 '"much given ... "' Bakeless, p. 46

p. 106 'By 1635 ... and trade' Alvin M. **Josephy**, Jr. (ed.), *The American Heritage Book of Indians* (New York: American Heritage Publishing Co., 1961), p. 214

p. 108 'The restructured ... old towns.' Ibid., p. 215

p. 108 'Rice ... and 90s' Visser, p. 180

p. 108 'The cultivation ... preferred.' Ibid.

p. 109 '"About the middle ... trees."' Catesby, quoted in Elman, p. 18

p. 109 '"actually between ... "' Catesby, quoted in Joseph **Kastner** *A Species of Eternity* (New York: Alfred A. Knopf, Inc., 1977), p. 17

p. 111 '"except that ... "' Catesby, quoted in Wayne **Hanley**, *Natural History in America* (New York: Quadrangle, 1977), p. 6

p. 111 '"I was much ... Beasts."' Catesby, quoted in Elman, p. 19

p. 111 'Among the many plants ... palmetto.' U. P. **Hedrick**, *A History of Horticulture in America to 1860* (New York: Oxford Univ. Press, 1950), p. 139

p. 111 '"protection against ... "' Douglas, p. 197

p. 112 'The effort cost ... American troops.' Josephy, p. 228

p. 112 '"broke down ... "' Mark **Catesby**, *The Natural History of Carolina, Florida and the Bahama Islands* (London, 1731–43), p 23

p. 112 '"Nature ... of chips."' Ibid., p. 16

p. 114 '"worthless swamplands ... Holland."' Broward, quoted in Douglas, p. 312

p. 115 '"Shall the sovereign ... "' Ibid., pp. 313–14

p. 115 'Miami real ... a year.' Douglas, p. 316

p. 115 'In 1928 ... houses in Miami.' Ibid., p. 340

p. 115 'By the early 1940s ... that rate.' Ibid., p. 382

p. 115 'The National Audubon ... 1920s.' Information from 'Pollution Poses Growing Threat to Everglades,' *New York Times*, 17 September 1989, p. 1

ACROSS THE SEA OF GRASS

p. 119 'The eastern ... paw to ground.' Matthiessen, p. 64

p. 119 '"A poor servant ... to do."' Francis Higginson, quoted in Cronon, p. 25

p. 119 '"an incredible amount ... "' Peter Kalm, quoted in Cronon, p. 120

p. 119 'The average New England ... 300 ft long.' Cronon, p. 120

p. 120 '"Our timber ... other fuel."' Benjamin Lincoln, quoted in Cronon, p. 114

p. 120 'Another tenacious ... the continent.' Lauren **Brown**, *Grasses* (Boston: Houghton Mifflin Co., 1979), p. 91

p. 120 '"Our Runs ... Interruptions."' Bakeless, p. 271

p. 123 '"land of ... in it."' John Filson, quoted in **Henry Nash Smith**, *Virgin Land: The American Land as Symbol and Myth* (New York: Vintage Books, 1957), p. 129

p. 123 '"so over ... "' Bakeless, p. 267

p. 124 '"intersected with ... "' Bakeless, p. 316

p. 124 '"I am at ... "' Lauren Brown, p. 6

p. 126 'To some Indians ... for both.' John **Madson**, *Where the Sky Began: Land of the Tallgrass Prairie* (Boston: Houghton Mifflin Co., 1982), p. 48

p. 126 '"obscure the ... "' William Faux, 1823, quoted in Lauren Brown, p. 11 and May T. **Watts**, *Reading the Landscape* (New York: Macmillan Co., 1957), p. 38

p. 126 '"It is a strange ... horse."' Gro. Svendsen, 1863, quoted in Edward S. **Barnard** (ed.), *Story of the Great American West* (Pleasantville, N Y: Readers Digest, 1977), p. 314

p. 126 '"It is a beautiful ... "' Bakeless, p. 308

p. 126 '"I was perfectly ... meadows."' Lauren Brown, p. 14

p. 130 '"the view is ... "' Washington Irving, quoted in John **Madson**, 'The Running Country', *Audubon Magazine* (July 1972), p. 16

p. 130 '"finer and fatter ... "' Hodge, p. 68

p. 130 '"They have a ... "' Ibid., pp. 382–3

p. 133 '"pishkins"' David **Lavender**, *The Way to the Western Sea* (New York: Harper & Row, 1988), p. 201

p. 133 'To most Americans ... Atlantic coast' Richard A. **Bartlett**, 'The Lure of the West', in *Exploring the American West 1803–1879* (Wash., DC: US Dept. of the Interior, 1982), pp. 8–9

p. 135 '"the Missouri ... "' Jefferson, 'Instructions to Capt. M. Lewis,' 20 June 1803, quoted in Charles A. **Miller**, *Jefferson and Nature: An Interpretation* (Baltimore: Johns Hopkins Univ. Press. 1988), p. 240

p. 135 '"to acquire ... "' Jefferson's instructions quoted in Lavender, *The Way to the Western Sea*, p. 391

p. 135 '"rich, covered ... "' Clark, quoted in Barnard, p. 38

p. 135 '"immense herds ... "' Lavender, *The Way to the Western Sea*, p. 129

p. 135 '"so gentle ... "' Clark, quoted in Kastner, p. 133

p. 135 '"generally associate ... "' Lewis quoted in Kastner, p. 130

p. 138 '"Capt. William Clark ... "' Lavender, *The Way to the Western Sea*, p. 297

p. 140 '"from oblivion ... "' Marjorie **Halpin**, *Catlin's Indian Gallery* (Wash. D C: Smithsonian Inst. Press, 1965), p. 7

p. 140 '"Nature has ... "' Catlin, *North American Indians*, vol. 1, pp. 288–95, quoted in Roderick **Nash** (ed.), *The American Environment: Readings in the History of Conservation* (Reading, MA: Addison-Wesley Co., 1968), pp. 7–9

p. 140 '"A settler regards ... "' John **Madson**, 'Grandfather Country', *Audubon Magazine* (May 1982), p. 46

p. 141 'Most eastern plows ... clinging loam"' Madson, 'The Running Country,' p. 17

p. 141 'There were commercial ... farming.' Ibid., p. 16

p. 141 '"For miles we ... "' J. H. Buckingham, quoted in *The American Land* (Smithsonian Exposition Books, New York: W. W. Norton & Co., 1979), p. 113

p. 141 '"As one stands ... "' *Harper's New Monthly Magazine*, 212 (Jan. 1868), p. 190

p. 142 'In order to ... sell to settlers.' Lamar, pp. 992–3

p. 143 '"when I first ... "' Catlin, quoted in Nash, *The American Environment*, pp. 5–6

p. 146 '"is the only ... "' Sheridan, quoted in Martin S. **Garretson**, *The American Bison*, 1938, p. 128; and Dee **Brown**, *Bury My Heart at Wounded Knee: An Indian History of the American West* (New York: Holt, Rinehart & Winston, 1970), p. 265'

p. 146 'Close to 4 ... and 1874'. Dee Brown, p. 265

p. 147 'With densities ... 1.5 million cattle.' Richard **Perry**, *Life in Desert and Plain* (New York: Taplinger Pub. Co., 1977), p. 87

p. 147 '"Real estate ... "' Barnard, p. 313

p. 147 'In the 1880s ... the new land.' Ibid., p. 317

p. 149 'Of the 70 000 ... by 1922.' Brokaw, p. 92

p. 149 'During the Dust ... disappearing prairie farms.' Boyd **Gibbons**, 'Do We Treat Our Soil Like Dirt?' *National Geographic*, vol. 166, no. 3 (Sept. 1984), p. 354

p. 149 'In little less ... eroding winds.' Peter **Farb**, *Face of North America* (New York: Harper & Row, 1963), p. 215

INTO THE SHINING MOUNTAINS

p. 151 'A complex series . . . the planets.' Farb, p. 135

p. 152 '"communication"' Jefferson, quoted in Miller, p. 240

p. 152 '"sterile . . . of cultivation."' Pike quoted in *The Conquest of North America*, p. 393

p. 152 '"become equally . . ."' W. Eugene **Hollon**, *The Great American Desert Then and Now* (New York: Oxford Univ. Press, 1966), p. 40; and Walter Prescott **Webb**, *The Great Plains* (Boston: Ginn & Co., 1931), p. 153

p. 152 '"terrestrial . . . of deer."' Pike, quoted in David **Lavender**, *The Rockies* (New York: Harper & Row, 1968), p. 54

p. 152 'best communication . . . rivers in a day.' Ibid., p. 55

p. 153 '"public high . . ."' Ibid.

p. 153 '"emence hills . . ."' Lewis, quoted in Don **Moser**, *The Snake River Country* (New York: Time-Life Books, 1974), p. 58

p. 153 '"ranges of . . ."' Ibid. p. 55

p. 153 '"Much fatigued, and . . ."' Clark, quoted in Moser, p. 59

p. 153 '"as wet . . ."' Clark, quoted in Lavender, *The Way to the Western Sea*, pp. 268–9

p. 153 '"When the discovery . . ."' Patrick Gass, quoted in Moser, p. 60

p. 157 '"a big horned . . ."' Reuben G. **Thwaites** (ed.), *Original Journals of the Lewis and Clark Expedition* (New York: Dodd, Mead & Co., 1905) vol. 2, pp. 72, 75

p. 157 '"The places . . . and sight."' Clark, quoted in Thwaites, *Original Journals*, vol. 2, pp. 73–4, 77

p. 157 '"the flesh . . ."' Lewis, quoted in Kastner, p. 133

p. 157 'In addition to . . . bows.' Thwaites, *Original Journals*, vol. 2, pp. 73, 76

p. 157 '"As they love . . ."' George Ruxton, quoted in John I. **Merritt**, *Baronets and Buffalo: The British Sportsman In the American West, 1833–1881* (Missoula, MT: Mountain Press Publ. Co., 1985), p. 63

p. 159 'By 1900 . . . size.' Information from 'Bighorn Profile,' *Audubon Magazine* (Nov. 1973), p. 4

p. 159 '"And then you . . ."' Henry Kelsey, quoted in Harold **McCracken**, *The Beast That Walks Like Man* (Garden City, NY: Hanover House, 1955), p. 69

p. 159 '"I must confess . . ."' Lewis, quoted in Kastner, p. 134

p. 159 '"will frequently . . ."' Ibid.

p. 159 '"ran at . . ."' Lewis, quoted in Hanley, p. 35

p. 162 '"better than . . . season."' Bakeless, p. 373

p. 162 'its use in cooking . . . baldness.' Pennant, p. 69

p. 162 '"The fat . . . quart of it."' Ibid.

p. 162 '"doubt their . . . activity."' Ibid., p. 70

p. 162 'To the Cree . . . "cousin."' McCracken, p. 38

p. 162 '"With these feathers . . . feathers."' Lewis, quoted in Thwaites, vol. 4, *Original Journals*, p. 160

p. 163 '"esteemed by . . . mentioned."' Ibid.

p. 163 '"The birdcatcher . . ."' Prince **Maximilian zu Wied**, *People of the First Man* (New York: Promontory Press, 1982), p. 251

p. 163 'Many of the villages . . . four months.' Ibid., p. 208

p. 163 'Maximilian's countryman . . . the world.' William H. **Goetzmann**, 'Explorer, Mountain Man, and Scientist,' in *Exploring the American West 1803–1879* (Wash., DC: US Dept. of the Interior, 1982), p. 60

p. 164 '"At certain . . ."' Alfred Jacob Miller, quoted in Barnard, p. 105

p. 167 '"Either this great . . ."' Timothy **Flint**, *Indian Wars of the West* (Cincinnati: 1833), pp. 36–7 (quoted in Wilcomb E. Washburn (ed.), *The Indian and the White Man* (Garden City, NY: Doubleday & Co., 1964), pp. 125–7

p. 169 '"For some time . . . mountains."' Edwin James, quoted in Maxine **Benson** (ed.), *From Pittsburgh to the Rocky Mountains: Major Stephen Long's Expedition 1819–1820* (Golden, CO: Fulcrum, 1988), p. 193

p. 169 '"A little above . . ."' Ibid., p. 222

p. 169 'We now know . . . arctic Russia.' Watts, p. 172

p. 170 '"nearly the size . . ."' James, quoted in Benson, p. 223

p. 170 '"We were surprised . . ."' Ibid., p. 225

p. 170 '"Falling upon . . ."' C. V. **Riley**, *Standard Natural History, II,* 1884, pp. 196–7

p. 170 '"a locust . . ."' C. V. **Riley**, *The Rocky Mountain Locust* (Wash., DC: Dept. of Agric., 1878), p. 332

p. 172 '"The road . . . underfoot."' J. K. Townsend quoted in Kastner, p. 279

p. 172 '"I never before . . ."' Ibid.

p. 173 '"Such beauties . . ."' J. J. Audubon, quoted in Hanley, p. 112

p. 173 'Gore's baggage . . . on demand.' Merritt, p. 94

p. 173 'There were over . . . 100 bear.' Ibid., pp. 93–4

p. 173 '"brother sportsmen . . . Pacific Ocean."' John **Palliser**, *Introduction to Solitary Rambles and Adventures of a Hunter in the Prairies* (London, 1853), quoted in Merritt, p. 69

p. 173 '"The atmosphere . . ."' Palliser, quoted in Merritt, p. 76

p. 177 '"that dash . . ."' Merritt, p. v

p. 177 '"The Rocky . . ."' Horace Greely, *An Overland Journey from New York to San Francisco in 1859* (1860), quoted in Peter **Yapp** (ed.), *The Travellers' Dictionary of Quotation* (London: Routledge & Kegan Paul, 1983), p. 953

p. 177 'It is estimated . . . their goal.' Lavender, *The Rockies*, p. 138; and Lamar, p. 242

p. 180 'In 1868 . . . 3.5 million.' Lavender, *The Rockies*, p. 242

p. 180 '"Denver is . . ."' Isabella L. **Bird**, *A Lady's Life in the Rocky Mountains* (Norman: Univ. of Oklahoma Press, 1960), p. 138

p. 180 '"They was mining . . ."' Ibid., p. 193

p. 180 '"Reverence for . . ."' W. Baillie-Grohman quoted in Merritt, p. 179

p. 181 '"no harm . . ."' Congressional Globe, 42nd Cong. 2nd Sess., 30 Jan. 1872, p. 697, quoted in Nash, *Wilderness and the American Mind*, p. 112

p. 181 '"the beautiful decorations."' F. Hayden, quoted in Nash, *Wilderness and the American Mind*, p. 112

p. 181 '"breathing place . . ."' George G. Vest, Congressional Record, 47th Cong. 2nd Sess., 1 March 1883, p. 3488, quoted in Nash, *Wilderness and the American Mind*, p. 114

p. 185 '"The best . . . are sold."' John J. Ingalls, quoted in Nash, *Wilderness and the American Mind*, p. 113

p. 185 '"Is it true that . . ."' Congressional Record, 49th Cong. 2nd Sess., 11 Dec. 1886, p. 94, quoted in Nash, *Wilderness and the American Mind*, p. 114

p. 185 '"in the great . . . capital."' William McAdoo, Congressional Record, 49th Cong. 2nd Sess., 14 Dec. 1886, pp. 152–4, quoted in Nash, *Wilderness and the American Mind*, p. 115

LIVING ON THE EDGE

p. 187 '"spiky."' Hodge, p. 348

p. 188 'Two other similarly . . . Mayo Indians.' Ruth **Kirk**, 'Life on a Tall Cactus,' *Audubon Magazine*, July 1973, p. 16

p. 188 '"Thorns are surprisingly . . ."' Johann Jakob Baegert, quoted in Kirk, p. 13

p. 188 '"It is easy to see that . . ."' Ibid.

p. 188 'Packrats often . . . a mystery.' Kirk, p. 15

p. 191 'wilderness', Hodge, p. 299

p. 191 '"grass like that of Castile."' Bakeless, p. 79; and Hodge, p. 349

p. 191 '"a method of . . ."' Coronado, quoted in Bakeless, p. 79

p. 191 '"It is a village . . . distance."' Hodge, p. 300

p. 191 '"For myself, they . . ."' Coronado, quoted in *The Conquest of North America*, p. 91

p. 194 'The agricultural tribes . . . food sources.' Noel **Vietmeyer**, 'Saving the bounty of a Harsh and Meager Land,' *Audubon Magazine* (Jan. 1985), p. 104

p. 194 'One of the Papagos' . . . 10 miles away.' Ibid., p. 105

p. 194 '"These people are . . . usually at work."' Hodge, p. 350–1

p. 194 '"They make the cross . . ."' Ibid., p. 351

p. 194 '"I am in a . . . tamarind, etc."' H. E. **Bolton** (ed.), *Kino's Historical Memoir of Pimeria Alta . . . 1683–1711* (Cleveland: Arthur H. Clark Co., 1919), vol. 2, pp. 265–6

p. 195 '"Hot countries . . . every stone."' Ignaz **Pfefferkorn**, *Sonora: A Description of the Province*, trans. and annot. by Theodore E. Treutlein (Albuquerque: Univ. of New Mexico Press, 1949), p. 125

p. 195 ' "There is a four-footed . . ." ' Juan
Nentrig, quoted in **Rudo Ensayo**, *A
Description of Sonora and Arizona in
1764*, trans. by Pradeau and
Rasmussen (Tucson: Univ. of Arizona
Press, 1980), p. 31

p. 197 ' "The most common and . . ." ' Ibid.,
p. 31

p. 197 ' "the benign . . . against misfortune." '
Pfefferkorn, p. 125

p. 197 'The town of Oraibi . . . in North
America.' Frederick J. Dockstader,
'The Hopi World' in *The Year of the
Hopi* (Wash., DC: Smithsonian Inst.
Press, 1979), pp. 7–9

p. 198 ' "Horses are the . . . enemy most." '
Castañeda, quoted in Hodge, p. 386

p. 200 'The Shoshone . . . encountered
Europeans.' Warren L. **D'Azevedo**
(ed.), *Handbook of the American
Indians – Great Basin* (Wash., DC:
Smithsonian Inst. Press, 1986),
p. 300

p. 200 'By 1690 . . . 300 animals.' Richard
White, *The Roots of Dependency*
(Lincoln: Univ. of Nebraska Press,
1983), p. 179

p. 200 ' "Sanorans are sworn . . ." '
Pfefferkorn

p. 200 ' "the behavior of a . . ." ' Pfefferkorn

p. 201 'The ocotillo or . . . a single year.' Farb,
p. 235

p. 201 'For most cactus . . . in place.' Kirk,
p. 16

p. 201 'Some of the plants . . . parent plant.'
Farb, pp. 246–7

p. 204 ' "with hospitable . . ." ' William
Becknell, in Archer B. **Hulbert** (ed.),
Southwest on the Turquoise Trail (CO:
Denver Public Library, 1933), pp. 56–
68; and in Ray Allen **Billington**, *The
Far Western Frontier 1830–1860* (New
York: Harper & Brothers, 1956), p. 24

p. 204 'The Santa Fe . . . each season.'
Barnard, p. 121

p. 204 'In 1824 . . . improve the highway.'
Billington, p. 27

p. 205 'In the decades . . . military outposts.'
Elna **Bakker** and Richard G. **Lillard**,
The Great Southwest (Palo Alto, CA:
American West Publishing Co., 1972),
p. 169

p. 205 ' "frightened horses and . . ." ' Jay
Monaghan (ed.), *The Book of the
American West* (New York: Julian
Messner, 1963), p. 99

p. 205 'During the Civil . . . of the Southwest.'
Ibid., pp. 97–9

p. 208 ' "It was impossible . . . they found." '
Castañeda, quoted in Hodge, p. 309

p. 208 ' "The upheavel was . . ." ' John Wesley
Powell, quoted in Elman, p. 183

p. 208 ' "more than four-tenths . . ." ' John
Wesley **Powell**, *Report on the Lands
of the Arid Region of the United States*,
U.S. House of Rep., Executive
Document 73, 45th Cong. 2nd Sess., 3
April 1878 (Wash., DC: US Govt.
Printing Office), quoted in Nash, *The
American Environment*, p. 29

p. 208 ' "only a small portion . . ." ' Powell,
quoted in Nash, *The American
Environment*, p. 30

p. 208 ' "the growth of timber . . ." ' Ibid.

p. 209 ' "The rain follows the plow . . ." '
Charles Dana **Wilber**, *The Great
Valleys and Prairies of Nebraska and
the Northwest* (Omaha, NB: 1880),
pp. 43–4, quoted in Henry Nash **Smith**,
*Virgin Land: The American Land as
Symbol and Myth* (New York: Vintage
Books, 1957), p. 182

p. 209 ' "sterile . . . of cultivation." ' *The
Conquest of North America*, p. 393

p. 209 ' "almost wholly unfit . . ." ' Stephen
Long, quoted in Hollon, p. 40

p. 209 ' "To a great extent . . ." ' Powell,
quoted in Nash, *The American
Environment*, p. 33

p. 209 ' "blossom as a rose." ' Isaiah 35:1

THE FIRST
AND LAST FRONTIER

p. 212 'Its vegetation . . . and birch.' **Dale
Brown**, *Wild Alaska* (New York:
Time-Life Books, 1972), p. 24

p. 212 ' "Good luck, thanks . . ." ' Steller,
quoted in Ernest **Gruening** (ed.), *An
Alaskan Reader* (New York: Meredith
Press, 1966), p. 18

p. 214 ' "The time here . . . work itself." '
Ibid., p. 15

p. 214 'For the next four . . . 46 men.' Barbara
and Richard **Mearns**, *Biographies for
Birdwatchers* (London: Academic
Press, 1988), pp. 352–3

p. 214 ' "so that one . . ." ' Steller, quoted in
Mearns, p. 353

p. 214 'Within 100 years . . . bird from life.'
Matthiessen, p. 100

p. 214 ' "like cattle . . . began eating them." '
Sven **Waxwell**, *The American
Expedition*, trans. by M. A. Michael
(London: Wm. Hodge & Co. Ltd,
1952), pp. 194–5

p. 214 ' "They are most . . ." ' Steller, retold in
Pennant, p. 209

p. 216 ' "This animal deserves . . ." ' Steller,
quoted in Frank Alfred **Golder**,
Bering's Voyages (New York:
American Geog. Soc., 1922–25),
p. 220

p. 216 ' "fairly good . . . suckling lamb." ' Ibid.

p. 216 ' "In Kamchatka . . ." ' Waxwell, p. 190

p. 216 'The Eskimos are believed . . . in
France.' Josephy, p. 270

p. 219 'The name Eskimo . . . "the
excommunicated." ' Ibid.

p. 219 'Scattered groups . . . Baja California.'
Bakeless, p. 399

p. 219 ' "Nothing can be . . . attractive
object." ' John R. Jewett, 1803, quoted
in Bakeless, p. 400

p. 222 ' "I was a boy of . . ." ' Hubert H.
Bancroft, *History of the Pacific States:
Alaska 1730–1885* (San Francisco: The
History Co. Pub., 1886), pp. 144–5

p. 222 'On the island . . . troops' Carl
Waldman, *Atlas of the North
American Indian* (New York: Facts on
File, 1985), p. 124

p. 222 'It is estimated . . . "war" ' **Richard A.
Smith**, *The Frontier States* (New York:
Time-Life Books, 1968), p. 14

p. 222 'There, from May . . . following year.'

Information provided by National
Marine Mammal Labs in Seattle

p. 222 'So excessive . . . over-saturated
market.' Bishop **Veniaminov**, *Notes on
Unalaska District*

p. 223 ' "to attract the . . ." ' Robin **Fisher** and
Hugh **Johnston** (eds.), *Captain James
Cook and His Times* (Seattle: Univ. of
Wash. Press, 1979), pp. 101–3

p. 223 'Further instructions . . . if provoked.'
Ibid.

p. 223 ' "very docile since . . ." ' E. J.
Martinez, quoted in Fisher and
Johnston, p. 103

p. 223 ' "to find out a . . . Baffin's Bay." '
John Frazier **Henry**, *Early Maritime
Artists of the Pacific Northwest Coast
1741–1841* (Seattle: Univ. of Wash.
Press, 1984), p. 63

p. 224 'Cook's crew discovered . . . in China.'
Bakeless, p. 402

p. 224 'In 1786 alone . . . in the area.' William
Fitzhugh and Aron **Crowell**, *Cross-
currents of Continents* (Wash., DC:
Smithsonian Inst. Press, 1988), p. 75

p. 224 ' "Two hundred and . . ." ' Louis
Choris, quoted in August C. **Mahr**,
*The Visit of the Rurik to San Francisco
in 1816* (CA: Stanford Univ. Press,
1932), p. 103, quoted in Henry, p. 39

p. 225 'It was used in . . . upholstered
furniture.' Richard **Ellis**, *The Book of
Whales* (New York: Alfred A. Knopf,
Inc., 1980), p. 13

p. 225 'At the peak . . . whaling expedition.'
David O. **Hill**, 'Vanishing Giants,'
Audubon Magazine (Jan. 1975), p. 79

p. 225 'Equally lucrative . . . single bowhead.'
Ibid. p. 107

p. 225 'It was used . . . and soap.' Ellis, p. 86

p. 227 ' "We cannot prevent . . ." ' Baron de
Stoeckl in a letter to Prince Gorchakov,
24 Dec. 1867, quoted in Gruening, p. 46

p. 227 ' "However spacious the . . ." ' Ibid.

p. 227 'It was undoubtedly . . . put together.'
The American Land, p. 254

p. 227 'The state has . . . at 20 320 feet.'
Dale Brown, p. 22

p. 227 ' "Seward's icebox . . . walruses." '
Richard A. Smith, p. 81

p. 227 'Today about 30 000 . . . moving
glaciers.' Robert A. **Henning** (ed.),
'Alaska's Glaciers,' *Alaska
Geographic*, vol. 9, no. 1 (1982),
pp. 32, 46

p. 228 'It is a . . . years old.' Dale Brown,
p. 33

p. 228 'Seventy thousand . . . other birds.'
US House of Rep. Com. on Merchant
Marine and Fisheries, Alaska National
Interest Land Conservation Act,
Report 96–97, Part II (1979),
pp. 98–101

p. 228 'So rich are . . . from Australia.' Ibid.
and Ira N. **Gabrielson** and Frederick
C. **Lincoln**, *Birds of Alaska* (Wash. DC:
Wildlife Management Inst.), 1959

p. 232 ' "They are harmless . . . great
violence." ' Pennant, p. 171

p. 232 ' "At the first sound . . ." ' Calvin
Leighton Hooper, quoted in John R.
Brockstoce, *Whales, Ice and Men*
(Seattle: Univ. of Wash. Press, 1986)

p. 232 ' "The natives of . . ." ' Capt. Frederick

A. Barker in a letter to the *New Bedford Republican Standard*, quoted in Brockstoce

p. 232 ' ''Fully one third ... must perish.'' ' Capt. Ebenezer Nye, letter to *New Bedford Republican Standard*, 2 Aug. 1879, quoted in Brockstoce

p. 234 'The Northwest ... or pottery.' Josephy, p. 277

p. 234 ' ''In all the world ...'' ' Tlingit tale quoted in Richard A. Smith, p. 34

p. 235 ' ''This being the fishing ...'' ' David Douglas journal entry of 20 June 1825, quoted in John **Davies**, *Douglas of the Forests* (Seattle: Univ. of Wash. Press, 1980), p. 41

p. 235 ' ''Both were purchased ... four pounds.'' ' Ibid., p. 42

p. 235 ' ''exceedingly fond ... of the fish.'' ' Douglas, journal entry of 19 July 1825, quoted in Davies, pp. 44–5

p. 237 'Douglas learned ... and raisins.' Josephy, p. 279

p. 237 'In all, Douglas ... bears his name.' Davies, p. 23

p. 237 ' ''the opportunity to ...'' ' Robert Kennicott, quoted in Herman **Viola**, *Exploring the West* (Wash., DC: Smithsonian Books, 1987), p. 188

p. 237 ' ''great land.'' ' Lamar, p. 19; and Gruening, p. 39

p. 237 ' ''which, in waters ... and gold.'' ' Charles Sumner, quoted in Gruening, pp. 38–9

p. 239 ' ''This is the Law ...'' ' Robert W. **Service**, 'The Law of the Yukon,' quoted in Gruening, p. 122

p. 239 ' ''Gold! We leapt ...'' ' Service, 'The Trail of Ninety-Eight,' in Gruening, p. 122

p. 240 'As many as nine ... killed at sea.' Glenn A. **Geiger**, 'The Saga of the Alaskan Fur Seals,' *The Explorer*, vol. 17, no. 2 (Summer 1975), p. 8

p. 240 'Kodiak, situated ... evacuated.' Bern **Keating**, *Alaska* (Wash., DC: US Nat. Geog. Soc., 1969), p. 103

p. 240 'In all, more than ... the globe.' Keating, p. 103; and Dale Brown, p. 83

p. 240 'Solar radiation ... Fahrenheit).' Dale Brown, p. 83

p. 240 ' ''The whole valley ...'' ' Robert F. Griggs, quoted in Dale Brown, p. 86

p. 243 ' ''There are resources ...'' ' Henry **Gannett**, *Harriman Alaska Report* (Wash. Acad. of Sciences and Smithsonian Inst., 1910–14), quoted in Gruening, p. 267

p. 243 ' ''a word of ... finest first.'' ' Ibid., pp. 267–8

SEARCHING FOR PARADISE

p. 245 ' ''and when they tried ...'' ' José Longinos Martínez, quoted in David **Lavender**, *California: Land of New Beginnings* (New York: Harper & Row, 1972), p. 2

p. 245 'Excavations of ... species of plant.' John M. **Harris** & George T. **Jefferson** (eds.), *Rancho La Brea: Treasures of the Tar Pits* (Los Angeles: Nat. Hist. Mus. of LA County, 1985), pp. 1, 15

p. 247 ' ''often covered with ...'' ' John B. **Jackson**, *American Space* (New York: W. W. Norton & Co., 1972), p. 183

p. 247 'At Rancho ... natural asphalt.' Harris and Jefferson, p. 9

p. 247 'From the pollen ... 8 million years ago.' Ibid., pp. 11 and 26–9

p. 249 'The Big Trees ... the Rocky Mountains.' François **Leydet**, *The Last Redwoods* (San Francisco: Sierra Club Books, 1969), p. 53

p. 249 ' ''plains and low hills ...'' ' Juan Crespí, quoted in Donald Culross **Peattie**, *A Natural History of Western Trees* (Boston: Houghton Mifflin Co., 1953), p. 21

p. 251 ' ''the trumpet-tongued press ...'' ' J. M. Hutchings, quoted in Francis P. **Farquhar**, *History of the Sierra Nevada* (Berkeley: Univ. of Calif. Press, 1965), p. 84

p. 251 'Five men took ... on Broadway.' Farquhar, p. 84

p. 251 'Another entrepreneur ... in 1866.' Ibid., p. 85

p. 251 ' ''a cruel ... purpose'' ' From 'An Immense Tree' in *Gleason's Pictorial Drawing Room Companion*, Vol. V, 1853, p. 216, quoted in Hans **Huth**, *Nature and the American: Three Centuries of Changing Attitudes* (Omaha: Univ. of Nebraska Press, 1957), p. 143

p. 253 'Before European contact ... lived in California.' Lamar, p. 149

p. 253 'Groups related by ... block of territory.' Lavender, *California*, p. 11

p. 255 'Life in the missions ... by force.' Robert F. **Heizer** (ed.), *Handbook of North American Indians – California* (Wash., DC: Smithsonian Inst. Press, 1978), p. 101

p. 255 'Their work grew ... *atole*.' Ibid., p. 103

p. 255 ' ''It is evident ...'' ' F. F. de Lasuen, quoted in Heizer, p. 102

pp. 255–7 ' ''I am very old ... alone.'' ' Heizer, p. 105

p. 257 'Before it subsided ... commonwealth.' Billington, p. 218

p. 257 'By May 1848 ... southern California.' Barnard, pp. 184–5

p. 257 ' ''The whole country ...'' ' *The Californian*, 29 May 1848, quoted in Paul R. **Wilson**, *California Gold: The Beginning of Mining in the Far West* (Cambridge, MA: Harvard Univ. Press, 1947), p. 19; and Billington, p. 220

p. 257 'By 1848 ... 2 miles wide.' Barnard, p. 185

p. 258 'By August 1848 ... in the east.' Billington, p. 222

p. 258 ' ''The accounts of ... public service.'' ' James Polk, Message to 30th Cong., 2nd Sess., House Executive Document, No. 1, pp. 10–15, quoted in Billington, p. 223

p. 258 'The Eldorado ... became realized.' These and other contemporary reports quoted in Ralph P. **Bieber**, 'California Gold Mania,' *Mississippi Valley Historical Review*, XXXV (1948), pp. 16–22

p. 258 'A New York clothier ... goldrushers.' Barnard, p. 184

p. 258 'Daguerreotype ... Gallup.' Billington, p. 224

p. 258 ' ''Oh Susannah ...'' ' For a sampling of California goldrush songs see Monaghan, pp. 520–5

p. 259 ' ''A sense of more ... passing army.'' ' John A. Crow, in *California As a Place to Live*, quoted in Leydet, p. 67

p. 259 'As the number ... in 1852.' Billington, p. 241

p. 259 'California changed ... (in 1852).' Lavender, *California*, p. 165

p. 259 'In 1853 ... children.' Ibid., p. 236

p. 259 ' ''a land of ...'' ' Joe Meek, 1833, quoted in Bil **Gilbert**, *Westering Man* (New York: Atheneum Pub., 1983), p. 142

p. 259 ' ''If a man were ... of California.'' ' Waddy **Thompson**, *Recollections of Mexico* (New York, 1846), p. 233, quoted in Billington, p. 88

p. 259 ' ''Lying on this ... care to hear.'' ' Emma H. **Adams**, *To and Fro in Southern California* (Cincinnati: W.M.B.C. Press, 1887), pp. 170–1

p. 259 'By the mid-1850s ... Indian converts.' Lavender, *California*, p. 232

p. 260 ' ''Los Angeles County ...'' ' R. W. C. **Farnsworth** (ed.), *A Southern California Paradise* (Pasadena, CA: 1883), pp. 9–10

p. 260 ' ''It is said that ...'' ' Ibid.

p. 260 ' ''Substantial private dwellings ...'' ' Jackson, p. 182

p. 260 'Frame houses ... tropical air.' Ibid.

p. 260 'San Francisco itself ... by 1853.' Michael L. **Smith**, *Pacific Visions: California Scientists and the Environment 1850–1915* (New Haven: Yale Univ. Press, 1987), p. 18

p. 260 'Though periodically ... from Australia.' Lavender, *California*, p. 235

p. 260 ' ''San Francisco seemed ...'' ' Bayard **Taylor**, *Eldorado: or Adventures in the Path of Empire* (1850), rpt. (New York: Alfred A. Knopf, Inc., 1949), p. 226, quoted in Michael L. Smith, p. 18

p. 260 'By 1853, there ... library association.' Lavender, *California*, pp. 236–7

p. 262 ' ''of the very commonest ... other museums.'' ' Spencer F. Baird, quoted in Lois Chambers **Stone**, *Birds of the Pacific Slope* (San Francisco: The Arion Press, 1986), p. 62

p. 262 ' ''You could readily ...'' ' Ibid.

p. 262 ' ''We reached the main ...'' ' Andrew Jackson Grayson, journal entry of 31 October 1853, quoted in Stone, p. 53

p. 262 ' ''Our great desideratum ...'' ' Baird, quoted in Stone, p. 64

p. 266 ' ''In the early days ... secluded localities.'' ' Grayson, quoted in Stone, p. 64

p. 266 ' ''I have found ... put together!'' ' Josiah D. Whitney, quoted in Michael L. Smith, p. 50

p. 266 'Between San Francisco ... to over 100 inches.' Michael L. Smith, p. 52

p. 266 ' ''there is from end ...'' ' David Starr Jordan, quoted in Michael L. Smith, p. 52

p. 266 'California afforded an ... to date.' Michael L. Smith, p. 7

p. 266 '"My plan was simply ..."' John **Muir**, *A Thousand Mile Walk to the Gulf* (Boston: Houghton Mifflin Co., 1916), pp. 1–2

p. 267 '"completely lost ... of inhabitants."' Ibid., p. 186

p. 267 '"Arriving by the Panama ..."' John **Muir**, *The Yosemite* (New York: The Century Co., 1912), p. 4

p. 267 '"It was the bloom-time ..."' Ibid.

p. 267 '"a lake of pure ..."' Ibid., p. 5

p. 267 '"rose the mighty Sierra ..."' Ibid.

p. 267 '"for public use ..."' Farquhar, pp. 122–3

p. 271 '"the terrestrial ..."' John **Muir**, *Our National Parks* (Boston: Houghton Mifflin Co., 1901), p. 74; *The Mountains of California* (New York: 1894), p. 56

p. 271 '"window opening into ..."' Muir, quoted in Nash, *Wilderness and the American Mind*, p. 125

p. 271 '"In the wilderness ... by Donatello."' Robert Underwood Johnson, quoted in Brooks, p. 22

p. 271 '"John the Baptist ..."' Linnie Marsh **Wolfe** (ed.), *John of the Mountains*

(Boston: Houghton Mifflin Co., 1938), p. 85

p. 271 '"The money-changers ..."' Muir, quoted in Stewart L. **Udall**, *The Quiet Crisis* (New York: Holt, Rinehart & Winston, 1963), p. 114

p. 271 '"As sheep advance ... poetry vanish."' Muir, quoted in Nash, *Wilderness and the American Mind*, p. 130

p. 271 '"Through all the wonderful ..."' Muir, quoted in Udall, p. 115

p. 271 '"to spare and cherish ..."' Horace **Greely**, *Glances at Europe* (New York: 1851), p. 39, quoted in Nash, *Wilderness and the American Mind*, p. 101

p. 271 '"The broad, fertile ..."' George S. **Kaime**, 'Where Our Lumber Comes From,' *Western Monthly* (March 1870), p. 191

p. 271 '"Must we stop ..."' Ibid.

p. 273 '"What if the supply ... given us."' Ibid.

p. 273 '"had to make way ..."' Muir, quoted in Nash, *Wilderness and the American Mind*, p. 136

p. 273 '"Thousands of tired ..."' John **Muir**, 'The Wild Parks and Forest

Reservations of the West,' *Atlantic Monthly*, vol. 81 (1898), p. 15; and *Our National Parks*; and Nash, *Wilderness and the American Mind*, p. 140

p. 273 '"worship with Nature ..."' Muir, quoted in Arthur A. **Ekirch**, Jr., *Man and Nature in America* (New York: Columbia Univ. Press, 1963), p. 83

p. 273 '"the grandest day ..."' Theodore Roosevelt, quoted in Linnie Marsh **Wolfe**, *Son of the Wilderness: The Life of John Muir* (New York: Alfred A. Knopf, Inc., 1945), p. 293

p. 273 '"explore, enjoy and ..."' Sierra Club founding document, quoted in Udall, p. 116

p. 274 '"That anyone would ... for anything."' Muir, *The Yosemite*, p. 260

p. 274 '"These temple destroyers ... heart of man."' Ibid., pp. 261–2

p. 274 '"Climb the mountains ... autumn leaves."' Muir, quoted in Udall, p. 125

p. 274 '"When we try ... the universe."' *John Muir* (Wash., DC: Nat. Portrait Gallery, Smithsonian Inst., 1971)

SELECTED BIBLIOGRAPHY

The following books are recommended for further reading on many of the topics discussed in this book. For a more specific bibliography and references to original sources used, see notes on pages 275 to 281.

Bakeless, John, *The Eyes of Discovery*, Philadelphia: J. B. Lippincott Co., 1950

Bakker, Elna S., *An Island Called California*, Berkeley: University of California Press, 1971

Bakker, Elna and Lillard, Richard G., *The Great Southwest*, Palo Alto: American West Publishing Co., 1972

Bancroft, Hubert H., *History of the Pacific States: Alaska 1730–1885*, San Francisco: The History Co., 1886

Billington, Ray Allen, *The Far Western Frontier 1830–1860*, New York: Harper & Brothers, 1956

Brockstoce, John R., *Whales, Ice and Men*, Seattle: University of Washington Press, 1986

Brown, Dee, *Bury My Heart at Wounded Knee: An Indian History of the American West*, New York: Holt, Rinehart & Winston, 1970

Chittenden, Hiram Martin, *History of the American Fur Trade of the Far West*, 2 vols., Stanford: California Academic Reprints, 1954

Cox, Thomas R., Maxwell, Robert S., Thomas, Phillip Drennon, & Malone, Joseph J., *This Well-Wooded Land: Americans and Their Forests from Colonial Times to the Present*, Lincoln, NB: University of Nebraska Press, 1985

Cronon, William, *Changes in the Land: Indians, Colonists and the Ecology of New England*, New York: Hill & Wang, 1983

Cumming, W. P., Skelton, R. A., & Quinn, D. B., *The Discovery of North America*, New York: American Heritage Press, 1972

Douglas, Marjory S., *The Everglades: River of Grass*, New York: Rinehart & Co., 1947

Driggs, Howard, *Westward America*, New York: Somerset Books, 1942

Dunbar, Seymour, *A History of Travel in America*, 4 vols., Indianapolis: Bobbs-Merrill Co., 1915

Ekirch, Arthur A., Jr., *Man and Nature in America*, New York: Columbia University Press, 1963

Ellis, Richard, *The Book of Whales*, New York: Alfred A. Knopf, 1980

Ewan, Joseph, *Rocky Mountain Naturalists*, Utrecht: Bohn, Scheltema & Holkema, 1981

Farb, Peter, *Face of North America*, New York: Harper & Row, 1963

Farquhar, Francis P., *History of the Sierra Nevada*, Berkeley: University of California Press, 1965

Fitzhugh, William and Crowell, Aron, *Crosscurrents of Continents*, Washington, D C: Smithsonian Institution Press, 1988

Galbraith, John S., *The Hudson Bay Company as an Imperial Factor*, Los Angeles: Berkeley Press, 1957

Goetzmann, William H., *Exploration and Empire*, New York: Alfred A. Knopf, 1971

Gruening, Ernest (ed.), *An Alaskan Reader*, New York: Meredith Press, 1966

Hanley, Wayne, *Natural History in America*, New York: Quadrangle/New York Times, 1977

Hedrick, U. P., *A History of Horticulture in America to 1860*, New York: Oxford University Press, 1950

Hodge, Frederick W. (ed.), *Spanish Explorers in the Southern United States: 1528–1543*, New York: Charles Scribner's Sons, 1907

Hollon, W. Eugene, *The Great American Desert Then and Now*, New York: Oxford University Press, 1966

Hordern, Nicholas, Dresner, Simon, and Hillman, Martin, *The Conquest of North America: The Encyclopedia of Discovery and Exploration*, Garden City, NY: Doubleday & Co., 1971

Hughes, J. Donald, *American Indian Ecology*, El Paso: Texas Western Press, 1983

Huth, Hans, *Nature and the American: Three Centuries of Changing Attitudes*, Omaha: University of Nebraska Press, 1957

Jackson, John Brinckerhoff, *American Space*, New York: W. W. Norton & Co., 1972

Jaeger, Edmund, *Desert Wildlife*, Stanford: Stanford University Press, 1961

Kastner, Joseph, *A Species of Eternity*, New York: Alfred A. Knopf, 1977

Lamar, Howard R., *The Far Southwest 1846–1912: A Territorial History*, New Haven: Yale University Press, 1966

Lamar, Howard R. (ed.), *The Readers' Encyclopedia of the American West*, New York: Harper & Row, 1977

Lavender, David, *California: Land of New Beginnings*, New York: Harper & Row, 1972

Lavender, David, *The Rockies*, New York: Harper & Row, 1968

Leydet, Francois, *The Last Redwoods*, San Francisco: Sierra Club Books, 1969

Lorant, Stefan (ed.), *The New World: The First Pictures of America*, New York: Duell, Sloan & Pearce, 1946

Madson, John, *Where the Sky Began: Land of the Tallgrass Prairie*, Boston: Houghton Mifflin Company, 1982

Matthiessen, Peter, *Wildlife in America*, New York: Viking Press, 1959

Merritt, John I., *Baronets and Buffalo: The British Sportsman in the American West, 1833–1881*, Missoula, M T: Mountain Press Publishing Co., 1985

Miller, Charles A., *Jefferson and Nature: An Interpretation*, Baltimore: Johns Hopkins University Press, 1988

Monaghan, Jay (ed.), *The Book of the American West*, New York: Julian Messner, 1963

Morison, Samuel Eliot, *The European Discovery of America: The Northern Voyages*, New York: Oxford University Press, 1971

Nash, Roderick, *The American Environment: Readings in the History of Conservation*, Reading, M A: Addison-Wesley Publishing Co., 1968

Nash, Roderick, *Wilderness and the American Mind*, New Haven: Yale University Press, 1967

Peattie, Donald Culross, *A Natural History of Trees of Eastern and Central North America*, Boston: Houghton Mifflin Co., 1946

Peattie, Donald Culross, *A Natural History of Western Trees*, Boston: Houghton Mifflin Co., 1953

Ricklefs, Robert E., *Ecology*, Newton, M A: Chiron Press, 1973

Rossi, Paul A. and Hunt, David C., *The Art of the Old West*, Denver: Denver Museum of Natural History, 1957

Schubel, J. R., *The Living Chesapeake*, Baltimore: Johns Hopkins University Press, 1981

Shelford, Victor E., *The Ecology of North America*, Urbana: University of Illinois Press, 1978

Shepard, Paul, *Man in the Landscape*, New York: Ballantine Books, 1967

Smith, Henry Nash, *Virgin Land: The American Land as Symbol and Myth*, New York: Vintage Books, 1957

Smith, Michael L., *Pacific Visions: California Scientists and the Environment 1850–1915*, New Haven: Yale University Press, 1987

Stone, Lois Chambers, *Birds of the Pacific Slope*, San Francisco: The Arion Press, 1986

Sturtevant, Wilham C., *Handbook of North American Indians*, 15 vols., Washington, D C: Smithsonian Institution, 1978–present

Thwaites, Reuben G. (ed.), *Original Journals of the Lewis and Clark Expedition*, New York: Dodd, Mead & Co. 1904

Turner, Frederick Jackson, *The Frontier in American History*, New York: Holt Rinehart & Winston, 1920

Udall, Stewart L., *The Quiet Crisis*, New York: Holt, Rinehart & Winston, 1963

Viola, Herman, *Exploring the West*, Washington, D C: Smithsonian Books, 1987

Visser, Margaret, *Much Depends on Dinner*, New York: Collier Books, 1986

Washburn, Wilcomb E. (ed.), *The Indian and the White Man: Documents in American Civilization*, Garden City, N Y: Anchor Books, Doubleday & Company, 1964

Webb, Walter Prescott, *The Great Plains*, Boston: Ginn & Co., 1931

White, Richard, *The Roots of Dependency*, Lincoln: University of Nebraska Press, 1983

Wolfe, Linnie Marsh, *Son of the Wilderness: The Life of John Muir*, New York: Alfred A. Knopf, 1945

Wormington, Marie H., *Ancient Man in North America*, Boston: Houghton Mifflin Co., 1947

INDEX

Numbers in bold indicate
illustrations

Adirondacks 56
aestivation 200–1
agave 194
agriculture
    California 253, 259
    Cherokee tribe 41, 44
    French Canada 62
    Great Plains 146–7, 149
    pre-European 18, 194–5
    Southwest 194–5, 200
aigrettes 114
Akootan Island scene 221
Alaska 211–42
    Aleut name 237
    Astoria 225
    Barrow 228
    birds 228
    Central Plateau 212, 236
    Cook expedition (1778) 223–4
    forests, coastal 211
    glaciers 212
    gold rush (1897–8) 237
    Good Friday earthquake (1916)
        241
    mineral resources 237, 239–40
    Nome 237
    North Slope 212, 241
    oil resources 241
    purchase 228, 237
    Russian sale to US (1867) 227
    size 227
    Spanish claim abandoned 223–4
Alaska National Interest Lands
    Conservation Act (1980)
    241
Albany River trading post 84
Aleut people 216, 219, 222, 224
Aleutian Islands 214, 215, 216, 223,
    241
Algonquian Indians 25, 38
alligators 88, 92, 104, 105–6
alpine plants 168, 169
Alta California 253
Amadas, Philip 25
American Fur Company 140, 167
American River, gold discovery
    (1848) 257
antelope, pronghorn 134, 137
Apache Indians 198, 204
Apalachee Indians, Florida 106
Appalachian Mountains 38, 41,
    42–3, 46, 61
    Catesby 109
    Cherokee departure 47
    natural barrier 123
    Rockies comparison 151, 153,
        157
    Spanish exploration 97
arbor-vitae (white cedar) 57, 68
arctic fox 76, 81
arctic hare 81
arctic poppy 80
Arctic Ocean 212, 241
Arizona, Indian cultures 194–8
Arkansas River 152–3, 204

armadillo, ice-age period 18
artesian springs, Florida 91, 92, 93,
    95
ash
    mountain 56
    white 68
aspen 56, 66, 212
Assiniboin Indians 163
aster 56
Astor, John Jacob 167, 225
Atchafalaya Swamp, Louisiana
    116–17
Athapaskan Indians 227, 232
atl-atl 95
Audubon, John James 114, 173,
    260
    books 173, 260
    paintings 53, 148 (above), 166
Audubon, John Woodhouse 148
    (below)
Audubon Society 114–15
avocet, American 143
auk, great 52, 53, 54
Aztec civilization 20

badger 147
    ice-age period 18, 249
Baillie-Grohman, William A.
    180–1
Baird, Spencer Fullerton 263
Baja California 219, 253, 262
baleen (whale bone) 225
balsam 68, 71
Barker, Captain Frederick A. 232
Barlowe, Arthur 25, 28
barren 124
Bartell, John 205
Bartram, William
    alligator encounter 105–6
    paintings 93
    Travels 92
bat, ice-age period 249
Beach, Rex 239
beans, Indian food 28, 44, 194
bear
    black 39, 66, 162
    grizzly 159, 160–1, 162, 165,
        212
    ice-age period 247
    polar (ice) 18, 20, 50, 52, 84, 87,
        232
    Rocky Mountains, 159, 162
beaver 44, 63, 64, 65–6, 68, 166,
    232
    dance 47
    ice-age period 18
    fur trade 68, 164, 167
Becknell, William 204
Bering Island 214, 216
Bering Sea, whale hunting 222,
    224–5
Bering Strait, land bridge 18, 219,
    251
Bering, Vitus 212, 214, 241
Bermuda 15, 16
Big Sur coast, California 244
Big Tree see sequoia, giant
bighorn sheep 157, 158, 159
Bimini Island, Bahamas 91

birch 66, 212
    yellow 56
    white (paper) 68, 69
Bird, Isabella 180
birdfoot violet 129
birds
    Alaska 212, 228
    Audubon's book 260
    California 260, 263, 266
    conservation societies 114
    extinctions 110, 112, 114, 214
    Grayson's collection 263
    migration 15, 20, 22, 26, 44, 228
    Newfoundland 51–2
    prairies 143
    Rocky Mountains 172–3
    Sonoran Desert 188, 191
The Birds of America (Audubon)
    173, 260
bison, wood 31, 123, 130
    ice-age period 247
    see also buffalo
Bitterroot Mountains 138, 153
blackbird
    red-winged 66
    yellow-headed 173
black-eyed Susan 118, 120
Blackfoot Indians 130, 163, 198
blueberries 66, 67, 68, 211, 237
bluebird, mountain 174
boa constrictor (buyo) 195
bobcat, 147, 248, 249
Bodega Bay, Russian trading post
    (1812) 225
Bodega, Juan Francisco de la 223
Bodmer, Karl 163, 165
bogbean (gentian) 72
Boyle, Robert, English chemist 57
Brief Recit (1545) (Cartier) 54
British Columbia 211, 237
British settlements
    expansion in 17th century 76
    Hudson's Bay Company 82–7
    Jamestown, Virginia 28–33, 38
    later colonists 24
    New England 68–70
    Roanoke expeditions 25, 27–8
brittlebush 201, 203
Brooks Range, Alaska 151, 212,
    228
Broward, Napoleon Bonaparte
    114–15
Bry, Theodore de 27, 104
buffalo 8, 72, 126, 131, 139, 204
    dance 47
    Great Plains 130, 133
    ice-age period 18
    protection reserves 146
    slaughter 11, 143, 146
Buffon, Comte de 65
bunchberry 56
butterfly, White Mountain 20

Cabot, John, exploration (1497)
    24
cactus 188, 189, 192–3, 201, 203
    barrel 193
    cardon 188, 191
    cholla, 188, 192

hairbrush 188
    ocotillo 202
    organpipe 188
    pitaya agria 188
    prickly pear 103, 194
    saguaro 188, 189, 191, 194
    senita 188
    sina 188
    teddy-bear cholla 192
California 245–74
    birds 260, 263, 266
    conservation 266–74
    fertility 259–60
    gold rush (1848) 257–9
    Grayson's bird collection 263
    Pacific coast 244, 252
    Spanish mission system 251,
        253–5, 257
    US jurisdiction (1848) 257
    US treaty settlement 142
Calusa Indians 92, 95, 100
    culture 102–3, 105, 106
camel
    ice-age 95, 205, 247
    introduction and use 205
Camp Wood, Missouri (start of
    Lewis and Clark expedition)
    134
Canary Islands 15
canoe, 30, 68
Canyon de Chelly 196
Cape Cod 15
Cape Mary's Island,
    Newfoundland 55
Cape May, bird migration 20
cardinal flower 72
caribou 68, 212, 234
    barren-ground 76, 77–82
    ice-age 18
    woodland 77–82
Carter, President Jimmy 241
Cartier, Jacques 60, 112
    Brief Recit (1545) 54
    Newfoundland (1534) 51–7
Cascade Range 152
Castañeda, Pedro de 130, 187–8,
    191, 198
Catesby, Mark 115
    Natural History of Carolina,
        Florida and the Bahama
        Islands 110, 111, 212, 213, 214
    naturalist 109, 111, 112
Catlin, George 9, 11, 13, 138, 140
    buffalo warning 11, 143, 146
    Indian paintings 131, 163, 167
    national park proposal 140
cattle 201, 209
    ranches 147, 204, 255
    Spanish introduction 198
Cavalier, Robert, Sieur de la Salle
    56
caviar 29
cedar, white see arbor-vitae
Central Valley, California 260,
    267
Champlain, Samuel de 66–8, 70,
    71, 112
Charles II, King, Hudson's Bay
    charter 76, 82

Cherokee Indians
  cultural beliefs 41, 44, 47–8
  Eighth Clan 47
Chesapeake Bay, Maryland 14, 28–9
  marine life 29–30
  waterfowl species 33
chicken, prairie 138
Chihuahua Desert 187
Choris, Louis 224
Christianity 46, 106, 194, 197, 201, 253, 255
Chugach Mountains 227
Chumash Indians 245
Cíbola, seven cities 187, 191
Cimarron Desert 204
Civil War 112, 114, 205, 227, 273
clams 54
Clark, William
  exploration 134–5, 138, 153
  grizzly bear encounters 162
  Rockies traverse 153
  Superintendent Indian Affairs 140
  see also Lewis, Meriwether
Clark's crow 139
Clatsop, Fort 138
Clearwater River 138
climate 120
  Alaska 211, 212, 227–8
  California 253, 259, 266
  Canadian winter 57
  Desert Southwest 187
  Florida 100
  Hudson's Bay 84
  Rocky Mountains 157
  Southeast 31
coachwhip plant 201
Coast Range, California 152, 262, 267
Cockqua, Chinook chief 235, 237
cod, Grand Banks 61
Codex Canadiensis 63
Colorado
  gold mining 177, 180
  sand dunes discovery 152
  settlement 124
Colorado River 153, 205, 208, 209
Colter, John 181
Colter's Hell 181
Columbia River 138, 225, 235
columbine 168
Columbus, Christopher 61
  manatee description 92
  voyage 15–17, 18, 274
Comanche Indians 130, 198, 204
conch 103
condor, California, 262, 263, 266
coneflower 121, 126
conquistadores 47, 106, 130, 191, 198
conservation
  Alaska legislation (1980) 241–2
  Alaskan seals 240
  California 266–74
  Everglades 114–15
  Massachusetts Audubon Society 114
  national parks 180–1, 185
  redwood forests 251, 253
  Rockies 159, 180–1, 185
  Sierra Club 273–4
  Southwest pressures 209
  US Soil Conservation Service 149

Continental Divide 15, 138, 152, 153, 154–5, 156, 164, 187
  Lenhi Pass 153
Cook, Captain James 223–4, 225
copperhead 100
coral islands 89
coreopsis, swamp 113
cormorant 51, 214
  Pallas's 214
corn, Indian food 28, 31, 44, 194, 200
Coronado, Francisco Vásquez de 105, 130, 187–8, 191, 194, 205
Corps of Discovery (Lewis and Clark expedition) 134–5, 138, 153
Cortéz, Hérnan 130
cottonmouth 98
cougar 124
cowboys 204
coyote 134, 136, 147
  ice-age period 247, 249
crab
  blue 30, 252
  horseshoe 22, 23
cranberry 66–8, 237
Crater Lake National Park 273
Cree Indians 162, 163
Crespi, Father Juan 249
crocodile, American 104, 105
crow, Clark's 139
Crow Indians 198
Cumberland Gap 122, 123
curlew, Eskimo 143, 148
cypress, bald 102
cypress swamps 88, 105, 112, 116–17

dandelion 120
  false 126
Davis, Jefferson 205
Dawson (Yukon) 239
Death Valley, California 186, 201, 266
deer 44, 66, 68, 106, 126, 253
  ice-age period 18
  white-tailed 31, 32, 40, 97, 106, 107, 108, 120, 123
Deere, John, plow inventor (1837) 141
deforestation 112, 241, 271, 273
  eastern forests 120
Denali (Mt McKinley) 227
Denver 180
Depression years 147, 149
desert 149, 187–209
  Cimarron 204
  Chihuahua 187
  Great American 124, 209
  Great Basin 187
  Mt Katmai 240
  Mojave 203, 249
  plants 201
  Sonoran 187–9, 193
The Discovery ... State of Kentucke (Filson) 123
diseases
  English colonists 33
  Indians 38, 47, 106, 255
  role in Indian mythology 44
  scurvy 57
  smallpox 38, 163
  tuberculosis 38

typhoid 38
Douglas, David 235, 237, 251
Dowd, Augustus 251
Dragging Canoe, Cherokee chief 47
Drake, Sir Francis 253
dromedaries, introduction 205
drought, prairies 149
drought-resisters (plants) 201
Dry Tortugas islands 91–2
duck
  Eider 214
  Labrador 53
Dust Bowl (1930s) 147, 149
Dutch West Indies Company 68
'Dutchman of Warre', slavery trader 38

eagle 162–3
  bald or white-headed 2, 162, 249
  golden 162, 249
  ice-age period 247
East Indies, search for 16
ecology
  Alaska 212, 241
  beaver communities 65–6
  California 266
  deforestation effects 119–20, 123
  prairie dogs 147
  prairies 124, 126, 143
  Smoky Mountains 41, 44
  Sonoran Desert 191, 200–1
  tundra regions 76
egret 66, 105
  great 114
  reddish 114
  snowy 114
eider, Steller's 214
Eldorado 187, 258
elephants, ice-age period 18, 247
Elizabeth, Queen
  American colonization 24–5
  Raleigh expeditions 25
elk 31, 44, 66, 68, 123, 127, 253
  tule 260
Elliott, Henry Wood 221, 240
Emerson, Ralph Waldo 181, 271, 273
English settlements see British settlements
environment see conservation
erosion, Grand Canyon 208
Eskimo (Inuit) 87
  in Newfoundland 52
  origin 216, 219
  starvation reports (1870s) 232
  walrus hunting 232
  whale hunters 224
Estévanico 95
Everglades 99, 100, 102–3, 105, 111
  bird losses 114
  drainage attempts 114–15
  fruits of 108
  national protection 115
expansionism 227
  Russia 253
exploration
  Cartier 51–60
  Catesby the naturalist 109, 111
  Champlain 66–8, 70–1
  Columbus' voyage 15–18
  Florida discovery (1513) 91
  Grand Canyon (1849) 205, 208
  Lewis and Clark 134–5, 138, 153

Long's expedition (1819–20) 169
  Northwest 212, 214
  Pacific coast 224
  Prince Maximilian zu Wied-Neuwied 163
  Radisson and Groseilliers 72–6
  Raleigh expeditions 25–8
  Rocky Mountains 151–3
  Southwest 187–97
  Yellowstone Hot Springs 181
Exxon Valdez oil damage (1989) 241

falcon 247, 249
Ferdinand Island 16
ferret, black-footed 147, 148
Filson, John, Kentucky account 123
finch, purple 93
fir 56
  Douglas 237, 260
  lowland 237
  noble 237
  silver 237
  white 237
fish, migration 22, 235
fishing
  Grand Banks 60–2
  Jamestown 33
fishermen 16
  Breton 54, 61
  Grand Banks 61
Flint, Timothy 167
Florida 89–115
  artesian springs 91, 92, 93, 95
  bird losses 112, 114
  Catesby's Natural History 111
  plantation system 108–9
  purchase, US government 111
  Ribaut's account (1563) 22, 24
  Spanish discovery (1513) 91
  springs 93
  transfer to English (1763) 84
Florida Big Bend, Suwanee R. 96
Flordia Keys 89, 91, 103, 267
flycatcher 20
Fontaneda, Hernando d'Escalante 103, 105
forests
  Alaska 211–12, 241
  Canada 54, 56
  deforestation 112, 119–20, 123, 241, 271, 273
  eastern 31, 41, 119, 130
  Midwest 123–4, 141
  use for fuel 119
Fort Clatsop 138
Fort Laramie, painting (Miller) 9, 165
Fort Mandan, Lewis and Clark expedition 9, 138
Fort Nelson 84
Fort Pierre 9, 143
Fort Severn 84
Fort Union 9, 140, 156
Fort Vancouver 172–3
fossils 89, 95, 245–7, 249, 253
fox 44, 52
  arctic 77, 81, 87
  ice-age period 247, 249
  kit 248
France, Louisiana/US settlement 133–4
Francis I, king of France 51

Franciscan missionaries 255
   Southwest 194–5, 204
Fraser, Simon 225
French settlements, Canada 70–1, 84
Frobisher, Martin 27
frog (Catesby drawing) 110
Funk Island 51
fur trade 47, 54, 57, 62–5
   Canada 71, 73, 77, 84
   early years 68, 76, 82
   Great Britain in Alaska 224
   Hudson's Bay Company 84
   North Atlantic 60
   northern fur seal **220**, 222–3
   Plymouth colony 68
   Rockies 164, 167
   Russian traders 216, 219
   sea otter 216, **217**, 219, 222
   US competition 167
   with China 224

Gabrielino Indians 245
Gálvez, Jóse 253
gannets 52, **55**
Gannett, Henry, Alaska survey
   conclusions (1980) 241, 243
Gaspé Peninsula 54, 77
Gass, Sergeant Patrick 153
geese, snow **36–7**
*The Genera of North American
   Plants* (Nuttall) 172
Generall Historie of Virginia . . .
   (Smith) 28–33
geysers 181
Gila monster 195, **196**
Gila River 191
Gilbert, Humphrey, settlement
   plans 24–5
glaciers
   Alaska 227–8, **210**, 212, 230–1,
      237
   Rocky Mountains 170
Glacier Bay, Alaska 227, 228,
   230–1
Gleason's Pictorial 251
goat, mountain **158**
gold 16, 24, 47, 54, 100, 191, 251,
   260
gold prospecting 256
   Alaska (1897–8) 237, 239
   California (1848) 257–9
   Rockies (1859) 177, 180
goldenrod 56, 120, **129**
Gore, Sir St George 173
Grand Banks 60–2
Grand Canyon 205, **206–7**, 208
Grand Canyon National Park 273
Grand Teton Mountains 150
Grant, President Ulysses S. 146,
   181
grass 124
   bluestem 124, **128**
   cord 29–30, 33
   late summer 29–30
Grasshopper Glacier 170
grasshoppers (locusts) 170
grassland, prairie 119–49
Gray, Robert 225
Grayson, A. J. 260, 262, 266
   painting **261**
Great American Desert 124, 209
Great Basin 198
Great Falls, Missouri River 138

Great Lakes, Canada 70, 72, **74–5**,
   100
Great Plains 119–49
   introduction of horse 133, 198
   Radisson's exploration 72
   transformation 146–7
   wildlife 126, 130
Great Smoky Mountains 38, **42–3**,
   46
Greater Antilles 95
Greely, Horace 173, 177, 271
Green Mountains, New England
   56
Griggs, Dr Robert F. 240
Gros Ventres Indians 163
Groseilliers, Médard Chovart,
   Sieur des 72–6, 77, 82
ground sloth 18, 95, 247
grouse
   ruffed 44, 123
   sage 173
   sharp-tailed 173
Guale Indians, Georgia 106
guayule, desert 201
guillemot 52
Gulf of California 187
Gulf of Mexico 15, 20, 73, 84, 89,
   91, 102, 266
Gulf of St Lawrence 52, 56, 70
Gulf Stream 16, 57, 91
gum tree
   sour black 111
   tupelo 111

haddock 61
Haida Indians 223, 232, 234
hairbrush cactus 188
Haiti 92, 95
hake 61
hammocks (small islands) 102
hare, arctic 77, **81**
Hariot, Thomas 27, 28
   Cherokee settlements 47
Harper's New Monthly Magazine
   141–2
Harriman, Edward Henry 273
Hartweg, Karl T. 251
hawk, ice-age period 247
Hayden, Ferdinand 181
hemlock, western 211
Hennepin, Louis, drawing 131
heron
   great blue **113**, 114
   green 114
   little blue 114
Hochelaga (Montreal) 54, 56
hog, razorback 100
homesteaders 141, 149
honeybees, European introduction
   57
Hopi Indians 197–8, 200
horse 130, **132**
   native species (extinct) 18, 247
   Spanish introduction 133, 198,
      200
hot springs, Yellowstone 181, **184**
Hudson, Henry 84
Hudson's Bay 72, **85**
Hudson's Bay Company 84
   Atlantic coast activity 82
   Fort Vancouver post 172–3
   Kennicott's expedition 237
   Pacific coast activity 225, 227,
      237

Hudson's Strait 84
human migration
   European discovery 20
   forced relocation of Indians 31,
      47, 130
   immigration flood 147, 149
   native Americans 20, 234
   western settlers 123–4
hummingbird
   Costa's 201
   rufous 173, 211, **213**
Huron Indians 54, 62–5
ibis 105
   glossy 114
   white 114
ice age 18, 20, 29, 41, 71, 77, 89,
   95, 123, 124, 130, 247
Illinois Indians 63
immigration
   California 259
   Great Plains 142, 147
Inca civilization 20
Indian 9, **104**
   abuse of 31, 106, 255
   agriculture 18, 44, 209
   archery proficiency 95
   Bodmer's paintings 163
   buffalo hunting 130, **131**, 133
   California 253, 255, 257
   Columbus' discovery 18
   corn 44, 194, 200
   crops 108
   deer hunt and ceremony 40
   diet 44, 103, 105, 143
   displacement 31, 38, 47, 130, 257
   dwellings 26, 44, 54, **199**, 200,
      234
   eagle, importance 162–3
   fishing techniques 26, 30
   horses adoption 198, 200
   mythology 41, 44, 234–5
   Northwest 234–5, 237
   pictographs 196
   prairie tribes 130
   relocation 31, 47, 130
   raiders (attack) 204–5, 267
   Roanoke settlement 28
   smoking 63
   Southwest 187–209
   snake dance 197
   totem carving, Sitka 233
   western decline 167, 169
   White illustrations 26
   wildlife affinity 162–3
Indian tribes
   Algonquian 25, 38
   Apache 198, 204
   Apalachee 106
   Arizona 194–8
   Assiniboin 163
   Athapaskan 227, 232
   Blackfoot 130, 163, 198
   Calusa 92, 95, 100, 102–3, 105,
      106
   Cherokee 41, 44, 47–8
   Chumash 245
   Comanche 130, 198, 204
   Cree 162, 163
   Croatean 28
   Crow 198
   Gabrielino 245
   Gros Ventres 163
   Guale 106

Haida 223, 234
Hopi 197–8, 200
Huron 54, 62–5
Illinois 63
Iroquois 62, 71, 73, 76
Mandan 163
Menomini 162
Micmac 54
Minnataree 163
Narragansett 49
Navajo 198
Nootka 223
Oawnee 204
Osage 130
Ottawa 62
Papago (Tohono O'odham)
   194–5, 200
Pawnee 130, 204
Pima 200
Pueblo 234
Sauk 162
Sheepeater 157
Shoshone 138, 198
Sioux 130, 142–3, 163
Timucua 106
Tlingit 223, 233, 234
Wichita 198
Yaqui (Mayo) 188
Zuni 191, 194, 200
indigo, introduction of 108
Ingalls, John J. 185
insects 18, 82, 126, 170, 201, 228
Inuit *see* Eskimo
iris 72
Iroquois Indians 62, 71, 73, 76
irrigation, Southwest 194–5, 209
Irving, Washington 130
Island of Birds (Funk Is.) 51, 52
Isthmus of Panama 18, 20, 259
ivy, poison 100

jackrabbit 134, **137**
Jackson Lake **150**
Jackson, President Andrew 167
Jackson, William Henry 181
James, Edwin 169
James River, fish abundance 29
Jamestown, Virginia, English
   settlement (1607) 28–33, 38,
   112
Jasper National Park, Alberta **175**
jay
   blue **213**
   Steller's 212, **213**, 214
Jefferson, President Thomas
   Lewis and Clark expedition
      134–5, 138
   Louisiana (1802) 133
   western exploration 152
Jefferson River, beaver dam 65
Jesuit missionaries 70, 255
   Southwest 194–5, 204
Johnson, President Andrew 227
Johnson, Robert Underwood 273
Jolliet, Louis 73
Joshua trees 203
*Joyfull Newes Out of the Newe
   Founde Worlde* (Monardes)
   27
junco 41, 44, **45**
Juniper Springs, Florida **93**

Kaime, George 273
Kalm, Peter 119

Kamchatka 214, 216
Katmai, Mt 238, 239–40
Kayak Island (St Elias) 212
Kelp, Pacific 219
Kelsey, Henry, on grizzly bear 159
Kennicott, Robert 237
Kentucky, settlement 123
Key Largo 89
Key West 89
Kino, Eusebio Francisco 194–5
Kissimmee River 100
kit fox 248
kivas 197
Klondike River 239
Kodiak Island
    Russian trading post (1784) 225
    volcano effects 240

La Brea Tar Pits 245–9, 246, 253
La Salle, Robert de 73
Labrador
    Cabot's exploration (1497) 24
    ice-age relics 20
Lachine (rapids) 56
Laguno del Espíritu Santo, El 100
Lahontan, Louis-Armand, Baron de 61–2
larkspur 126, 258
Lassen Peak, Sierra Nevada 249
Laurentian Hills 56
'The Law of the Yukon' (Service) 239
Le Clercq, Chrétien 70
Le Moyne de Morgues, Jacques 27, 40, 105
Lenhi Pass 153
Levi Strauss 258
Lewis, Meriwether 134
    eagle feathers, importance 162–3
    grizzly bear encounters 159, 162
    page from notebook 139
    Rockies traverse 153
    western exploration mission 134–5, 138, 153, 225
    see also Clark, William
limestone, Florida 91, 93
Lincoln, Benjamin 120
lion, ice-age period 18, 247
Livingston, Robert 133
lizard, beaded 195
lobelia 72
locusts, Rocky Mountains 170
London, Jack 239
Long, Major Stephen H. 169, 209
Los Angeles 205, 259
    tar pits 245, 246, 247, 249
Louis, Nicolas, illustrations 63
Louisiana Territory 138, 152, 204, 227
    French acquisition (1682) 84
    US acquisition (1802) 133
Louisiana tanager 139
lynx 57, 167, 176

McAdoo, William 185
Mackenzie, Alexander 138, 164, 225
The Mammals of North America (Audubon) 173
Mammoth Hot Springs 184
mammoth 246, 247
manatee 92, 94, 95
Manatee Springs 92

Mandan Indians 163
mangrove 101, 102
mangrove swamps, Florida 102
Manhattan 22, 68
Manifest Destiny 271
Manual of the Ornithology of the US and Canada (Nuttall) 172
maple 56, 58–9
    sugar 57, 60
    syrup harvest 57–60
Marco Island artifacts 106
Mariposa Grove of Big Trees 267
marmot, yellow-bellied 171
Marquette, Jacques 73
marten 57, 167
martin, purple 120, 191
Martínez, Estéban José 223
Massachusetts Audubon Society 114
mastodons 18, 247
Mather, Cotton 120
Maximilian zu Wied-Neuwied, Prince 163
Maya civilization 20
medicinal plants 27, 44, 57
Mendenhall Glacier, Juneau 210
Menomini Indians 162
Menzies, Archibald 251
Mesa Verde National Park 273
mesquite 191, 194, 253
Mexico
    Grayson's birds 263
    independence (1821) 204, 255
    US treaty settlement (1848) 142
Mexico City (Tenochtitlán) 130, 204
Mexican war 205
Miantonomo, Indian chief 49
Micmac Indians, trade 54
Midway Geyser Basin 182–3
migration
    altitudinal 41, 44
    bird 15, 20, 22, 26, 33, 44, 143, 228
    caribou 82
    fish 22, 235
    post ice-age 18, 20
    see also human migration
Miller, Alfred Jacob 164, 165, 167, 172
minerals
    Alaska 237, 239–40
    California (1848) 257–9
    Ribaut's account (1563) 22, 24
    Rockies discoveries 177, 180
Minerva Terrace, Yellowstone 184
mink 66, 68, 166, 167
Minnetaree Indians 163
missionaries
    Florida 106, 108
    Franciscan in California 255
    French 219
    Indian resistance to 255
    Jesuits in California 255
    Spanish in Alaska 223
Mississippi River, French discovery 73
Mississippi valleys, settlement 123–4
Missouri Fur Company 167
Missouri River 163, 178–9
    Lewis and Clark expedition 134
Mojave Desert 187, 249
Monardes, Nicholas 27

Monroe, James 133
Montezuma's Castle, Arizona, 199
Montreal (Hochelaga) 54, 56, 73, 77
moose 66, 68, 72, 123, 212, 232
Moran, Thomas 181
mosquito 66, 82
Mt Edith Cavell, Jasper 175
Mt Katmai 238, 239–41
Mt McKinley (Denali) 226, 227
Mt Rainier National Park 273
Mt St Helens eruption (1980) 241
Mt Washington, ice-age relics 20
Mt Whitney, Sierra Nevada 264–5, 266
mountain men 204
Muir, John, conservationist 266–74
murres 51, 52
musk ox 76, 78–9
    ice-age survival 18, 20
muskeg (sphagnum bogs) 72
muskrat 18, 19, 66, 68, 105
mustang 132, 205

Napa Valley, vineyard 256
Napoleon Bonaparte, Louisiana US settlement 133–4
Narragansett Indians 49
Narrative of a Journey Across the Rocky Mountains (Townsend) 172
Narváez, Pánfilo de, expedition (1528) 95, 97
NASA 239, 240
National Audubon Society 115
National Geographic Society
    Mt Katmai expedition 240
National Parks
    establishment of 140
    Banff 63
    California 267, 273–4
    Crater Lake 273
    Everglades 99, 115
    Glacier 273
    Grand Canyon 273
    Grand Tetons 150
    Jasper 175
    Mesa Verde 273
    Mt Katmai 238, 240
    Mt Rainier 273
    Olympic 243, 273
    Sequoia 273
    Smoky Mountain 42–3, 46
    Yellowstone 140, 180–1, 182–3, 184, 185
    Yosemite 267, 270, 273, 274
National Wildlife Refuge 114
The Natural History of Carolina ... (Catesby) 111, 212, 214
nature reserves 140, 159
    bison/buffalo 146
Navajo Indians 198
New Amsterdam (New York City) 68
New England
    Cabot's exploration (1497) 24
    colonists (1628) 48–9
    wildflowers 120
New France 70–1
    exploration 72–6, 82
New Jersey, bird migration 22
New Mexico (1840s–50s) 205
New Netherlands 77

New Orleans 84, 133–4
New York City 22, 267
Newfoundland 15, 16, 24–5, 77
    bird migration 15
    Cabot's exploration (1497) 24
    Cartier's exploration (1534) 51–2, 60
    discovery records 15–17 (map)
    seabirds 51, 54
night-heron 114
Niña, discovery voyage 15–16
Nome, Alaska 237
Nootka Indians 223
Nootka Sound 225
North Carolina
    bird losses 112
    Ribaut's account (1563) 24
    see also Roanoke
North Dakota, bison reserve 146
North Slope, Alaska 212, 228, 241, 247
North West Company (fur trading) 225
Northwest Passage 54, 60, 224
    Cook expedition (1778) 223–4
    Hudson's Bay Company charter 82
    Lewis and Clark expedition 134
Nova Scotia 24, 60
Novarupta volcano 240
Nuttall, Thomas 172–3

oak 56, 96
    blue 258
    live 258
    poison 100
    water 111
Oawnee Indians 204
ocotillo 201, 202
Odobenidae (walrus) 228
oil formations
    Alaska 241
    California 247
Okeechobee, Lake 100, 115
Oklahoma, bison reserve 146
'Old Faithful' geyser 181
old growth (forests), Northwest 241
Olympic National Park 243, 273
Ontario, Lake 71
opossum 18, 33, 35, 44
Oraibi, establishment 197
orange 272
orchis, purple-fringed 72
Oregon, US acquisition (1846) 142
Osage Indians 130
osprey 66, 72
Ottawa Indians 62
otter, 18, 44, 63, 66, 105, 167
    sea 216, 217, 219, 222, 240
An Overland Journey from New York to San Francisco (Greely) 177
owl
    burrowing 147, 249
    elf 191
    great horned 60, 72
    snowy 77, 85
oxen, musk 77, 78–9
    ice-age period 247
oysters, Chesapeake Bay 30

Pacific coast 211–42, 245–74
Pacific Fur Company 167, 225

Pacific Northwest 211–42
  British claims 225
  native culture 234
  US claims 225
packrat, Sonoran Desert 188, 191
Palliser, John 173
palmetto 102, 111
Papago Indians (Tohono
  O'odham) 194–5, 200
parakeet, Carolina 110, 112
Partridgeberry 56
Pawnee Indians 130, 204
Peale, Charles Willson 138
Peale, Titian 172
pelagic sealing 239–40
pelican 106
  brown 90, 106, 114
  white 72, 92
Pelican Island, Florida 114
Penn, William 68
Pennant, Thomas 162, 232
Pennsylvania 68, 123
Pérez, Juan 223
permafrost, Alaska 227–8, 237
Pfefferkorn, Ignaz 200
pig, wild
  ice-age period 18
  Spanish introduction 97–8
pigeon, passenger 112
pika 170, 171
Pike, Zebulon 204, 209
  Rocky Mountains expedition
  151–3
Pike's Peak 151, 169, 171, 172,
  177
Pilgrims 38
  American journey (1620) 27
  New England settlement 48–9
Pima Indians 200
pine
  lodgepole 237
  piñon 191, 194
  white 27
Pinta, discovery voyage 15–16
pitaya agria cactus 188
pitcher plants 113
Placentia, fishing village (1684) 61–
  2
plantation system 38, 108–9, 255
Platte River 152–3
Pleistocene mammals 18, 245–9,
  246
plover 22
  black-bellied 143
  hunting 112
  lesser golden 143
  piping 143
  semi-palmated 143
  snowy 143
plow invention (1837) 141
Plymouth Rock 38, 76
Pocohantas, Indian princess 38
Polk, President James K. 258
pollution, wildlife recovery 22
Ponce de Léon, Juan, Florida
  discovery 91, 95
poppy
  arctic 80
  California 201, 203, 268–9
porcupine, ice-age period 18
Port Valdez, oil pipeline 241
Portugal, fish import duty (1506)
  61
Powell, John Wesley 205–9

prairie dog 135, 138, 147
  black-tailed 137
prairies
  California 260
  common tern on 144–5
  cornfields 118
  Dust Bowl period 149
  evolution of 124, 126, 141
  fire 126, 129, 141
  grasses 124, 127, 128, 130
  immigration 141–2
  livestock ranches 147
  Midwest 119–49
  settlers 126, 141–2
  wild flowers 121, 129
Pribilof, Gavril 222
Pribilof Islands 240
prickly pear 194
priests, Indian 197
Prince William Sound 224, 241
promyshlenniki 216, 219, 223
Prudhoe Bay, oil pipeline 241
ptarmigan 77, 81
Pueblo Indians, 234
Pueblo Revolt (1680) 197–8
Puerto Rico, Ponce de Léon
  expedition (1513) 91–2

quail 120
  California 173
Quebec City (Stadacona) 54, 70
Queen Charlotte Islands 234

rabbit
  cottontail 120
  ice-age period 18, 249
racoon 33, 34, 167
Radisson, Pierre Esprit 72–6, 77,
  82
railroads (1828–69) 142–3, 209
rainforest, Olympic National Park
  244, 266
Raleigh, Sir Walter 24
  Roanoke expeditions 25, 27–8
  settlement charter (1584) 25
  tobacco introduction 38
rancherias, California 253, 255
Rancho La Brea Tar Pits 245, 246,
  247, 249
Raton Pass 204
rattlesnake 100, 109, 195, 196, 197
raven 87, 249
  Indian artifacts 233
  Indian mythology 234–5
Red River 152, 198
redwood, California 249, 251, 260
Rendezvous 164
Report on the Lands of the Arid
  Region of the US (Powell)
  208
rhinoceros, ice-age period 18
Ribaut, Jean, wildlife report
  (1563) 22, 24
rice, South Carolina 108
Riley, C. V. 170
Rio Grande River 153
River Glades (now Everglades) 102
Roanoke Island
  discovery reports 25
  attempted settlements 25, 27–8,
  38, 112
robin 112, 120
rockchuck 171

Rocky Mountains 151–85
  Appalachians comparison 153,
  157
  bighorn sheep 158
  Continental Divide 154–5
  fur traders 164, 167
  goats 158
  gold rush (1859) 177
  Grand Tetons 150
  ice-age relics 20
  Lewis and Clark traverse 153
  Mt Edith Cavell 175
  tourism encouraged 173, 177
Rolfe, John 38
Roosevelt, President Theodore
  114, 273
Round Island, walruses 229
Royal Horticultural Society,
  Douglas' plant collection
  237
Rupert River trading post 84
Rupert's Land 82
Russia
  fur traders 216, 219, 222
  US expansion protest 227
Russian America 223, 225, 227
  sale to US (1867) 227, 237
Russian-American Company 227
Ruxton, George 157, 159

saber-toothed cats 18, 95, 247
Sacagawea, Shoshoni guide 138
Sacramento River 257–8
Sacramento Valley 260, 266
saguaro catcus 188, 189, 194
St Augustine 91, 108
St Elias (now Kayak Island) 212
St Elias Mountains 227
St Lawrence Bay, Alaska 232
St Lawrence River 54, 71, 73
St Louis, Missouri 134–5, 138, 140,
  260
St Peter 212, 214
salmon
  California 253
  Indian totem carving 233
  Northwest regions 235
salt-tolerant plants 29–30
San Francisco 204, 239, 257, 259,
  260, 263, 266, 267, 273
San Joaquin Valley 259
San Rogue (Columbia River) 225
sanderlings, migration 22
sandpiper 22, 112, 143
Santa Fe 204
Santa Inez Spanish mission 254
Santa Maria, discovery voyage
  15–16
sassafras 20, 27
Sauk Indians 162
'Sault La Chine' (Lachine rapids)
  56
sawgrass 100, 102, 111
Say, Thomas 172
Sea of Cortéz (Gulf of California)
  187
sea cow 92, 95, 214, 216
sea lion, Steller's 218, 219
seal 63, 220
  hunting 221, 222–3, 239–40
  ice-age period 18
  northern fur 222–3
  treaty 240
Secotan Indian village 26

Seminole Indians
  culture 108
  lake names 100, 102, 114–15
  war and relocation (1835–42)
  111–12
Sequoia National Park 273
sequoia, giant 249, 250, 251, 271
Service, Robert W. 239
Seven Cities of Cíbola 187
Seven Years' War (French and
  Indian) (1763) 84, 123
Seward Peninsula, Alaska, gold
  rush 237, 239
Seward, William Henry 227
'Seward's icebox' 227, 228, 237
shark 103, 219
sheep
  bighorn 158
  Dall's 212, 218, 226
Sheepeater Indians 157
Sheridan, General Philip Henry
  146
Shining Mountains (Rockies)
  151–85
Shoshone Indians 138, 198
Sierra Club, founding 273
Sierra Madre Oriental, Mexico
  151
Sierra Nevada 151, 152
  formation 257
  gold rush (1848) 257–9
  wildlife 249
silver 54
  California 257
  Mexico 204
  Rockies 180
Sioux Indians 130, 163
  buffalo slaughter 142–3
Sitka, Russian trading post (1799)
  225
Skagway, Alaska 237, 239
skunk, ice-age period 18, 249
skunk cabbage 60
slavery
  early record (1619) 38
  South Carolina 108
  southern Florida 106
sloth, ground 18, 95, 247
Smith, Captain John 28–33
Smithsonian Institution
  Grayson's expedition 263, 266
  Kennicott sponsor 237
Smoky Mountains (Smokies) 38,
  41, 42–3, 46, 111
snake dance, Hopi 197
Snake River 138
soil conditions, Florida 89, 91
Sonoran Desert 187–91, 193, 211,
  266
Soto, Hernando de
  cruelties 106
  expeditions 47, 97, 100
Spain
  Alaska expeditions 223
  Alaskan claim abandoned 223
  California mission system 251,
  253–5, 257
  Catholic missionaries (1635)
  106, 108
  land acquisition 84
  West ownership 133
Spanish expeditions
  Alaska 223
  California 253

Florida 91, 95
  missionaries 106, 108, **254**
  Southwest 187–209
Spanish settlements 198, 204
speculators 209, 259
spoonbill 105, 114
  roseate **113**
spruce 71
  black 212
  sitka 211, 237
  white 212
squash, Indian food 28, 44, 194
squirrel 44
  flying 33
Stadacona (Quebec City) 54
Standard Natural History (Riley) 170
Steller, George 212, 214, 216
Stewart, William Drummond 164, 167, 172
Stoeckl, Baron de 227
Stony Mountains (Rockies) 151–2
sturgeon 72, 235, 237
  Chesapeake Bay 28, 29
  migration 22
Sumner, Charles 237
Susquehanna River 29
Sutter, John A. 257
Superior, Lake 72, **74–5**
Suwannee River 92, **96**

Tait, Arthur F., painting **129**
Talan, Jean Baptiste 71
Talleyrand 133
tamarack 68
Tamiami Trail 115
Tampa Bay 91, 95
tanager, western **139**
tar pit lake, Los Angeles 245, **246**, 247, 249
Taylor, Bayard 260
tectonic plate activity 240–1

Tenochtitlán (Mexico City) 130, 204
tepary bean 194
tern
  arctic 228
  common **144–5**
Texas, US annexation (1845) 142
thermal springs, Yellowstone 181, **184**
Thompson, David 225
Thoreau, Henry David 181, 271
thrush 20
  varied 173
timber doodle (woodcock) 123–4
Timucua Indians 106
Tlingit Indians 223, 232, 234
  artifacts **233**
tobacco
  cultivation, Jamestown 38
  South Carolina 108
  use of 38, **63**, 225
Tohono O'odham *see* Papago Indians
Townsend, John Kirk 172–3
'The Trail of Ninety Eight' (Service) 239
Trail of Tears 47
transportation
  railroad 142–3
  river steamboats 142
Travels (Bartram) 92
Treaty of Breda (1667) 76
Treaty of Guadalupe Hidalgo 257
Treaty of Paris (1763) 84, 133
tundra 76–87, 143, 212, 228
turkey 44, 72, 108, 123
turtle 66, **107**
  alligator snapping **99**
  box **26**
  green sea **90**, 91–2, 106
  slider **104**

Umnak Island 222
US Soil Conservation Service (1935) 149
US War Dept. 205

Vaca, Cabeza de 95, 97, 130
Valley Glacier, Juneau **210**
Valley of Ten Thousand Smokes **238**, 240–1
Vancouver, George 224, 225, 251
Vancouver Island 225
Verrazzano, Giovanni 25
Vikings 16
violet, bird's foot 126, **129**
Virginia
  British settlement 28–33
  tobacco origins 38
volcanic activity 240–1
voyageurs 72

walrus 52, 228, **229**, 232
wampum 65
warble flies 82
warbler 20
  Cape May **21**
water moccasin **98**, 100
weasel, ice-age period 18, 247, 249
weaving, Navajo and Hopi 198
West Indies 38, 91, 102, 108
whale
  bowhead 225, 228
  humpback **221**
  industry 224–5
  killer 219
  right 224–5
whaling, Bering Sea **221**
White, John
  illustrations 26, 27–8
  Roanoke colony failure 27–8
Whitehorse (Yukon) 239
Whitney, Josiah 266

The Whole and True Discovery of Terra Florida (Ribaut) 22, 24
Wichita Indians 198
Wilhelm, Frederick Paul 163–4
Wilson, Alexander, *American Ornithology* 139
Wind River Range, Wyoming **168**
wolf 44, **86**, 106, 133, 134
  caribou predator 82
  ice-age period 247
  Indian mythology 234
  prairies 134, 147
  timber (gray) 124
wolverine, ice-age period 18
woodcock 123–4
woodpecker
  Gila **190**, 191
  ivory-billed **110**, 112
  Lewis's **139**
Wrangell Mountains 227
wren, cactus 188
Württemberg, Duke of *see* Wilhelm, Frederick Paul

Yakutat, Russian trading post (1787) 225
Yaqui (Mayo) Indians 188
yarrow, **118**, 120
Yellowstone, Mammoth Hot Springs **184**
Yellowstone National Park 140, 180–1, 185
  Midway Geyser Basin **182–3**
Yellowstone River 138, 152–3
Yosemite
  National Park **270**, 274
  Valley 267
Yukon **236**
  gold rush (1897–8) 237
Yukon River events 237, 239

Zuni Indians 191, 194, 200